I Was a Monster
Movie Maker

OTHER WORKS BY TOM WEAVER AND FROM McFARLAND

A Sci-Fi Swarm and Horror Horde (2010)

I Talked with a Zombie (2009)

Earth vs. the Sci-Fi Filmmakers (2005)

Eye on Science Fiction (2003; paperback 2007)

Science Fiction Confidential (2002; paperback 2010)

John Carradine (1999; paperback 2008)

Science Fiction and Fantasy Film Flashbacks (1998; paperback 2004)

It Came from Horrorwood (1996; paperback 2004)

Double Feature Creature Attack (2 vols. combined 1994/1995; paperback 2003)

Poverty Row HORRORS! (1993; paperback 1999)

Science Fiction Stars and Horror Heroes (1991; paperback 2006)

Interviews with B Science Fiction and Horror Movie Makers (1988; paperback 2006)

Universal Horrors: The Studio's Classic Films, 1931–1946 (and Michael Brunas and John Brunas; 2d ed., 2007)

I Was a Monster Movie Maker

Conversations with 22 SF and Horror Filmmakers

Tom Weaver

McFarland & Company, Inc., Publishers
Jefferson, North Carolina, and London

Dedicated to

Casey Adams	Faith Domergue	Aubrey Schenck
William Alland	David Duncan	Lee Sholem
Lewis Allen	Harry Essex	Curt Siodmak
John Archer	Gene Evans	Randy Stuart
John Ashley	Gene Fowler, Jr.	Gloria Talbott
Billy Benedict	Albert Glasser	Don Taylor
Doug Benton	Sidney Hayers	Harry Thomas
Edward Bernds	Rose Hobart	Shirley Ulmer
Tom Boutross	Howard W. Koch	Ray Walston
Lloyd Bridges	Maureen O'Sullivan	Marie Windsor
Richard Denning	Patricia Owens	
Edward Dmytryk	Gil Perkins	

The present work is a reprint of the illustrated case bound edition of I Was a Monster Movie Maker: Conversations with 22 SF and Horror Filmmakers, *first published in 2001 by McFarland.*

Library of Congress Cataloguing-in-Publication Data

I was a monster movie maker : conversations with 22 SF and horror filmmakers / [reported] by Tom Weaver.
        p.   cm.
Includes filmographies and index.

ISBN 978-0-7864-6444-9
softcover : 50# alkaline paper

1. Science fiction films—United States—History and criticism.
2. Horror films—United States—History and criticism.
3. Motion piction producers and directors—United States—Interviews.
    I. Weaver, Tom, 1958–
PN1995.9.S26 I19 2011   791.43′615—dc21   2001023432

British Library Cataloguing data are available

© 2001 Tom Weaver. All rights reserved

No part of this book may be reproduced or transmitted in any form or by any means, electronic or mechanical, including photocopying or recording, or by any information storage and retrieval system, without permission in writing from the publisher.

On the cover: Bird-men and coneheads were just part of the menagerie of monsters harassing Anne Helm in the fantasy adventure *The Magic Sword*.

Manufactured in the United States of America

McFarland & Company, Inc., Publishers
Box 611, Jefferson, North Carolina 28640
www.mcfarlandpub.com

Contents

Acknowledgments vi

Phil Brown 1
Booth Colman 16
Faith Domergue 29
Michael Forest 44
Nelson Gidding 61
Anne Helm 78
Candace Hilligoss 88
Michael A. Hoey 96
John Kerr 112
Phyllis Kirk 122
Suzanna Leigh 132
Yvonne Lime 141
Norman Lloyd 151
Maureen O'Sullivan 180
Paul Picerni 194
Anthony M. Taylor 211
Shirley Ulmer 227
Ray Walston 250
Joan Weldon 257
June Wilkinson 270
William Read Woodfield 283
Dana Wynter 294

Index 309

Acknowledgments

Abridged versions of the interviews featured in this book originally appeared in the following magazines:

Phil Brown: "The Jedi's Uncle," *Starlog* #261, April 1999; **Booth Colman**: "Booth Colman," *Cult Movies* #28, 1999; **Faith Domergue**: "Keeping the Faith," *Fangoria* #133, June 1994; **Michael Forest**: "Michael Forest—An Interview," *Classic Images* #282, December 1998, and "Who Yearns for Adonais," *Starlog* #274, May 2000; **Nelson Gidding**: "The Original Ghostwriter," *Fangoria* #185, August 1999; **Anne Helm**: "At the Helm for Horror," *Fangoria* #175, August 1998; **Candace Hilligoss**: "Stolen Souls," *The Astounding B Monster* #18, March 1998, and "Soulless Carnival," *The Astounding B Monster* #31, April 1999; **Michael A. Hoey**: "Michael A. Hoey Remembers *The Navy vs. the Night Monsters*," *Midnight Marquee Monsters* #60, Summer 1999; **John Kerr**: "Interview: John Kerr," *Chiller Theatre* #11, 1999; **Phyllis Kirk**: "Heroine in the 'House,'" *Monsters from the Vault* #10, Winter/Spring 2000; **Suzanna Leigh**: "The Deadly Biz," *Fangoria* #192, May 2000; **Yvonne Lime**: "I Was the Girlfriend of a Teenage Werewolf," *Classic Images* #284, February 1999; **Norman Lloyd**: "Times Traveler," *Starlog* #257, December 1998, and "Norman Lloyd: Working With Hitch," *Classic Images* #298, April 2000; **Maureen O'Sullivan**: "Maureen O'Sullivan—Our Favorite Jane," *Films of the Golden Age* #21, Summer 2000; **Paul Picerni**: "Hero in the House" and "Wax Nostalgic," *The Astounding B Monster* #31, April 1999; **Anthony M. Taylor**: "Raising the Incubus," *Video Watchdog* #53, 1999; **Shirley Ulmer**: "Shirley Ulmer," *Cult Movies* #25, 1998; **Ray Walston**: "Ray Walston Meets Bela Lugosi," *Cult Movies* #26, 1998; **Joan Weldon**: "A Human's Life," *Starlog* #258, January 1999; **June Wilkinson**: "Voodoo Doll," *Chiller Theatre* #9, 1998; **William Read Woodfield**: "William Read Woodfield on Creating *The Hypnotic Eye*," *Chiller Theatre* #10, 1999; **Dana Wynter**: "The Lady Elegant," *Starlog* #270, January 2000

This book could not have been written without the generous assistance of many of the same people who have helped me in the past: Sincere thanks go out to John Antosiewicz, Buddy Barnett (*Cult Movies*), Marty Baumann (*The Astounding B Monster*), Ted Bohus (*SPFX*), Pat Broeske, Ginny Brown, Arianné Ulmer Cipes, Robert Clarke, Kevin Clement (*Chiller Theatre*), Glenn Damato, Joe Dante, Erin, Tigger, Rufus and Clint A. P. Fresco, Michael Gingold (*Fangoria*), Susan Hart, Joe Indusi, Tom Johnson, Joe Kane (*VideoScope*), all the nice folks at Lincoln Center (Louis Paul, Christine Karatnytsky, Dan Patri, Dave Bartholomew, Brian O'Connell, Christopher Frith), Tim Lucas (*Video Watchdog*), Kevin McCarthy, Dave McDonnell (*Starlog*), Boyd Magers, Barry Murphy, Ray Nielsen, John Parnum, Jeanne Provost, Oconee Provost, Rich Scrivani, Tony Timpone (*Fangoria*), Brian Weaver, Lucy Chase Williams, Wade Williams, Robert Wise and Marc Zubatkin.

Mark Martucci, owner of the world's most fabulous video collection, was always there when I needed him, as were research associates Mike and John Brunas. John Cocchi and Jack Dukesbery furnished invaluable assistance with the many filmographies. More extra special thanks to Michael Fitzgerald, who conducted and transcribed the Faith Domergue interview.

Phil Brown

*In my long life in films, there are ones I'm proud of
and those I'm not proud of.
The Jungle Captive and Weird Woman fall into the latter category.*

New to the autograph show "scene" in 1997 is *Star Wars*' Uncle Owen, the scowling, careworn moisture farmer who ekes out a living on the desert planet Tattoine (with the reluctant help of footloose nephew Luke Skywalker) in the opening reels of the 1977 space saga. Fans line up for actor Phil Brown's signature, hear his memories of the making of *Star Wars*, peruse his résumé—and try to read the film titles that have been crossed off this list of credits. In this interview, Brown remembers *Star Wars*, the 1940s horror movies he'd just as soon forget (*Weird Woman* and *The Jungle Captive*), and describes the real-life horrors of his brush with the House Un-American Activities Committee.

Born in Cambridge, Massachusetts, Brown was the son of a doctor whose work took the family all around the country. After majoring in dramatics at Stanford University, Brown played some of his earliest stage roles as part of New York's Group Theatre. When it folded, he and other Group Theatre vets headed to Hollywood, where Brown made his movie debut (1941's *I Wanted Wings*) and helped found the fabled Actors' Laboratory. His association with the Lab came back to haunt him later in the decade, when its members fell under the scrutiny of HUAC, and Brown was eventually compelled to relocate with his family to England. It was overseas that he was able to resume work on stage, TV—and on the sandy surface of Tattoine, under the supervision of *Star Wars* director George Lucas.

How did you land your part as Luke Skywalker's uncle in Star Wars*?*
I'm a working actor who lived in England for 40 years and worked there a lot. George Lucas came over to England to cast a lot of the roles in *Star Wars*, and in the normal course of events I went around and met him and he said, "You got the part."

What were your first impressions of this project you were getting involved with?
Well, I didn't really know. The script was kind of minimal, because a lot of

the stuff was going to be put in as special effects and so on later. So [in the script] you had short bursts of scenes. The whole section that I'm in, the early part, was all spelled out in dialogue and *where* we were and *why* we were there and so on. But then, as you got further on into the script, into the big battle sequences and so forth, it was kind of minimal. I didn't get an idea of the shape of the whole thing until ...well [*laughs*], until I saw it on the screen!

Your desert scenes were shot in Tunisia.

I had known Alec Guinness before *Star Wars*, and we just happened to end up together on the plane which was taking the few [actors] who worked in Tunisia, plus the whole crew. I sat next to him and we were chatting, and we both said, "What's it all about??" [*Laughs*] It didn't seem quite clear at the time; as I said, it wasn't clear to me until I saw it. It was just a job for me, that was all—just another job. I'm grateful it turned out so nicely.

What was Tunisia like?

Tunisia was a very interesting place for me. I'd been to other parts of Africa, the northern parts, but I'd never been to Tunisia before. We were out in an oasis near this desert where we were shooting. It was an attractive little village, very primitive, but with a nice hotel. We were quite a long distance from any place, it was out in the boondocks. I wasn't working the whole time—my shooting days were not many, because it's not a long sequence. I had a lot of time off, but I wandered around the town a bit, and I had my typewriter. I've forgotten what I was writing, to tell you the truth [*laughs*]—that was a long time ago!

And the weather?

The weather was fine. It was a time of year when it was not terribly hot, so that was not a problem. People always ask me that, they ask, "Wasn't it terribly hot?", because they think of Tunisia as being roasting all the time. Well, it isn't—it has summer and winter like any other place. We were fine.

Your impressions of George Lucas?

George is a very interesting man. He's a genius, as you know—he has a special genius for inventing and putting together these fantasies. And then there's his great knowledge of the technical side of these things. He is not a great "actor's director" (and he doesn't *claim* to be), so you are allowed a great deal of freedom as to what you do. He was very pleasant to work with, but he was shy, and I didn't spend a lot of time with him off-screen, at the hotel. But he was busy anyway—a director's always twice as busy as all the actors put together! So I didn't get to know him terribly well, except that he's a very nice man. That's about the size of it.

"Uncle Owen" is a "moisture farmer." What exactly is a "moisture farmer"?

I wish you knew. If you find out, tell me [*laughs*], 'cause I don't know! It's a question I didn't ask! I just played a man who had certain characteristics which I could get my fingers on easily enough. I didn't ask a lot of questions, I'm sorry to say—I suppose I should have! But I didn't think it was going to help my performance, let's put it that way. I had scenes to play with human beings, thank God: My wife [Shelagh

Irascible Uncle Owen (Brown) contends with Jawa used droid salesmen in *Star Wars*.

Fraser], my charge Luke Skywalker [Mark Hamill] and so forth.

What was Mark Hamill like at that point?
He was a very nice chap. To me, he seemed terribly young—which he was! I was 60 or 65, and he was barely 20. He seemed very nice and lively and brash, and very talented, pleasant to work with.

Uncle Owen is a gruff character. Was that spelled out in the script, or something you brought to it?
No, no, it was pretty much there in the script, he plays that function in the storyline. He has to be gruff with this young man, trying to prevent him from going off to join the wars. He's selfish, because he wants the boy to stay there and help him work. And he is trying to convey that idea to the boy, and make him feels it's important. So he comes out as a gruff man.

Any memories of the various actors playing the Jawas?
The Jawas were little Tunisian kids.

The interior scene, where the family is eating—where was that shot?
The interior was shot back in London, after we got back from Tunisia. You made your entrances and exits through holes in the ground or holes in the wall in Tunisia, and then you came out in London [*laughs*]!

What did you think of Star Wars *when you first saw it?*
Oh, I was enormously impressed with it. Since George had not bothered

to detail (and why should he?) the special effects things, it all came as a great surprise to me. I was very impressed with his inventiveness, his ability to imagine all these technical things, and then to cause them to be conceived, and then get 'em made and put it all together. I think it's fantastic.

Take a break from science-fiction and tell me how you came to help found the Actors' Lab.

The Actors' Lab came about because there were a number of us in Hollywood who had been in the Group Theatre and who had been trained in the Stanislavsky approach to acting. People around Hollywood heard that we were there, so we began to offer "classes" for younger people. Now, I was never a teacher, but some of the other people were—I was just a part of the whole thing. We used to have a little studio above a café over on Franklin Avenue; then when the War came along, our "leader," the man who organized things more than anybody else, a man named "Bud" [Roman] Bohnen, thought we should be doing something towards the war effort. Somebody like (say) Bob Hope or Bing Crosby could go out as a single and entertain the troops; well, we could only contribute by doing plays. So we did a whole series of plays which were done without any scenery, just a suitcase full of props. We cast them, directed them and sent 'em out through an outfit called the USO. They sent these things around the world to all kinds of military installations overseas and in this country.

The character of the school changed when the war finished. There were a lot of returning servicemen to whom we wanted to offer training under the G.I. Bill of Rights. Naturally, most of the students were going to be men, and we needed women to partner them. Again Bohnen came up with a bright idea: We would ask the studios to supply us with young starlets and would ask them to pay a much larger sum than the G.I. Bill was supplying for the men, in order to make a go of the project. About the same time, we started to do a series of plays in our tiny 200-seat theater to raise money for the project as well. That's where I came in—I was much more interested in production, direction, I built scenery, I did everything.

In the great city of Los Angeles where there was no proper theater except the occasional road show in a big house downtown, we developed a nationally famous theater—albeit with only 200 seats. We did a great variety of plays, Chekhov, O'Casey, Tennessee Williams, Arthur Miller; our production of Ben Jonson's *Volpone* had a feature article in *Life* magazine and a photo on the cover. It said, "In a small theater behind Schwab's Drug store, you can see some of the finest acting in America today."

Now that I hear you talk about the Actors' Lab, something I can tell you're very proud of, I begin to understand why you've got movies like Weird Woman *and* Jungle Captive *scratched out of the résumés you hand out!*

[*Laughs*] They were just jobs, nothing I could particularly be proud of. In my long life in films, there are ones I'm proud of and those I'm *not* proud of. *The Jungle Captive, Weird Woman* and a thing called *Pierre of the Plains* [1942] fall into the latter category.

You did films like these with the attitude of "I'm an actor and this is a job," correct?

Yes. Actually, I had been to Hollywood once before: When I was in New York, I was cast in a very small role in the very first film I played in, *I Wanted Wings* [1941], a film about the training of flyers. I was brought out to Hollywood to make that movie. Then when the Group Theatre broke up and we all moved out here, well, then, naturally, I just proceeded to put myself "on the market" and got film parts.

Once you had moved to Hollywood, what was your first movie? Was it H. M. Pulham, Esq. *[1941]?*

That would be it, yes. That was a reasonably good role, and the film had a lot of quite important actors in it. And King Vidor directing. So that was a good one.

Were you under contract to any studio during the early '40s?

No. I was about to be put under contract to Metro, who used me quite a lot. They were talking contract when

Lon Chaney, Jr., gave Brown (*and* his tweed jacket) a working-over in *Weird Woman*.

Uncle Sam picked up my option, and I went into the Army!

What memories of Lon Chaney, the star of Weird Woman?

I had a strange relationship to Universal. I was hired on two or three Chaney pictures, because Chaney had mainly played monsters, and now Universal wanted him to play doctors and other intellectual types. So they hired me to help him learn his lines and develop characters. The first morning when I showed up at his dressing room about ten o'clock to start work, he handed me a large glass of whiskey. Now [*laughs*], I'm not a prude, I like to drink with the best of them, but that was not my idea of the best preparation for a hard day's work! It was crazy working with him, really quite crazy, but he was a very nice guy and we got on well.

In *Weird Woman*, Chaney and I had a fight scene. I took a poke at him and he knocked me down, and we were down there on the floor when the director called "cut." In the course of this fake fight, he tore the sleeve of my jacket. Our faces were close together, and he whispered, "Look, kid, don't worry about that jacket. I'll getcha a new one." And he ripped it some more. What he didn't know was, it was *my* jacket—my own!—and the studio was not going to buy me another [*laughs*]! And it was a good jacket, a *damn* good tweed jacket of my own wardrobe! Somebody there sewed it up and gave it back to me.

One of the Chaney movies where you worked as dialogue director was Dead Man's Eyes. *That and* Weird Woman *were directed by Reginald LeBorg.*

He was a strange man. Perfectly pleasant—but rather arrogant. He thought he was a bigger man than he was, that was all. (That's not unusual in Hollywood!) I gather he's become a kind of cult figure, too. I remember another funny story about one of those films, I've forgotten which one, on which I was a dialogue director for Lon Chaney. I had just received the script—it was probably *Dead Man's Eyes*, which I wasn't in. I came on the stage the first day, and as I walked in from the outdoors, the whole stage was empty, except for Chaney sitting waaaay on the opposite side talking to somebody. And as I walked across, I said, in a very loud voice, "Look, Chaney, who the *fuck* wrote this hunk of shit?" Chaney turned casually, indicating the man he had been talking to, and said, "Meet the author!" Well [*laughs*], what could I say? I think it's a hunk of shit and I'm sorry! I'm sorry for you and I'm sorry for all of us!

And The Jungle Captive? *Did you think that was better than* Weird Woman?

I just saw both of 'em, but I couldn't really say which was the better of the two—I'd rather not be committed on that [*laughs*]! They were both pretty low on my scale. But it was money, and I had a wife and two very small children. Otto Kruger, who was the star of *Jungle Captive*, was a very nice man. I feel sorry for him that he had come down [the Hollywood ladder] so rapidly, because he used to be a big leading man. Then to be playing that crazy doctor in *Jungle Captive* was quite a comedown. Rondo Hatton, who played Kruger's henchman in that, was also a pleasant man.

You spent about 40 years in England

Brown (trapped by villains Otto Kruger and Rondo Hatton) says he appeared in movies like *The Jungle Captive* simply to support a wife and kids.

once your blacklist troubles began—but your first trip there was several years earlier.

I went to England first to play in *The Glass Menagerie* [on the stage] with Helen Hayes, directed by John Gielgud. That was 1948. Then I came back to Hollywood, and by that time the Lab was under attack. I knew that eventually I was going to be attacked one way or the other. I was never a member of the Communist Party, but that didn't make any difference at all. After that first trip to England, I came back under contract to Columbia as a dialogue director, with a promise that I was soon going to have a film to direct. It wasn't "soon"—it took a year and a half, but I eventually got the film *The Harlem Globetrotters* [1951] to direct. Which I enjoyed doing very much. But when that was over, even though it turned out eventually to be an enormous box office success, Columbia let me go. Usually when a young director does a first picture and makes a success of it, they keep him under contract. When they let me go, I knew I was on the skids.

My agent was Ingo Preminger, Otto Preminger's brother. He was a wonderful agent and one of the few men who fought the blacklist. He put me in touch with Eddie Lewis, who was starting a television series called *Schlitz Playhouse of Stars* with Irene Dunne as mistress of ceremonies. These were little half-hour things, and I directed two or three of those for Lewis, and directed her in her "bridging" things—she introduced each playlet. (That's another story, and a wonderful one.) Anyway, eventually Eddie Lewis called me in and said he'd had a letter from the Schlitz Brewing Company. The American Legion had got in touch with Schlitz, saying that if *Schlitz Playhouse of Stars* used me any more, they'd see to it that every American Legionnaire in the country stopped drinking Schlitz Beer. Well, that's a pretty tough thing for a young producer like Eddie Lewis to face. But he was very honest with me, he told me about it…and he had to let me go.

The day he told me this, he walked out of the office and got in his car and went home, and I went back to his office, lifted the letters out of his desk and had 'em Photostatted. I had no intention of using them against Lewis, and never would have, of course. But I wanted to have anything I could have in my hands, and I'm glad I did. It didn't do me any good, of course—*no*body won in those days. Nobody. If you fought the Un-American Committee boys, or anybody who was on that side of the fence, you were dead, you were finished.

The blacklisters may have thought they had me on the ropes, but I was determined to fight. I was advised by a lawyer-friend to pursue a plan of meeting all the groups and individuals who had determined that the great American public should not be "corrupted" by entertainment I had anything to do with. I had no success, not even with the unions to which I belonged, who should have been helpful—the Screen Directors Guild and the Screen Actors Guild. Ronald Reagan was at that moment president of SAG, *and* a secret FBI informant. What a laugh: I had a meeting asking for help with a man who was secretly informing the FBI what an undesirable character I was.

I am certain Reagan never admitted how wrong his position had been, but recently all three of the so-called talent unions [actors, writers and directors] called a meeting at the Motion Picture Academy Theatre at which the present heads of all three groups publicly apologized for their total lack of support for us members who had been wrongly attacked in those dark days. We blacklisted people were seated in a special section of that auditorium and were asked to stand to receive the apology. Most welcome, but just a bit late—like, 50 years.

When you made your first trip to England for The Glass Menagerie—*was it on that same trip that you co-starred in the movie* The Hidden Room?
Yes, it was.

That was directed by Edward Dmytryk, who (needless to say) had his own blacklist problems.
My relationship to Dmytryk is a long one. I admired him for refusing to give in to the Un-American Activities Committee, when the Hollywood Ten were all on the hot seat. But I didn't like him for what he did afterwards. He was the only stool pigeon amongst those ten. There were a few other stool pigeons

As the abducted American in the suspenseful *The Hidden Room*, Brown had one of his best English movie roles.

later on, whom I won't name, but Dmytryk I don't mind naming. The interesting thing about my relationship to Dmytryk is that I didn't particularly like him when I was *working* with him. I had been his assistant on a film called *Give Us This Day* (1949), made in England from a famous novel of the period, *Christ in Concrete* by Pietro Di Donato. Sam Wanamaker played the lead, and I was Eddie's general dogsbody on that. I'm also in it, in a tiny, tiny, tiny part, just because they needed somebody at the end.

Then afterwards he cast you in The Hidden Room?

That's right, and when that film was over, I never saw Dmytryk again. After Dmytryk served his term in jail, he made that drastic decision, open to anyone who wanted to get their job back: He informed on his friends. Naturally I had no wish to talk with him.

My only contact with him after he joined the opposition occurred obliquely, when I was confronting the American Legion. They informed me that they had learned I had been "cool" to several men who had decided to become stool pigeons. The two men turned out to be Dmytryk and Richard Collins. I'm not sure what kind of long distance temperature recording devices either man has built into his body for them to gauge the temperature of my feelings toward them—I have never seen Dmytryk since I returned to Hollywood in 1952 and never saw Collins since I briefly met him the first time, socially, way back in 1941.

This was one of the reasons I hated Dmytryk so badly: He just *made this up*, and he made it up for the simple reason that he *had* to. You see, people like Dmytryk and Richard Collins decided to change their stripes—they were Communists, and they decided they wanted to get back in the picture business. The way they did that was, they confessed, *but*—they also had to be "on call" for the American Legion, or for anybody else who wanted to say to 'em, "We got a new man coming up here. What do you know about...Brown?" And Dmytryk and Collins couldn't say, "Oh, he's a nice guy. Don't worry about him."

They had to have some derogatory thing to say about anybody they were asked about?

Exactly—that was one of the "rules of the game"! Once they decided to become stool pigeons, they *had* to be on call to answer the boys' questions. If the American Legion wanted a reference, they'd call [Dmytryk and Collins] up, and they couldn't say anything *nice* about somebody! *Both* men said to the American Legion that I had been "cool" to them. Anyway, let's get off it. That's enough, isn't it?

Almost—I do want to hear a little more about The Hidden Room. *What did you think of that part?*

I enjoyed it very much. It was a good film, cleverly written, and Dmytryk directed it very well.

Did you enjoy Robert Newton, who imprisons and torments you in the movie?

Oh, yes, he was a charming man. The only problem with Newton was that he was a reformed drunk. He used to be a real terrible drunk, but he was a *reformed* drunk by the time I worked with him. The poor man felt that he was no longer of interest to anybody, he felt that he was no longer interesting. Which is probably one of the reasons he used to drink—to *make* himself interesting! But he was just perfectly charming.

Any time Dmytryk talks about The Hidden Room, *he mentions Newton being a drinker, and says that he was very nasty when he was drunk.*

I find that baffling, because I don't remember Newton drinking at *all* during our picture. I never saw him under the influence of alcohol during production. Newton had been known around London as a colorful drunk for years, but he certainly never appeared drunk [during the making of *The Hidden Room*], and I was on the set every single day of the shoot. I don't know what the hell Dmytryk's doing bad-mouthing him at *all*.

Your best scene in the movie is the black humorous one where you and Newton are having the friendly discussion about how he should dispose of your body.

[*Laughs*] Yeah, that *was* kind of interesting. Actually, *my* favorite scene is my favorite because it's funny. At the very end of the film, my mistress [Sally Gray] comes into my hospital room with a little dog, and the dog is supposed to jump onto the bed and make love to me because we were such great friends while I was imprisoned. Well, the co-producer was a man called Nat Bronsten, who didn't like to spend money. He didn't get a trained dog, he just went to his publican's wife and bought that little dog 'cause it looked right [for the part]. The dog was not trained at all, and it cost us days and days of shooting because the dog wouldn't do anything it was supposed to! (It wasn't *my* money, *I* didn't give a god-damn!) Well, in that last scene where I'm in the hospital bed, the little dog wouldn't jump up and lick my face, so I put some bacon in my ears. The little dog didn't like bacon. I put some pieces of chicken in my ears, I put everything I could find! Liver in my ears! But the little dog didn't like any of those things. So finally what they did was they made the shot with me in the frame and just *threw* the dog in onto the bed. And I started to kiss the dog, and that was the whole scene. The dog was supposed to be kissing *me*, but *I* was kissing the dog!

It's obvious how tightly you're holding onto that dog.

Oh, sure! The dog was tryin' to get away, he didn't like me at *all*!

The beard you wear in Hidden Room—*was that your beard or makeup?*

That was makeup, because it had to get progressively longer—Newton had me imprisoned for about six months, and that was one of the ways of proving the length of time. [Makeup man] Stuart Freeborn was charming, but it was a great bore having that thing put on every morning!

He was later one of the makeup men on Star Wars. *Was he your makeup man on that, too?*

No, he was not out in Tunisia.

The few times I've been on movie sets, I've been bored out of my gourd by how slow everything happens. And I'm told that English crews are much slower.

Yes, it's a slow business. I like directing films, but not acting in 'em very much. 'Cause you're really not doing anything but sitting around. Yes, the English crews *are* a little slower, but by the time I was in England I was a little older and I was a little more patient. I learned to take along books or a typewriter or whatever, and so I managed all right.

Jump back about ten minutes and tell me the "wonderful Irene Dunne story" you mentioned.
You have to have seen the *Schlitz Playhouse of Stars* program to understand this fully, but I'll try and explain it: She was to be the mistress of ceremonies, and each little playlet each week had a different star. And she would introduce them and give a little background to help induct people into the story more quickly. Well, one of the principal writers on this series was a man called Luther Davis; the most recent thing he's written was a musical called *Grand Hotel*. Luther had a marvelous sense of humor, and he said, "Christ, we've got this wonderful actress. Let's make her work, let's not just have her sit in a chair." So Luther devised a series of little introductions in which Irene Dunne played a character who led you into the film you were about to see. Eddie Lewis, Luther and I went out to her house to convince Irene to do this. She said, "Oh, I can't do that sort of thing!", but I shamed her into it! I said, "Please, just give us a chance. I'll come up without these other two chaps, and you and I will work on these things. If you can't do it, you don't have to do it. But I can get you to do it."

A couple of days later, I went out to her home again and we had tea, and we began to work on these things. She had a wonderful sense of humor, and we really hit it off beautifully, she and I. Then when it came to shooting these things, we shot all 26 of them in one day! They were just a minute each, but she had to go and change clothes and so on. In one of 'em she would be dressed in a football uniform (shoulder pads and all!); another time she played an old hag, like a witch out of *Macbeth*! It was just a wonderful day—I sort of acted as her dresser, and went back to her dressing room and helped her change her clothes, and we were like a couple of kids! And, I swear, I don't think anybody in the world except me could have gotten out of her that many minutes of film, with changes of costume, in one day. 'Cause that was all we had, one day—Eddie Lewis said, "This is what you gotta do. You gotta get it in." So...we did!

I've read that you lived on a houseboat for most of the time that you were in England.
There's a story behind that. When you come into England as an actor, you're given a labor permit. This permit limits you to doing the job that you were brought into England to do. When I finished any given assignment, I was [supposed] to leave the country; a little policeman used to come around and keep telling me to get out of the country [*laughs*]! Fortunately I had a good friend in Parliament who (quite legally) got my papers buried at the bottom of some basket of a department that was trying to get me out of the country.

Having this Sword of Damocles over my head, I never could think of staying permanently; we moved from furnished flat to furnished house to furnished flat to furnished flat. We were living down close to the Thames in a place called St. Peter's Square, and I had a crazy idea that if I could get some kind of a place to live, that if I *owned* something, the Home Office would allow me, oh, six months or something to sell it. Well, one day my two sons, who were then about seven or eight, came running into the house and said, "There's a houseboat for sale!", just a few yards away. So we went down and looked and, by God, there was a first World War Canadian motor torpedo boat which had been converted and was being used as a domicile. They were small boats, about 70 feet long, and carried about four torpedoes. So after going down and looking at it, we bought it and we fixed it up. Eventually, a couple of years later, we had a little note from the Home Office saying we could stay as long as we wanted. It worked like magic!

How long did you live on the torpedo boat?

We stayed on it for about 15 years. I used to do all the repairs *in situ*; the tide would go out, and I'd just put my boots on and go to work. But there were a couple of planks which were too much for me, and so I took it to the Chelsea Boat Yard to get some repairs done on it. And instead of repairing it, they *sank* it!

With all your possessions on it?

Oh, yeah, we lost everything! So we started all over again—we bought a steel barge, totally empty, about 80 feet long and 24 feet wide, and we constructed a house out of it, a *beautiful* place. It had three flats: ours (the main one), and two other self-contained flats with bathrooms and kitchens and so forth.

What happened to your homes when the Thames got rough?

In the case of the first boat, we were the inboard boat of three moored parallel to the shore. The roughness didn't get to us—the other two boats shielded us from the wash and from the waves and from the wind. But when we bought the *second* boat, it was moved into the outboard position of the three boats. It was steel, and as part of the construction of it, I put 50 tons of concrete into the bottom as ballast, to keep it from bobbing about. Also, I wanted to heat the concrete, which I did—I think it's the only barge in the world with a heated floor. We lived on that for the next 30 years, and we sold it recently when we back came here [to the U.S.].

In general, was there enough work for an American actor in England during the years you were there?

It wasn't great, no. And I refused to try to play an English role at all. No, that would have been stupid. Other people may have been able to do it, and they *have*, but *I* couldn't. So, no, it wasn't great. I played a lot of leading roles in the theater shortly after I got there—the lead in *Teahouse of the August Moon* and *The Tender Trap* and *Oh, Men! Oh, Women!* and *Sabrina Fair* and so on and so forth. And then I began to direct in the theater there, and eventually I directed in television. So I was able to keep the wolf from the door, but it was not great. Not great.

The era of the blacklist ended, of course, back in the '60s. Why didn't you come back home sooner?

I came back once, just to dip my toe in the water, and I didn't really like what I saw. I got some jobs, and (believe it or not) one of the jobs that I got was with Richard Collins! I played a role which any Hollywood actor could have played, *any*, dozens and dozens and dozens of 'em. I'm sure he only took me on because he felt guilty. That was on a *Bonanza*. Terrible, terrible role. Anyway, to answer your question "Why didn't I come back?", it looked like I was going to have to start all over. I at least had a career going in England, producing and directing television shows and acting and directing in the theater. Here I would have had to start all over again. And I just didn't fancy that somehow, so I went back. And stayed until I returned here a couple of years ago.

Do you intend to act again?
I don't really want to act, but Richard Hatch, who is very big in *Battlestar Galactica* circles, is trying to revive that TV series, and he shot a kind of "teaser" to interest the studio. He asked me to play a cameo, and I did.

You've mentioned in a couple of interviews that you're a curmudgeon. Why do you say that about yourself when you're obviously not?
[*Laughs*] It's a role I play.

If Edward Dmytryk can write a book, which he has, when are you going to write your autobiography?
I'm working on a book, it's just taking me a long, long time to write it. I suppose the reason that I think I'm making a little progress now is that I have a new kind of incentive: I now have a website [www.philbrown.com], run by some people up in Walla Walla, Washington. I really have nothing to do with it except they send me pictures, I sign 'em and they send me money! And they've put my face on a T-shirt and all that kind of crap. So I'm eventually going to try and sell my book through that website. Presently it's called *Without Regrets: An Ancient Premature Anti-Fascist Glances Back at the Hollywood Blacklist*. And that's what it's about.

Phil Brown Filmography

I Wanted Wings (Paramount, 1941)
H. M. Pulham, Esq. (MGM, 1941)
Calling Dr. Gillespie (MGM, 1942)
Hello, Annapolis (Columbia, 1942)
Pierre of the Plains (MGM, 1942)
The Impatient Years (Columbia, 1944)
Weird Woman (Universal, 1944)
State Fair (*It Happened One Summer*) (20th Century-Fox, 1945)
Over 21 (Columbia, 1945)
The Jungle Captive (Universal, 1945)
The Killers (Universal, 1946)
Without Reservations (RKO, 1946)
Johnny O'Clock (Columbia, 1947)
If You Knew Susie (RKO, 1948)
The Luck of the Irish (20th Century-Fox, 1948)
Moonrise (Republic, 1948)
Salt to the Devil (*Give Us This Day*) (Eagle-Lion, 1949)
The Hidden Room (*Obsession*) (Eagle-Lion, 1949)
The Harlem Globetrotters (Columbia, 1951)—director
The Green Scarf (British Lion, 1954)
A King in New York (United Artists, 1957)
The Camp on Blood Island (Columbia, 1958)

John Paul Jones (Warners, 1959)
The Counterfeit Traitor (Paramount, 1962)
The Bedford Incident (Columbia, 1965)
The Boy Cried Murder (Universal, 1966)
The Adding Machine (Regional Films/Universal, 1969)
Operation Cross Eagles (Noble/Triglav Film/Continental, 1969)
Land Raiders (*Day of the Landgrabber*) (Columbia, 1970)
Togetherness (General Film Corp., 1970)
Tropic of Cancer (Paramount, 1970)
Valdez Is Coming (United Artists, 1971)
Ooh...You Are Awful (*Get Charlie Tully*) (British Lion/TBS, 1972)
Scalawag (Paramount, 1973)
The Romantic Englishwoman (New World, 1975)
The Pink Panther Strikes Again (United Artists, 1976)
Star Wars (20th Century-Fox, 1977)
Twilight's Last Gleaming (Allied Artists, 1977)
Silver Bears (Columbia, 1978)
Superman (Warners, 1978)
Reds (Paramount, 1981)
Chaplin (Carolco/TriStar, 1992)

Booth Colman

*The [Planet of the Apes makeup] was horrendous.
I've never cared much for spirit gum and sticking things on
and all of that—and this was that in spades!*

A veteran of almost half a century in the film and television industry can't help occasionally dabbling in the horror and science-fiction categories, and actor Booth Colman is no exception. Colman co-starred as the malevolent Mories in the future-set *World Without End* (1956), conspiring against twentieth century time travelers; on TV, he has guested on dozens of sci-fi and suspense series, from classics like *Thriller* and *The Outer Limits* to more recent genre fare like *Galactica 1980* and *Star Trek: Voyager*. He also played the wily orangutan scientist Dr. Zaius on CBS' short-lived *Planet of the Apes* teleseries (1974).

These credits just scratch the surface of the career of the prolific Colman. Born in Portland, Oregon, and educated at the Universities of Washington and Michigan, he served in the Japanese Language Division of U.S. Military Intelligence during World War II. After his discharge, Colman began acting on the New York stage, rubbing elbows with many acting legends (Boris Karloff and Basil Rathbone among them); in 1951, he headed to Hollywood to make his film debut. Between movie and TV assignments, Colman keeps active with theater work; since 1981, he has played Ebenezer Scrooge (*A Christmas Carol*'s contemptuous cheapskate) more than 500 times on the stage of the Meadow Brook Theatre in Rochester, Michigan.

I more or less always wanted to be an actor. I acted in plays at school, and after I came out of the Army, I stayed in New York City. I joined the Equity Library Theater, which was just beginning, and did two plays for them [*Maria Stuart* and *No More Ladies*]. I was approached by an agent and got started fairly quickly, understudying and playing two small parts in an Irwin Shaw play, *The Assassin* [Colman's Broadway debut, 1944]. Then I did auditions for various people, among them Margaret Webster, a distinguished theater director in New York. She happened to have been born in New York City, but her parents were Dame May Whitty and Ben Webster—a theatrical family of 300 years in England. (They were playing in New York when she was born.) Margaret

Webster referred Maurice Evans' company to me. They came to see me in the Shaw play, and I met with them and auditioned and so forth. I joined him for *Hamlet*, which played for a number of months; I played Guildenstern and understudied Laertes. Then I was with him on the radio that year, with Helen Hayes—she had her own program. I remember narrating *Romeo and Juliet* when the two of them did that.

What lured you to Hollywood?

I worked on the Broadway stage and around New York until 1951. In '51, I was with [Basil] Rathbone in the summer tour of *The Winslow Boy*, and I had a chance to come out here for a test for Howard Hawks. That was my first picture, it was called *The Big Sky* [1952] with Kirk Douglas. That went on for a good many weeks, and then I stayed out here because other jobs presented themselves. I didn't go back to New York until '55, and then I did a long tour with the Robert Shaw Chorale. We went to 125 one-night stands, except for Chicago and Toronto, where we were *two* nights.

Jump back a bit and talk about The Winslow Boy *and Basil Rathbone.*

It was produced by the Theater Guild. The London company was playing on Broadway, and as soon as they closed, we opened in Westport, Connecticut, at the Theater Guild's summer theater there. We were supposed to play two or three dates of a week apiece, but frankly the company was so good that it got bookings and went on for a number of months. Basil Rathbone had taken over the direction of the play—they had had a disagreement with whoever it was who began it. It was a very fine production and he was wonderful in the part. Of the various people who played the part, I think he was probably the best in it.

Did he play the boy's father?

Oh, no, he played the great lawyer. (The boy's father in our company was Colin Keith-Johnston, who had been in the original company of *Journey's End* in London.) Rathbone was easily the best in the [lawyer] part because he had that icy, "fish" quality that it needed [*laughs*]. We had David Cole, a young English boy who made a hit in *The Innocents*, and Meg Mundy, who had been in *The Respectful Prostitute* on Broadway. It was a very good company. I used to—I can't say *correspond* with Rathbone, but I had several exchanges of letters with him, and as the years went by, I saw him several times, though I never was in a picture with him. I saw him out here—when he came here, he was old and tired and working in some Grand Guignol [stage] show that they did here, in the Santa Monica High School, I believe. It was *awful*, a terrible comedown for him. I can only gather that he needed the money. (He had earned a great deal in his day, but it wasn't there when he was old and tired.) It had very little merit and it had very little *publicity*. Phil Tonge, a great friend of his and mine, and Phil's wife and I went to see the show, and we picked up Basil afterwards and drove him to his hotel. That was the last time I saw him, because he went back to New York. He didn't look very well, and I don't think he *was* very well.

What kind of a part did he have in it?

I don't remember anything about the show. He was the lead, whatever that was, but the show itself just... meant nothing. It was awful, it was a

Colorful character actor Booth Colman, a veteran of over 50 years on stage, radio, TV and film.

Grand Guignol play with the side of someone's face being fried in a pan and all that. It was *unfitting* to see him doing that stuff. I was so sorry that he felt he had to.

And as a director, how did you enjoy working with him?

He was fine, a wonderful director. I didn't see him afterwards in New York because I came out here, but I *did* see him here when he came here to work. That was also true with Boris Karloff. I met him the first time during *Hamlet* rehearsals, because he was a silent partner of Maurice Evans, he was an investor in the show. And Boris was courting one of the ladies in the company. She wasn't an actress, she was an English lady who handled Evans' business and personal details. Boris and Evie were married when we were on our break-in tour. In our company, playing Osric, was Morton DaCosta, who later became a very important director—*Auntie Mame* [1958] and *The Music Man* [1962] were some of his [film] credits. I remember he sent Evie a telegram for the wedding: DON'T LET HIM SCARE YOU OUT OF BED. [*Laughs*] I saw the Karloffs for, oh, 20-odd years after that, whenever they came out here. We were very friendly. Eventually he moved back to England, but he'd come here when there was work.

Was Karloff still married to his wife Dorothy when you first met him?

No, I think they were divorced. Dorothy was the mother of his daughter Sara; I think Dorothy came from Portland, Oregon. I believe her family were bakers. *She* was a schoolteacher. Apart from that, I don't know anything about her. Boris was married several times in his life.

Everybody talks about what a kind, gentle, poetry-reading soul he was—and yet he was married about as many times as Elizabeth Taylor!

I think *seven*. I never heard him say a word about [his multiple marriages]; it's not something that he would have discussed with his young actor-friends [*laughs*]!

What was Evie Karloff like?

She was a very charming English lady. She'd been married to a comedian named Tom Helmore, and they were divorced. She and Karloff were married for the rest of *his* life. Several years ago, the Academy of Motion Picture Arts and Sciences had a retrospective on Boris Karloff, and they invited her and they brought her over from England for the weekend. I was invited to the little cocktail party they have for friends and so forth, before the members and the public come in. Someone [invited me] because they knew I had been with Karloff in a couple of his undertakings; there were others like me there. When I was introduced to her, I said my name and mentioned Maurice Evans, and that brought back [to her] a memory. She was then in her advanced 80s, a very old party, but she was very cordial and very nice. Also there was Boris' daughter Sara Jane, whom I hadn't seen since she was a little girl. I had a nice conversation with her and met her son, who is an attorney. Sara Jane is a very lovely lady who lives out in the desert. I've been in touch with her a couple of times recently, during the time she was trying to get the Post Office to issue the [Classic Movie Monsters] stamps. She did a lot of work on that, and I managed to get the petitions into the three actors' unions here. Everyone signed them, as I'm sure thousands of people did all over the country. She called me when she heard that the campaign was successful—Karloff appears on two of the stamps, *Frankenstein* and *The Mummy*.

You were also on Karloff's Thriller *TV series.*
Yes, a couple of times. He occasionally played in it—he didn't play in the episodes I worked in, but he was the host. We also worked together in a series at the old Roach studio, *The Veil*—which Karloff later told me he was never paid for! Those pictures are probably still in some vault.

A bunch of them were spliced together into "movies" and shown on TV.
Karloff told me that nine or ten were made, and then they ran out of money or something. I was in a couple of live television shows with him, too, I guess in the '50s. An amusing little story: On one, the actors were taking a smoke break and Karloff joined us as we were talking about our agents, complaining about something. He said [*in an English accent*], "Well, you know, I'm with MCA. MCA has offices all over the world. And when I'm out of work, I'm out of work *a-l-l over the world*!" [*Laughs*] I've always remembered that!

You had a pretty good part in one of your two Thrillers, *"Waxworks."*
It was a "remake" of *Mystery of the Wax Museum* [1933]. I was the homicide inspector and my assistant was Ron Ely. We must have looked like Mutt and Jeff [*laughs*]—he's about six-four, something like that, a very tall fellow, and I'm five-nine-and-a-half. I played with him again later, down in Mexico, when he was [TV's] *Tarzan*.

What was it you liked about Karloff?
Well, just about everything. He was a wonderful friend with a great sense of humor, and he loved his work. He always had great stories to tell, like Lon Chaney giving him a ride home one day when Boris was looking for extra work at Paramount! He had great stories and he *relished* his success, which came to him fairly late in life—he was past 40 when he got *Frankenstein*. He reveled in it, he enjoyed the success—he'd worked very hard for it.

Did you ever see him on stage?
Oh, yes, I saw him in *Arsenic and*

Old Lace and *The Linden Tree*, which Maurice Evans backed, and *Peter Pan*. I wish I could say I was *in* one of them—I wasn't, but I did see him in those things, and I would see him afterwards.

When Karloff was working in Hollywood in the '60s, did they have a home to stay at, or were they put up in hotels?
I think at that time that he stayed with Evie at the Chateau Marmont, which is a hotel on the Sunset Strip. Whether he owned property here, I don't know; I would doubt it, I think he probably gave all that up when he went to New York and played on the stage so much.

Apart from talking about "the business," what else would Karloff talk about? What were his interests?
He was a great cricketer, and in his halcyon days here he was a member of the British cricket set. Sir Aubrey Smith was the head of it, and *all* the British players—there was a tremendous colony here in those days. I've learned since that a certain amount of snobbery existed, the caste system that they brought with them; some members of the British colony here just sort of disassociated themselves from it, like Charles Laughton and others. But Karloff seemed to be comfortable with all of that. He came from a rather distinguished judicial family: I think there were seven boys, of which he was the youngest. They were all connected with the bar in England. But Boris wanted to be an actor and ran off to Canada, and I gather that (until he became a big success) he didn't have too much contact with them. I could be wrong about that, I don't know his family details *that* well.

Did he ever talk politics?
Not to my knowledge. In fact, I don't think he became an American.

I recently interviewed a guy named Aubrey Schenck, who produced a couple Karloff pictures, and he also sang Karloff's praises. And then, out of the blue, he threw in the comment that Karloff was "the stingiest guy who ever lived."
That was not my experience, although I certainly can't claim to have been *out* with him a lot. [The Karloffs] were fond of me, I feel, but I didn't share any intimacies with them or go out socializing or anything else. I could have been his *son* in terms of age. But I was never aware of anything of the sort. And on the rare occasions that we had coffee or something, he certainly *paid*. I remember riding in a taxi cab with Maurice Evans in New York; we were doing *Hamlet* and, between the matinee and the evening, we had the Helen Hayes radio show to tape. The cab fare was 80 cents, and he said [*in an English accent*], "Let's see now...here's *my* 40..." [*Laughs*] So *he* was rather like that! Sometimes I wondered, "Now, why would he *do* that?" It may have been that he was just basically *cheap*; but also it could have been to make a young actor feel that he was an *equal*. But if the places were reversed, I would have just paid the bill and forgotten about it! But, you know, these people grew up in a different milieu, under different circumstances, and I suppose there was a day in their lives where sixpence or two and six *meant* something [*laughs*]!

You mentioned Lon Chaney before, and I know you have a second-hand Chaney story that involves Joan Crawford.
I worked in an episode of *The*

Virginian, and the director of that show was Robert Gist. I'd known him from New York days—he was in the original company of *Harvey*—and he knew I enjoyed anything about Chaney. So he got her to talk about Chaney one morning, when we were sitting around in a little circle rehearsing lines. She started to talk about Chaney and she got *emotional*: She said that he was the greatest actor she'd ever been with in her career, including all the MGM leading men and everything else. He had opened up the world to her, taught her to *think* and to *react*, not to just pose and all that.

She *still* did a lot of posing [*laughs*] but, however, she had great admiration for him—her sentiments were obviously true. He must have been amused by her and, although it was a silent picture, he probably taught her not to just react with those big eyes, but to think about what she was supposed to be saying and doing.

Any memories of playing a small part in Them! *[1954]?*

I was a newspaperman in that; it was directed by Gordon Douglas, who had worked years before with Laurel and Hardy. I remember the interview to

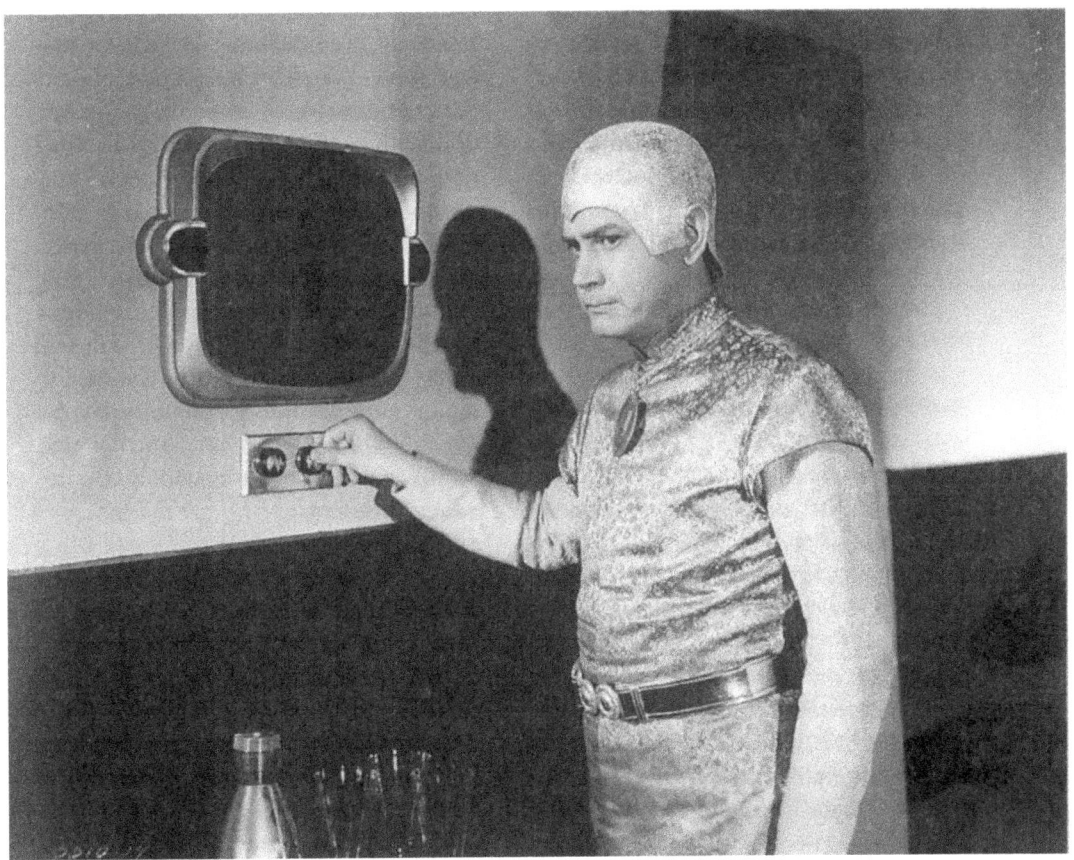

Don't let the floral pattern on his costume give you the wrong idea! Booth Colman was responsible for some man-sized acts of villainy in *World Without End.*

get the job: I was sitting on a bench in the casting office, next to a tall kid who was also waiting to go in and see Solly Biano, Warners' casting man in those days. We spoke to pass the time, and he said [*in a Texas drawl*], "I'm from Texas. I come here to be a movie star." He didn't say he was here to be an actor or to look for work, he was coming here to be a *movie star*. He got into the picture, too. Well, a short time later, Walt Disney sent for a print of *Them!* because he was interested in [*Them!* star] Jim Arness for the part of Davy Crockett [on the Disney TV series]. He saw the scene that this Texas kid played—he was in a psycho ward because he insisted he had seen these monster ants. He played the scene very well, and Disney said, "Who's that?" They had to find out his name, and Disney said, "I want to talk to him." And *this* kid got the part of Davy Crockett. His name was Fess Parker. That was his start—one of those "happy accidents."

Do you remember how you got your part in World Without End*?*

If I'm remembering right, the agent read it and suggested me for it, and I went over and auditioned for them and got the part. I can't remember very much about it: It was a quickie, it was done in eight or ten days I would say. The Australian actor, Rod Taylor—I think it was his first job here. He subsequently went over to MGM. And the director, Edward Bernds, was a very nice man. I saw the picture recently because someone gave me a tape of it, and…it's just a quick job of the day. I'm sure it did very well, I'm sure they made a lot of money on it. The *actors* didn't [*laughs*]!

Of all your movies that I've seen, you had the biggest parts in World Without End *and* Raiders from Beneath the Sea *[1964].*

When I look at those things now, I realize how much I had to learn [about acting in movies]. I had to learn to do less in front of a camera. *My* training was all on the stage, where you have to project your voice and your actions for the balcony. Of course, in pictures you have to do just the opposite.

I've just played a lot of small parts in a good many of these pictures; I suppose [my biggest part] *was* in one of those…sort of…*dumb* pictures [*laughs*]. Years after *World Without End*, a friend of mine, Nancy Galloway, was Sam Peckinpah's secretary at Warners. They had been great friends—Peckinpah was best man at her wedding. I had a lunch date with her and I came up to get her at his office. She introduced me to him, and he said, "Oh, hello, Booth. You don't remember me, do you?" And I didn't. He said, "I was the assistant director on *World Without End*," and I was embarrassed because, after all, I should have known that. (But I didn't!) He was a very pleasant man, quite unlike his reputation with the booze and the swearing and the carrying-on. And he was very nice to *her*—she was with him quite a long time.

In the early '60s, you made a few films overseas.

I spent one year in Rome—the year we had an actors' strike here. I worked there in two American pictures [*Under Ten Flags*, 1960, and *Romanoff and Juliet*, 1961] and two Italian-Yugoslav co-productions. I also did a lot of dubbing of Italian movies [into English]—I was quite busy that year. They had a small Anglo-American community there, professional actors, or somebody's husband or wife [*laughs*], and they were pretty good. I dubbed quite a few pictures into the English-language version. They had to dub *every*thing—there was a French company and a German and so forth.

Do you remember the titles of the Italian-Yugoslav movies you mentioned?

No, I've tried to do that before and I can't. I remember going to Dubrovnik and once to Zagreb, and in one scene, about *four languages* were used. You learned where your cue was and that's when you spoke. Of course, everything was dubbed later, so it didn't matter. They had an Italian speaking Italian, I spoke English, and there was a Serbian and someone else, German, I think [*laughs*]. They were lousy horror pictures, but I don't remember much about them.

Were there any other Americans in them?

Not to my knowledge. Unless they were hiding behind accents or something [*laughs*]!

You worked on a lot of different TV series in the '60s, including Tarzan *and* Voyage to the Bottom of the Sea.

Tarzan was in Mexico, and I think I did two episodes back-to-back. If the show had had a third season, my character would have been repeated. But I understand they had arguments over salary and they didn't continue it, so they had only the two seasons and I was only on the two episodes of the final season.

I remember Irwin Allen [producer of *Voyage*]—he also *directed* the episode you mentioned. He was a very pleasant man to me. I did a couple of jobs for him later on, like a pilot that didn't sell.

He had had a successful show called *The Time Tunnel*, and he sort of revamped it and called it *Time Travelers* [1976]—the same idea of a professor sending the two leading men back into the past. I did the part of the professor. It didn't sell, for what reason I don't know; it was as good as any of the other junk made at the time [*laughs*]! I would have been a regular on the show if it had taken off.

You were a regular on the short-lived Planet of the Apes *TV series.*

At the time it was being cast on the Fox lot, they saw a great many people. I had an appointment in the ordinary way and I had to read a scene, and they seemed to like the way I did that. I was called back (I think *twice*), and I finally read for the assembled "supreme court." They liked what I did; one of the men said, "Would you feel claustrophobic in that kind of makeup?" Trying to be funny, I said, "Well, I think Lon Chaney's ghost would come down and protect me," or some idiot remark like that. Which they thought was good! And the next thing I heard was that I had gotten the job, as Dr. Zaius. I certainly enjoyed it, but if you'd said at the time that 27 years later people would still be interested, I would have been amazed!

They told you that you had the job before you were involved in any makeup sessions?

Yes, that's right. *Then* they did a plaster cast of my head, my face and all of that. At the auditions, the thing was, "Could he say the lines? Could he have intensity?" or whatever it was they were looking for. (That's what *I* would look for, anyway.) So, no, there was no makeup session first—that would have entailed a lot of time and money.

TV star Colman had to rise at 3:45 A.M. to be in the makeup chair at five every day that he appeared as *Planet of the Apes'* Dr. Zaius.

Do you remember who else was up for the part?
No, I don't, but I can tell you that there were a great many.

What was the makeup ordeal like the first time?
Well, it was horrendous. I've never cared much for spirit gum and sticking things on and all of that—and this was that in spades! But you get used to *any*thing. I was made up every morning by Frank Westmore, the youngest of the first generation of Westmores. When I got used to it, it wasn't so bad.

"Walk" me through a busy day for you on the Apes *set.*
I had to get up around quarter to four in the morning, to be there at Fox, in Frank's chair in the makeup department, at five o'clock. And I was ready at eight, with about a half an hour or so off in the middle, when they'd bring me in breakfast. At eight o'clock, I'd be on the set, after the wigs and the clothes and all the rest of it. I'm sure they were Maurice Evans' costumes [from the movies], 'cause the studio had everything there. We were more or less the same size. I like to think that I got the job because I did it well, but it may have been because the clothes would fit [*laughs*]!

Then we'd do the day's work, whatever it was. They got very good at it as time went on, and I'd be through in the early afternoon. But, when we first started, there were days when I was there all day long. Of course, you get very tired; I don't think I could handle it today. You'd go home tired and study whatever you had to do tomorrow. It wasn't something where you'd be working constantly, morning, noon and night at it; after all, it *was* a television show.

And lunch?
You couldn't have lunch, except something through a straw. I tried to eat a sandwich one day, but you *can't*. You had to eat like an animal, with your "other mouth" out in front of you. And you couldn't rinse your mouth or anything. So I gave that up. I'd have breakfast, and then very little at lunch and dinner.

Had you seen any of the Apes *movies?*
I saw the first one, and maybe one of the others. That's all.

Roddy McDowall said that after a while, because of all the rubber appliances, his face was like hamburger.
Well, yes. And some people are sensitive to acetone and those things, which they use to remove the makeup. I know I had problems, too. After two or three days of it, your face is very irritated. If you have a day or two off, it heals quickly—at least in *my* case it did. But he had skin problems of some kind. They'd spend about 15 minutes taking the makeup off, because they did it very carefully in order to use it on "atmosphere people" the next day. They used human hair and yak hair on me, so it was an expensive proposition and they saved the pieces. I would get new stuff every day—

And, once they were peeled off you, they became "hand-me-downs."
That's right. I don't know if they could do that today; it's probably unhygienic [*laughs*]! Roddy was very pleasant to me and we did our scenes very well. But we were never really formally introduced. One day I was talking to him with*out* my makeup, and suddenly he said, "Oh!" and he started to laugh. I guess my voice was a giveaway and he

Colman has been starring since 1971 in the yearly Meadow Brook Theatre (Rochester, Michigan) production of *A Christmas Carol*.

The eyes are the only thing of your own [that are showing]. You have to learn to use your voice so it doesn't sound too muffled—you have to "throw your voice," like a ventriloquist. Your body posture and your walk and all of that sort of thing—that's all you can do. After all, you're completely hidden otherwise.

You visited a zoo for pointers on how to play an orangutan.

Yes, I did, I went to the zoo here and watch them. They walk, you know, in a different way, their *structure* is different.

The reviews of the first episode were universally awful. Variety *called it "retarded"!*

I thought that was the best one they had [*laughs*]! And I still *do*! I guess the reviewers felt it suffered by comparison with the movie, and perhaps that it so. But it wasn't so bad. I think it was the best script they had.

Were you disappointed when it was canceled after only 14 episodes?

I certainly was. Not because I thought it was a great artistic achievement, but it was a very nice *job*. I was hoping that it would get two or three seasons, and it *might* have, under other circumstances.

For years now, you've been playing

realized who I was—and *I* realized that he didn't know what I looked like without my makeup on [*laughs*]!

McDowall also said he had to depend on his eyes and facial movements to do any sort of acting through all the makeup.

Scrooge in a Michigan stage production of *A Christmas Carol.*

I've been going to that theater [the Meadow Brook Theatre at Rochester] since 1971. My friend Terry Kilburn was the artistic director there; he recently retired after 25 years. He directed me in [the play] *The Andersonville Trial* here in Los Angeles in 1961, and in '71, when he was at the Meadow Brook Theatre and decided to repeat *Andersonville Trial,* he sent for me to come and do the part, which I did. Then I did *Inherit the Wind, A Man for All Seasons, The Caine Mutiny Court Martial, Death of a Salesman, The Merchant of Venice*—a lot of different plays. And finally he decided to do *A Christmas Carol* 16 years ago, and it was a big hit and a moneymaker for them. (Terry was in the 1938 MGM version of *A Christmas Carol*—he played Tiny Tim.) I've done it every year since; last year [1997] was the fifteenth time. It's a wonderful part—it *isn't* just some silly nonsense about a cranky old man. You see a *metamorphosis* of the man—it's a morality play, and it has a great deal to say. It's done very well there, I must say, and it's a "big thing"—a lot of locals are used, and every year there's competition among the children for the jobs. There's a nucleus of regulars—a couple of people have been with me all 15 years in it. And from time to time I do another play there, *Camping With Henry and Tom,* a play about Thomas Edison and Henry Ford and President Harding. I play Tom Edison.

What else would you like to add, as we wrap this up? Anything?

No, not really [*laughs*]! I'm here waiting for the next job, waiting for the next phone call. I don't intend to retire, not as long as I can learn the lines and move around.

Booth Colman Filmography

The Big Sky (RKO, 1952)
Julius Caesar (MGM, 1953)
The Silver Chalice (Warners, 1954)
Living It Up (Paramount, 1954)
The Human Jungle (Allied Artists, 1954)
The Adventures of Hajji Baba (20th Century–Fox, 1954)
Secret of the Incas (Paramount, 1954)
Ring of Fear (Warners, 1954)
Them! (Warners, 1954)
Moonfleet (MGM, 1955)
Flight to Hong Kong (United Artists, 1956)
World Without End (Allied Artists, 1956)
My Gun Is Quick (United Artists, 1957)
Auntie Mame (Warners, 1958)
The Beast of Budapest (Allied Artists, 1958)
The Case Against Brooklyn (Columbia, 1958)
Under Ten Flags (Paramount, 1960)
The Errand Boy (Paramount, 1961)
The Comancheros (20th Century–Fox, 1961)
Romanoff and Juliet (Universal, 1961)
Raiders from Beneath the Sea (20th Century–Fox, 1964)
Fate Is the Hunter (20th Century–Fox, 1964)
A Global Affair (MGM, 1964)
Kisses for My President (Warners, 1964)

Youngblood Hawke (Warners, 1964)
Harlow (Paramount, 1965)
Wild on the Beach (20th Century-Fox, 1965)
Runaway Girl (United Screen Arts, 1966)
Maryjane (AIP, 1968)
The Lawyer (Paramount, 1970)
The Great White Hope (20th Century–Fox, 1970)
Scandalous John (Buena Vista, 1971)
Norma Rae (20th Century-Fox, 1979)
Return to the Secret Garden (2000)

Faith Domergue

I was black-and-blue, from shoulder to feet,
when I was battling [the Metaluna Mutant]...
That man in the monster suit really had me beaten up!

Born in New Orleans, Louisiana, Faith Domergue was 15 years old when she was signed by Warner Brothers, who sold her contract to industrialist-movie producer Howard Hughes several months later. Hughes gave her a big publicity buildup but didn't allow her to star in a movie until *Vendetta* (1950), a historical melodrama with a problem-fraught production history more intriguing than the movie itself. The dark-eyed beauty went on to play everything from murderesses (*Where Danger Lives*, *The Duel at Silver Creek*, *This Is My Love*) to a scientist battling mutants in outer space (*This Island Earth*). She also contended with a giant octopus in *It Came from Beneath the Sea*, and even played a monster herself—a slinky snake woman who charmed and then chilled her victims in *Cult of the Cobra*. Domergue, 74, died of cancer in Santa Barbara, California, on April 4, 1999.

This interview was conducted by Michael Fitzgerald, with questions prepared by Fitzgerald and Tom Weaver. Michael is the author of Arlington House's *Universal Pictures*, co-author of McFarland's *Westerns Women* (with Boyd Magers), and is the organizer of the annual Universal Players Reunion. He lives in El Dorado, Arkansas.

When you first got into pictures, was your "Southern" accent a problem?

Well, I never had an accent! My parents and I left New Orleans was I was two. Like many others during the Great Depression, we wound up in California. Southerners stick together, it seems, for everybody who came to our house was from the South. Although my parents and their friends had accents, I never had one. I did have a lisp, and it was my second grade teacher who corrected it—by having me read poetry! I enjoyed it, and I was so good at it that I was asked to read at various places.

How did your contract with Warner Brothers come about?

There was a place in Santa Monica called, I think, the Del Mar Beach Club. My parents didn't like it, but I did. One day, Mr. Hamilton (I've forgotten his first name) told me, "You are such a

Glamourous Faith Domergue first went under contract (to Warner Bros.) at age 15.

beautiful young girl. You really should be in pictures." Well, that line was used on *every*body, but this time, it turned out to be legitimate! He introduced me to Henry Willson, an agent with the Zeppo Marx Agency. It was Mr. Willson who took me to Warner Brothers, and Steve Trilling, and then to Sophie Rosenstein, the great drama coach at Warners. It was that simple. I was signed to a term contact, with the approval of my parents and the courts. Of course, I had already done a great deal of little theater (I loved it), and I had studied at the Bliss-Hayden Academy.*

At such a young age, what was life like at a studio?
It was an eight-hour day that included four hours of school. Joan Leslie and Gloria Warren, a singer in the Deanna Durbin vein, were the only other girls in class with me. Miss Horne was the teacher, and when we weren't studying our ABCs, we studied acting and anything else that might help us in a career. I was coached and often watched films being made, but never had so much as a walk-on at Warners.

Your picture appears in a 1941 Photoplay, *and you were referred to as Faith Dorn. Was that a mistake?*
No. Jack Warner was too stupid to pronounce Faith Domergue, so he had my name changed to Faith Dorn. Anyway, I only stayed there [at Warners] for eight or nine months. I signed in April 1941, was renewed in six months, and then two or three months later, Mr. Howard Hughes asked to buy my contract, and they agreed.

And you still made no films, not until you were finished with school.
Then, for the experience, I was given a small role on loan-out in a Jane Russell picture, *Young Widow* [1946]. I had third billing but only two scenes. It got me used to the camera and everything. You can study, but it is experience that is needed.

Are all the stories about the making of Vendetta *really true?*
Well, it really did take years to make. We started it in 1946, after I finished *Young Widow* [with Max Ophuls directing]. But shortly thereafter, Mr. Hughes was in that terrible plane accident where he crashed into several homes in Beverly Hills. Anyway, we shot it on location about two hours north of Los Angeles. Preston Sturges [Hughes' partner at the time] for some reason took advantage of the fact that Mr. Hughes was incapacitated, and he took absolute control—of the script, and almost everything else. Preston was always on the set, and he wouldn't even let Max Ophuls direct. Max might be able to say "Action" or "Cut," but it was Mr. Sturges who kept calling the shots. Six weeks later, they had spent a million dollars, and had no film to show! Finally, a recovering Howard Hughes got wind of it and fired both Max and Preston. He hired Stuart Heisler to direct. We then started from scratch—new script, new costumes, but the same cast. Four months more went by. There was a layoff. Then Mel Ferrer came on the scene to direct retakes. This went on and on. By 1948, I had married Hugo Fregonese, a director from South America, and I told them I was moving to Buenos Aires. I agreed to further retakes, but I wanted nothing more to do with motion pictures. On January 1, 1949, my daughter Dianna was born [in Buenos Aires], and in April we fled back to the U.S. because of political unrest. My husband was trapped down there, but he did manage to escape later on.

What happened then?
I wanted to go back to work. Henry

---

*Character actor Harry Hayden and his actress-wife Lela Bliss owned and operated the acting school.

Reluctant planet-hoppers Rex Reason and Domergue grapple with one of Metaluna's insect-men (Reg Parton) in *This Island Earth*.

Willson came out and told me of two offers. Feeling an obligation to Howard Hughes, who now owned RKO, I took the RKO deal and I began work on *A White Rose for Julie*—which was the working title for *Where Danger Lives* [1950]. I played a homicidal maniac who murders her husband, Claude Rains, by suffocation! She almost does the same thing to her lover, Robert Mitchum!

Career-wise, did things start to go better for you at this time?

Well, sort of. Mr. Hughes had both films completed, but never released them! He did give me a huge publicity build-up. I am told he spent five million dollars publicizing me—but with neither film in release, it was all wasted. By the time he finally did release them, I had to tell him I couldn't attend the New York premieres—I was expecting my second child. Naturally, he was furious. All that money spent promoting a glamour girl who was in actuality a mother and a mother-to-be. He hid me out in Palm Springs, until one day Louella Parsons got hold of it and told the story. I then asked if I could go back to Los Angeles.

Is that when you signed with Universal?

I sat around RKO for two years, doing nothing. Then I was finally loaned out to Universal for *The Duel at Silver Creek* [1952].

Wasn't it peculiar that in all your first roles, you were villainous?

Perhaps. It seems that dark-haired girls were portraying that type more so than blondes. Actually, in *Vendetta* I was more of a menace than a villain—but Hillary Brooke was the blonde good girl. The meanies always give you more to do than the sweet little ingenues.

How did you get out of your RKO contract?

My husband was going to England to direct *Decameron Nights* [1952] starring Joan Fontaine. I wanted to be with him, and I asked Perry Lieber, head of publicity at RKO, to help me obtain my release, and he did.

You didn't stay in England long, did you?

No—over there, the director's wife was virtually nothing. I had been a star, a *somebody* over here, and I wanted to be again. So I returned to America, signed a two-pictures-per-year contract with Universal, and started working steadily. In fact, every week in 1954 and 1955 I was working, either in a film or on television.

You've mentioned that This Island Earth *[1955] is your favorite sci-fi film.*

Yes, very much so. Whenever there is a film festival in Europe, it seems they always run that one. Unfortunately, some of the footage that was shot seems to be missing from the prints—on television as well.

They created the dying planet of Metaluna on the old Phantom of the Opera sound stage—the largest sound stage in Hollywood. Although there were technically "no accidents" on the picture, I was black-and-blue, from shoulder to feet, when I was battling that monster [the Metaluna Mutant, played by stuntman Regis Parton]. And much of that sequence is what seems to be missing from prints today. Maybe it was edited at the time, but I don't recall that it was.

Did any of the black-and-blue marks need to be covered by makeup?

No. Remember, I was wearing that form-fitting suit—all the resulting bruises were covered up in that uniform. But that man in the monster suit really had me beaten up! And, oh, remember when Rex Reason and I go into that lake? Well, it was freezing cold and not clean. They had the explosives, so we *had* to go underwater! I've always said that special effects try to kill me. And then, 20 years later, it ironically did happen to a friend. I worked on a *Combat* [TV episode] with Vic Morrow, and years later the special effects on *Twilight Zone—The Movie* [1983] went wrong, and he was decapitated. Very, very frightening.

Had you worked with special effects before?

Oh, my, yes. In *Vendetta*, there was the scene where I have to be shot. Well, Stuart Heisler was the director during this episode, and he wanted it *real!* They wired gunpowder underneath my heart, to show the explosion when I'm shot. One guy hiding behind a bush had a wire that controlled it. Another man had another wire that would pull me back, just as if I had actually been shot. Well, when we did the take, it exploded and I was pulled back all right, but my dress was on fire! The harness that the explosives were connected to kept me from being burned, but it made me mad as hell! Then another time, we had lots of fog (I call it smog), made of ammonia and dry ice. Well, those ammonia fumes really got to me. My mouth was swollen, I just couldn't handle it. And the smell! They put Black Narcissus perfume on the smog, and it was even worse. Yes, special effects have always tried to kill me.

What memories of Jeff Morrow? You worked with him twice.

I did? What was the other picture?

Legacy of Blood *[1973]*.

Oh, that's right. Oooh, the special effects on that—the actor [John Smith] who had those bees all over him. Well, I wouldn't have been able to have done that. I have never seen the picture, although I thought that it was pretty good at the time.

And how was Morrow to work with?

He was a man of the interior, very inside. Sweet, dear. He took his work seriously, and wouldn't budge on a point. He'd argue with the director because he thought he was right. He always stayed by himself—like a young Claude Rains. He ate at the commissary by himself. In the second picture [*Legacy of Blood*], which was years later, he did loosen up a little, but he never did open up.

And Rex Reason?

Rex was fun, giving, charming. We got along, just like buddies. We endured all those special effects hazards together. Oh, back to the water scene. Of course it was shot from different angles, many times. But, the first time we had a take, I just couldn't bring myself to go under. Rex literally pushed me under that icy cold water. Universal's back lot, after dark, got extremely cold.

Were all your scenes shot at Universal?

Yes, either on the sound stage or on the back lot. No locations at all.

Did you realize This Island Earth *was "a classic in the making"?*

No, you never know that it's going to be. But I could tell it was something good. It took much longer to make, and [Universal] kept pouring money into it. I knew it was going to be something spectacular. And after I saw it, I was very impressed. I recently looked at it again, and it still holds up very well!

Where did you first see it?

The studio screened it for us on the lot, and I *loved* it! And the special effects, they were all perfectly wonderful. My children had seen Reggie [Parton] in the monster outfit [on the set], without his monster head on. I assumed they would identify him when he was on the screen, but oh, no. Both were small, and they began screaming! I had to get up and take them out of the theater! I really shouldn't have let them see the film, because they became hysterical. But I really did think they'd recognize Reggie.

Both Jeff Morrow and Rex Reason thought the inclusion of the Mutant was a bad idea, that it cheapened the movie. Did you have an opinion about this?

I don't agree! I thought the Mutants

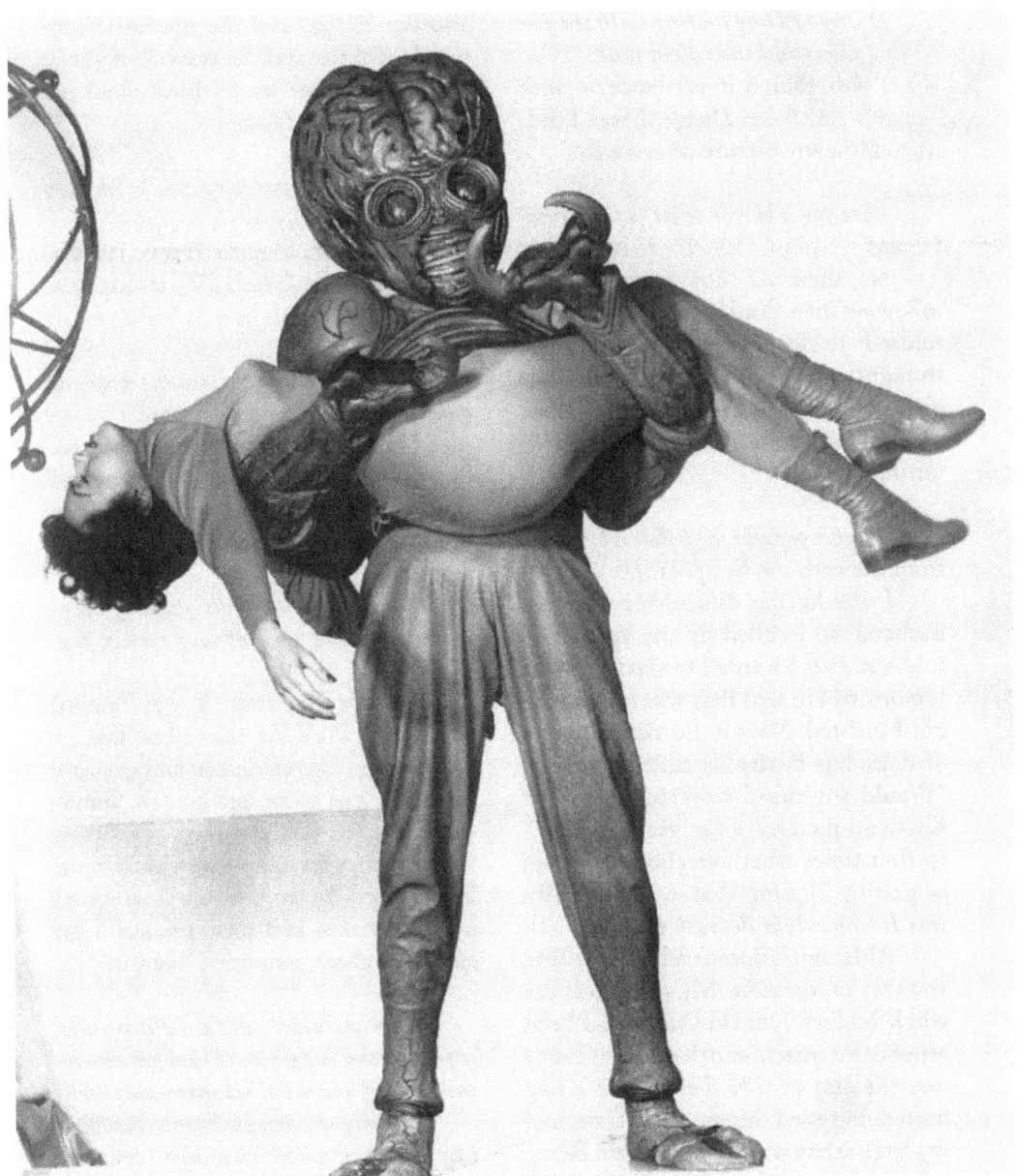

"Black-and-blue, from shoulder to feet" after duking it out with the Metaluna Mutant, Domergue gets a well-earned rest in her opponent's arms.

were wonderful—look how many were in *Star Wars*. And ours were the *first*. And, you know, Steven Spielberg must like our picture, because a few years ago I was watching *E.T.* [1982] with my daughter in Santa Barbara. To my surprise, when E.T. turned on that television, there were Rex and I [in *This Island Earth*], being pulled up into that flying saucer! It was very exciting!

Did you do any touring with the picture, as Universal stars often did?

I only toured in conjunction with *Vendetta* and *Where Danger Lives*. I didn't tour on any picture afterwards.

Were you a horror or sci-fi fan growing up?

No, there was not much of a cult following then. And besides, my parents refused to let me see them. They thought it might frighten their little girl. Strange as it sounds, I had never seen one of those classics of the 1930s until much later.

Another popular sci-fi flick is It Came from Beneath the Sea *[1955].*

I was having difficulties with my husband, so I called up my agent and told him that I wanted to start working tomorrow! He said that was impossible but I insisted. Now, it did take a couple of days, but finally he called up with, "Would you mind working on a Sam Katzman picture? I can get you three-to-four times what everybody else will be getting." I jumped at it, and the film was *It Came from Beneath the Sea*.

Although it doesn't look it, the film was very inexpensive. My salary was the whole budget. Donald Curtis had been around for years, and Kenneth Tobey was the star of *The Thing*, but I had been doing good things at this time, and my large salary was the end result. Being a "name" certainly paid off. We were actually on that submarine, and being the only lady aboard, it presented a little problem when it was time to use the ladder. I would always say, "Gentlemen, please. Clear away!" We also went to San Francisco to shoot but, you know something?, they wouldn't let us use the Golden Gate Bridge! We had to use another bridge, and the special effects people did the rest. I always thought it was strange that we couldn't shoot on the real Golden Gate.

Where did you stay while in San Francisco?

At the St. Francis Hotel. It's the one used for the *Hotel* [TV] series a few years ago.

Did you have any trouble with the quickie nature of the production?

I had no trouble with the quickness. Besides, it was well done. Katzman had tiptop production crews and actors. The production flowed quickly—and well.

Compare the "no-frills" shooting experience to making some of your earlier, bigger pictures.

On the big stuff, I was babied, pampered. We'd do take after take. It was boring. On the lesser budgets, my initiative had to be put into it. Sometimes I even did my own wardrobe, when I felt what they had wasn't right. I rehearsed by myself, so I wouldn't make mistakes and need retakes. I got quick, brighter, smarter. I liked it!

Your character was a very assured, self-sufficient lady—until danger threatened, and of course she fell apart completely!

She was an entirely liberated, highly intelligent marine biologist, smarter than the men. But she was also a woman—so she swooned [*laughs*]!

What were your impressions of Kenneth Tobey?

Very nice—I just wish he'd gone further, he was a good actor. I recently saw him in *The Thing*—it had been colorized. He was very good.

Did you meet Sam Katzman?

A lovely, roly-poly, full-of-beans, get-up-and-do-it man. Not terribly refined, but smart! He got quality for small money.

Were you impressed with It's *special effects?*

No. The special effects were run of the mill. The picture was good, the story, the approach, the suspense. Excellent actors. But the special effects, just so-so.

When you started doing the sci-fi films and the budget Westerns, you must have realized that your chances for "top stardom" were being relinquished. Was it a tough decision, making the move into these smaller movies?

Definitely it was a tough decision. But I had two children to support. I had a big house, a nurse, a maid. My husband gave me nothing—not even child support. You can't fight for the best films when you have to fight for the moment—you take whatever is offered. I had no choice. I had to have money for the bills.

Do you have any anecdotes about Cult of the Cobra *[1955]?*

Yes, that was very interesting. I had been on location is St. George, Utah, shooting *Santa Fe Passage* [1955] with John Payne for Republic. We were there over a month, and that picture turned out to be my favorite of the features I did, with *This Island Earth* coming in second. Anyway, we were back at Republic, doing the interior shots, when I got a call from Universal telling me I had to report immediately for a movie already in production called *Cult of the Cobra*. It seems that Mari Blanchard was playing the part of Lisa Moya, but she just wasn't coming over, and they thought I'd be perfect.* I told [Universal] I wasn't finished with *Santa Fe Passage*, but since I had signed that two-pictures-per-year pact, they told me to report on my noon hour for costume fittings! Luckily, Republic and Universal are near each other in the Valley, so that wasn't as much of a problem as it could have been. This kept up, and then the day after I finished at Republic, I was to report to Universal. Well [*laughs*], I showed up for work the next day—at Republic, where they told me, "Miss Domergue, you finished the picture yesterday." I couldn't believe it, but going back and forth so much confused me! I hurried over to Universal, and it was the only time in my life that I was late for work. They were very nice and understood the predicament.

Through lighting, they gave my eyes that eerie, "snakey" quality. Luckily, I have green eyes, because had they been brown, the technique they used just wouldn't have worked. And as you know, I didn't transform into a snake like, say, Lon Chaney, Jr., changed into the Wolf Man, so I was lucky in that way.

I assume that it wasn't you in the temple scene, wrapped in a snake outfit and weaving in and out of that jar during the "snake dance."

No, that wasn't me. She was a dancer with the Carlssons, as I recall.

---

*Domergue misremembers the situation (or was misinformed by Universal). Mari Blanchard did screen-test for the lead, but Domergue was signed to play the part over the October 23-24, 1954, weekend, several days before the movie went into production.

Sultry Domergue played one of her most sizable film roles in the Lewton-esque chiller *Cult of the Cobra*.

In Cult, *you're both villainous and sympathetic at the same time.*

Yes, perhaps I was, but you must remember that I was playing this terrible person, carrying out those hideous deeds. She couldn't have gotten off, even if she did have second thoughts about it all. I do agree that it was sad at the end, when Marshall Thompson walks slowly away from her lifeless body, finally realizing it was she who had committed all those murders.

So you enjoyed playing the snake woman.
Yes, it was lots of fun! Everybody was friendly. Because of doing the two pictures together, I would be tired, and sometimes forget my lines. Everyone was so patient and understanding.

Did you have to work with the cobras?
Absolutely not! There were real cobras on the set, but they had people there who knew how to handle them. I didn't get close!

Kathleen Hughes, who's also in Cult of the Cobra, *remembers that the director Francis D. Lyon gave her a hard time. Do you have any memory of him?*
He was quiet. A dear. I later did *Escort West* [1959] with him. He was a simple little man, and we got along fine together. There were no problems at all.

What did you think of the finished film?
When I saw it, I was so pleased—with the film and myself. I was going through a divorce with Hugo, and with all this trauma, it didn't show at all in the performance. I didn't let it get to me. Yes, it was really rather good.

What about the movies you made in England in the mid-50s?
For *The Atomic Man* [1956] with Gene Nelson, I had to have a work permit, and Gene had to have a permit as well. But Lee Patterson, my leading man in *Spin a Dark Web* [1956], was a Canadian and thus exempt! I thought the premise of *The Atomic Man* interesting, but it wasn't a very good picture.

Director Ken Hughes went on to bigger, better things. What can you recall about him?
He was very English. He had bright, quick ideas about things. I later saw him in America—he'd come over to replace somebody on a Kim Novak movie. He had remained the same—a little on the Cockney side.

Compare making a picture in England with working in Hollywood.
Things move *slower* in England than in the U.S. When I did the picture with Zachary Scott, *Violent Stranger* [1957], there was a woman in the cast who couldn't remember her lines. We shot all afternoon long without film in the camera, just for her. They would *never* do that over here! But anyway, I went back and forth to do the pictures—I wasn't living over there full time during those periods. I did a lot of TV work in the '50s and '60s, and it was through the experience of television that I felt I really learned my craft. In fact, the most favorite thing I ever did was an episode of *Bonanza* entitled "The Lonely House." It was directed by William Witney, and was so well-received that *TV Guide* did a cover story on it!

Let's talk a little about a few of your other leading men. In Where Danger Lives, *were you afraid of Robert Mitchum, considering his then-recent publicity?*
I was terrified of him! It was so important to me to do good on this film. But Bob put me on ease within three days on the set. He was divine, intelligent

and witty. We became great friends. In fact, on the last day of shooting, Mitchum and John Farrow, the director, took me to lunch. They presented me with a beautiful gold bracelet. When you turned it over, the inscription read, FROM THE OTHER MEN IN YOUR LIFE.

What about Claude Rains, who played your husband?

He was formal. Very difficult to know. He'd rehearse until he'd drop, but then he hurried on back to his dressing room. I never warmed up to him, or really got to know him.

*One actor you worked with didn't seem to get along off-camera with anybody—Audie Murphy [*The Duel at Silver Creek*].*

I have heard that, and at first Audie was quiet, very stand-offish. Then, for some reason, he decided I was "okay." He came over and asked my advice on a cooking stove he and his new wife were about to buy. We became friends, and I have him all the homey advice he asked for, never letting on that I wasn't the least bit domestic, as he had assumed. Audie was very easy to work with—much more so than, say, Stephen McNally [in the same movie], who was "tense," "tight." Now, the director, Don Siegel, was good, marvelous. A much better director than I am an actress.

What about Voyage to the Prehistoric Planet *[1956] with Basil Rathbone?*

That was a Russian film, and they took the [scenes of] Russian actors out and put us in—using the same backgrounds, exteriors and such. At the time I signed to do it, I was unaware of what it was going to be. Basil was charming. A lovely man, so professional. Ouida, his wife, was unfortunately not on the set. I would have enjoyed seeing her. She was a legendary hostess.

And director Curtis Harrington? Any recollection?

Vaguely. Not too much. I've blocked it out of my mind. I just did it for the money, as did Basil Rathbone. But when we were making it, over at Robert Altman's studio, I wandered into the prop department and came across a sculptured head of my first husband! I had given it away when we split, and it was rather startling, running into his "head" at this time!

Prehistoric Planet *is available on video tape. Would you like a copy?*

No, thank you.

Psycho Sisters *[1972], with Susan Strasberg?*

That was a fun picture. I enjoyed working with Susan Strasberg and Sydney Chaplin, I had a great time with them—but I have no desire to ever see it! [Director] Reginald LeBorg was kind of cranky. I did a *Bronco* or maybe a *Sugarfoot* with him years earlier and, you know what?, he was crabby in *that*, too! *Psycho Sisters* is not a good movie. I fought the whole time and they were trying to violate SAG rules about time off between shooting and having to be back on the set. I told them I would have to report them for breaking those rules. And I refused to do retakes!

What more can you remember about Legacy of Blood?

I saw the rough cut without the music. It needed work, but I thought it was good. It was short, so they had to add some scenes, trim some others. I thought *Legacy of Blood* was one of my best jobs! I have never seen the completed version, though.

How did you wind up in The House of Seven Corpses *[1973]?*

I was about to move to Europe with my husband [Paolo Cossa], and I wanted to do one final picture. I heard about this picture, I called my agent and told him to get me an interview. I went to the interview, and was very serious. When I was leaving, the director, Paul Harrison, said, "Goodbye, Smiley" [*laughs*], and I knew I got the part! *House of Seven Corpses* was fun to do. We shot it in Utah, because it was partially backed by Mormons. There was always one of the Salt Lake City Mormons on the set, to make sure that there was no smoking or alcohol around. Coca-Cola, okay. Wine, *no way*. Now, I'm a Catholic, and I do like wine with dinner. But you had to buy your own wine, and sneak it into the restaurant in a brown paper bag. The waitress would bring me a glass, but she wouldn't pour it!

How did Mormons happen to finance a horror film?

They were good businessmen, I guess. They knew a surefire investment when they saw it, so they took it! It was shot in a huge Mormon house—a museum piece that is open to the public, in Salt Lake City. I never saw the movie, but I have it here and have yet to run it. It was my last film.

Is shooting on actual locations better or worse than working on a sound stage?

Shooting at an actual location is the best! When you're shooting at a real place, it adds to the atmosphere and the performance. The real is much better for the characters—and the film.

You worked twice with John Carradine, Legacy of Blood *and* Seven Corpses. *When you think of Carradine, what comes to mind?*

A very embarrassing situation. John was a lovely man. However, when we were reading for *The House of Seven Corpses*, he was "in his cups" [drunk]. But when we were working, he was absolutely splendid. He had arthritis from the top of his head to the tip of his toes. This didn't prevent him from doing a magnificent job. He had a long monologue that was just great! I admired him very much. Later, however, John Ireland and I were having dinner at a restaurant, and I commented about Carradine, "I was pleasantly surprised how wonderful he is—considering he was tight during the reading of the script." Well, a man at the next table stood up, turned around, bowed and left. It was John Carradine! I was never so humiliated in my life! He never mentioned it afterwards, and I've always wished that it hadn't happened.

Do you mind the fact that some of your biggest fans are fans of these horror and sci-fi films of yours?

Heck, I don't mind. It's nice to have fans who enjoy you and your work, no matter what pictures they like.

With all the horror films you did, which did you think was the most terrifying?

Actually, to me the most terrifying experience of all was *live TV*. I call that "30 minutes of *hell*." On that, you had un-coverable mistakes. Did I just coin a new word, "un-coverable"? It was the anticipation that was most frightening, knowing that any and every mistake would be seen by millions of people. And, unlike the stage, there was no way to cover up the blunders. I would think to myself, "Why am I in this business?" while waiting the countdown to air time.

How about your life today?

By the early '60s, Hugo and I were long divorced, and in 1987 he passed away. I had to read about it in the paper. In 1963, I met Paolo Cossa, and he became the love of my life! We were married in 1966, and in the early 1970s we finally settled in Europe—Rome and Geneva. Since his recent death, I have decided to move back to the States, and am currently in the midst of looking for a home.

What led to your retirement from acting?

My husband, a former agent, was connected with the Bulgari Jewelers in Geneva. They are possibly the largest jewelers in the world today. When we moved to Europe, he asked if I would mind giving up the career and help him with this new business. And I did.

Did you ever see your films on TV in Europe?

Well, very seldom. And they were dubbed.

Did you do any of your own dubbing?

No, I never did. The French have their own actors—very professional—who do their dubbing. They are so careful about it. And the Italians always shoot without sound—it is later dubbed in.

Finally, are there any plans to resume your career?

I don't think I will—but one must never say never. Let's see, would I do character parts? Mmm. No, I don't think so. I have been asked recently, and said no. Right now, my children, my friends and my future home are important. But if something was amusing, fun—perhaps...

Faith Domergue Filmography

As Faith Dorn:
Dancing in a Harem (Featurettes, Inc., short, 1941)

As Faith Domergue:
Young Widow (United Artists, 1946)
Vendetta (RKO, 1950)
Where Danger Lives (RKO, 1950)
The Duel at Silver Creek (Universal, 1952)
The Great Sioux Uprising (Universal, 1953)
This Is My Love (RKO, 1954)
This Island Earth (Universal, 1955)

It Came from Beneath the Sea (Columbia, 1955)
Santa Fe Passage (Republic, 1955)
Cult of the Cobra (Universal, 1955)
The Atomic Man (*Timeslip*) (Allied Artists, 1956)
Spin a Dark Web (*Soho Incident*) (Columbia, 1956)
Il Cielo brucia (1957)
Violent Stranger (*Man in the Shadow*) (Anglo-Amalgamated Film Distributors, 1957)
Escort West (United Artists, 1959)

California (AIP, 1963)
Track of Thunder (United Artists, 1967)
The Gamblers (U-M Film Distributors, 1970)
One on Top of the Other (GGP, 1969)
The Man with Icy Eyes (1971)
Psycho Sisters (*So Evil, My Sister*) (Prism Entertainment/Hollywood Home Entertainment, 1972)
Legacy of Blood (*Blood Legacy*) (Universal Entertainment, 1973)
The House of Seven Corpses (International Amusement Corp., 1973)
This Island Earth clips featuring Domergue are seen in *E.T. The Extra-Terrestrial* (Universal, 1982).

Michael Forest

The first day Frank Wolff and I got to Greece [to star in the movie Atlas*], we were reading the script in the hotel room. ...[Writer Charles Griffith] came in to kind of sit there and get some impression as we were reading it. ...Finally Chuck got up and left. At which point, Frank said, "This is a real piece of shit!" and threw the script right out the window.*

Six-foot-three and weighing in at a lean, mean 215, Michael Forest was a rugged-looking addition to the Corman brothers' list of leading men during their corner-cutting 1950s heyday. Forest film-debuted as the whip-cracking barbarian Zarko in Roger's disaster-plagued *The Saga of the Viking Women and Their Voyage to the Waters of the Great Sea Serpent* (1957) and soon rose to star status in Gene's *Beast from Haunted Cave* and Roger's *Ski Troop Attack*, both shot in the winter of 1959 in the snowy expanses of South Dakota. Forest was also up to his biceps in action in the made-in-Greece *Atlas* (1960), Roger's flimsy attempt to cut in on the mythological muscleman craze sparked by Steve Reeves' *Hercules* (1959).

In between battles with beasts and Viking women, Forest was a stage actor who worked in Shakespearean plays and other legitimate productions as classy as his real name (Gerald Michael Charlebois). Born in Harvey, North Dakota, he moved with his family at a very early age to Seattle, attended the University of Washington for a year and then made his way south to the sunnier campuses of San Jose State. Graduating with a B.A. in English and drama, Forest came to Hollywood in 1955 and started acting on TV and on stage at the Players Ring. In 1957, he began to study with veteran actor-acting teacher Jeff Corey, in whose classes Forest first encountered Roger Corman. Forest worked extensively on TV and in films (many made in Europe), but—for his American fans, at least—few of his acting credits are as well-remembered as his TV stints on *The Outer Limits* and *Star Trek* and his notorious "Corman quartet."

At what point did you decide that acting was what you wanted to do for a living?

It really started back in Seattle. One day when I was maybe 14, a friend of mine came by and he said, "I'm on my way to the theater." I said, "You're on your way to *where*? What's this all about?" He began to tell me, and I went to the Seattle Repertory Playhouse to see him perform. And he was an incredibly good actor, even at 14, one of those prodigies. All of a sudden I saw this adulation being heaped on him, and I said, "Gee, *I* want to get some of that!" So that's kind of what prompted me to get into acting, it was through *him*. By trial and error, I made it my life's work whereas, good as he was—*incredibly* good as he was—he went into commercial art!

What was your first film?

The first film was a real *winner* [*laughs*]—it was with Roger Corman, and it was called *Viking Women and the Sea Serpent*. And, boy, what a real turkey *that* was! Curiously enough, I met Roger at Jeff Corey's classes, because Roger was in the same class with me. The reason he was there was because he wanted to be a little more familiar with acting. He had never been a drama student at Stanford University, he was in engineering, so it was not like he had grown up in the theater or anything. So this was a way by which he could learn more about it. (And it was to his credit, because he was already producing and directing pictures.) That was where I met him, and one day he said to me, "Look, Mike, do you want to do this picture [*Viking Women*]? It'd be nothing more than kind of a glorified stunt man, but if you want to do it, fine." I said, "*Sure!*"

You're seen in the picture quite a bit.

[*Laughs*] I positioned myself at all times alongside Dick Devon, the number one heavy in the piece, so that it appeared like I was his number one henchman. At one point Roger asked me, as he was about to shoot a closeup with two or three people, "Mike, were you standing there in the last shot?" I said [*casually*], "Yeah, this is where I was," and he said [*dubiously*], "Okay..." I made sure I was always right there, featured in the shot—

Whether you should have been or not?

Whether I should have been or not! I had a lot of fun doing it, in spite of the fact that it was a real piece of dreck—which I'm sure Roger would be one of the first to admit!

Riding a horse and all the other physical stuff you do in the movie—was that all up your alley?

Oh, yeah. I'd been an amateur boxer, and I was pretty physical in terms of keeping myself in shape and so forth. And riding horses was something I'd been doing since I was a little kid. All of that came pretty easy to me.

Memories of some of the other cast members?

The girls on the show were really nice to work with and we had a lot of fun. They were good sports. Betsy Jones-Moreland was one of them, a very nice girl and a good actress (although you can't tell from *that* picture!). Abby Dalton was working with Jeff Corey at the time, too, and I knew her from those classes. And Lynn Bernay I remember—Lynn and Betsy and Abby and I got along real great. It wasn't that I *didn't* get along with the others, but Lynn and Betsy and Abby were the ones I was always pushin' around or hitting with my cat-o'-nine-tails. We had a lot of fun jokin' about *that* [*laughs*]. And Gary Conway was a *very* nice guy, everybody got along with Gary. A beautifully built guy and a very *pleasant* guy, as I recall.

Brad Jackson? Richard Devon?

Brad Jackson—well, now, *there* was

Michael Forest spent much of *Viking Women and the Sea Serpent* **applying his cat o'nine tails to young actresses. ("We had a lot of fun jokin' about that.")**

a strange young man. Nobody quite knew what he was doing or what he was "on"—he was so aloof. He stayed to himself all the time, *so* withdrawn, and nobody understood him. He would go eat by himself, he wouldn't *talk* to anybody. And when he *did* say something, everybody kind of rolled their eyes. I don't know what his problem was, I really don't. As far as I know, *no*body got to know him, he was just kind of a strange person.

He had an actor-friend named Ken Miller who says that Jackson was very much into the occult.

Well, that could very well be—it doesn't surprise me to hear that, because he did seem *so* spaced-out. I don't know if he was on drugs, and I'm not suggesting that he was or wasn't—I just don't know. But he was *strange*. I thought

Dick Devon did fairly well in that picture, considering the situation and everything. In fact, he was *quite* good—he's a very good actor.

Richard Devon has an active dislike of Corman that began, I think, on that picture, because he saw no precautions being taken and people were getting hurt left and right. Including him.

I did several pictures with Roger, and I *will* say this about him: He was a bit cavalier in the way he would do things and the way he would allow the actors to take the chances that they did. But I must also say *this*: Roger was right there. I mean, if he asked you to climb up something and you said, "*Where* do you want us to climb?", *he'd* climb up and show you—"This is what I want you to do." It wasn't as if he was saying, "Go out there and battle that tiger, I'll just

Time to burn! Forest prepares to drop one of the *Viking Women* into the fiery sacrificial pit.

stand back here and watch you do it"—you know what I mean? He was pretty good about that. But he *didn't* really protect the actors that much from getting hurt, not in the *early* days, anyway. I never really got seriously hurt—I banged up my knees a couple of times and got a few bumps and bruises, but nothing serious, nothing more or less than you'd get when you were doing some of the Westerns at Warner Bros.

It was sort of a "gag" in the picture that Jonathan Haze and I were always fighting: Here I was, this big guy, beating the crap out of Jonathan, and of course at the end of the picture I get my comeuppance when he drowns me in the ocean. Curiously enough, that final fight was done on the first day of shooting and, I must tell you, that *was* pretty tough—I ended up with a sprained ankle and a sprained wrist. That was a little bit tough, that day!

Your fault? Jonathan's fault?
No, it was just one of those things. I came flying off the horse at him and we went tumbling down into the water. There were pretty good waves there, so we were getting slapped around. And when you're fighting in water, you don't have all of the stability that you might have on land—you kind of stagger around and fall. It makes it *look* pretty good, but can get yourself banged up. As I said, I sprained my ankle and sprained my wrist, but it was no big deal.

I have to take my hat off to Jonathan Haze. For a little guy, he really threw himself into all those fight scenes.

He was a nice guy to work with and we had a lot of fun. We were lookin' out that we didn't really hurt each other too badly. Well, for one thing, we had bare skin, we didn't have any clothes we could put pads underneath. When we went crashing down onto a floor or onto that stony ground, it was right straight down on bare skin and bare bodies!

The last cast member I want to ask about is Jay Sayer, who played Richard Devon's sissy son. I don't know if he has any credits other than Corman movies like Viking Women.

And he should never have made *that* one [*laughs*]! He...was...*weird*! And he certainly didn't endear himself to anybody in that company! He was *all right*, nobody took real offense to him, but he was not much of an actor, that's for sure!

How tall were you and what did you weigh in those days?

I guess I'm about 6'3" and I weighed around 215. That's about what my weight is now, I've stayed pretty much the same.

Do you recall how you were picked to star in Roger and Gene Corman's South Dakota movies?

The director of *Beast from Haunted Cave*, Monte Hellman, was someone I knew quite well—I knew him as Monte *Himmelbaum*, which is his real name. He called me one day and said, "Listen, we're gonna do this picture in South Dakota, and Frank Wolff is gonna be on it, and you can be on it too. I want you to go down and meet Gene Corman." I said, "Fine," and I went to the office and I met Gene Corman. Roger was also there and we talked and so forth, and it was like a done deal even before I walked in because Monte wanted me to do the picture. *Beast from Haunted Cave* and *Ski Troop Attack* were done back-to-back: We did *Beast* first; then Roger came up the day we were finishing *Beast*, we had one day off and started the *next* picture!

With the same cast, the same everything.

Yeah, the same people, with the exception of just a *couple* who went back to L.A. We did two pictures in five weeks.

How did you know Monte Hellman?

I was living in the same apartment building that he was, and I had met him briefly about four years before, when he came to San Jose (I was at San Jose State at the time) looking for some actors for his [theatrical] company, the Stumptown Players. Then, just by chance, we were living in the same apartment building and I ran into him again. We got to be friends, and he just wanted me to do the picture.

If Viking Women *was done sort of Mickey Mouse, what was it like making Corman movies in the snows of South Dakota?*

Those two pictures were really tough—what was taking place was pretty tough on us physically. The first morning of shooting on *Beast*, we had to go up on a ski lift to Terry Peak. Terry Peak was a ski area where a lot of the real heavyweight skiers liked to go; it wasn't that well-known and yet it was good skiing, so they would go there rather than to some of the more popular places, which were quite crowded. That first morning it was 20 degrees, and it "warmed up" to about 25 [*laughs*]! We had to go up on a ski lift, and Monte said, "Okay, Mike, you and Sheila [leading lady Sheila Carol] go up in the first lift." She was kind of nervous about going on the ski lift, so Monte told me, "You go up with her, kind of calm her down a little bit." I said fine. So we take off in the first gondola and we go up a little ways into the air—and we stop. And we're swingin' in the breeze. Well, they were loading the equipment on each gondola that came around, and then they'd send us up a few more feet and we'd stop *again* as they loaded *more* equipment onto *another* gondola [*laughs*]! And I thought, "What in God's name are we doin' here?" They couldn't shoot with us up at the top, not until the equipment was set up, so why were we going up? We should have stayed down below and waited 'til *a-l-l* the equipment got up there, and *then* gone up in one turn of the damned ski lift! So *that* was not too well planned-out! I have to tell you, by the time we got up there, I don't think I had anything that was warm on me *at all*—it was *so* cold!

The hotel seen in Beast from Haunted Cave—*is that where you stayed?*

That's right. And it was a pretty good place—the accommodations were okay, and we had a lot of fun there. I must tell you, there was one morning—Saint Patty's Day, 1959—when Frank and I didn't have a call on the picture until about two o'clock in the afternoon. (By that time, we had gotten into *Ski Troop Attack*.) We both came down in the morning and we said, "What are we gonna do for Saint Patty's Day?" We thought about it, and we went into the bar—the bar and the restaurant were right there—and we decided we had to do *some*thing. So we went down to a dime store, a little five-and-ten, and asked them if they had anything *green*—hats and horns and so forth. The gal said, "Well, I don't think so. Why?" I said, "Well, it's Saint Patrick's Day!" "Oh," she said, like she'd never heard of it before [*laughs*]. Well, we got all of the balloons and everything they had had from Halloween—it was all sitting in the back. We bought hats and funny ribbons and all this stuff.

Look out, *Beast from Haunted Cave*—Michael Forest is ready for action.

We brought it back to the "family restaurant"/bar and set it up, and the word got out that we were handing out hats and horns to all the kids and celebrating Saint Patty's Day. Well, you can imagine, the place was *loaded*. And the guy who ran the place loved it, because people were comin' in and here were the actors from Hollywood having a Saint Patty's Day party. By the time Roger's assistant came down to get us at around one o'clock or two o'clock, Frank and I were [*laughs*]—we were *deep* into the booze! "Jeez, you guys," the assistant said, "Roger wants you up on the hill!" We said [*slurring his words*], "Come on, come on in here and have a drink!" "No, I can't! You guys gotta—" "*Come on* and have *one* drink, or we won't go!" So he said, "Okay, one drink," and he came in and had a drink. And then we jumped in the car (with drinks in hand!) and rode up to the top of the mountain where Roger was, and we *staggered* out of the car yelling [*drunkenly*], "*Roger!*" And he said, "Oh, my God! What have you guys been doin'?" I said, "We've been havin' a few little drinks, Roger. It's Saint Patty's Day!" Well, Frank and I had to do just a ski-by. And you can imagine the two of us tryin' to ski when we were not really able to stand up [*laughs*]! But we did it—finally!—and then we said, "Come on, Roger! Let's get out of here! Come on! Fold it up for the day! It's too cold, it's gettin' too dark" and so forth. And Roger was a pretty good sport about it; we said, "Come on, Roger, we're gonna buy you a drink down below." We all bundled in the car and went down and continued the party at the bar, and we got Roger down there to join us.

What else did you do in your spare time up there? What is *there to do in Deadwood, South Dakota?*

There wasn't much to do, believe me. And, to tell you the truth, you didn't want to. By the time we got done each day, we were exhausted—I mean, *really* physically exhausted. You just didn't want to do too much afterwards. We might have *drank* a little too much, but that was just to get the *chill* out of our bones. That was *medicinal* [*laughs*]! And sometimes we even started out in the morning with a quart of brandy, and we had *that* finished by about 11 [*laughs*]! We *had* to, it was so *cold*!

You and Frank Wolff?

Frank and I, and a couple of the others would join us. Dick Sinatra [Frank Sinatra's actor-cousin] was always willing to accept a drink at the drop of a cork [*laughs*]!

Can you compare and contrast Roger and Gene Corman?

Well, Gene was not a director, Gene was the producer, and he left the directing chores to whoever he had chosen. That's the way it was at *that* point in my relationship with him; it may have changed afterwards, I don't know, but at that time, that's the way it was. Roger, of course, was not only a producer but he was a director. I don't want to compare the two and say that one was "better" than the other, but I think Roger had more input on the films than Gene did, because Roger wore both hats. That was the major difference between the two of them.

Was Gene Corman a "hands-on" producer? Was he there at all times?

He was there, yes, but Gene was good in the sense that he made the thing *work* but he didn't *interfere*. He was there and you felt his presence, but it wasn't like he was hovering over you or anything like that.

So he wasn't back at the hotel having hot cocoa or anything while you guys—
Oh, no, no, nothing like that. He did his job and he did it well.

Did you have enough of a crew up there?
They had a local crew come in from Chicago, and it was a good crew, hard-workin' guys. And Monte Hellman was a very good director. Monte had been an actor himself and he understood the problems of actors and so forth, and he had a great relationship with all of us. I *always* liked Monte.

I thought Sheila Carol was very good in both pictures. What did you think?
Sheila was very good. Sheila had had a lot of...personal problems that I didn't know all about. But she was a *very* nice person and a hard worker and a good sport, considering the conditions under which we were working.

And Chris Robinson, who played the Beast?
We didn't *see* much of Chris. Chris had made some kind of a deal to build the monster, and he stayed pretty much to himself. Dick and Frank and Monty and Wally Campo and I—we were all kind of together most of the time. It wasn't as if we were shunning Chris or anything like that, but he was kind of involved in keeping his monster together. I didn't know what he was doing, and I barely saw him when we were there.

There isn't a good look at the Beast in the whole movie. Standing there right next to it and lookin' at it, what were your impressions?
I kept lookin' at it and thinking, "*This* doesn't scare me at all!" [*Laughs*] But it was *supposed* to, I guess! Now, I'm not trying to make a bad situation for Chris, Chris was doing the best he could under the circumstances, trying to make this thing *walk* when he could hardly *move* in it. It was supposed to be something that we were terrified of and shooting at it when it was attacking it. Well [*laughs*], you could *walk* faster than *it* could move!

The cave in the movie—where was that?
That was a mine that had been abandoned. They opened it up for us to shoot in there, and it was a bit of a dodgy situation. There was nothing shoring it up, and it was a *huge* cavern—they literally had hollowed out a mountain. We were shooting guns, and just that reverberation was enough to set off some problems there—stuff falling off the ceiling and so forth. I was always a little bit nervous about working in there. And one of the other problems we had was the air—it got very bad in there, it got very stale quickly. They tried to pump air in there, but they didn't really have the kind of equipment that would take care of it sufficiently.

What were you paid to star in Beast from Haunted Cave *and* Ski Troop Attack*?*
[*Laughs*] I got the big bucks on that. I got $500 a week. I think at that time, minimum weekly was 350 and I got 500—I held out for big bucks!

Five weeks to shoot two pictures, so...2500?

Big bucks. And thought I was in the tall clover [*laughs*]!

Any quick observations about Ski Troop Attack?

That was probably tougher than the other one because of some of the things that we had to do—climbing up mountains and hanging over open pits and things like that. That was a tough picture from that standpoint. Right at the beginning, on the first day of shooting, we had to climb up underneath that bridge that we were supposedly blowing up. We were climbing the support braces—you know, those iron girders that support a bridge. In that cold and with the ice and snow and all, *that* was a little bit much, to be doin' that. But we were careful and nobody got hurt. Because if you fell, boy, that was a long drop down there! There were no stunt guys doin' *that* for us. There *were* some ski things that were done by local skiers who did some stuff that required more ability than *we* had. In those cases, they had the stunt skiers, but most of the time we were the ones who were doin' it. And it was some tough stuff, I'll tell you. *Really* physical stuff, and *very* cold.

Did you have any contact with writer Charles B. Griffith, who wrote three of your Corman pictures?

Oh, I bumped into Griffith several times over the years. He has spent a lot of time in Australia, and he comes back and forth. I didn't think too much of some of his writing, particularly *Atlas* [*laughs*]—I didn't think too much of *that*! As a matter of fact, the first day Frank Wolff and I got to Greece, we were reading the script in the hotel room. He had a copy and I had a copy and we were both going over it, and Chuck came in to kind of sit there and get some impression as we were reading it. I turned to Frank and I said, "I'm on page 14," he said, "I'm on 16." A little while later: "I'm on 30," "31." And finally Chuck got up and left. At which point, Frank said, "This is a real piece of shit!" and threw the script right out the window [*laughs*]. We called down to the bar and we ordered quadruples to be brought up *immediately*—one quadruple Scotch and one quadruple bourbon. The young man came up with a tray full of drinks, four glasses of Scotch, four glasses of bourbon, a whole tray of ice and soda water, and he said, "Where is the party?" We said, "*We* are the party!" [*Laughs*] And that was the beginning of *Atlas*!

How did Atlas *come about?*

I think it was because the *Hercules* pictures had become such a big thing. I think Roger wanted to kind of capitalize on that, and so he figured he was gonna make a poor man's version of *Hercules*. And [*laughs*] that's what *Atlas* turned out to be. That's basically *it*—he just called me one day and asked me if I wanted to do this. At the time, I was doing a lot of [TV] work on the CBC in Canada, up in Toronto, and it worked out that [right before Forest had to leave for Athens] I was going to be doing a show up there in Toronto. I think I finished on a Saturday, and then on Sunday I flew from Toronto to Athens.

Originally Roger wasn't sure where he was going to shoot the picture, and he wasn't quite sure *what* the picture was going to be [*laughs*]! At one point in time, he was talking about shooting it in *Stockholm*. I couldn't imagine shooting *Atlas* in Stockholm, although you

Forest leads his soldiers into battle in Roger Corman's *Atlas*.

could conceivably do that. But, obviously, shooting in Athens was the better choice.

Just as the film was about to go into production, Corman called it his "first million dollar production." How many hundreds of thousands of dollars was he off by?

An *awful* lot. You could cut that in half and *still* be exaggerating [*laughs*]!

Did he try to give you the impression that Atlas *would be a big picture? That was his standard operating procedure with some of his actors.*

Yeah, one assumed that, if we were going to Greece, if Roger was putting out the kind of money it takes to bring us all over there, that he was going to make it pretty lavish. But obviously it *wasn't* very lavish. I think he got some of the Greek Army for practically nothing. They came in and did their stuff, banging their cardboard shields with their wooden swords [*laughs*]! It had some funny moments, that's for sure! But when Roger was shooting a picture, you just accepted the way he was gonna do it, or you didn't do it at all.

According to Dick Miller, he was offered the role of the tyrant in Atlas.

That I didn't know. I remember that they had to shoot some additional scenes for *Atlas* over at UCLA, and Dick Miller was in more fights than you could shake a stick at. I never saw him, I never had anything to do with the additional stuff because I never shot here at all. In the picture, you see Dick killing somebody and *being* killed every five minutes [*laughs*]!

You stayed in Athens during the making of the movie, correct?

Right, in a hotel on Venizelou Street. It was right in the heart of Athens, not far from the Grand Britannia, the major hotel in Athens. Nice location, and not a bad hotel. It had a good view of the Acropolis. And of course it was a wonderful experience to be in Athens. When I was in school I studied the Greeks, and now to see and to be part of all of those antiquities was really a thrill for me. My wife came over, too, and she was there for most of the picture. We saw the Acropolis (of course), and we took a side trip to Crete and visited the ruins of Knossos and Mallia. That was quite fascinating, because we actually were in the throne room in the Palace of Knossos and sat on the oldest Western throne that is extant. That's something you no longer can do, they now have it roped off and they don't allow people to even *touch* it any more. (And I don't blame them!) It's 4000 years old and we actually sat on it. Frank and I and my wife went to Knossos, and it was *fascinating*. That, of course, was where Homer wrote about the Labyrinth.

Did Barboura Morris, your leading lady, tag along on these excursions?

No, Barboura didn't, I guess she had other things that she was doing. Barboura was a great gal and I always liked her. She was married for a while to Monte Hellman, and when we were doing *Atlas*, they were still married. I remember Monte saying, prior to my leaving for Toronto, "You take care of her now! Take care of her!" I kind of looked after her as much as I could, but she was pretty independent and she could take care of herself with no problems.

I remember one little incident one morning: We were all coming down in the hotel elevator and Roger said, "Well, Mike, I think we've gotten rid of some of the worst problems. I think today's gonna be one of our better days." Well, that was the kiss of death! We had to go shoot in a park right in the center of Athens, so all the cars pull off the road in this very hilly, mountainous park. Everybody starts taking off, going up the hill, and I say, "Roger, where are we *going*?" He's walking away from me and he says, "Get up to the highest part of the hill up here. That's where we'll be." I say, "Roger! *Where*?" He says, "The highest part of the hill!"—he's yelling back at me as he's racing up this hill. (I'm waiting for Barboura, she's trying to get her costume on and get her stuff together.)

Everybody disappears, and Barboura and I start climbing up this hill. I don't see anybody, I can't *hear* anybody. We get up to the highest part, and I mean the *highest part*, and there was a huge boulder up there. I ask Barbara, "Do you see anybody?" and she says, "No." "Do you *hear* anybody?" "No." We start *yelling*, "Roger! Roger!", and nobody's answering us back. I climb up on this huge rock, and now I am the highest thing in this park, nothing is higher. There's nobody there.

Finally, about a half-hour later, somebody comes hollering: "Michael! Barboura!" It was the assistant, looking for us. He says, "What are you guys doin' *here*?", and I say, "*We* were told to come to the highest point on this hill. There's nothing higher than where we are right now. Where *is* everybody?" "Well," he says, "we're down here..." So we walk down, down, down, a *long* ways down to a spot where they were shooting.

That's where "the highest point" was to Roger [*laughs*]! He says [*excitedly*], "Where *were* you guys?" and I said, "*Roger*! You said the highest point and, by God, that's where we were! Now don't tell me we weren't, because *that's where we were*." And he mumbles, "Oh, well, okay..." Barboura was not happy about all this, but I just kind of rolled with the punches. You have to keep in mind, "This is Roger!" [*Laughs*] I later reminded him of his "Today's gonna be one of our better days" comment, I told him he never should have said that, and he said, "You're right. I'll never say it again!"

Where were the ruins where you shot the movie?
We actually shot at the Acropolis, right *on* the Parthenon. Now they have it cordoned off; you can (obviously) *look* at it, but they don't allow the tourists to get up on the Parthenon itself any more.

Did you feel you had the physique to step into a Steve Reeves-type part?
[*Sighs*] I was fairly well-built, but not on *that* level. I was never that kind of a bodybuilder. But, I figured, if Roger felt that I had the build for what he wanted, then, fine. But I never kidded myself that I was gonna scare Steve Reeves [*laughs*]!

Did you work out while you were over there?
Yeah, I did, I sniffed out a gymnasium there and I became the only English-speaking member of that gym. Through sign language and so forth, I was able to communicate with people. I used to go and work out there every chance I got. I still have the card that shows that I'm an honorary member of that athletic club.

I can tell from watching the movie how windy it was when you were shooting.
Yeah, every once in a while we'd get some wind blowin', because that was in the summertime and once in a while you'd get some of those breezes blowing out to sea. There were some strong winds blowing, almost like Santa Anas. And it was *hot*—it could get *very* hot there. But it was an enjoyable experience. I liked the Greek people, and it was an interesting experience just to be part of that society.

Did you learn to speak any Greek?
Not really. I speak Italian and French, but I don't speak Greek. Maybe a few words. That language is much too difficult for me. We had enough people around who spoke English. We had one young man who was working as an assistant, a Greek who had been born in Alexandria, and he spoke about seven languages. He spoke English just like you and I would speak it, and he also spoke Greek, he spoke Arabic, he spoke French, he spoke German, he spoke Italian...! He was terrific, and a great guy to work with.

What was Frank Wolff like?
Frank was the kind of guy who... well, to *meet* him was to *like* him. He had that kind of personality. He was very outgoing and very honest, and an extremely good actor. Some of his best work was done after he went and lived in Italy. I saw a couple of the films that he did, and he was *exceptionally* good. In one he played Count Ciano, Mussolini's son-in-law, and he was wonderful in it, and in the other he played a Sicilian bandit. He literally was cast right off the street: Some director was walking down the street and saw Frank, and Frank

looked just like the bandit. So he was cast right off the street! He did wonderful work in those two pictures, which I saw back-to-back; Frank had a screening of both of them for his parents, who had come to Italy. Unfortunately, he was a suicide. It wasn't pleasant, it wasn't good. He was a very close friend, and it was a very sad situation. That's all I would like to say.

Did you go see these Corman movies when they were new?

I did, because I was curious. They were just about what I expected. Every once in a while I'd cringe a little bit— "Ewwww, God, what did I *think* I was doing there?" (I think actors are very critical of themselves!) But then, every once in a while I'd say, "Well, *that* wasn't bad. I can live with that." But most of the time I wasn't too pleased [*laughs*]!

I noticed in a mid-'60s press item about you that A House Is Not a Home *[1964] was listed as your first film. Were you making an effort to "lose" those early Corman credits?*

Oh, no—I would never have done that. You accept what you've done, the good and the bad. I don't know where *that* came from, I really don't!

Any memories of The Outer Limits *and* The Twilight Zone?

The *Outer Limits* episode ["It Crawled Out of the Woodwork"] was directed by Gerd Oswald, and there was nothing outstanding that took place in that as far as I was concerned. One of the things I had to do was react to this monstrous form of energy that was coming towards me. Gerd said, "This is something that is absolutely scaring you to death. You *can't* go too far with it, with the fear. Unfortunately, you're not gonna be able to *see* anything, you just gotta imagine it." So I had to really "let it all out" and react to something that I wasn't even seeing. I didn't want to look ridiculous, but Gerd said, "No. *Believe* me. You've got to 'sell' it." And *The Twilight Zone* ["Black Leather Jackets"] was fun. [Lee Kinsolving, Tom Gilleran and Forest] played aliens on motorcycles in that, and I used to ride motorcycles. They gave me a bike that had a regular foot clutch, which was the old-fashioned kind that *I* was used to riding. So they gave me this 1939 Harley frame with a brand-new engine and a foot clutch—they call it a "suicide clutch." The other bikes had the hand clutch, which of course all bikes have now. It was fun because they were *very* hot bikes, and we did "wheelies" a couple of times, which we weren't supposed to do. But we got fooling around, and it was a fun episode to do.

Do you happen to know how you were selected to play Apollo in the Star Trek *episode "Who Mourns for Adonais?"?*

They wanted to find a Shakespearean actor who was fairly well-built. They had even gone as far as London to look for an actor of that type. Then they called down to San Diego, to the [Globe Theatre] Shakespeare Festival there, and asked if there was an actor there that could properly fill the bill. They said no, not at that time, but they said there *had* been an actor [Forest] who had worked there previously, and that he was probably in Hollywood. They gave the *Star Trek* people my name, and they in turn called me and had me come in. That is how it all came about. I had quite an extensive background in Shakespeare, and of course they wanted somebody who had that sort of classic training.

Did you even know what Star Trek *was when they first approached you?*

I knew about it because I was friendly with Leonard Nimoy before he *got* the show. As a matter of fact, he and I did a small low-budget picture together [*Deathwatch*, 1966] and during the making of that picture we had a slight break, three or four days, in the shooting schedule. That break allowed Leonard to go and test for a new sci-fi television show [*Star Trek*]. When he came back, he said to us [*dubiously*], "You won't believe this show that I tested for. They had me wearing these funny rubber ears. I don't know…I don't know if *this* show will ever go!" [*Laughs*]

Did you have to test for Star Trek?

I didn't test on-camera, but I did have to go in and read for them. I went in at least twice; I went in the first time, and then they called me back. They were looking originally for a British actor and had even looked in London, and they said that they wanted me to do it in a British accent, when I was auditioning for them. I said, "It would be rather false for me to try and do a British accent. I can *do* a British accent, but it won't be *me*, it won't *really* be the character." I had been trained in the theater and I had good theater speech, what we call "mid-Atlantic"—kind of in between American speech and British speech, but good, solid theater speech. I said, "I will give you *that*. I think that that should be what you look for, particularly in light of the fact that it is not written in the British idiom. It is written more in the American style of dialogue, albeit with classic overtones to it. I think you'll be satisfied with good, solid theater speech." And they accepted that idea.

Forest now flies a plane, plays tennis and dosen't have "the pressure of trying to get a job any more."

Were you still in good-enough shape at that time, or did you have to work out before you played the part?

I've always worked out, I was in very good shape. One of the things they wanted me to do during one of the readings was, they said, "We'd like to see how physically well-built you are. Will you take your shirt off?" I said, "Well, that's fine, I can do that." And I *was* in pretty good shape—I've been working out since I was in my early teens, and am *still* doing so. They saw that I was pretty well-built—nothing like an Arnold Schwarzenegger or anything like that, but certainly sufficient for what *they* were looking for.

Did you have an "approach" to the role of Apollo?

My whole thing as far as acting was concerned was, you put yourself into the situation where your character finds himself, and you just extend yourself into those given situations. That's all you can really *do* as an actor, you can't do any *more* than that. Shakespeare, in one of Hamlet's speeches, wrote, "Suit the action to the word; the word to the action." *That's* always been very meaningful to me, as to what acting is all about. As a matter of fact, to digress for just a moment, *through* that play and *through* that moment in *Hamlet*, Shakespeare was really telling his contemporaries what acting was all about. At that time, acting was very declamatory, very broad, and Shakespeare used that speech of Hamlet's to tell his contemporaries what acting was really *about* and how they should go about it. And that's the way I've always approached acting—"Suit the action to the word; the word to the action."

In my limited experience interviewing Star Trek *veterans, I've found actors who barely tolerated William Shatner, and others who didn't like him at all.*

In later years I've gotten to know Bill better than I did then, and I think Bill has changed a great deal. It's always too easy to say, "An actor has a tremendous ego," "He's a rather strange person as far as his ego is concerned"—but you have to take into consideration the fact that there's a lot of pressure on actors in a situation like that. You have to cut 'em a little slack. Sure, he may have had an ego that was bigger than all outdoors, but at the same time there are certain things going on in an actor's life and you have to make a little excuse for them from time to time. I've done a couple of live shows of his, shows that he does for incapacitated children every year. He's very generous about that sort of thing—it's a kind of a rodeo-type of thing that he does at the Equestrian Center here. And I know he's done other charitable work. So...he's a good man.

And your fellow guest star Leslie Parrish?

Oh, she was *lovely* to work with, a *wonderful* person. *Very* easygoing. As a matter of fact, she wasn't very comfortable being an actress in Hollywood. She was *good*—it wasn't that she wasn't good—but she wasn't comfortable with the whole *business per se.* I don't know exactly what the situation was, but she said to me once, in kind of a casual way, that she just wasn't happy with Hollywood. And after she did that segment, it wasn't long before she got married and left the business entirely. And probably was much better *for* it! She was a lovely person, a *very* very nice, nice person—probably *too* nice to be in the business. I think you need a little more toughness than she had, and that was just not *her*—she was a very sweet person.

In the '80s you had your last two sci-fi roles to date, King Kong Lives *[1986] and a thriller called* Deep Space *[1987], which I haven't seen.*

Do yourself a favor—don't [*laughs*]! And *King Kong Lives*, the only good thing about it was that we had a lot of fun doing it. Leon Rippy, Hershel Sparber, Wallace Merck and I were the redneck bad guys in it and we had a lot of fun doing it. The director was John Guillermin and he had nothing but problems on that show—technical things, everything was going wrong, one thing after another. But *we* used to bring a smile to his face, 'cause when we came in there, we did good work for him. We had a good relationship with him and it was fun doing it, even though the picture wasn't particularly good.

I'm a fan of yours because of the Corman pictures, and I'm sure other people know who you are because of Star Trek. *Has any of this worked out to your satisfaction? Is this the kind of stuff you wanted to be remembered for when you got into acting?*

[*Laughs*] Well, not really. Not *really*! I look back and it certainly hasn't been what you might call a *distinguished* career, but on the other hand, it hasn't been *bad*. Some of the things that I've done, I take a great deal of pride in. But, like all actors, you do work in material and situations that are not what you *want* and you try to make it the best you can. Acting has its ups and its down.

You said there are things you take pride in. Let's take a break from this science-fiction stuff and let me ask you what those are.

Well, some of the work I've done in the theater particularly. I don't know if that is pertinent to what you're writing—

No, but I want you to talk about it anyway.

What I take pride in are the things that I've done in the theater—some of the groups I've been with and some of the work I've done, particularly in San Diego, at the Shakespeare Festival at the Old Globe. In some of the plays that I did there, I thought I did quite well and I'm quite proud of the work. I also did a production of *The Crucible* in Milwaukee with a wonderful, wonderful cast and I felt that I did some very good work in it. The reviewers said that the entire cast was excellent in this production. So things like that, *that* kind of work, I really feel proud of.

Any wrap-up comments on your movie-TV career?

I don't think there's anything terribly memorable in what I did. I think I did a workmanlike job in most of the roles that I played, and I'm proud of that. I would like to have had a big role in some film that was a little more important, but that never happened. But over a period of 40 years, I had a pretty good career from the standpoint of working most of the time. Of course, I did a *lot* of work in Europe.

Did you enjoy the European phase of your career?

Immensely. I never regretted a moment of that over there. It gave me an opportunity to go places and see things and meet people, and I would never have had those opportunities had I not been in the acting profession. I did Westerns and costume things, and also some modern cops-and-robbers-type pictures. But those were films that weren't seen here [in the U.S.] with the exception of a couple, like a big picture I did in North Africa, *Mohammad, Messenger of God* [1977].

I used to work at a film rental company that got a bomb threat because we carried it.

There were a lot of threats going around when the picture was going to be released. But it was a wonderful experience. I was on the picture for over a year and there were 22 countries represented in that picture, between the actors and the production people and all of that. And in all that time, with the exception of maybe one or two minor little things, *nobody* had a problem. There were Arabs working with Jews and Arabs who didn't like certain other Arabs and so forth, but never a problem. It was quite an interesting experience, to say the least.

So you had a better time during your "overseas" career than you did in Hollywood?
Yes, I did, I had better roles there, they had more depth to them, and I felt my work was better there than here.

But, as I said, those pictures were never *seen* here!

What are you doing acting-wise today?
Mostly what I do today is voice work. I do voice replacements and background voices and stuff like that. I'm not really interested in working in front of the camera any more, I'm basically retired and I kind of like it. If somebody were to offer me a job, that's fine, but I don't pursue the business any more. I just don't want to. I'm perfectly content with the way things are at the moment. I fly a plane and play tennis and rather enjoy my life, and I don't have the pressure of trying to get a job any more.

Michael Forest Filmography

The Saga of the Viking Women and Their Voyage to the Waters of the Great Sea Serpent (AIP, 1957)
Shoot Out at Medicine Bend (Warners, 1957)
Beast from Haunted Cave (Filmgroup, 1959)
Ski Troop Attack (Filmgroup, 1960)
Valley of the Redwoods (20th Century-Fox, 1960)
Atlas (Filmgroup, 1960)
A House Is Not a Home (Embassy, 1964)
The Glory Guys (United Artists, 1965)
The Greatest Story Ever Told (United Artists, 1965)
Deathwatch (Beverly Pictures, 1966)
The Sweet Ride (20th Century-Fox, 1968)
The Money Jungle (Commonwealth United Entertainment, 1968)
100 Rifles (20th Century-Fox, 1969)
The Last Rebel (*L'Ultimo Pistolero*) (Larry G. Spangler [Italian/American/Spanish], 1971)
Ettore lo Fusto (1971)
The Dirt Gang (AIP, 1972)
The Assassination of Trotsky (Cinerama, 1972)
Desperado (*Now They Call Him Amen; I Bandoleros della Dodicesima Ora*) (Balcazar De Barcelona [Spanish/Italian], 1972)
The Loves and Times of Scaramouche (*Scaramouche*) (Avco Embassy, 1975)
Mohammad, Messenger of God (*The Message*) (Anthony Birley/Tarik Film Distributors, 1977)
King Kong Lives (De Laurentiis Entertainment Group, 1986)
Deep Space (TransWorld, 1987)
Border Shootout (1990)
Body of Evidence (MGM, 1993)
Cyber Ninja (voice only; 1994)
Cast Away (20th Century-Fox, 2000)

Nelson Gidding

I thought [the house seen in The Haunting*]
was a wonderful house, just perfect...and the way
Bob Wise shot it was great. He made the house a character.
...It was actually a hotel; before it was a hotel,
I don't know what it was. But it had its own private ghost!*

Noises in the hallway beyond a closed door. A weird configuration on an ornate bed frame. An area of cold air. A door, once locked, now standing open.

These might sound like mild (perhaps even improbable) ingredients for a full-fledged fright film, and yet they add up to almost unbearable suspense in *The Haunting* (1963), the classic haunted house melodrama based on Shirley Jackson's novel *The Haunting of Hill House*. Director Robert Wise and his cast (Julie Harris, Richard Johnson, Claire Bloom, Russ Tamblyn) have received full marks for their contributions to this masterpiece of unseen terror, but too often neglected is the excellent screenplay by Nelson Gidding, who went beyond Jackson's 1959 novel to furnish the film with its most spine-tingling scenes.

Born in New York and educated at Phillips Exeter Academy and Harvard, Gidding says that he has been interested in writing ever since he was a child and had a poem published in the Boy Scouts magazine ("That was as recently as the mid-'20s [*laughs*]!"). A POW during World War II, Gidding began writing his first (and only) book *End Over End* while in prison camp; after the war's end, he segued into TV work and ultimately into movies. His list of film credits includes such well-respected titles as *Odds Against Tomorrow* (1959), *The Andromeda Strain* (1971) and, with co-writer Don Mankiewicz, the Oscar-nominated screenplay for 1958's *I Want to Live!*, the story of the last years of real-life prostitute Barbara Graham (Susan Hayward) and her gas chamber execution on murder charges. *I Want to Live!* was Gidding's first film for director Wise, with whom he has worked on several subsequent occasions—most memorably on the screen's greatest ghost story.

How did you segue into writing for television and the movies?

Through my book [*End Over End*]. I had a friend named Paul Monash who was writing for television and who had done a novel, and he was telling me that they were paying three, four, five hundred dollars for writing a live television show. He said it was very easy; [because of] my book, which had some small reputation, he said he could get me a job easily. So he did, and I got the $500 and I went to the island of Haiti. I had flown over it while going overseas during World War II, and I saw from the air the most beautiful place I had ever seen, a tropical paradise. And when I was in prison camp, lying in my bunk thinking of various tropical paradises which I might or might not eventually get to, I always dreamed of Haiti.

What was that first TV show?
It was live and it had Sarah Churchill, Winston Churchill's daughter, in it. It was about Harriet Quimby, the first woman to [fly] solo—she soloed about 1916, and her instructor was a fellow called André Houpert, who had been in the French Escadrille, a flyer in World War I. I said they had a love affair—nobody else did [*laughs*]! That was my first script, live TV out of New York, NBC.

Was there more TV before you got into movies?
Oh, yes, there was quite a bit more, a *lot* of TV—old shows like *Danger* and *Suspense* and *Kraft Playhouse*. I came out to California and I did the pilot for a show called *Sergeant Preston of the Yukon* for a dreadful man who also owned *The Lone Ranger*. He was an old man from Detroit, George Washington Trendle. He was a horror! He invented—or he *said* he did, I don't think he did—*The Lone Ranger* and *Sergeant Preston of the Yukon*. Those were his two radio programs, and he also owned the television rights. I was the head writer for [TV's] *Sergeant Preston*—I did the pilot, which was picked up, and it became a television show. So I was given a contract and came out to California to supply 26 episodes—or maybe it was 39. "Supply" meant that I could do what I wanted, I was in charge of the writing, and I thought I'd write a great many of them. When I came out, I thought I was just gonna be out here for maybe less than a year, do these scripts and go home rich. But I couldn't a second script past Trendle! This old fart, he read *everything* and he dotted all the i's and crossed all the t's, and I couldn't get my second script through. (And I thought this was a good script—as good scripts on *Sergeant Preston* went [*laughs*]!) *Finally* Fran Striker, the head writer of *The Lone Ranger*, said he'd *tell* me why I couldn't get that script through: He said that in that second script, I had a French-Canadian, and Trendle could not *abide* the French because his wife could speak French and *he* couldn't, and she rubbed his nose in it all their 50 years of marriage [*laughs*]! But *I* didn't know that! I believe he created the Lone Ranger, this writer Striker who worked for Trendle for years, but Trendle got all the money.

We used to have to take Trendle out to Hollywood and Vine so he could watch women going past in slacks. This, to him, was exciting—he was from Detroit, he was an old man [*laughs*]! He was rich before World War I, he had *banks* before World War I. And the reason I mention that is because Fran Striker's son got a brain tumor—Striker, whom *I* think created the Lone Ranger and possibly Sergeant Preston of the Yukon. Striker worked for Trendle for years and they knew each other for years. Trendle told me to buy some TV scripts from Striker so that Striker could use *that* money to pay his son's doctor bills.

Writer Nelson Gidding progressed from low-budget TV series like *Sergeant Preston of the Yukon* to the film classics *The Haunting*, *The Andromeda Strain* and the Oscar-nominated *I Want to Live!*

Trendle wouldn't just *give* the money to him. Imagine that! I don't know if Trendle was a *billionaire* in those days, but he certainly had a great deal of money; this fellow Striker was his head radio writer; and Trendle wouldn't even help him to the extent of just paying for his son's operation. He was a mean old bastard.

After that inauspicious start, you moved over to Warner Bros.

I started to write television shows for Warner Bros., for Bill Orr, who was head of the television department at that time. He was Warners' son-in-law. The main studio was on one side of the street and the television outfit was in another building across the street, *not* on the main lot. They were drunk one night (as usual) up at [Jack] Warner's house, and Warner was talking, saying what a terrible time they were having doing a movie about the life of Helen Morgan—they couldn't get a screenplay [done]. And Bill Orr said, "Well, *I've* got a writer, I'll send one of my top boys over there and *he'll* do it for you." So he sent me over there, and Mike Curtiz was the director. I had my interview with Curtiz, and I was told ahead of time by my *very* good agent that I had to dress as fastidiously as I could, 'cause Curtiz was very fussy about people dressing. I did as well as I could, because generally I look something like a Liverpool slum [*laughs*]! I was sitting there and my agent kept pointing at my foot—I had my ankle on my knee and he kept tapping it and looking at it. I didn't know what he meant. *Finally*, I looked down and I had a hole in the bottom of my shoe [*laughs*], and my agent was trying to tell me, "For God's sake, put down your foot!"

It was a remarkable interview: Everything I said, Curtiz said no. Every time I said, "I intend to do so and so...", Curtiz (who had a strong Hungarian accent) would say, "No! I do eet like *diss*!" So I suggested *another* idea and he said, "No, no, no! I do eet like *diss*!" At the end of the interview, I got up and I figured it was all over and that it was a complete shambles—and Curtiz threw his arms around me and said to my agent, "I haff to haff this boy!" And I got the job!

A writing job on an "A" picture.

That's right! The first feature I'd ever done was an "A" feature [*The Helen Morgan Story*, 1957]! Next I did a picture called *Onionhead* [1958], which had a very good actor in it, Andy Griffith; and then I became a contract writer at

Warner Bros., in the worst times of the studio. But I was fired twice in one week! First they told me that they weren't gonna renew my contract, but they wanted me to finish the script I was working on at the time—I was writing a Western for a producer called Jules Schermer. They said, "We like the script, you'll finish that." But at the end of the week, they said, "No, we're not gonna finish that either." So I was fired twice in one week [*laughs*]! I felt *very* bad because I'd had this sinecure, this contract, and we all got pretty good money. But I said, "To hell with it!", and I went to Tahiti [*laughs*]! I went with my wife and little boy, who was very small then, and we had a glorious time in Tahiti—and pretty well went through our savings. But when I came back, I got *I Want to Live!* I had been recommended by a very good writer, and *that's* the best recommendation, of course, a recommendation from a good writer. (Charlie Schnee, who is now gone.) Walter Wanger, the producer, took me to Bob Wise and we had a meeting of the minds and got along *very* well. We both had the same idea of doing a jazz score. After *I Want to Live!*, my career was launched.

Barbara Graham, who went to the gas chamber for murder and was played by Susan Hayward in I Want to Live!—*was she guilty?*

I don't think she actually killed the old lady, but she certainly was an accomplice in *some* way. But I believe she was not in the house when the old lady was murdered.

Talk about The Haunting—*how did you get the job of adapting Shirley Jackson's book for the screen?*

Bob was sent the book and he gave it to me to read, and he asked me what I thought. I said it was great, and he said, "I think so, too. Let's do it. We'll do it as a ghost story." I worked on that with him, and in the middle of that process, when I was halfway through it, it dawned on me that this wasn't a ghost story *at all*. It's about a woman who's had a nervous breakdown and has been institutionalized. The haunted house is actually the institution, the sanitarium where she is a patient. And Markway, the head of the experiment in the haunted house, is actually her doctor. Theo is her nurse, and Eleanor is a patient. This is all true; I did quite a bit of research once I had this idea. A cold spot is shock treatment; I understand that, when you undergo shock treatment, you feel cold, *very* cold afterwards. And of course the violence of the shock treatment itself is the noise and the banging of the haunted house. And people were always opening and closing doors because it was a locked institution. [In the movie, the doors of Hill House open and close by themselves.] It worked perfectly. I could give you chapter and verse, I had a very good case for it.

How did you intend to get across to the audience the fact that the haunted house was actually a sanitarium? With a scene at the end?

I suppose we would have, but I don't know—I didn't get that far. We had written a ghost story and it was supposed to *be* that, and we weren't going to change it drastically. But we figured this might be the real meaning. Bob said, "Let's go and see Shirley Jackson," and we *did*—we went from California to Bennington, Vermont, where her husband [literary critic Stanley Edgar Hyman] was a teacher. We had a meeting with her, had lunch with her, and told her this idea. And she said no—she said, "It's a good idea, but—that isn't it. [*The Haunting*] is a ghost story." And that was that.

And yet there's a whiff of that left in the movie you wrote. The audience never quite knows if the ghosts are real or if—
That's right, it's left hanging, it's "open." Is Eleanor [Julie Harris] disturbed, or are these [ghosts] the real thing? That's the one thing Bob and I didn't agree on: I believe in the supernatural, something that is not explained *yet* but we will have an explanation *someday*. He doesn't believe, he'll have no part of the supernatural. But he *can* easily stretch his imagination to anything in space, flying saucers or anything like that. *That* he can understand and believe in, but the supernatural? He does *not*.

What was Shirley Jackson like?
She was wonderful, a very smart woman. We spent a few hours with her, and she was gracious. I had liked her work before—*The Haunting* wasn't the first time I had come across her work. She wrote a *very* good, very *famous* "long short story" called *The Lottery*.

When The Haunting *was first announced, it was going to be made for United Artists.*
Yes, but I think the budget for it was a million dollars and [United Artists] said that was too much in those days. That *wasn't* a lot of money, even then. So Bob took it to England and did it on the Eady Plan. And of course England worked *perfectly* for New England. We found this marvelous haunted house, a wonderful place which indeed *had* its own ghost—they *claimed*. And that's the house you see in *The Haunting*.

Were any of the interiors shot inside the house?
No, I don't think so. They were shot at a studio in England.

If you had had more money in your budget, would you have wanted "bigger" stars?
Oh, no, no! *Very* wonderful actors we had. Richard Johnson worked perfectly as the professor who is from England, and who works now at an American college. Julie Harris was a stage actress, and she was wonderful—and still is now!

How long did it take to write the script?
It wasn't fast. It was probably something over six months. When I started, I believe Bob was working on *West Side Story* [1961].

Did you pass pages along to Wise as you finished them, as many writers do?
No, not as I finished them. I passed them along to him as I wanted him to read them, just to show him how it was coming along. To give *him* confidence and to give *me* confidence in the project. Also, keep in mind that I had already done a complete treatment, so there were no surprises in it.

According to a Hollywood Reporter *item, you initially went after Susan Hayward to star in* The Haunting. *Does this ring any bells?*
Maybe they did try to get her, because she'd been in *I Want to Live!*, which was very successful; in fact, she

won an Academy Award for it. But we couldn't have had anybody better than Julie Harris. Susan Hayward was a very good actress, but she would have been *different*, a much, much more dynamic person, much more forceful. I can't imagine anyone other than Julie Harris in the part.

The Hollywood Reporter *didn't say what part she was going to play...maybe she was being offered the part of Theo, which she might have been good in. Would you agree with me on that?*
Yes. But I think the picture [as is] turned out to be beautifully cast.

Were you in England when they made the movie?
Yes, I was there and I saw the house—I thought it was a wonderful house, just perfect. The house itself was great and the way Bob *shot* it was great. He made the house a character. The book also did that, and so did my screenplay: It made the house a character, one of the *main* characters. And Bob did it superbly well. It was actually a hotel; before it was a hotel, I don't know *what* it was. But it had its own private ghost!

When Robert Wise was starting out as a director in the '40s, he made a couple of pictures for a producer named Val Lewton.
Val Lewton was his mentor.

Do you think his work with Lewton influenced the way he approached The Haunting?
I think it had an effect on the way he made *all* his pictures. He admired Val Lewton enormously because he was given his start by Lewton, the chance to direct. And to Val Lewton, the all-important thing was the script, and so the script's *always* been important to Bob. He has enormous respect, he has *reverence* for the scripts and for the written word, and that's why he's such a good director for writers to work with. Val Lewton had that, too.

I tell you, Bob is very generous. On *I Want to Live!*, we were interviewed for television, and the interviewer asked him, "Mr. Wise, where does a director get the wonderful idea that you had at the end, where the reporter [Simon Oakland] turns off his hearing aid after he's heard that Barbara Graham has been executed?" Bob said, "It's very hard, but once in a while you're lucky. I looked in Nelson Gidding's script and it said, 'The reporter turns off his hearing aid'—and I did it." There aren't many directors who'll say that. Bob would be the first director to say, "If I don't have the script, I can't do it."

The way The Haunting *ends, the viewer is left to wonder whether the house is haunted—*
Or whether Eleanor *is* psychotic. There's plenty of evidence in there to show that she is...but there's *also* plenty of evidence to show that these [supernatural] things *are* happening. *My* belief is that the house *is* haunted.

Do you believe in ghosts?
I believe that this house was haunted, and I believe there *could* be such a thing as a haunted house. But it *could* be paranormal, and that the things that happen [in haunted houses] will be explained someday.

There is *a hint in the movie that the ghosts are real: Julie Harris continues to narrate the movie after she's dead. That's not in the novel.*

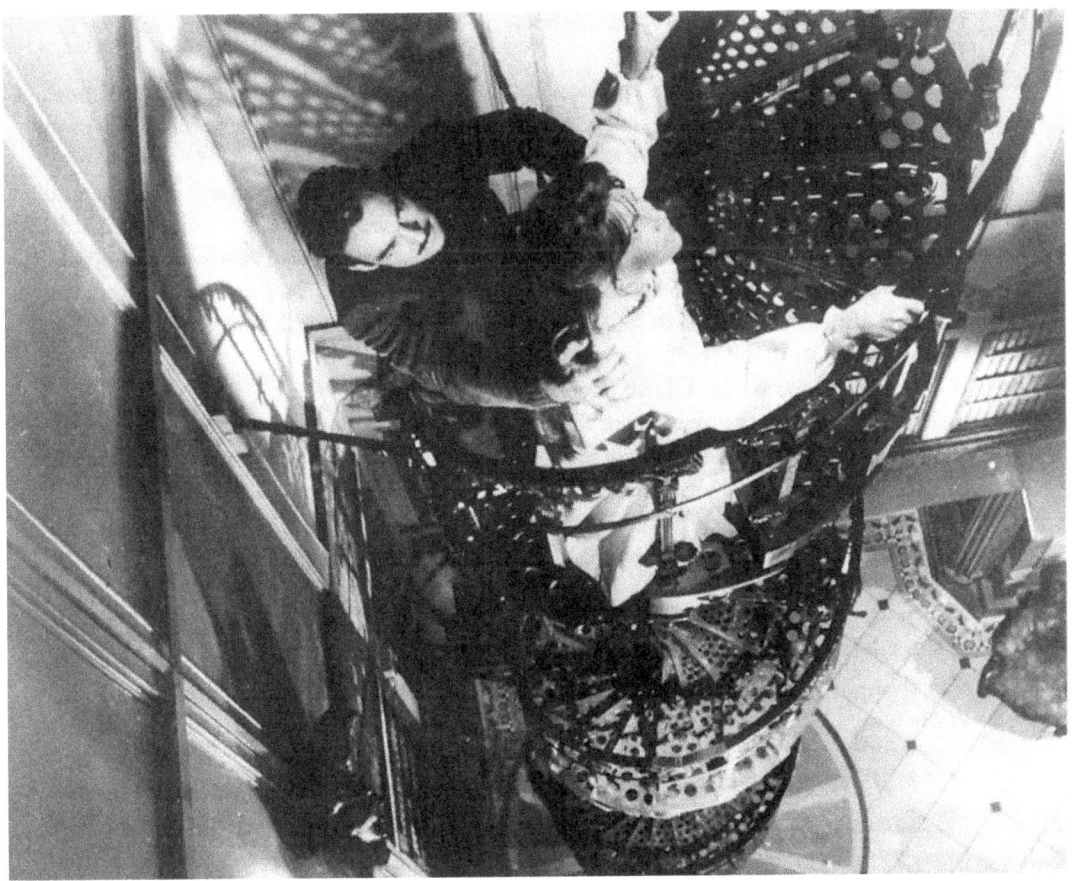

While Gidding altered some sections of the Shirley Jackson novel, he nonetheless maintained the spirit of the story. (Richard Johnson, Julie Harris pictured.)

No, it's not. And, you're right, that's a clue that the house *is* haunted. The house goes on being haunted, and she's now one of the people—maybe the *main* person—haunting it.

"We who walk here, walk alone," she says at the end.

Yes! Glad you caught that.

I'd like to try to get you to agree with me that most of the changes you made to Jackson's novel were for the better.

I think they *all* were [*laughs*]! I wouldn't have *made* them if I didn't!

You didn't get much help from Jackson's book dialogue-wise. Some of her characters' dialogue is almost jabberwocky.

I don't write anything without humor. I feel humor is most effective when it's least expected. There's quite a bit of humor in [the script of] *The Haunting*, and there's none in the book. I did that in *I Want to Live!*—there's humor in *I Want to Live!*, which is hardly a comic setting. The humor in *I Want to Live!* is either ironic or sardonic, but there's humor in it *of its kind*.

Was there any hesitation on anybody's

part about bringing the hints of lesbianism from the novel to the screen?

I felt the taint of it in the novel, and we put it in. We had to be very careful of it in those days, but we sketched it in because we felt it *should* be there as part of…well, the *un*natural. We had the supernatural, and in those days [lesbianism] would be considered *un*natural. But now, it's almost unnatural to be *straight* [*laughs*]! We shot for the beginning of the movie a scene where Claire Bloom's girlfriend is leaving the apartment where they live, and Claire is throwing things out the window. It's a small scene, just mostly a shouting match from Claire in the window to her girlfriend in the car.

Why was it cut from the movie?

Maybe for reasons of length. Maybe they thought it wasn't up to snuff. I don't know why.

One of the scariest scenes in the movie—the pounding on the walls and doors—comes from the book. But most of the other highlights aren't in the book.

The hand-holding scene [between Harris and Bloom] *is* and it *isn't*. In one part of the book, they're holding hands and they're together. But I separated them—put one on one side of the room and the other on the other, and I wrote the line, "*Whose hand was I holding?*" That is *not* in the book.

Nor are any of the scare scenes you added at the end. The first time you saw the picture with an audience—do you remember their reaction?

I don't—that was a long time ago. But I do know that we got a scream from audiences every time Mrs. Markway's face showed up in the trap door at the top of the stairs.

Who doesn't get enough credit for The Haunting?

The performances are very good, especially Julie Harris, Claire Bloom and Richard Johnson. It's a very good cast, and they made it very credible and they make it funny. You couldn't ask for a better cast. I also think that the cameraman, Davis Boulton, was good, and so was the production designer, Elliot Scott.

You wrote it, and you were there when it was shot. Do you find The Haunting *scary, or were you too close to it?*

Sure, they're *all* frightening, before they open [*laughs*]!

But does it spook you? Or can't you be spooked by something you made yourself?

I don't think I am spooked by it, I know too much what's coming. By the way, I wrote a movie called *The Hindenburg* [1975] and they had a preview of it in Houston. I sat there, and there was a little boy who was sitting in front of me, a child. The moment the main credits came on, he clapped his hands to his ears and held them there. And he sat there. And after the first half-hour, I realized he wasn't gonna take them down. So I tapped him on the shoulder and I said, "Little boy, don't be frightened. I'll *tell* you when it's going to blow up!" [*Laughs*]

What other ghost movies do you like? Were there any that inspired you at all?

No. I know the one movie that frightened me as a boy was *Phantom of the Opera* with Lon Chaney. I *like* ghost stories, though.

Robert Wise seemed glad to get back to making movies in the U.S. after The

Haunting. *He complained in a 1963 interview about British union rules that were antiquated.*

That's right, you had to get permission to break at certain times. And permission *not* to break. If tea time is at 4:15, in the middle of a very expensive shot that's taken you half a day to set up, *they* will quit—it's up to *them*! So you have to get permission. And if you forget to say "Please" or "Thank you," some of them won't do what you're asking! *That* didn't bother Wise because he's very civil and he's naturally polite, a thorough gentleman in every sense of the word. But it's a pain in the ass, nevertheless!

You've also written some science-fiction movies. The first one I need to ask you about is Skullduggery *[1970].*

I would prefer you didn't! It was good at one time, but…on the screen, I think it's my worst picture, to tell you the truth. The script was pretty good, but there's a sad story connected with it. This movie has a tortured history and a mutilated existence [*laughs*]!

I got Otto Preminger interested in the novel [*You Shall Know Them*] by Vercors. Preminger always wanted me to write a movie for him, ever since I did *I Want to Live!*, so I got the book and I brought it to him. It was being done as a play at the time, so we went to the French town of Carcassonne and saw the play. He spoke fluent French, and I spoke some French. Preminger bought the rights to the book and said, "We'll do it as a play."

In English, in America.

Yes. The novelist was Vercors, and he did the play too. Vercors was a hero of the French Resistance, and he *published* during the French Resistance—underground publishing. He did some well-known books at the time. Anyhow, we saw the play, and I went to work on it for Preminger. He was in Venice at the time, and I went to Venice and worked there with him. But then he became interested in doing a movie called *Bunny Lake Is Missing* [1965] and now he didn't want the play at that time. So it was bought for Saul David by ABC Pictures, a company that had just started—this was gonna be their first movie. And so I worked on that. At the time, I was very enthusiastic. It was a comedy, a *philosophical* comedy, which are really, in some ways, the best kind; all *good* comedies have some serious matter.

We went to New Guinea—when ABC picked it up and they were going to do it with Saul David as the producer, as their first major movie, we went to New Guinea, 'cause that's where it takes place. And I had a good connection there, because during World War II, in North Africa, I got to know an Australian captain. We became friends, and I would take him out to the airfield; he'd fly missions with us, he *wanted* to. He was a wild-ass Australian. He would be smuggled on the airplane, and there was no record of him. [These missions] were dangerous—as a matter of fact, I *did* get shot down, although he wasn't on that mission. Anyhow, we went to New Guinea and he had connections. He was a general by then, and one of his classmates at the Australian West Point was in charge of New Guinea, of the *military*. There were two parts of the rule of New Guinea, there was the civilian and there was the military. And of course the military's always the stronger, 'cause they've got the transportation and they've got the men. So he helped us, his friend took care of us in New Guinea, gave us guides, and he was going to let us use the Australian Army, the troops that were in New Guinea at the time.

And you set up everything in anticipation of shooting there.

Yes. The movie is about a Missing Link, in a sense, it's about a strange group of creatures and you don't know *what* they are, whether they're human and apes. They're actually something *between* men and apes…whatever *that* is. As a matter of fact, the epigraph of the novel was written by a man called D. M. Templemore, and it says, "All Man's troubles arise from the fact that we do not know what we *are*, and do not agree what we want to *be*." So we don't know whether these creatures are human or not, because we don't know what "human" is, completely. Finally a man [Burt Reynolds] says he killed one of the creatures, a baby, and he is to be tried for murder, which will prove whether the creatures are human or animal. And that's important, because an Australian billionaire [Paul Hubschmid] is enslaving these creatures because he has found out that they can do small tasks, like assembly line tasks, and they're

Studio interference and other monkey business made *Skullduggery* **(with ape woman Pat Suzuki) a movie Gidding would just as soon not talk about.**

doing that kind of thing for him. If Reynolds is guilty of murder, then the creatures are human; if he's not, if he's declared innocent of murder because the creature is animal, then there's no crime. That's the point of the picture. *What* is human, *we* don't decide, because that's too big a question—as a matter of fact, the picture ends when the jury is out. Which was sort of a cheat, but... [*Laughs*]

How did the movie go from ABC Pictures to Universal?

We came back after the trip to New Guinea, and the day we came back, the head of ABC movies was about to go to Europe. He wanted to see Saul David, it was very *important* that he see Saul, because we were about to start shooting. The executive was leaving at 11 o'clock that night and he wanted to see Saul that afternoon. And Saul said he couldn't see him, he wouldn't go. The executive was wild, he said it was important because they were about to spend several million dollars on this movie, but Saul said, "No, I can't come, I can't come." The reason Saul David wouldn't come was because his daughter was in the hospital with multiple sclerosis and was *dying*, as she had been for some years, and he saw her when he was in the States. But he wouldn't *tell* this executive that, he was a man of fierce and strict, unbending pride. I begged him to, but he *wouldn't*. The executive was outraged, and he put the picture in turnaround and then he sold it—he didn't want to do it because he didn't want to have anything to do with Saul David, because he was so angry. So it went over to Universal.

And did Universal want to shoot in New Guinea?

No, they decided they didn't, even though we had it all set up—we had the use of the army and the troops. New Guinea was a wild place—still *is* a pretty wild place, as a matter of fact—but we would have had security there. But Universal said no, it's too expensive, and they decided to go to Jamaica, where it would be cheaper and easier. Which was emasculating the picture, in many ways, because it would have been very interesting to have shot this picture in New Guinea.

At least one of the Skullduggery *reviews said that there was a second unit shooting in New Guinea.*

When we were there, we probably *did* do some photography. But Universal had us shoot [the bulk of the picture] in Jamaica.

In the cast, there was an actress called Susan Clark, who was the Lindsay Wagner of her day—she had been a very beautiful model and she starred in a lot of commercials, and this was her first part. Susan Clark was very good-looking, and had some ability. Not a great actress, but certainly a good actress. Burt Reynolds was *excellent* in it, he had just the kind of cynical manliness that we wanted in the part. The first day of shooting, we had a director called Richard Wilson, whose best picture was called *Al Capone* [1959]—quite a good picture. He had been a member of the Mercury Theatre, Orson Welles' group, and he was now directing. I had many discussions with him about the picture, and after the first day of rushes down in Jamaica, Saul David *fired* him! He thought the rushes were so bad, he fired him! It was kind of an unfair thing in a way; the rushes *weren't* very good, I'll grant you, but it was the first day! There they had the whole company down in

Jamaica, waiting, and they got a director called Gordon Douglas. I *knew* Gordy Douglas, we were sort-of friends—I knew him in London, we used to use the same pub. As a matter of fact, he practically *lived* in this pub, called the Audley, a very good, well-known pub, rather a posh pub. So I phoned him up and I said, "You wanna talk about the picture?" He said, "I'm leaving [for Jamaica] tonight." I said, "Well, I'll come over this afternoon—" "No," he said, "I haven't read the script. I'll read it on the plane." He was a *very* casual director and he has done a *lot* of pictures, *none* of them good [*laughs*]. This picture was done in Jamaica and it was brought in on time because he would tear pages out of the script and throw 'em away.

Karl Malden wanted to play the part of Otto Kreps, a drunk, a member of the expedition who sleeps with a Tropi [an ape woman]. He's a very important character in the novel and in the play, and he's very fat. And I *kept* it that way. Malden in those days wasn't as heavy as he is now (not that he *is* a heavy man now); in those days, he was tall and certainly not fat in any way. So Saul David wouldn't cast him. Malden was very anxious to play the part, he said, "I'll *play* it fat"—you know, a good actor *can*, just like a good *young* actor can be *old* and an *old* actor can be *young*. And not all depending on makeup and padding, which of course is very easy to do anyhow, to *make* him look fat. Malden said, "I'll *play* him fat," with that mentality, but Saul David wouldn't sit still for that. So we got another actor [Roger C. Carmel], an actor who was stout, and when he turned up in Jamaica, he was *thin*, he had lost weight! So we lost Karl Malden because he wasn't fat, and now *this* actor turns up thin because he wanted to be attractive to girls [*laughs*]! I wasn't angry about *that*, but I was angry because in this case it didn't make any difference whether the actor was fat or thin. Sometimes it might—I don't think you'd want a skinny Falstaff. I now teach a class in screenwriting at USC Film School, and I always tell my students, "Do not write too much physical description. Write about the interior of the character and the qualities and the personality—but don't say much about the physique." And I tell 'em why—because *we* lost Karl Malden.

And that's the history of the picture. So the picture is nothing like what it would be, and it was a disappointment. It's my worst picture, in a way, but in *some* ways it's the noblest, the way it started off. It was a good book, a good play and a good *script*, but you can't tear whole pages out of it and change things around for comfort and convenience, like you would outfit an automobile. So that's the sad story of *Skullduggery*. I'd like to see it again, although I know I was appalled when I first saw it. There were pages, *whole pages* missing, and there was not much done about the transitions.

Whose idea was making a movie of Michael Crichton's The Andromeda Strain?

I think Universal came to Bob Wise with it and asked, "Do you want to do it?" He read it and he liked it, and he asked me if *I* wanted to do it. At that time, the first landing on the Moon was about to happen, and the facility in *Andromeda Strain* is modeled to a certain extent on the facilities they were using for the first Moon shot. People at that time, 1969, were very worried about disease and germs and organisms being brought down from the Moon. Remember when the astronauts debarked after they landed? There was an airtight tunnel to take them from the craft, so the Earth wouldn't be exposed to their germs—the astronauts went from there into what they called "a clean facility." So *The Andromeda Strain* was very much "under the influence" of the first Moon shot.

Did you have to get government permission to make a movie like that?

No, but we had government cooperation to a certain extent. Well, not "government"; we had technical advisers from Jet Propulsion Laboratories and I suppose we had some from NASA. So we had help in that sense.

There were no stars in the picture, just "character people." A decision was made not to have any "name actors" in the movie?

Bob Wise prefers to get actors who will be identified with the parts. (He *has* worked in his long career, of course, with a great *many* stars.) What we *did* have in *Andromeda Strain* was a woman [character] who wasn't in the novel, and *she* turned out to be "our star" because she was very good.

Kate Reid. Why did you change a male character from the book into a woman?

Because I thought it would "bring everything up" to have all these scientists relating to a woman, I thought it would provide different points of view. I thought it would make it much better. And I had to *fight* for her—oh, boy, yeah! When I first brought it up, Bob said, "Nelson, I'm surprised at you." He thought it was the old Hollywood trick, "Get a sexy woman in [the movie], get a babe!", but it wasn't that at all—I mean, look at the person [Reid] who played it. At the time, there were a lot of women chemists and scientists of various kinds, but it was nothing like it is today, when they're common. I said, "No, no, no! This will be a scientist." Bob didn't know if this would lend credibility, and I said, "Well, it'll certainly bring out qualities in the script and in the situations."

Both the novel and the movie assert that they're based on an actual event. Is there any *truth to that?*

None. None at all. Other than it's based on the fact that people were worried about the shot to the Moon, that organisms and other dangerous things could come from outer space. We knew very little about it—*still* we know very little. We had three technical advisers from J.P.L., and Dr. Richard Green was, I think, the head man. I had a lot of trouble with them. They would knock out things that I wrote, because they couldn't "prove" it, or they'd say, "This or that couldn't *happen* within 300 miles of the Earth." Finally I got desperate and I said, "For God's sake, you're supposed to *help*. You're not supposed to give me obstacles, you're supposed to *help* me." "Well," Green said, "if you send the satellite beyond the 300-mile limit, you can do anything you want." I said, "That's *it!*"—they hadn't said that! 'Til then, I had been hidebound by what Crichton had written in his novel—it wasn't written in stone, but he had put the satellite out 300 miles and we had stuck with that.

So by putting the satellite further out into space, you got these persnickety advisers off your back.

That's right, Green said, "Put it out in deep space, and you can write *any*thing." And by the time we got through,

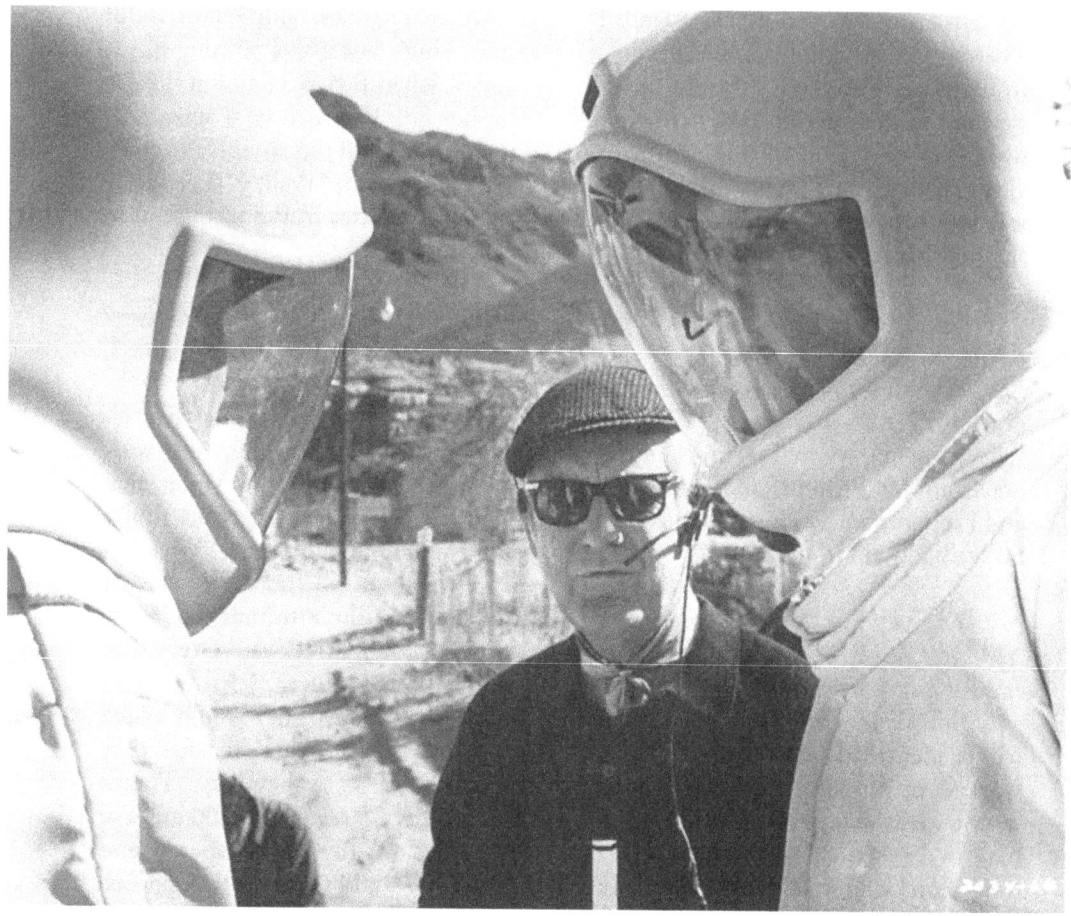

The Andromeda Strain producer-director Robert Wise gives instructions to James Olson and Arthur Hill during location filming at Shafter, Texas.

[the technical advisers] were coming to me with ideas for science fiction shows—ideas that *I* thought were unbelievable.

Where was Andromeda Strain *shot?*
It was shot at Universal, except for location things in Texas, like the opening scene of the picture where the people are killed by the mysterious organism.

There's a lab scene in the movie where a monkey "dies" on-camera. Any memory of how that was done?

He was the best actor in the film—no offense meant to the others, but that was a magnificent performance [*laughs*]! The way it was done was, we couldn't kill the monkey, or any *other* creature—you're not supposed to, in *any* film. The Humane Society always has someone on the set. So what we did was take the air out of the set, and at the last moment, as the monkey ran out of air and collapsed, a person on the crew would dash in and grab the monkey. So that's how we got that "performance" out of the monkey.

Did you get to meet Michael Crichton? What was he like?

Well, the first thing I'd have to say is, he's very tall [*laughs*]—almost seven feet tall! And very smart. He did tell me one remarkable thing: He would come to the set fairly often, and I would be down on the set once in a while, and he said to me, "Have you ever directed a picture?" I said no. "Well, you're foolish," he said, "it's *easy*." He'd never done a picture. In fact, I don't think he'd ever sold anything to the movies before; *The Andromeda Strain* was his first successful novel. But, he said, "There's nothin' to it [directing]." And, by God, he did direct a picture very soon after that, *Westworld* [1973], and he's directed quite a few since then. He doesn't bother now, I don't think.

He was 20-something when he wrote The Andromeda Strain. *I find that unbelievable.*

Michael Crichton has always been ahead of the curve. He was *very*, very smart, a bright and intelligent man. And a *good* man.

*The last movie I want to ask you about is one that's probably not very high on your list—*The Mummy Lives *[1993].*

I don't remember it. [*Laughs*] Oh, that was terrible. What happened there was, the movie that you see, *I* didn't write most of it. When I got involved in it, at the very beginning, it was a good project, and we were supposed to have a good actor in it, but he died before the first day of shooting—Tony Perkins. I worked with Perkins, I went up to his house and worked with him.

On the script?

Well, no, not on the *script*, but I met him and talked with him and found out how he felt about things and got to know him. He was very pleasant, a man of great charm and high intelligence. He had a lovely house, and I spent some time with him—not a great deal, but I would say I had maybe three or four meetings with him and tried out things with him and so on. One of the big studios was supposed to do it, but then Perkins died and we "lost" the picture. It ended up, years later, being shot in Israel with Tony Curtis, and it's very, very bad. The movie says it's adapted from a Poe short story ["Some Words With a Mummy"]—

But it's actually a half-assed remake of the old Boris Karloff Mummy.

That's right. The producer [Harry Alan Towers] was a guy who was very fast on his feet, and he has done a lot of pictures like that—I was not the first victim [*laughs*]! In fact, I think I had to sue 'em to get my money, to get my final payment.

So The Mummy Lives, *the movie I've seen, is nothing like the script you wrote.*

No, nothing like it. I've never seen the movie, but I hear it's awful.

For the last several years, various filmmakers have been threatening to remake The Haunting—

And now they've done it. We think it's too bad. They're going to take the glory of the picture, where you see nothing, and fill it with all kinds of wild special effects. And it'll be over-produced, we feel.

"We" as in you and Mr. Wise.

I've talked about with him and, yes, he opposed it for years. And I think it's too bad, too. What the hell, our picture was our picture, and nothing's gonna change it. But it's too bad they have to take this story. Why can't they find one of their own…?

And, by the way, even if we'd had more money, we would *not* have had special effects, we didn't *believe* in them for this picture. That's the "trick" of the picture, that's what's so good about it: You don't see *any*thing. You hear things and you sense things and you use your imagination—but you *see* very little or nothing. What do you see in this picture that's so frightening?

Not a thing.

Exactly. So we did without the special effects—which weren't so important in those days. Nowadays you make special effects and try to get a story to get with them. We *could* have shown [ghostly manifestations], but we didn't *want* to. The whole point was, we thought it was more frightening *not* to see anything, to be frightened by what's going on in your own mind. You can "see" the things, but you just *don't* see them, if you follow me. It's in your mind's eye. People don't walk up to me to try to touch the hem of *my* garment, but they constantly do that to Bob Wise, and many people tell him, "This is the most frightening picture I've ever seen." *The Haunting* has survived through the years well, and I'm pleased about that. It wasn't all that successful when it first opened, but it has its glory now.

[The 1999 remake of *The Haunting* from director Jan de Bont was released a few months after the preceding interview was conducted. In this brief follow-up interview, Gidding shares his thoughts on the new *Haunting*.]

Where did you see the new Haunting*? Were you invited to the premiere?*

No, I just went on my own once it had been released. I don't know if Bob Wise was invited to the premiere or not. You know, the whole thing isn't worth talking about much. It's a bad movie, and there's no sense flogging a dead piece of horse shit!

[Laughs] You told me going into this interview that, out of respect for your "fellow filmmakers," you were going to "take it easy" on the new Haunting.

I *am* [*laughs*]! My considered judgment is, it's a bad movie. And most of us have *done* a bad movie…present company excepted! But they went in exactly the wrong direction. They took a *very* good picture, a classic which was well-done, a good adaptation, and they took it and ran in the wrong direction. They made it so that the audience *saw* everything. Well, *you* saw it at a preview, *you* saw it before *I* did, and you told me there were "bad laughs" coming from the audience.

The audience I saw it with in New York laughed at the "scary" parts and slept through the rest.

Well, those "bad laughs" were still resounding on the West Coast when *I* went to see it.

Moviemakers today who have access to special effects simply can't resist using them.

That's exactly the problem. The [failure of the new *Haunting*] is a cautionary tale: It shows that special effects can ruin a movie as well as "make" it. They ruined the concept, they paid no attention to our version. I guess they were afraid we'd sue them, or they might even have to give credit to Wise and me. So they used as little as they could and they did just the opposite of what we did. They showed *every*thing, which is exactly what we didn't want to do and which we *didn't* do. We left it up to the *mind*.

They did use the line "Whose hand was I holding?", but—

But they used it meaninglessly! They did take certain things—they apparently figured, "These people [Wise, Gidding, etc.] must have known *some*thing," so they took certain things, but they didn't seem to know why we *did* what we did. "Whose hand was I holding?" was a high point in our picture.

What more can you tell me about the reaction of the audience you saw it with?

What I did was, I went to a performance comparatively early in the afternoon so I could sulk alone—there weren't that many people there. (It probably would have been hard to find a performance where there *were* people—the movie didn't do at *all* well!) You heard a few murmurs, you know …"piece of shit" [*laughs*]…and the "bad laughs."

I think The Haunting *had a pretty good opening weekend—it seems like most movies do these days. But after that, it didn't do much business at all.*

It did *some* good, though: They sold a lot of the old *Haunting*s in video stores. In the comparisons, people said what a good movie the former one was, and so there was some spurt in sales!

Anne Helm

I really just wanted to do wonderful parts and I wanted to be part of the creative stream. And I ended up doing a lot of roles that I would probably have been better off not doing.

In the 1950s, Anne Helm was New York's top teenwear model. She danced at the Copa, starred in commercials, appeared on prestigious live TV series and acted on and off-Broadway. Known as "the American Brigitte Bardot," she "went Hollywood" in the late '50s. While the career that followed (11 movies and numerous TV appearances) wasn't what she would call spectacular, it was almost like "a dream sequence" for Helm, who along the way played a princess (*The Magic Sword*, 1962), co-starred (and dallied off-screen) with "The King" (Elvis Presley, *Follow That Dream*, 1962)—and ran afoul of a Hollywood queen (Joan Crawford).

Born in Toronto, Helm's entire Canadian "show biz" career consisted of playing *Alice in Wonderland* at camp and acting in a Christmas pantomime at Montreal's Her Majesty's Theatre. When she was 14, she and her mother relocated to New York, where teenage Helm studied ballet and began modeling for John Robert Powers. The title role in a *Shirley Temple Storybook* TV production of "The Sleeping Beauty" lured her to the West Coast, where she subsequently landed roles in the fantasy and horror films *The Magic Sword*, *The Couch* (1962), *Nightmare in Wax* (1969) and William Castle's *Strait-Jacket* (1964)—a job she lost when star Joan Crawford decided she wanted her friend Diane Baker to play Helm's part.

Once you started modeling, your ballet career seemed to fall by the wayside.

Yeah, I really did well with the modeling, and it sort of swept me away from ballet. Ballet is such a disciplined profession, and my heart really wasn't in it. I loved to dance, but I didn't want the regimentation of having to work *so* hard every day! Not at *that* age—I was so young. And then I started making all this money, so modeling kind of got me away and ultimately got me into show business.

How did you break into TV in New York?

One of my friends got an acting part as Miss America on *The Phil Silvers Show* [*Sergeant Bilko*] and I got the job of doubling for her as a dancer—they needed a ballet dancer who could do the point work. Then she got sick, and I stepped in for her at rehearsal time. And they *preferred* me, which was really quite awful, a *terrible* way to be introduced into the business, because I sort of bumped my friend off. (Although she *was* quite sick, and it was doubtful that she could come back.) Anyway, I took over, and that was my very first acting part.

How did you land the role of Sleeping Beauty on Shirley Temple Storybook?

They wanted me to come out [to Hollywood] for a reading—I think they had read one of my reviews in a play. So my mother brought me out here for that, and I auditioned and I got it. Then work just started *happening*. I had done a few shows back in New York—I'd done *The U.S. Steel Hour* and *Studio One* and "The Human Comedy" [on *Du Pont Show of the Month*] with my half-brother David DeEyre, who played the lead and was only six at the time. It was an unprecedented thing, doing that live, coast to coast, with a very young child. He played Ulysses and I played his sister.

How did you enjoy doing live TV out of New York? Was it nerve-wracking?

It was like doing theater—and I *had* done theater. So it was exciting. You felt a rush, always, because there was always pressure to get it right.

An Anne Helm glamour shot, before she began screaming on screen.

Was Shirley Temple Storybook *your first big break?*

Yes, probably, in terms of television shows. They had a lot of publicity on this; I was supposed to be on the *Life* cover, and then some disaster came about! So I was bumped off the cover, but I had a really nice spread in *Life* magazine. It was fun, because there was a lot of attention paid to this show. Judith Evelyn was in it, Alexander Scourby, Nancy Marchand...

Did you meet Shirley Temple?

No, I didn't meet her. *Never* did.

And I did about *three* of them, I believe! It was sort of like when they did *Alfred Hitchcock Presents*—he wasn't around either. I finally did meet him at a party, but very casually. I didn't meet him on the show at all.

What was the experience of working on Hitchcock's TV show like?

I loved the show because it was well-done for a half-hour series, and it always had fascinating stories, sort of like *The Twilight Zone*. Robert Florey, who directed me in one of them ["Change of Heart"], also directed a lot of movies. In that one, I was the granddaughter of a clockmaker [Abraham Sofaer], and at the end it turns out that he killed me and put a ticking clock inside of me [*laughs*]! When my lover comes back, he sees me sitting in the chair and it's sort of like a *Psycho* moment—he comes running up and the camera pans in and you hear this "tick-tock, tick-tock." The grandfather wanted to possess me, and that was the only way he could, by making me into a clock. I would love to have really *met* Alfred Hitchcock and talked with him about things.

I've talked to a couple of actresses who said they got very nervous and tongue-tied around him. I wonder if he didn't somehow do that to them on purpose.

He probably did. And he was a very *secretive* man, from what I understand. I heard that he was very interested in me for some film; while I was doing *The Swingin' Maiden* [1963] over in England, he ordered a lot of my films. I never knew if that was true or not, but I was just *delighted*, 'cause I thought, "Oooh, maybe I'll get to do a *movie* with him," which would have been wonderful. He did the same thing with Tippi Hedren: He had sort of a "film fest" of her, and then hired her. But it was all very secretive, sort of the way Howard Hughes used to work. I always thought of Alfred Hitchcock as being the same style of man.

Some of your early publicity made you out to be "the American Brigitte Bardot." Was that the kind of career you wanted to carve out for yourself at the beginning?

Well, I was so flattered in New York, when I was working off-Broadway, when that happened, when this critic started writing things like that. I played sort of a coquette-ish part off-Broadway in a play called *Claremhard*, and that's where that came from. And other people picked it up. It followed me a *little* bit, but I was very fortunate in that I always had various roles that I played. I never seemed to get typecast. I played so many wonderful characters—Southern girls and schoolteachers and nymphomaniacs [*laughs*]. Just the gamut! I loved the idea that people looked at me as a Brigitte Bardot, such a beautiful person, 'cause to me she was just a goddess. She was certainly a goddess in *most* men's eyes in those days

How did you get involved on The Magic Sword?

I think it just happened with an interview, or [producer-director] Bert Gordon had seen me in something, because all of a sudden I had the part. It sort of was one of those "parts given"; I didn't really have to work or test for it or anything. I understand that *Magic Sword* is thought of as one of Bert's better pictures. I didn't really know a lot about Bert when I started working with him; it wasn't until later that I found out he really was very well-respected by many in the business in terms of what he was able to do with so little money and the special effects that he was able to pull off in those days.

Bert Gordon was a sweetheart, he was very nice to work with—I enjoyed him. He was always preoccupied, I think, 'cause he really did a very good job for such a low budget. And he had wonderful people in it, you know—Basil Rathbone and Estelle Winwood were real pros. I unfortunately didn't get to know Basil that well. He was a very quiet, reserved man—I don't know if he was a *shy* man, but he seemed to keep to himself. It was very formal every morning, and we didn't have any conversations, really. But he was a gentleman, and Estelle Winwood was delightful. And I had a lot of fun with Gary [Lockwood]— Gary was an old friend, so we really just had *fun* as the prince and princess. Gary and I hung out together during that film, and he was crazy [*laughs*], he was fun. We used to date a lot, and we hung out with the same group of people—my brother Peter and I used to know Tuesday Weld, and Gary knew Tuesday, and we would just all be crazy. Gary laughed a lot and he liked to make jokes and fool around. I just remember it was always fun, it was like party time when Gary was around.

Helm and Gary Lockwood, real-life pals, played medieval lovers in Bert I. Gordon's *The Magic Sword*.

Your first scene was an outdoor pond scene that was shot in January. How cold was that?

It was pretty cold out there. It was on the back lot of 20th that we did that, and it wasn't pleasant—I do remember it being quite chilly!

Where else was The Magic Sword *shot?*

Most of it was shot at Goldwyn, and then we went out to the back lot at 20th. The castle [courtyard] scene with me and the dragon was also shot on the

20th back lot, I'm pretty sure. The original title was *St. George and the 7 Curses*, but it ended up being *The Magic Sword*.

Where did you see Magic Sword *for the first time, and what did you think?*

I probably saw a screening of it. I liked it, I thought it was really well-done. I was quite amazed by it. I loved the fantasy parts, probably because I didn't have a really normal childhood. So [*laughs*], I think I got to live my childhood out in a lot of parts that were given to me!

What was "not normal" about your childhood?

I grew up really fast—like, I was in New York studying at the Met and basically taking care of my whole family at a very early age. And I didn't go to school—my mother didn't believe in schools, and kept me out. So I grew up fast and became an adult sooner than I should. If I could do it over, I would do it differently. I missed a lot by not going through the normal stages of growing up. I think that's what was wonderful about acting for me: I felt like I was a kid again.

Also, your father wasn't around, correct?

My father left when we were very young—I was about two and a half.

Later on, did you make public appearances or tour with The Magic Sword*?*

No, I didn't. I did it with *Desire in the Dust* [1960], and for *The Interns* [1962] the producer had me go to France and that was lovely. I spent a whole week there doing publicity.

Back in the early '60s, you got a lot of publicity over inheriting a million dollars.

Oh, I inherited this trust from my grandfather, and it got *so* out of whack in the newspapers. I have a lifelong trust that my grandfather left me and my brother and it's *worth* a million dollars, but I don't have a million dollars in the *bank*, no!

Well, you got a lot of press out of it.

I did, yeah. But a lot of people thought I was rich, and never believed me when I said I wasn't [*laughs*]!

Any memories of your supporting role in The Couch *with Grant Williams?*

I don't remember a lot of it, because I had a very small part in that, playing some kind of floozy. I knew Grant Williams and I *dated* Grant—he was a very gifted pianist, I remember *that*. He did concerts and things, and I often wondered why he'd gone into the acting profession because he could have done a lot as a pianist.

The Couch *was written by Robert Bloch, who also wrote both your* Hitchcock *episodes.*

He was a *wonderful* writer, *very* good. He also wrote *Strait-Jacket* and I got to know him on that movie—I really just enjoyed him so much. (I hadn't met him on the other shows.) What was great about *Strait-Jacket*, and very *sad* for me too, is that I felt very much like family. They brought me in very early on, when Joan Blondell was scheduled to star, and then Joan Crawford got a-hold of the script. She had a great deal of money in those days because he had been married to the president of Pepsi-Cola, so what she did was basically buy Joan Blondell's contract out and bump her off and get the part. I found this out later—*much* later, after *I* had left the picture. That's when I heard all these horror stories.

When Joan Blondell and you were scheduled to star together, did you meet Blondell?

No, I did not, but I went in for rehearsals and everyone was telling me what was going on. Then all of a sudden Crawford was going to do it. Of course, I was *delighted*—I had no idea that Joan Blondell had been bumped off. And Blondell had a nervous breakdown over this, 'cause *Strait-Jacket* was a very big break for her. She had had a large lull in her career, and I think it pretty much devastated her [to lose *Strait-Jacket*]. But, anyway, I was delighted, I thought, "God, *Joan Crawford*! I can learn so much from her"—I had that much admiration for her. But it came to be that she really disliked me intensely, she was very jealous, and got *me* bumped off, too.

So you did get to meet Crawford.

Oh, yes, I got to rehearse with her for a few days, and it was *hell*—it was not a good situation! It was a lot of hypocrisy, and a lot of times I had no idea what was going on. I was very "innocent" in those days in terms of not seeing through things, not understanding what was really happening. She just didn't want me on the movie. And they all loved me—[William] Castle and Bloch loved me, and we had been working together very intimately on the part, which was a wonderful part. I was really disappointed—I was really *shaken* by it, actually. I never once thought I would *ever* want to leave the acting profession, 'cause I loved it so much, but it *so* hurt me on a personal level that I really considered wanting to get out of the business. I also wondered if I had the "stuff" to *be* in the business. It brought out a lot of self-doubt and insecurities for me. And up to that point, I just *loved* acting! But this sort of knocked the wind out of me. It was a good lesson for me, it gave me some "building blocks" of strength and helped me start looking at things in a different way. And *not* to be entirely trusting of everybody [*laughs*]! But that comes from being young, our innocence and our trusting of other people.

What was Castle like?

He was great. He was my "friend" up to a point, but Crawford was certainly the "meal ticket" on that for him. I was disappointed—*very* disappointed—by everyone concerned. But I was just some little pawn who was used by *her*, I felt. She really wanted her friend Diane Baker in the part—and Diane was wonderful in the part.

Can you give a for-instance of how Crawford made life on the set hell for you?

She didn't like the fact that I brought a Diet Coke on the set, she made a big issue of *that*. She pulled all this technical stuff with me in rehearsals, where she wanted me to say the line *right* at the moment she (let's say) dropped an ice cube—this was in the first rehearsal. She was just a very hypocritical person. And I was privy to a lot of things—conversations of hers that I heard on the set. She really wanted me off the picture, and I knew that. But by that point, there was no way I even wanted to *be* on the picture. She was a very sick woman. She pushed all *my* buttons for sure! (In fact [*laughs*], I was delighted when her daughter came out and said all these dreadful things about her in *Mommie Dearest*. It was many years later, but it made me feel less bad!) Bette Davis called me after this happened and she told me what a bitch Crawford was, so *that* made me feel good. I saved all the letters from Joan Crawford and I have them in my scrapbook. She sent these loving, sweet, saccharine letters to me and sent me flowers—and I felt like she had *murdered* me [*laughs*]!

This was afterwards?
Yes, after I left the picture. She was *so* sorry "it hadn't worked out" and all this stuff [*laughs*]—it was just nonsense! It was bizarre, the whole event was very bizarre for me.

And Crawford was such a name that nobody had enough gumption to stand up to her, I guess.
To them, it was wonderful that they had a huge *star* in this movie. I think the most difficult part of the business is the *impersonal* part of it. This was one of those situations where I got to see a lot of devastation—and then I became *part* of it! But look at Joan Blondell: *She* had a nervous breakdown, and, my God, she'd been *around* for a while!

Were you friendly with Bette Davis?
No. A designer friend of mine was *very* close to Bette Davis and had done a movie with her, and this friend had told her what had happened. Crawford and Bette Davis had had this huge feud—they had just finished *What Ever Happened to Baby Jane?* [1962] and their feud was all over the papers. So Davis was just fueling the fire, I think, when she called me [*laughs*]. It was one-upsmanship for her, another feather in her cap to just say, "The woman's a bitch!" But it was a wonderful call for me, because Crawford just crushed my ego. I really looked up to Crawford, and I didn't realize I was dealing with a sick woman. I took it very, very personally. But, again, in retrospect, it was probably a wonderful thing that happened to me 'cause it made me stand back and see the business from a different perspective. I had stars in my eyes about everyone—"God, *Joan Crawford*!"—and I didn't know that there were people *like* her out there. It took that real strong wallop for me to grow up and face facts about some of the people out there. You *have* to be aware of that, otherwise you can get crucified in this business. Or *any* business, for that matter!

Do you ever wonder what would have happened in your career if you had been in Strait-Jacket? *It did turn out to be a big moneymaker*
I've often wondered that about certain parts; if I had done *this* part or *that* part, what would have happened. I always remember the movie Haskell Wexler directed, *Medium Cool* [1969]—my agent had me turn it down. I really wanted to do the part, but they couldn't come up with the money because it was a low budget. I really always regretted not doing that; it would have changed the course of my career. That was one of my regrets, I would *love* to have worked with Wexler, 'cause he was really an artistic man.

Are you someone who still watches their own stuff?
Sometimes I'll watch 'em—but I get bored [*laughs*]! I get more of a kick out of it if my daughter has not seen it. Sometimes people will send me shows that I haven't seen in years and years, and I'll share them with my daughter. *That's* fun.

But the idea of sitting there by yourself, watching yourself—that doesn't float your boat?

No. That's somewhat depressing [*laughs*]! It's like anything: You look back and you wish you could redo it, you think you could do a better job. I *always* think that.

Do you have any recollections of Mother Goose a Go Go *[1966]?*

I was pregnant then, and it was sort of funny 'cause here I was bikini-clad—the sexual aspects of the movie were so ridiculous. They had my boobs hanging out and me laced up in all these tight frocks, and I was three and a half months pregnant. I only remember the movie because it was an exciting time for me, it was my first child. I don't think *Mother Goose* ever got a release, that's how bad it was. But now I have it on tape so it's sold in video stores, I'm sorry to say [*laughs*]!

What do you remember about Nightmare in Wax *with Cameron Mitchell?*

Oh, Lord, I don't even want to talk about it [*laughs*]! Remember the scene at the wax museum where we're trapped in boxes? It was such a low-budget film that the boxes they had us caged in, the boxes that we supposedly could not get out of, were made out of cardboard. We were all hysterical in these boxes, and any time we moved—any time we *breathed*—the whole box would move with us! It was so silly, the whole thing, that it was hard to stay serious in the "drama" of it all. I remember breaking out in giggles all the time. That last part of the movie was shot in a factory somewhere, a huge mausoleum of a building. We also filmed some scenes in someone's house.

Poor Cameron Mitchell ended up making a lot of movies like that.

I *know*—and he was *such* a talent, wasn't he? I worked with him on an episode of *The Beachcomber*, and before that he did a *lot* of good movies. But *Nightmare in Wax* was one of the lowest-budget movies I think I've ever been in. It was *really* low! That was a movie that was difficult to do, just because they didn't have very much money. The sets were tacky, and we were all pretty silly. I mean, *you* saw the movie—did *you* take it seriously?

No. I thought it was pretty dreadful, actually!

It's one of the worst movies I think I've ever seen. Everything was done in one take—that was it! Because we didn't have time. I think it was probably shot in a week [*laughs*]!

In recent years, you've been doing more TV than movies?

Right. I haven't been working in a while, I've been pretty much retired from the business, although I'm starting to get back into it now. I really want to work creatively if I'm going to work in the business, because the pressures of working in episodic TV are just too great—I don't want to step into that arena again. I'm talking about silly little parts where you go in for two days; there's just so much pressure that it doesn't interest me any more. When you get into high-gear shows where there's a lot of money at stake, it's more difficult for the artist. At least it is for me. Maybe it's just a psychological barrier I have with that. But I would almost prefer to work for free, in what I love doing. I don't like to mix it up with money. (I'm talking very idealistically now!) But that's

Anne Helm today.

how I started out in the business: I really just wanted to do wonderful parts and I wanted to be part of the creative stream. And I ended up doing a lot of roles that I would probably have been better off not doing. I just got kind of caught up.

What was your last TV show? Was it Amazing Stories?

Yes, I think so. That was a fun show and a wonderful part. I loved the part, it was one of those "fantasy" parts, and the director [Phil Joanou] was very creative. Just the whole story, the way it was written, was wonderful—it was very much like a *Twilight Zone*.

Actually, that script was written for The Twilight Zone.

Really? Richard Matheson wrote it, and he had done a lot of *Twilight Zone*s and other fantasy things. For *Amazing Stories*, they made a doll, a replica of me, and one of John Lithgow. And he fell in love with my doll when he saw it and I fell in love with *his* doll. So we were destined to be together, and it was through the dolls that we met. John was delightful, and I just had the best time working with him. A real professional and a very caring being—it was just lovely. It was a nice "last show" to do, one of my favorites. And I still have my little doll—I have her sitting in a doll's rattan chair in my living room [*laughs*]. She watches TV with me!

You were billed "Annie Helm."

That was a name I went back to after my divorce. I just like being *called* Annie, so for a while I used Annie. But I think I'm going to use Anne from now on. Some people get confused.

Have you enjoyed your life in Hollywood?

I did, while I was doing it, and it was a great stepping stone and a catalyst for me becoming an artist. I really "found myself" more through the physical arts than I did through acting. I love working with my hands, and I work in all kinds of media—I do clay, I sculpt. And I really like where I am right now: I'm writing children's books and illustrating them. That's where my interests lie. I taught *children* for many years when I was up in Topanga, after my children were born, and I actually worked as a teacher with an afterschool program in Santa Monica. And *I* learned a lot from the children—a lot of the [art] work that I do is very childlike, I'm a "primitive." I do unicorns and magical gardens and very childlike places, and I think I'm just sort of recreating the childhood I didn't have.

The acting was a wonderful experience and it was *given* to me, and so I was very spoiled that way—I didn't have to work very hard for the parts I was given. It seemed like all the doors just opened for me. I'm a fatalist and I believe in fate and destiny, that it's pretty much *written*. There's no formula to being in the business. To me, it was just sort of a wonderful weaving of fate. But it's like anything: When you're going through it, you don't appreciate it. Not until you get away from it. I look back on it almost as a dream sequence.

Anne Helm Filmography

Desire in the Dust (20th Century–Fox, 1960)
The Magic Sword (United Artists, 1962)
The Couch (Warners, 1962)
The Interns (Columbia, 1962)
Follow That Dream (United Artists, 1962)
The Swingin' Maiden (*The Iron Maiden*) (Columbia, 1964)
Ready for the People (Warners, 1964)
Honeymoon Hotel (MGM, 1964)
Mother Goose a Go Go (*The Unkissed Bride*) (Jack H. Harris/VIP Distributors/U.S. Films, 1966)
Nightmare in Wax (*Crimes in the Wax Museum*) (Crown International, 1969)
Hide in Plain Sight (MGM/United Artists, 1980)

Candace Hilligoss
on the *Carnival of Souls* remake

I thought, "This is the kind of movie that I would pay *them not to let me in the theater." I would give them eight dollars* not *to allow me inside, because the agony of sitting through this crap is so great that it would be worth eight dollars to me to be permitted to stay far, far away!*

Near the top of the list of cult horror movies of the 1960s stands *Carnival of Souls*, the haunting, "Occurrence at Owl Creek Bridge"-like story of a church organist (Candace Hilligoss) who survives a watery car crash only to discover that she now lapses into weird spells during which no one can see or hear her.

During the film's 1989 theatrical re-release, and for several years afterwards, Hilligoss tried to get Hollywood interested in a follow-up film, which has now been made and released (directly to home video) by Trimark. But, like her old screen character, Hilligoss is not seen or heard in the 1999 movie she instigated—for the very *un*-supernatural reason that the new film's producer froze her out. In the first half of this interview, Hilligoss talks about the raw deal she got from the makers of the old *and* new *Carnival*s; in the second half, she rates the remake.

When did you get the idea to do another Carnival of Souls?

In 1989, when they had the *Carnival of Souls* reunion in Lawrence, Kansas, I said to Herk Harvey [writer-producer-director-co-star of the 1962 original], "Wouldn't you love to do a sequel?" He said, "If the first one had made money, I might be interested." I told him I wanted to pursue it, and he said, "If you want the headache, you pursue it." I did. I sat down and wrote a treatment, and Reza Badiyi was very interested in getting involved. (Reza was one of the original cameramen on *Carnival of Souls*, and he's a director now.) Then, a year later, I expanded the treatment into a screenplay. Reza loved the script and he thought it would be a great idea. At the time, Reza's agency set up a meeting for us at Shoreline Pictures in Century City. In June 1993, we brought it to them, and that's where we first met Peter Soby. None of them at Shoreline had ever heard of *Carnival*, and the reason they were interested was because I had spent the past four years publicizing the movie with appearances at film festivals, interviews with major papers across the country and even with Leonard Maltin on *Entertainment Tonight*.

They screened [the original movie]. Once all of them had viewed it, they were interested in doing this project with Reza and me. However, since Shoreline did not seem to have the money to launch any film, we decided to move on to other places. Peter Soby later called me and told me he had left Shoreline and he wanted to know if anyone had taken *Carnival of Souls* over. I said no, it was still available and I was still trying to see people about it. Then he asked if he could join in some way, to create interest and to produce it. I met with him and he said, "I would love to do something with it." So I spent a year and a half helping Peter. We met a number of times at a local restaurant in Hollywood to discuss ideas for the movie. I gave him the screenplay I had written for the sequel. He took copious notes on my suggestions as to whom to contact, who would be most helpful and other names to drop.

Toward the end, he asked me if he might speak directly to Herk Harvey, to reassure Herk that he had a sincere interest in it. I called Herk Harvey and I said, "I don't *really* know who he is," because Peter's one film credit was, he was a bookkeeper at Lorimar. But Herk said, "I'll talk to him." And for some reason, when Peter Soby talked to Herk Harvey—I don't know what Peter had in his hip pocket, but somehow he convinced Herk to give him an option. And they did not include me in the option. Peter never told me what had happened, that he had done this. In fact, he sort of disappeared. Then, many months later, I read in *Variety* that Peter was doing *Carnival of Souls* with Trimark. And I was no longer his partner, as he had other people. At that point, Peter said that he had been chosen by Herk Harvey, out of everyone, because he was so wonderful. And that Herk died knowing it was in great hands with Peter Soby.

And, of course, Herk is no longer around to tell his side of it, to talk about the phone conversation with Soby and how you got dealt out.

Herk's wife Pauline is just sick about it. She said, "I assume that Herk [who was dying of pancreatic cancer] was not himself, and just assumed you were part of it." But, who knows?

What about Herk Harvey's partner, John Clifford, the guy who wrote the original movie? What's his attitude?

John had no loyalty to me. Once he saw the dollar signs, he didn't care who brought it to him. He didn't care that I was connected, he didn't care about all I had done.

Did you have any sort of contract with Soby?

I did have a signed agreement with Peter, which was very loose. It showed that we had met and that I was to be a participant.

When you found out that Carnival of Souls *was being made for Trimark, what did you do then?*

I contacted Peter and told him that the widow of Herk Harvey said that an option had been signed because they assumed I was part of it; I asked, "Could

Like pearls tossed before swine, Candace Hilligoss' story ideas were ignored by the makers of the 1999 *Carnival of Souls* remake.

I please see the option?" He never answered me.

What contact have you had with him since then?

Cut to a year, year and a half later, to about mid-July [1997]. All of a sudden Peter calls me out of the blue, because now he wants me to play a one-day cameo in *Carnival*. I said, "Peter! I thought we were partners. What is going on?" Well, there was a lot of harrumphing and stalling, and he said, "I thought that was only if we were going to do your sequel. We're doing a remake." I said, "Oh, no, Peter, I brought the project to you and helped you. And introduced you to Herk Harvey. You never even knew about *Carnival*." In fact, I don't even think he was born when we were making *Carnival*! I told him I was really disappointed in him, because for a year and a half I helped him. He fumbled around and then he said, "Well, I'd really love you to come down and do a cameo." I said I wasn't interested.

Then he had the publicity company that's handling the new *Carnival* call me up: "We'd like you to come down and pose with the cast," etc., etc. I said, "Why would I want to do that?" The guy said, "Well, we think it would be a lot of *fun*." "Fun? Fun to help someone who stabbed me in the back and stole a project from me? You have the nerve to call me and ask me to go down and push your picture?" The guy said, "I don't understand. Peter says you're very nice!" I said, "Of *course* I'm nice—I spent 18 months helping him. I'm sorry that he turned out to be such a shark, but I guess they learn fast in Hollywood."

Did you ever see a script, or get an idea what this new film will be like?

I don't know. They never sent me a script, Peter Soby never discussed it with me, never wanted me to know anything about it. All he wanted was to get my face on film so he could use the good will that I had generated with *Carnival*. Let this be a lesson to anyone in the film world who has an idea, who wants to go around and peddle it. Here I thought I was protected by friendship—but friendship means nothing. Frankly, I felt totally betrayed by Herk Harvey and John Clifford. I thought that they were totally on my side, and I was stunned that when they saw an opportunity, they didn't care any more.

What's the lesson in all this? What do you hope happens with the new movie?

I hope that Peter Soby is exposed for what he is. I wish I could say to him…

Say it to him now!

Okay, I'll tell you what I would say: To be an artist, one must search for the truth. If he, as a filmmaker, is consumed with how to cheat and connive, there is no room to be an artist, because he is no longer in a position to search for the truth. You cannot possibly do anything worthwhile if you don't have that soul in you. Since he doesn't, there's no way it could be any good.

[The remake of *Carnival of Souls*, made by producers operating under the auspices of sleazemeister Wes Craven, languished on the shelf for nearly two years before slinking onto the video market virtually unnoticed (February 1999). Actress Bobbie Phillips (*Showgirls*) took on what was, ostensibly, Candace's original role, while standup comic Larry Miller appeared as a sadistic clown. In flashbacks to the Phillips character's childhood, she watches as Miller murders her mother; upon his prison release years later, Miller returns to terrorize her. The producers thoroughly "Cravenized" the original plot, tossing in these elements of rape and brutality, as well as incongruous creatures that Candace aptly describes as "pink fetuses in bubble gum body suits." In this follow-up conversation, she makes plain her opinion of this odious "remake."]

What were your first impressions of the new Carnival of Souls?

Well, that it had nothing to do with my *Carnival of Souls*, and I'm sorry they used the title because they've *ruined* the title of our original film. Their remake says in the opening credits, "A Film by Adam Grossman." I don't know who he is, but the audience should now know that if they ever see "A Film by Adam Grossman" on any movie, it should be a cue to run for the nearest exit! He wrote and directed it. And Wes Craven, I think, should be hung by his thumbs at Hollywood and Vine for movie fans to stone, because he's so devastated the intent of the original.

Do you happen to know how much Craven had to do with it?

It doesn't matter. It's under his umbrella, and he's got his name pasted all over it.

Plot-wise, it really is more like one of his typical movies than it is like your Carnival of Souls.

Yes, his signature crap is written all over it, too. They keep saying that [leading lady] Bobbie Phillips is "from *Showgirls*"—a fact which I would *hide*, rather than play up! I did see *Showgirls*, but I couldn't remember which nude she was. I didn't recognize her, maybe because she now has clothes on.

In fairness to her, I want to say that I thought she—and some of the other actors—were a lot better than this new Carnival of Souls.

Yes, and it's a shame that (with one clinker like *Showgirls* in her career) she now gets thrown *another* clinker. It could set her career back four or five years. These are the kind of things that *ruin* actors who aren't big enough stars to override bad movies. She should have gotten in something *good* before she got cursed with this one.

Did any part of it scare you? It left me completely unfazed.

I know exactly what you mean. Take for example the lost souls that are meant to spook the audience and the heroine. Do we blame Craven or director Grossman for this idiotic portrayal of the lost souls? Giant fetuses that looked as if they were covered in pink bubble gum, having epileptic seizures—so silly. The only thing that scared me was the fact that these people who made this movie thought that this would sell [*laughs*]! That was the most frightening part of the whole thing.

It's come out on home video, but they originally planned to put it out theatrically, correct?

Of course. When no one wants to release a movie, when no one is willing to take a movie off your hands or give you a distribution deal, you're forced to go direct to video to get any money back.

How long ago was it made?

It was made the summer before last—the summer of '97. So it took almost two years to come out.

Did they have the nerve to take anything at all from your treatment?

No, because they were too stupid. It shows how dumb they were—I threw my pearls before swine here. And they were too stupid to know what the pearls were.

They had no idea why the first picture worked. That was the most aggravating thing about the new Carnival.

They didn't understand, they weren't on the same level. It was almost as if they actually weren't even in the same genre!

It reminded me more of Cape Fear *[1962], with horrific "dream scenes" thrown in, than it did of your* Carnival. *If it had had a different title, I'd have watched it for an hour before your* Carnival *crossed my mind.*

A friend of mine told me that the ripoffs of *Carnival* that he's seen were better done than the remake. The one with Zohra Lampert, for instance [*Let's Scare Jessica to Death*, 1971], and *Jacob's Ladder* [1990], and even *Sole Survivor* [1982]. In the new *Carnival*, their idea of a brilliant opening was to have a little girl watching a clown [Larry Miller] rape and batter her mother, and then twist and break the mother's neck. I thought, "This is the kind of movie that I would *pay* them not to let me in the theater." I would give them eight dollars *not* to allow me inside, because the agony of sitting through this crap is so great that it would be worth eight dollars to me to be permitted to stay far, far away!

The main character, the girl Bobbie Phillips played, didn't have the right quality for this new story.

It was strange how they tried to make her a real '90s girl: She's a heavy smoker, she says the f word and she runs a beer joint, setting up drinks for old geezers. *That's* their idea of a '90s woman. She's the grown-up version of the little girl we saw in the first scene, the girl whose mother was murdered by the clown. Years later, the clown comes back and he turns up in the back seat of Bobbie Phillips' car and shoves a gun down her throat. Then he makes her drive, and the car goes off the pier and crashes into the river. All of a sudden she wakes up in her bathtub—

Giving the audience the indication that the scene in the car was all a dream.

Yeah! Then she goes into the longest

car wash that I've ever been through [*laughs*]—it went on forever and ever—and the car fills with water. It fills up and fills up until her face is shoved against the roof, then suddenly she's back on land again. I thought, "Well, what happened to the truck? Did something get left on the cutting room floor?" Then we flash back—or maybe forward?—to a scene where she's at the carnival, but she's still driving the truck and it's in tiptop condition after both of them "drowned" in the car wash!

After a while, I wasn't even trying to make sense out of it any more. In your version, you were a girl that strange things were happening to. In this version, she was just a girl who was having nightmares.

What I always think is a "cheap shock" is, every time you put your heroine in trouble and don't know how to get her out of it, have the alarm clock ring and have her wake up in bed. And the audience goes, "Oh, by golly, it was just a nightmare!"

That lets the screenwriter off the hook every time.

Right—and that's all they did here, they got off the hook every time by having her "wake up" someplace else. The thing that made it so bad film-wise, technically, is this: Not only did they have these odd "jumps" where the audience has to ask themselves, "Did it really happen to her, or was it her nightmare?", but they also intercut flashbacks of her as a child, with that stupid clown. They were constantly going forward and back, forward and back—

Into reality, out of reality—

And then they're also doing back story "fill," to let the audience know more about the clown from the beginning of the movie, the guy who murdered her mother. In flashbacks, we see how the mother *met* the clown and so on and so forth. And remember the love scene

Hilligoss makes an eerie reappearance from the river that swallowed up her car, in the one and only *true* version of *Carnival of Souls.*

between our heroine, played by Miss Phillips, and the good-looking young harbormaster [Paul Johansson]? They go off on his boat, and she wants to get some comfort, some sympathy from this handsome man. Soon they start in kissing and so on and so forth—then, all at once, it ends up with such hot, heavy panting and tearing at clothes that you would have thought they were on the *Titanic* and were gonna be sinking any second [*laughs*]! I thought, "What is the panic? Why?? Who was going to interrupt them in the middle of the ocean?"

My problem with the new Carnival *is that it's one of these lousy "dream" horror movies, filled with dream sequences and all kinds of weird stuff. My attitude is: In a movie where any*thing *can happen...who cares what* happens?

That's why the audience loses interest. The audience was constantly being shown that what she seemed to be experiencing didn't really happen; every time she got in trouble, the next thing we knew, she'd awaken or "land" somewhere else. Like the scene where she goes to a carnival, and the wranglers come after her. The audience doesn't have a clue why these strange people are stalking her and making her run away. I thought, "Well, at least they're not the fetuses in pink bubble gum. But why are all the carnival people turning on her?" Once *again*, she wakes up in bed, and we just excuse it as another nightmare.

The thing that (to me) was the real nightmare for the character was having to run that tavern. Remember how many leaks and floods there were, and how they had to tramp around in the basement, and how things in this joint were always running out?

I love the scenes where the tavern ceiling is leaking because (obviously) a pipe is broken somewhere upstairs—but instead of fixing the pipe, they just keep fixing the ceiling. It takes a special kind of stupid to write stuff like that.

Someone so stupid that that's how *they'd* try to fix that leak!

Were you offered a part, or just the opportunity to be photographed with the cast?

Peter Soby called me up and said, "How would you like to come down for one day to play a cameo?" Well, after my conversation with him, he realized I had no intention of coming down. I wonder what they would have had me play; I might have been one of those pink fetuses in a bubble gum body suit [*laughs*]! What *could* they have had me play? Some drunk at the bar that Bobbie Phillips sets up a drink for? Puhleeze! I don't know what they had in mind for me to do.

I'm soooo glad you weren't in it!

Oh, it was so awful. The funhouse scene looked to me like a description of an LSD nightmare. She gets a gun and aims at the clown and overkills him—and then, as usual, she wakes up *again*. But, hocus pocus, she's back at the car wash, only to wake up again at home. This girl seems to spend a lot of time in bed! Now suddenly, she's back at the carnival. This is a cinematic lesson in how to confuse and to annoy an audience all at the same time.

It put me *in the mood to start goin' to sleep and wakin' up.*

Well, this is why it got boring. I lost track of the number of times she got in trouble and woke up. And as an audience, you no longer knew what was supposed to be real and what wasn't. So you no longer cared. Maybe Wes Craven would have done better to remake one of those *Perils of Pauline* flicks.

And your prediction is that the movie will lose money.

I don't even think they'll make back their costs. I hope it ends their careers. The producers, I mean. God forgive the actors; they weren't casting *Hamlet* that week, and actors need jobs. So forgive the actors. But the *producers* and the *writer* and the *director*—may it end their careers. That would be a just punishment for trying to "put one over" on an audience, for having the presumption to think that their catastrophe was anything like the original, as directed by Herk Harvey.

Michael A. Hoey

*Once the title was changed to
[The Navy vs. the Night Monsters],
we knew that when the movie came out,
the reviews were going to be, "Navy 0, Nightcrawlers 4"!*

In 1965, writer-director Michael A. Hoey brought to the screen *The Navy vs. the Night Monsters* (an adaptation of Murray Leinster's novel *The Monster from Earth's End*), in which deadly walking trees—spawned in the "Hot Lakes" region of Antarctica—overrun an island naval base off the South American coast. The Mamie Van Doren-Anthony Eisley-starring film got some good reviews on its initial release (*The Hollywood Reporter* called it "a class vehicle in every detail"), but it subsequently toppled into the "so bad it's good" category, where it remains to this day. In this interview, Hoey describes the uphill battles involved in making *Night Monsters*, and pleads his case that the movie didn't become a Golden Turkey until after it left his hands.

Hoey, the son of character actor Dennis Hoey (Insp. Lestrade in the Universal *Sherlock Holmes* series), was born in London and relocated to the U.S. as a child. Growing up in the shadows of the Hollywood studios, he decided he wanted to get into the business and began his career in the editing room. Branching out into production, he formed a company (Bardin Productions) in partnership with actor Britt Lomond and in 1961 announced their intention to film the Leinster novel (Hoey's title was *The Nightcrawlers*); the project was sidelined when Hoey became a Warner Brothers producer. Four years later, after the end of his Warners stint, Hoey made the film for low-budget specialist Jack Broder—who interfered throughout production, and subsequently hired Arthur C. Pierce to write and direct new scenes for inclusion in Hoey's finished film. Here Hoey tells *his* side of the surprising story...

When did the idea of making The Navy vs. the Night Monsters *first occur to you?*

Around 1959, I read a book called *The Monster from Earth's End* by Murray Leinster. I was very taken with it and thought, "Gee, this could be an exciting film." What appealed to me about it was, I was a great fan of *The Thing*, Howard

Hawks' film, which I felt had a wonderful style and an interesting premise: A group of people cut off from the outside world, facing an unknown entity, have to decide on their own how to deal with it and how to survive. That was pretty much the premise for *Monster from Earth's End*. I managed to get an option on the book and I sat down and I wrote a screenplay.

Did you deal directly with Leinster?

No, actually, I went to my attorney, who spoke to Leinster's agent. I never had any direct contact with Leinster at all, at any time. By the time the film was completed, I would have been ashamed to talk to him, because of what happened. Which was not of my doing. We'll get into that.

I wrote the screenplay and tried to peddle it around. At that point, I was working as an assistant film editor at Warner Brothers. Then, because of a situation which occurred on a picture called *The Chapman Report* [1962], Jack Warner promoted me to producer. So I jumped from assistant film editor to producer, and spent the next two years developing scripts at Warner Brothers—only *one* of which was produced, *Palm Springs Weekend* [1963]. Then I began a relationship with a wonderful man and director by the name of Norman Tau-

"Are you hinting my apples aren't what they ought to be??"
A Night Monster on the prowl!

rog, who I ended up doing about 12 pictures with. He directed *Palm Springs Weekend*, then we did an Elvis Presley [*Tickle Me*, 1965] on which I became sort of a writer and production assistant to him. I was on six [Presley pictures] altogether, and I got writing credit for two of them, *Stay Away, Joe* [1968] and *Live a Little, Love a Little* [1968]. But I also did a lot of rewriting on *Tickle Me*, *Speedway* [1968], *Spinout* [1966] and *Double Trouble* [1967].

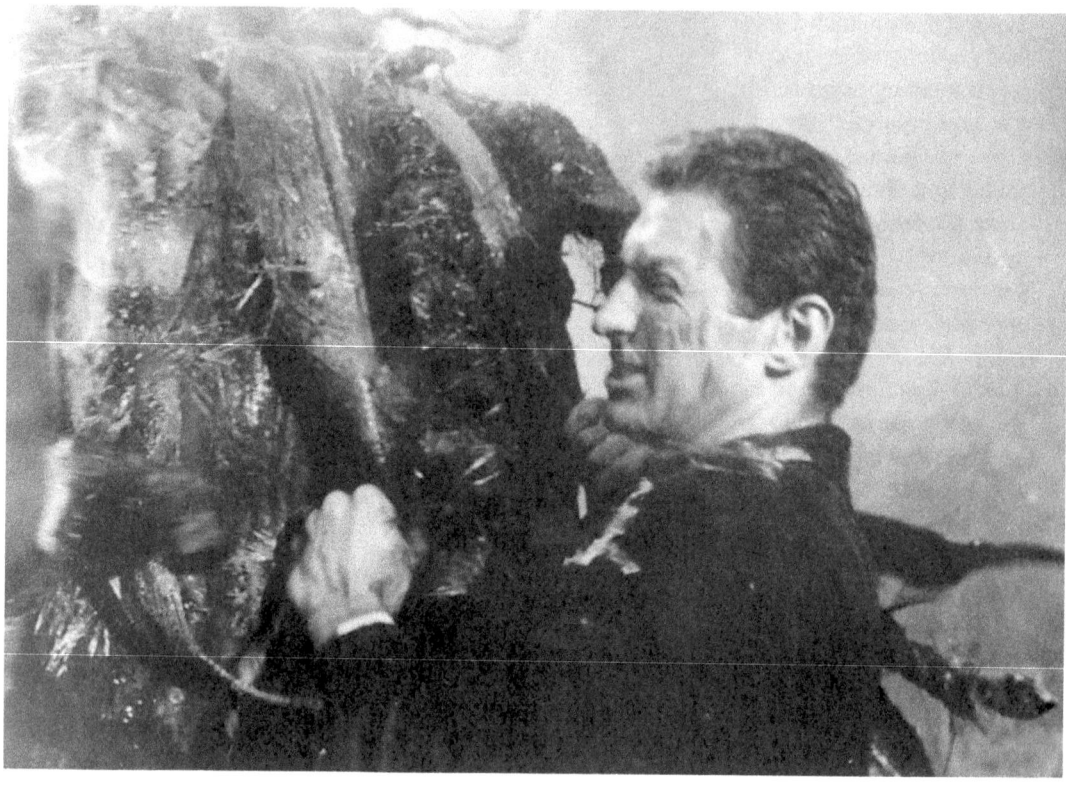

Mike Sargent is about to be "absorbed" by one of the tree monsters.

When you first announced your film way back in 1961, you were calling it The Nightcrawlers.

That was the title that I gave my screenplay. There's an irony to all this: When I bought the book, I thought, *"Monster from Earth's End*...that's too exploitative a title. I'd like another title." One day I'm driving down the street and I see a sign on some guy's lawn, NIGHT-CRAWLERS FOR SALE. Obviously *he* was talking about worms, but I thought, "Boy, that's a great title for this project!" So I called it *The Nightcrawlers.* But Jack Broder, who was the executive producer, retitled it *The Navy vs. the Night Monsters*, which is an abominable title. I remember the day when I was rehearsing and Broder walked in and announced what the new title was going to be. The entire cast was ready to walk out—they were furious that he would give it that title. Such an exploitative, dumb title.

According to one of the trade papers, it went from The Nightcrawlers *to* The Navy vs. the Nightcrawlers *to* The Navy vs. the Night Monsters.

Once the title was changed to *The Navy vs. anything*, we knew that when the movie came out, the reviews were going to be, "Navy 0, Nightcrawlers 4" [*laughs*]!

Jumping back a minute: How much did you pay for the rights to the book?

It seems to me that it was a horrendous sum, like around $4000. By the way, the story was based on an actual premise: They really *did* find underwater springs in Antarctica, they *did* find vegetation. What Leinster did was take some actual incidents and build on them.

Back in 1961, when you were going to make it for your own "Bardin Productions," a couple of actors, Britt Lomond and Taggart Casey, were going to be your co-producers.

Taggart was a friend of mine who was involved with a couple of low-budget films. *Terror in the Haunted House* [1959] was one of them—he had something to do with the production end of it. He made an attempt to put the *Nightcrawlers* package together [in 1961], but he ended up just being one of the actors *in* it. Bardin Productions was a company that Britt Lomond and I formed.

He was also going to star.

Britt was an actor who had done a lot of things, including Monasterio on [the Disney TV series] *Zorro*. He and I got to know one another while I was working at Disney, and we actually wrote a screenplay called *Only the Sea Is Neutral*, a story about a German submarine which got into Scapa Flow during the early part of World War II. When that came along, we decided to try to put a company together. Then we ended up *making* a [semi-documentary] called *The Legend of Mandinga* [1961] which I went down to Colombia, South America, to direct. That was done under the Bardin Productions banner. "Bardin" was actually Barbara and Diane, our wives at the time.

So in 1965, after Navy *had been on the back burner for several years, things started coming together.*

It was while we were doing the mix on *Tickle Me* that I got a phone call from a guy by the name of George Edwards, who ultimately was the producer of *The Nightcrawlers*. He called me and said, "I've read your script and I think there's some interest in making it as a film. Would you be interested in selling it to us? We don't have a lot of money." I said, "Well...what *do* you have?" He said, "Let me just ask you one thing: Would you be interested in directing it?" And I told him, "You just said the magic words!"—I mean, if *that* was the case, they could get the film for virtually nothing! Which is about what they *got* it for. The whole "package" for the screenplay and my services as a director I think came to $10,000. Four thousand went to Murray Leinster, 2000 went to the Directors Guild, another thousand went to my agent [*laughs*]—by the time I got through, I didn't exactly get fat on it!

George Edwards was working with Jack Broder at this time.

That's right. George was a "hired gun"—he was hired by Jack Broder because Jack had this sudden whim to make movies. They ended up making two films literally back-to-back, *Women of the Prehistoric Planet* [1966] and *Navy vs. the Night Monsters*; one [*Women*] finished and the other one [*Navy*] started within a week or two, using the same crew. Broder was smart enough to know that he couldn't produce 'em himself, I guess, so he hired George Edwards to be what we now call a "line producer." But George was *much* more than just a line producer, he was a *very* talented guy, *very* creative. George was a terrific guy; I really, really liked him. Of all the experiences, bad and good, that I had on that film, certainly the George

Edwards experience was a good one. He was a good producer who tried to keep things away from you while you were on the set; keep the picture moving forward smoothly; keep oil on the waters. And at the same time make creative decisions that made sense, which was the antithesis of what Jack Broder did. George was a lovely guy and we remained friends the rest of his life.

It was shot at Producers Studio in Hollywood.

Right. And we shot two days on location up at Agua Dulce Airport, near Vasquez Rocks. That was the plane crash sequence.

The plane was stock footage, correct?

Not actually. The plane coming in was a C-47 which we hired. We actually had a fly-over—that shot of the plane coming in, banking, coming in, and you see that it's got its wheels up and it's about ten feet off the ground. *That* we shot. Later, after the picture was out of my hands, they changed the story and what I shot that day was no longer appropriate, so they *had* to stick in a piece of stock footage of a plane doing a belly landing that didn't even match the plane we had in the picture. We were using a C-47 and the stock shot was a totally different airplane. And as I recall, the stock shot was in black-and-white, so they had to tint it [*laughs*]. But this is from the man [Broder] who once said to me, "Why is it costing so much to build sets?" What he had in mind was to try to use the same sets, the same everything for my picture and *Women of the Prehistoric Planet*. Well, obviously, *Women of the Prehistoric Planet* and a story about a Navy base on an island off the coast of South America don't exactly match! But I was able to use the jungle set that they built, and I think we used it to rather good advantage thanks to Stanley Cortez, who was a fine cameraman.

You're not the first person to complain to me about Jack Broder.

They published the initial budget on the movie and Jack had a look at it, and I guess it was more than he intended to spend. I seem to recall that he wanted to make the picture for $125,000, which people were doing in those days. Anyway, the budget came out, and the art director had put in the budget the cost of building Quonset huts, the buildings that these people lived and worked in. Broder saw that and wanted to know why we needed to build the exteriors of the Quonset huts. He said, "I know there are hundreds and hundreds of feet of film of Quonset huts in stock footage." I was thrown by that—I was sitting in the office, across the desk from him, thinking *fast* 'cause I don't want to start an argument immediately. I said, "Jack, *that* might work for a couple of shots, just to establish the Quonset huts, but when we get into these scenes where people come from the inside of the Quonset hut out, or they go from the outside in, we've got to walk them into the buildings. Otherwise, how do we do that?" He said, "Well…why don't you put up a process screen and project the shot of the Quonset huts on the screen? Then all you gotta do is build a door." I said, "You mean, cut a hole in the screen and build a door?" and he said, "Yeah!" Well [*laughs*], I said, "Okay, Jack—lemme get *back* to you on that!" I think that gives you some idea of Mr. Broder's film knowledge!

And he'd been in the industry for years!

Well, only as an exhibitor. He'd never really been a producer. Except for *Bela Lugosi Meets a Brooklyn Gorilla* [*laughs*].

In the early '50s, when Broder had another moviemaking fling, he used to let his son read the scripts, and if the son didn't like 'em, Broder ordered them rewritten. The son was ten years old.

And Broder made his daughter Madelynn, who was in her late teens or early twenties, the associate producer of *Navy vs. the Night Monsters*! She was an associate producer in name only—I think I saw her *once* on the film.

Tony Eisley told me that the extra scenes Arthur Pierce wrote and directed screwed up the whole picture. What was your original premise?

It was set up at the very beginning of the film that Tony Eisley's commanding officer had left the island on some sort of a special tour, he was off on the mainland. So, in effect, the lieutenant commander [Eisley] was in charge. He was *not* the head of the base, but suddenly he was thrust into this position of having to run the place. Well, it *looked* like it was going to be a very easy thing to do 'til all the trouble started—at which point *he* had to deal with it, he *had* to figure it out. Why?, because [in the Hoey footage that Pierce and Broder deleted] the plane came in, belly-landed and knocked over the radio tower, leaving itself crashed on the runway. They couldn't fly any planes in or out and they couldn't *talk* to anybody else, 'cause the radio tower was down. So until they could do one of two things (move the plane or put up the tower again), they were on their own. *That* was the premise. The way the picture ended up once Broder added the new scenes, Tony Eisley makes a phone call and gets *told* what to do [by the military brass in Washington], and then does it.

Then your *footage resumes, with Eisley acting like every decision is up to him, and he's really sweating it out.*

Well, of course, because that's the way we originally *shot* it.

Why did Broder make so many changes and shoot so many extra scenes after you "wrapped"?

Broder had said to me, "I need a 90-minute picture" and I delivered him a 78-minute film. I didn't really believe that it *had* to be 90 minutes for him to sell it to television, which is what he was maintaining. So, when I left the picture, he had Arthur Pierce, the director of *Women of the Prehistoric Planet*, come in and shoot added scenes. Well, what Arthur did was not just shoot added scenes, but change the whole premise. He added *allll* those scenes of those navy officers in that base on the mainland, the scenes where people would say, "[Eisley] wants to know what to do," "Well, tell him to do *this*." Then Pierce would cut back to the base where, all of a sudden, things were starting to happen. It completely *ruined* the premise of what I had in mind, which was very much like *The Thing*: a case where people had to figure out for themselves what was going on, and *deal* with it under intense pressure and under limited resources.

I'm going to guess that the comedy scene of the dumb soldier inflating the weather balloons was also not yours.

Oh, God, no. Oh, God, no. Oh, God, no. Oh, God, *no*.

How about that long opening scene of

the three men b.s.'ing in the cockpit of the airplane?

No. See, my premise was that you never went on board that plane until after it crash-landed. Then, when you *came* on board, all you saw was the pilot [Mike Sargent] sitting in a catatonic trance in the pilot's seat. Everybody else had disappeared. The premise that I functioned under was "less is more," and if you don't show it, the audience's imagination would create a much more vivid monster than we could ever create visually. I intended to show the monster in the most limited form at the very end of the picture. The end of "my" picture was when they surrounded the nightcrawlers in the cliff area and burned 'em up.

The book goes on from there a bit. Help arrives, but they think everybody on the island imagined it all. I thought that was dumb.

I did too, obviously, so I figured that the climax of the film should be the destruction of the trees. Presumably there were probably still some nightcrawler buds out there somewhere that might grow, but we left that [open]. It was a very typical 1950s-1960s kind of science fiction ending—"Watch the skies!", that kind of thing.

You keep talking about all the things Broder did after you wrapped. Did he also interfere during production?

Broder had writers all over the place—he would send pages down to me on the set. It was usually after I'd shot the scene, so I could just say, "Too late." And all through the preparation, he kept saying, "I've got this writer, why don't we let him try it?" I just had to bite my tongue and press on.

In the Leinster book, the pilot blows his brains out. You had him come back as a kind of zombie.

Yeah, because I wanted to develop a red herring. I didn't want the audience to get ahead of us, which they could very quickly do because it was a pretty basic plot.

And also they'd seen the poster with the walking trees on it before they came into the theater, I'm sure!

I hadn't any idea that it was gonna be *quite* that obvious in the publicity. When I set out to write the story, I wanted to create as many tensions and moments of uncertainty as I could. The pilot became a red herring, which worked well for the Ed Faulkner character, who blames the pilot for *everything*. The pilot also creates a couple of scare moments, like when he attacks the nurse [Kaye Elhardt].

I also like the book. One of the cleverest things about it was that the commander kept thinking the monsters were in the trees and it drove him nuts that he couldn't find them. Not until the end does he and the reader realize that the monsters are *the trees.*

Exactly. We tried to do that in the film to some extent—in the early parts, you saw movement, like when the dog gets killed and when Pamela Mason gets killed.

Was the comedy of Bobby Van part of your contribution?

Yes, Bobby was something that I wrote. We even went so far as to do a sort of a parody of the Paul Henreid character from *Now, Voyager* [1942], lighting two cigarettes at the same time for himself and Kaye Elhardt. That was done just for fun, we just sort of thought it would be a cute little touch. Purely tongue-in-cheek. It leads right into the sequence where Kaye leans against the Quonset hut wall and gets burned by the corrosive liquid.

In the book, the commander was named Drake. Whose idea was it to change it to "Charlie Brown"?

Mine [*laughs*]!

I like it. The fact that Bobby Van makes fun of his name throughout the movie made me like it.

Tony Eisley [Lt. Charlie Brown] and I knew one another at Warner Brothers while I was producing there and he was doing [the TV series] *Hawaiian Eye*. His name came up in a casting session. He was not our first choice, I was hoping to get a bigger name, but when it became evident that we couldn't and *his* name came up, I said I thought he would be an excellent choice. I knew he could do a good job, and I thought he did an excellent job.

Who were some of the actors you had in mind but couldn't afford?

I can't remember any more, it's been so many years. But, yes, there were a lot of people that I would have liked to have seen. I think we were thinking in terms of Dana Andrews or somebody like that at the time.

Mamie Van Doren?

Roger Corman was a sort of a "secret partner" in this — Roger had some connection with this project. What the connection was has never been absolutely clear in my mind, but there was no question that Roger either put some money up or made some kind of a deal with Broder. I think that George Edwards may have been put there by Roger to "mind the store" (which George did, very, very well). Also, Roger had a commitment with Mamie Van Doren and he passed on the commitment to Jack Broder, and I "inherited" Mamie. There was a wonderful incident: Mamie was supposed to be a navy nurse, as I think she was in the book. The island was a support base for the International Geophysical Year, a sort of a "halfway point" and a naval supply depot, and Mamie was supposed to be a navy nurse. When it came time to do the costuming, the wardrobe person, George Edwards and I got together and we looked at pictures of navy nurse uniforms and said, "That's fine." Then I got a phone call from George saying Mamie wanted us to come to the house 'cause she'd like to discuss wardrobe. Okay, fine, up we go...and Mamie has had all her costumes made. And they look like pinafores! She came out in this one outfit with these deep pockets on this pinafore and she said, "See, it's very functional. I can keep all my thermometers in here, and..." I was biting my tongue — I was *not* angry, I was absolutely ready to burst into laughter!

It got to a point where she said, "I *will* not wear the uniform." So we eventually arrived at a compromise where I said, "We'll make her a civilian. There are enough other civilians on the base that I guess having *one* civilian nurse won't be a big deal" — although the Kaye Elhardt character was a nurse *with* a uniform but Mamie was a nurse who *wasn't* in a uniform. I think we got rid of about 95 percent of her costumes. I wasn't a *fool*, so I put her in a tight sweater and a pair of slacks for about 50 percent of the time, and a couple of the other times she wore the least disturbing of all of the wardrobe that she had created. And we got away with it, it wasn't too bad.

Actually, Mamie tried very hard. We worked hard on a couple of the scenes, to try to get a performance out of her, and she was terrific. She certainly did everything that I asked her to do.

Eisley's memory is that she was ticked off throughout the whole movie!

[*Laughs*] Now, see, sometimes actors know things that directors *don't*, 'cause they're talking while I'm off worrying about other things. Maybe she never was happy about the wardrobe, and whatever else was going on. My recollection is that she pretty much did what she was asked to do, and I remember leaving the picture feeling that we had a fairly good relationship.

In an interview, she said that her boyfriend, a baseball player named Bo Belinsky, was supposed to be in the picture with her.

No, no. Maybe what got her annoyed is that Roger sold her commitment; maybe she expected to do something totally different. None of which was I privy to. As far as Bo Belinsky was concerned, there was never any mention of Bo being in the picture.

Were you satisfied with the trees?

No. Jack Broder wouldn't hire the guy who we originally had meetings with, a guy who could have done a marvelous job. In 1965 we were certainly far more limited with our technology than we are today, but there were people around who were capable of doing decent jobs. I wanted the [monster] trees to look like the *other* trees, so that there wouldn't be the feeling that they stood out like sore thumbs, which is what those stupid things did. Broder hired some guy who did them for $1.98. When they showed up on the set the first day, I refused to film them, I was so upset.

What an area to skimp in—a monster movie's monsters!

At that point, Broder was trying to make it a $125,000 movie, even though we were already well into production. I kept asking to see what was going on [with the trees] and no one would ever show anything to me, and *finally*, on the day that I was to shoot this thing, they brought 'em in. I was even more upset by that than I was the day he came down and announced the title change. It was just ludicrous. They brought in one tree where a guy could get inside and wiggle his arms, and two other "dummy" trees which just stood there. Stanley Cortez and I looked at each other and said, "How are we gonna shoot this?", and I said, "How 'bout no lights?" And he said, "Well, that's probably the only way we *can* do it." So we literally tried to light it so that it was *so* dark that the only time you would see the trees was when the Molotov cocktails were exploding around them. Well, Broder didn't like that and he had that scene "printed up" [brightened] so that the trees are vividly lit. But that was never our intention of how we would show 'em. As I said, my idea from the very beginning was that what you *can't* see frightens you far more than what you *can*. I intended to do the film in as subtle a manner as possible. Well, "subtle" was a word that went out very early in the game [*laughs*]! For the scene where the pilot is "absorbed" into the

On the MGM back lot, Hoey is flanked by director Norman Taurog and Susan Hart during the making of *Dr. Goldfoot and the Bikini Machine*. (Courtesy of Susan Hart.)

tree, they created a flap in the tree [for him to squeeze in through]. I thought that didn't work *too* badly. It was not what I had originally intended, but it was okay.

What about the little tree stumps that walk on the beach at the end?

That was stuff that Jon Hall shot. I had nothing to do with it.

The Jon Hall?
Yes, Jon Hall, *the* famous Jon Hall from *The Hurricane* [1937]. In later years, he had a production company, and

apparently he made a deal with Broder and he went out and shot more stuff of the nightcrawlers. This is the part I *love*: Here is a story about trees that only moved at night, and suddenly [in the scenes Hall shot] they started moving in the daytime [*laughs*]. Because Jack Broder didn't care about *that*, either! This was all created under the "guidance" of Jon Hall: That one shot of a couple of guys in a white Jeep who get out and look through binoculars, those shots of the stubby stumps walking across the sand (they looked like garbage cans with a couple of feathers on them), and then the stock shots of the navy acrobatic aircraft.

You're talking about the stock shots of the Blue Angels, representing the jets that are supposedly bombing the Night Monsters.

That's right. The picture ends with a stock shot with the four Blue Angels, with multi-colored streamers going out the back. No combat plane in its *life* ever did anything like that! It was footage from an air show. The logic that went into it was almost non-existent!

I thought Stanley Cortez's photography and lighting were very good.

Oh, he was marvelous. Stanley was known as "The Baron." This was my second feature—I'd done *Legend of Mandinga*—and I thought, "Boy, how am I gonna relate with the guy who did *The Magnificent Ambersons* [1942] for Orson Welles?" The first day, we shot the stuff with Billy Gray, which was really the opening of the movie—the opening of *my* movie was the Bobby Van character leaving the barracks, driving down, walking into that radar center and finding out that there was a plane coming in. The shots downstairs with Billy, with that kind of reddish-bluish light, were the first things we shot the first morning. I had laid it out and Stanley set the shot, we got it lit and we did the thing. About 11 o'clock that morning, he came over, put his arm around me and he said, "We're gonna be okay, kid." And I thought, "Oh, God...!" He never was anything *but* terrific.

Do you remember who you wanted to build the trees?

No, I don't. The guy who built the trees got the special effects credit, Edwin Tillman. He was a guy who had a garage somewhere, that's all. And he really did it for $1.98.

Between the time that you bought the rights to the story and the time you made the movie, The Day of the Triffids *came out. What did you think of it?*

Well, that was a much more expensive movie than mine. You have to remember that *Nightcrawlers*, in 1965, was a ten-day shooting schedule, *with* a union crew, and it came in for $178,000.

Any other memories of your cast?

It was a terrific cast. After *Father Knows Best*, Billy Gray had sort of been having a tough time; he straightened his act out but was still having trouble getting back. Our casting director, a lovely guy named Ross Brown, came to me and said that Billy Gray was looking for work, and I said, "It'd be marvelous if he would play Twining." So they made an offer and he accepted. Ed Faulkner I asked for; I thought he'd be very good playing the heavy. He was a big John Wayne co-star—he did *The Green Berets* [1968] and a whole bunch of other films. He was a good friend of John Wayne's.

And he was in Tickle Me.

And *Tickle Me*, exactly! There are also two "Memphis Mafia" guys in *Nightcrawlers*, [Elvis Presley hangers-on] Sonny West and Red West. Sonny was the sailor who's standing guard on the plane when he's killed, and Red and Sonny *both* were a couple of the firemen who put on fire suits and go out to meet the plane when it crash-lands. Pamela Mason had a talk show in town at that point, and of course was James Mason's ex-wife. Somebody said, "We'll give her the part, and maybe she'll do a little publicity for the picture." It wasn't a big role, so I had no real strong feelings about it. She *obviously* felt that it was beneath her, but she was a pro and she did what I asked her to. But what Tony Eisley said about Mamie [that she was ticked off] was *my* impression of *Pamela*.

Walter Sande was my ideal choice to play the biologist; when the name came up, I said, "In a minute!" I'd been a fan of Walter's for years, I'd watched him in so many films. Like my father, he was a good, solid character actor, and I was thrilled with the idea of him playing that role. He did an excellent job. Russ Bender was an old friend of mine and—as was the case with Taggart Casey—I said, "I want these two guys to play the petty officers." So that was sort of an "automatic." Phillip Terry was a gentleman, a lovely man, and I liked him very much. He was wonderful in what he did in the film, he was a professional and a delight to work with.

Some of the original cast members came back for the extra scenes, and also Biff Elliot as a naval commander—talk about miscasting!

I don't think very much thought was given to any of that stuff, they just jammed it in there. Those scenes are dreadful. Kind of broke my heart.

Your assistant director, Wyott Ordung, is a guy who came across like a bit of a "character" in an interview he gave.

Wyott was a screwball, and I had a lot of problems with him. Wyott was Jack Broder's man, and was always on the phone telling him what I was doing wrong. I have no great respect for Wyott Ordung. The makeup man was Harry Thomas, a dear old guy who did an excellent job. Remember the body they find in the jungle? We took an extra, and Harry did [the burn makeup] in one morning and we did the shot.

Why weren't you asked to shoot the extra scenes?

I was out of town—after I left what I thought was the final cut with [editor] George White, I went off to do a picture for AIP called *Dr. Goldfoot and the Bikini Machine* [1965]. So I was in San Francisco shooting second unit when they did what they did. When I came back, George showed me what had been done and I raised hell. But Broder said that was the way it was going to be and that I'd had my cut, and that I no longer had any control over the film. So I more or less had to swallow my pride. If I wanted to have anything further to do with the film—and I *did* want to see it through the final mix and all—I would have to accept what he had done.

The irony is, years later, when Broder sold the films to television and never paid us anything, I took it to the Writers Guild and the Directors Guild, and

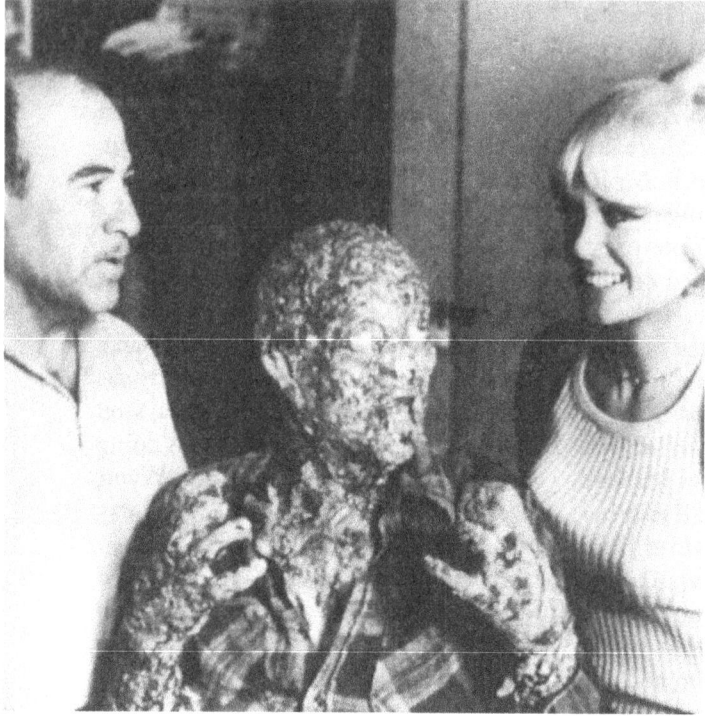

Makeup man Harry Thomas and star Mamie Van Doren with Thomas' newest creation, burn victim Charles Kramer.

I was responsible for Arthur Pierce getting a *lot* of money when he desperately needed it. And I forgave Pierce...more or less. I've always blamed Jack Broder *more* than Arthur Pierce, although I thought that Arthur's abilities were somewhat limited. That certainly showed in the stuff that he did on my film.

Well [laughs], on his own films, too! Pierce also wrote the extra scenes, right?
I guess so. I certainly didn't. I think he did, 'cause he wrote and directed his films. I'm assuming that what Broder figured is that he could make a deal and get Pierce to do both jobs.

Marvin Miller is the unbilled narrator. Did you write the narration?

No. Actually, I happen to like that narration, it kind of fit in. It made sense to me and I liked it, and Marvin's voice was wonderful. And the stock shots at the beginning I thought were okay. It wasn't what I had intended, but that didn't bother me.

By the way, Jack Broder's grandson is trying to do a book about his grandfather, and he recently called me.

[Laughs] I'm sure he can use your *contribution!*
Well, I don't know what he'll use of it, but I didn't say anything to you that I didn't say to him. I have *never* had a fond spot in my heart for Jack Broder, for many of the things he did—*plus* the way he treated me, which was quite unpleasant during the whole relationship in the making of the film. Also the way he tried to cheat me later, by not paying me any money.

I didn't realize he mistreated you. I thought you just didn't like his interference.
He was a very gruff man, not a pleasant person to be around. The whole nature of his being was adversarial, and he just dealt with people that way.

A producer named Herman Cohen told me Broder always had his right hand in his pants when he was talking to people.
[*Laughs*] You know, I think you're right—I had forgotten that! But, I

mean, Broder was just what he was. Broder began life with Realart Films, and my first memory of Realart Films was a movie which I *loved* called A *Walk in the Sun* [1945] that Broder somehow got the rights to and reissued as *Salerno Beachhead*. I went to see *Salerno Beachhead* and said, "I've *seen* this movie!"—I realized that it was a rip-off. And that kind of tells you what the guy was like.

Do you wish that Arthur Pierce had gotten a co-credit?

Uh…I don't know. I mean, I just wish Arthur Pierce hadn't *done* it [*laughs*]! Incidentally, when the picture first came out, it got excellent reviews, which surprised the hell out of me.

The Hollywood Reporter *review was practically a rave.*

If you want to read a *really* nice review, read the review that Kevin Thomas wrote for *The L.A. Times*. It was absolutely amazing. And, as I recall, both reviews start off by saying, "Don't be turned off by the title," which was kind of a nice thing after all that had happened.

My career as a director really didn't take off until some years later, and that was more in television than in features. It was because of my involvement with a television series called *Fame*—I was the supervising editor the first season, and then the second year I was an associate producer and a writer, and starting in the third year I became a writer-director on the show.

If you don't mind, I want you to talk about your dad, Dennis Hoey, a bit. Why did he move from England to Hollywood in the '40s?

Well, actually, he came to Broadway first. We came over just about the time the War was starting, and I think a couple of things combined to bring us over: *One* was that he had an offer to appear in a play on Broadway, and *two*, he saw the storm clouds brewing [over Europe]. He just decided to move to New York, so we lived in New York for about four, five years. He was quite successful—he toured with Katharine Hepburn in *Jane Eyre*, playing Rochester.

In recent years, Hoey has served as an executive producer of the Creative Arts Emmy Awards shows.

But she found [the play] *The Philadelphia Story* during the tour, and she decided she'd rather take that to Broadway than *Jane Eyre*. Who knows what effect [being on Broadway in *Jane Eyre*] might have had on his career! At any rate, he got a lot of notice and offers, and I guess when they played in Los Angeles, he decided it was time to come out here. He had an agent [Earl Kramer, Stanley Kramer's uncle] who wanted him to move out here, so we moved to California. That was around the beginning of 1941. And he started working immediately, playing Englishmen. Of course, the war films were starting, and in the early '40s he made a career of playing Nazis in three or four movies! Then Sherlock Holmes came along, and there we were.

Did you ever go onto the sets of any of your dad's movies when you were a kid?

Oh, a *lot* of them, yeah—I was on the sets of the Sherlock Holmeses several times. In fact, I remember being on the set of *The Pearl of Death* [1944] in the scene in the London museum where Miles Mander steals the pearl. At one point in the scene, Miles Mander's stuntman ran across the room and crashed out through this great big plate glass window, which *I* thought was very exciting. *Then* I found out that the plate glass window was made of candy, which is what they used in those days. The director, Roy William Neill, gave me a piece of the candy window to take home with me [*laughs*]! I was probably about nine at the time. I also was on the set of *Wake of the Red Witch* [1948] and got to meet one of *my* heroes, John Wayne—that was a very exciting experience for me.

Why did your father retire from pictures so many years before he passed away?

He left Hollywood because he remarried—he married a woman of some wealth, I must say! A woman who lived in New York, and also had a home in Tampa, Florida. He continued to work in New York through (I would guess) around the mid-'50s. Someone sent me not too long ago an [episode of TV's] *Omnibus* that was done around '56, a study of the great detectives of literature. James Daly played the "host," a character who flowed through the whole thing, and they created this situation where the fictional detectives came in to solve a murder. And they had my father play Sir Arthur Conan Doyle, which I thought was kind of fun [*laughs*]!

Getting back to Navy vs. the Night Monsters—*I'm not saying this to butter you up, but I can see the makings of a good science-fiction picture in what's left of your stuff.*

Yep. It broke my heart when I looked at it again not too long ago and I saw all that *crap*, that ridiculous blowing-up-the-balloons scene at the beginning and all the stuff on the plane and all the added stuff at the end. Not only were they *bad*, but they took away from the moments that *I* had tried to create. What's amazing to me is that suddenly it's become sort of a cult film.

The Navy vs. the Night Monsters (1966)

Realart/Standard Club of California Productions, Inc./A Jack Broder Production; Associate Producer: Madelynn Broder; Produced by George Edwards; Directed by Michael A. Hoey; Additional Scenes: Arthur C. Pierce & Jon Hall; Screenplay: Michael A. Hoey; Based on the Novel *The Monster from Earth's End* (1959) by Murray Leinster; Photography: Stanley Cortez (De Luxe Color); Production Manager: Richard Dixon; Assistant Director: Wyott Ordung; Art Director: Paul Sylos; Set Decorator: Clarence Steensen; Special Effects: Edwin Tillman; Costumer: Patrick Cummings; Makeup: Harry Thomas; Hair Stylist: Jean Austin; Post-Production Supervision: Master Film Editors of Hollywood; Supervising Editor: George White; Sound Effects Editor: Del Harris; Music: Gordon Zahler; Music Editor: Igo Kantor; Special Photographic Effects: Modern Film Effects; Casting Consultant: Marvin Paige; Property Master: Al Joyce; Sound Mixer: Clarence Peterson; Script Supervisor: Wandra Ramsey; Shooting titles: *The Nightcrawlers* and *The Navy vs. the Nightcrawlers*; British title: *Monsters of the Night*; 90 minutes

Mamie Van Doren (Lt. Nora Hall), Anthony Eisley (Lt. Charles Brown), Bill Gray (Petty Officer Fred Twining), Bobby Van (Lt. Rutherford Chandler), Pamela Mason (Marie), Walter Sande (Dr. Arthur Beecham), Edward Faulkner (Bob Spalding), Phillip Terry (Doctor), David Brandon (Lt. Rogers), Del [Sonny] West (West), Kaye Elhardt (Diane), Biff Elliot (Commander Arthur Simpson), Taggart Casey (W.O. Holly Hollister), Russ Bender (C.W.O. McBride), Mike Sargent (Miller), Red West (Fire Control Party Member), Charles Kramer (Burned Body), Marvin Miller (Opening and Closing Narration), William Meigs, Garrett Myles, Paul Rhone.

John Kerr

*My agent called me one day and said,
"I got you this job in* Pit and the Pendulum.*"
They were going to have a three-week
shooting schedule, and they had offered
a certain amount of money. My agent thought it was
per week, and they thought it was for the whole picture!*

The career of an actor can hold many surprises. The biggest surprise for John Kerr is that, after landing key roles in deluxe Hollywood movies, his best remembered acting stint may be skulking the plush corridors and dank secret passageways of Vincent Price's Spanish castle as a glumly determined young man investigating the death of his sister. The movie is *Pit and the Pendulum*, arguably the highpoint of Roger Corman's celebrated cycle of Poe films of the '60s.

The son of June Walker, a Broadway actress, and Geoffrey Kerr, a stage and screen actor turned writer, Kerr seemed predestined for a theatrical career. Within several weeks of his 1952 graduation, Kerr landed a leading role in the Broadway play *Bernardine*. He won an award as outstanding newcomer, then went on to an even more conspicuous success, playing opposite Deborah Kerr in Robert Sherwood's theatrical blockbuster *Tea and Sympathy*. John's sensitive performance as a student falsely accused of being a homosexual (only to be seduced by the headmaster's wife) earned him critical recognition and more awards. (He and Kerr repeated their roles when *Tea and Sympathy* was adapted for the screen under Vincente Minnelli's direction.) More film work followed, including a major role in the big screen version of Rodgers and Hammerstein's milestone musical *South Pacific* (1958).

Despite his impressive résumé, Kerr felt his career was running out of gas. Changing his venue from the stage to a courtroom, he embarked on a legal career, specializing in medical malpractice, personal injury and defective products cases.

My father was a playwright. He started as an actor, and his father had been an actor-manager in London in the '20s, Frederick Kerr. [Frederick Kerr also appeared in Hollywood movies like James Whale's Waterloo Bridge *and*

Frankenstein, both 1931.] My father came to this country I guess in the '20s and he and my mother were married in the mid-20s. He was an actor, and one of the successful plays that he was in was called *Just Suppose*, which had to do with, "What if the Prince of Wales should fall in love with an American?" [*Laughs*] I think that Leslie Howard was in it, and my father played his best friend.

I was born in New York in 1931, and then he went back to England not very long before the War. I think it had to do with the fact that their marriage was very rocky, and he went back home. (They subsequently were divorced, *after* the War was over.) I grew up in New York; my mother was a single parent, and I went to a lot of boarding schools. Actually, that was the best thing in the world for me. I went to some very good schools—I went to a school outside of White Plains called the Harvey School, which was an excellent school, and from there I went to Exeter [Phillips Exeter Academy in New England], and from Exeter I went to college.

Did you have your sights on an acting career throughout your youth?

I don't think I really focussed, but I think that *was* sort of what was in store for me. When I was in college, I worked at the Brattle Theatre in Cambridge [Massachusetts] and I worked in summer stock, and I did do a lot of acting. At that time, certainly, acting was what I *wanted* to do.

When you were at the Brattle, did you know [future horror film star] Bryant Haliday?

Oh, I knew Bryant, Bryant was one of the founders of the Brattle. I don't know where his money came from, but he was one of the two quite-wealthy people who started it; Miles Morgan was the other, Miles Morgan of the J. P. Morgan family. I had a lot of respect for Bryant and I thought the world of him. He had one of the most beautiful voices that you'd want to hear, and he played all the Shakespearean leads, the young male leads. And he was just wonderful.

A producer named Guthrie McClintic came up to see me in a play at the Brattle Theatre and he asked me to try out for *Bernardine*, a [Broadway] play that he was going to produce that fall. I did, and I got the job, and that was the start of my career.

Did you also do TV in New York?

Yes, I did quite a bit of *live* TV. There were those hour-long dramatic series, and I was in every one of those at least once. I also did [the plays] *Tea and Sympathy* and *All Summer Long*, and from *All Summer Long* I went out to Hollywood and did *The Cobweb* [1955]. And then I had a two-picture deal to do *Gaby* and *Tea and Sympathy* [both 1956] at MGM.

But your film debut was in The Cobweb.

Right. It was made around the turn of the year, December 1954-January 1955. I think I got that because Jimmy Dean was supposed to be in it, and then he did *Giant* [1956] instead.

In an old interview, you said that the negative reviews that the movie South Pacific *[1958] got set back your career, and the careers of everybody else who was in it.*

I think that's true.

I was under the impression South Pacific *was a very well-received movie.*

It was a popular success, no question about that. It ran for two years at a first-run theater in London, for example, and I think it ran quite a long time in New York and Los Angeles—the major cities. But the critics were very negative towards it. They thought that it should have been cast with, like, Doris Day instead of Mitzi Gaynor. And they didn't like the colored filter shots. There are points throughout where they racked a colored filter across the camera lens—sometimes yellow and sometimes red. (They were [ordinarily] used for photographing surgery, to get a better definition of the vessels and so on.) *That* was universally condemned by the critics, they didn't like it at all. Also, there was sort of a sense that the movie wasn't as good as the show [the Mary Martin-starring stage musical]. So the critics were very negative about it and, really, I think it *did* affect everyone.

You were offered the role ultimately played by Anthony Perkins in Friendly Persuasion *[1956]. Do you think your career would have benefited if you had taken that part?*

[*Pause*] Nobody's ever asked that before...how did you know about *that?*

I do my homework!

Well, lemme put it this way: No, it probably would *not* have made that much difference. What you *start out as* doesn't really make that much difference in terms of 10, 15 years later. Unless you were in something really extraordinary, like Jimmy Dean. But *who* remembers the first movie that Marlon Brando was in? Do *you* know?

The movie where he was the G.I. who comes home in a wheelchair. I can't think of the name of it...

The Men [1950]. But *who* remembers *that?* What you remember is Marlon Brando, the great actor, from his *great* movies. So I don't really think that it matters, down the road, what your first choice was—although it's very important at the very *beginning* [*laughs*]! I really *loved* the story *Friendly Persuasion*, and they wanted me very badly—Jessamyn West, who wrote the original novel, called me and talked to me. I would have loved to work with [director] William Wyler, I would have loved to work with Gary Cooper, I would have loved to have *that* kind of a "package." But would it have made any difference 15 years later, would it have affected my decision about staying in the business or changing professions? I don't think so. And I don't think that it would have led to different types of roles. I think I was considered for *Psycho* [1960], for example. I *think* I was, because everyone *was*. Tony Perkins was a friend of mine, and I think Tony was wonderful in *Psycho*. But *after Psycho*, he was always only identified with that. So I would have steered clear of *that*.

One more hypothetical question: You can turn the clock back and either be in Friendly Persuasion *or the movie version of* Tea and Sympathy. *Which would you pick?*

Oh, *Tea and Sympathy*! *Tea and Sympathy*, every day. But *that* was not what the choice was, the choice was *Gaby* or *Friendly Persuasion*. I had an MCA agent at that point, he was a good agent and no fool, and he said to me, "Do you wanna be a supporting actor [in *Friendly Persuasion*] or do you wanna be a leading man? These MGM roles are leading man roles," blah blah blah blah. But I would never have *not* played

Tea and Sympathy—I mean, [playwright-screenwriter] Bob Anderson had approval of cast, and he would not have agreed to anyone else but me. Unless I was dead, I guess!

Do you remember the circumstances leading up to your co-starring role in Pit and the Pendulum?

It's a funny story: My agent Bill Robinson called me one day and said, "I got you this job in one of these Edgar Allan Poe things, *Pit and the Pendulum*." They were going to have a three-week shooting schedule, and they had offered a certain amount of money. My agent thought it was per week, and *they* thought it was for the whole picture [*laughs*]! So *that* had to be resolved!

I knew that *House of Usher* [1960] had been very successful with Vincent Price, and I really *liked* Vincent Price—I'd met him slightly and I got to know him a little bit. He was a wonderful, wonderful man, erudite about art and everything. And so I thought, "Why *not*?" I knew it wasn't going to be something that you were going to hang on the wall as one of the greatest things you ever did, but it was a *job*.

Well, I saw it just recently—one of my fans sent me a tape of it. I knew that it had become kind of a cult movie, so I watched it and I thought, "Jesus, this is really not that bad. In fact, it's pretty *good*!" My character's always climbin' up and down stairs, sayin', "What was that noise?" [*laughs*]—I *really* was a straight man there! But the movie *is* effective, and psychologically it's grotesque, it's bizarre. And *I* thought it was kinda good! I can't say that I'm *proud* that I was in this movie, but I'm glad I was a part of it. The acting was excellent, the way it was shot was really good, and I thought that (with one or two exceptions) I did a pretty good job in it.

Well, that begs the question: What would those exceptions be?

One of them was at the very end, when they untie me off of the pendulum slab and I'm mumbling, "Gee, he thought I was Sebastian..." As I recall, that was Roger Corman's choice, *he* wanted me to be dazed and *not* in a great emotional turmoil. He just wanted me to be dazed...and then get off! And I did. So I don't think I did that moment very well. And there were maybe one or two other moments throughout the rest of the picture—for instance, I don't think that I was serious enough about breaking down the wall to get to Barbara Steele's coffin. But Roger didn't *want* dramatics.

Your character really is very dour and touchy from one end of the movie to the other.

I didn't mind that. I came to Spain with one purpose only, and that was to find out what happened to my sister [Steele]. That was driving me. There's an indication of some attraction between me and Luana Anders, a little scene where I say, "If things had been different, perhaps we might have gotten to know each other in another way," something like that. But there wasn't any foolin' around, no romance, no hanky-panky going on as far as *my* character was concerned. I was just there to find out what happened to my sister, *by God*! I was gonna do that come hell or high water. And I thought it played.

Vincent Price had a reputation for being a bit of a prankster.

Oh, Vincent kept breaking me up.

I'd be trying to look sternly at him, saying to him, "What's going on?? What's happened to my sister? You haven't answered my questions!", blah blah blah. And he'd just give me one of those funny looks of his [*laughs*]! I remember one time we were rehearsing and he said, "What ever happened to Baby LeRoy?" and I just fell over laughing at that. I had to bite the inside of my cheek in order not to grin!

I didn't think that on a Corman picture like that, there'd be much time for rehearsals.

Oh, yeah, we would rehearse the scenes. As I recall, Roger had gone to (or *was* going to) some kind of acting classes, and so he was conscious of the actors' need to rehearse and adjust and "make it his own" and everything. And so we *got* that [rehearsal] time. He shot very fast and they *lit* it very fast.

When you talk about rehearsing, you mean that you rehearsed each scene just before you shot it.

That's the way it usually works. We

Kerr feels that the professionalism and ingenuity of B-movie makers (like the *Pit and the Pendulum* team) would have improved some of the *A pictures* he was in.

didn't sit down and rehearse for a week before we got onto the stage, we did it right then and there before we shot it—the whole movie was shot in only three weeks, and that's fast, *really* fast, for a color [movie].

On your bigger movies, the MGMs and South Pacific, *did you rehearse the whole thing before shooting began?*

No. The only one I ever rehearsed before we started shooting was a picture with Anne Francis called *Girl of the Night* [1960] We had three or four days where we went over the scenes and rehearsed. I've never had it in any other.

What were some of the other differences between making Pit and the Pendulum *and working at a major studio?*

Let me tell you frankly that they could have made *South Pacific* the way they made *Pit and the Pendulum*, to *South Pacific*'s advantage. We shot *South Pacific* very fast, but with very little real rehearsal, but *that* was because of the weather. They were constantly trying to get it shot before it'd start raining again—this is the exterior shots I'm talking about, of course. They would have profited from the professionalism and the knowledge and the experience of the people who made those low-budget pictures and knew how to get it done fast. But on *South Pacific* they had such a lot of equipment, and cameras with the big wide lenses and stuff like that. And once we got to it, there was very little rehearsal and very little shooting. We'd do four or five takes and that would be *it*, print it. Really, I don't think I'm exaggerating—a very low number of takes for what was involved in *South Pacific*, like the songs and some other things. *Very* few takes. And it was *very* unusual that you would do it in *that* few takes. You hear stories about people like William Wyler, who'd get up to Take 35...!

And how many takes on Pit and the Pendulum*?*

Also under ten, because that's part of "the deal." You get actors who can "deliver," and that's it.

How did you like working for Corman?

Roger was very quiet, very intense. And he was very supportive of the actors—he would let the actors go. Obviously he had to keep a very tight rein on the staging, because of the constrictions of time. If there was *anything* about that film that you could criticize, there was a certain lack of humor. (Of course, it's hard for criticize it for *that*!) I thought, maybe, there could have been just a *little* bit—but there just wasn't *any*. But those [Corman-Poe] movies are classics. I *know* they're classics because I was *told* they were classics!

Did you see any of the other ones?

No. I never saw *House of Usher*, or any of the later ones.

Mark Damon, the young leading man of House of Usher, *now tells people that he actually directed* Pit and the Pendulum.

I have no recollection of him being there and doing things that one associates with the directing. That's not to say that he could not have met with Roger, [outside of] the working day, and helped to plan shots and things like that. But *on the set*, I have no recollection of anyone except Roger Corman.

Any temptation on your part—or anybody's part—to employ an accent?

I was playing an English character, the brother of the English wife of Vincent Price. *I* don't remember any discussion about it, but there *may* have been some thought about having me put on some kind of English accent. But, as you've noticed, there isn't any accent—I just tried to speak well, maybe a little bit clipped.

What memories of the pendulum scene?

I think they did a very good job of hiding the fact that the blade that hit me was balsa wood, and that I had a piece of steel strapped across my chest so that I wouldn't be hurt. And I remember that the pendulum was huge [*laughs*]—it really *was* huge! And they did swing it and have it come down as I was lying there looking at it. Even though I knew it wasn't gonna hurt me, it really *was* imposing. The scene was very broken up, a little of this and a little of that, so when we were shooting it there wasn't any sense of the scene rising to a climax—it was all put together in the cutting room. But, yes, the pendulum set was impressive—I thought *all* the sets were very good. And then there was the one exterior we did, where they added a painted castle onto the film of the carriage driver and me on the beach. That was shot somewhere south of Los Angeles, on the beach. We spent about a half-day or three-quarters of a day doing that.

Did you have a double at any point during the pendulum scene?

Absolutely not. This was three weeks, low-budget.

And Price was a nice guy all throughout shooting?

Oh, he was a wonderful man. A *wonderful* man. Just the most charming, gentle, humorous, lovely, lovely person.

How about some of the other cast members?

I didn't get to know Luana Anders particularly, but I enjoyed working with her—I enjoyed working with *all* of them. I didn't get to know anyone. [Barbara] Steele was interesting, and had kind of a sense of humor. Also, she complimented me about the way I wore tights, so naturally I liked Steele [*laughs*]!

Are you someone who socializes a lot on a set, or do you stay to yourself?

It depends on my mood. I saw a picture of Ricardo Montalban in the paper over the weekend, and I was reminded that I was in a television show with Ricardo at Universal years ago. I didn't like the show (even though it was a pretty good show!), but when Ricardo would hit the stage in the morning, his whole personality would *expand*. He just *loved* it, he *loved* being there. He could be in his dressing room, he could be getting coffee, he could just be sitting around, but he just *loved* being on the stage, it brought him *alive*. It was like, "This is the meaning of life!", you know. And…I never *had* that [*laughs*]! When I saw him, I thought, "Oh, Ricardo, I wish [acting] made me feel the way it makes *you* feel. I really wish I loved it the way *you* do. But all *I* think of is, 'Oh, jeez, I'm gonna get up three hours earlier than I usually get up, and hopefully I get there okay, and (if you'll pardon me!) I hope I'll be able to have a bowel movement!'" [*Laughs*] All of that stuff that has to do with changing your routine. I thought, "I *wish* I could enjoy it like Ricardo, he just loves it," but I *didn't*.

And was that one of the reasons you got out of the business?

Opposite: Kerr (hit, manhandled and then nearly halved by *Pit and the Pendulum*'s Vincent Price) later pursued a career as a personal injury lawyer (!).

Stage, TV and movie actor John Kerr (rhymes with star) in his heyday.

I was seguing into that. A number of things happened—my mother passed away, after I'd been helping take care of her, and I had come to a point in my life where I just wanted to do something different than being the kind of actor I was in the Hollywood of the early 1960s. My agent Jimmy McHugh also represented Leo Penn, the actor who became a director, and Leo was a *dear* man—really, what a nice man. Jimmy got me to work as an apprentice with Leo, directing. I worked on the Ben Gazzara TV show...*Hey, Stop Running*, or whatever it was called...

Run for Your Life.

That's the one. And the director had to do *every*thing. They'd take a picture of a note pinned to the wall, and he's got to say [*dramatically*], "...*Action!*" [*Laughs*] And I thought, "Oh! I can't do this. I just can't do this either." I had directed on the stage and, actually, I had done some *very* good work, but this was just completely different. I just figured I'd better get out of it. So I did: I went up this hill from where I lived to the UCLA Law School and applied, and I was fortunate enough to be accepted.

You also played a number of lawyers on TV, both before and after.

[*Laughs*] Yes, I did. As a matter of fact, at that time I was in the original *Peyton Place* TV series, playing a lawyer. And then subsequently, my agent Jimmy McHugh (who knew that I was gonna change careers, who knew he was never gonna ring the bell with me) continued to represent me and got me work for *years*—it must have been for at least four or five years after I became an attorney. I would moonlight as an actor and make extra money. I was originally with a firm but after that I was on my own, and I needed to make the money. On [TV's] *The Streets of San Francisco* I was one of the D.A.s.

What kind of law do you specialize in?

I do personal injury and medical malpractice trial work, although I'm hoping to phase out and be able to retire in the first three or four months of next year [2000]. I've been doing it for about 30 years.

I once pestered Sam Arkoff to name some of his favorite AIP movies, and after some hemming and hawing he finally said Pit and the Pendulum.

Well, that's nice. It's really nice to have been in a...in a...in an underground movie [*laughs*]! The thing that is interesting to me is that people go *back* to see it and *back* to see it, and it's still being run on television. And I've done one or two autograph shows, and people come up to me with photos from...guess what? They bring me the posters and this and that. If you had told me years ago that *Pit and the Pendulum* would be *The* One—out of allll the stuff I've done, if you had told me that *this* would be *the* cult-type movie that people would be collecting memorabilia on, I would have said, "You're out of your gourd." Just... no way. *Noooo* way...

John Kerr Filmography

The Cobweb (MGM, 1955)
Gaby (MGM, 1956)
Tea and Sympathy (MGM, 1956)
The Vintage (MGM, 1957)
South Pacific (Magna Theatre Corp./ 20th Century–Fox, 1958)

The Crowded Sky (Warners, 1960)
Girl of the Night (Warners, 1960)
Pit and the Pendulum (AIP, 1961)
Seven Women from Hell (20th Century–Fox, 1961)

Phyllis Kirk

I bitched and moaned and told
[Warner Bros. executive] Steve Trilling
that I was not interested in becoming
the Fay Wray of my time. And I was told, "Tough titty."

Vincent Price may have failed to immortalize Phyllis Kirk in wax in the 1953 chiller *House of Wax*, but the experience did immortalize her on film for generations of horror movie buffs. This was an odd turn of events for Kirk, who (given her druthers) would have turned down the top role in the 3-D thriller—a remake of *Mystery of the Wax Museum* (1933)—because she had no yen to become a 1950s screen queen.

Danish by descent (real name: Phyllis Kirkegaard), a native of Syracuse, New York, Kirk had jobs as a waitress and a perfume counter clerk before she began a modeling career. Stage roles ensued before Hollywood beckoned; she was a contract player at MGM and then Warner Bros., where she was stalked on the studio's "New York Street" and other locales by Vincent Price's maniac sculptor in *House of Wax*.

Kirk's talents were better showcased on the small screen, where she had good dramatic roles on many of the era's prestige series (and consequently made the covers of *TV Guide* and *Life*). Her signature TV role was as Nora Charles, the daffy, fast-talking wife of Peter Lawford's *The Thin Man* (the 1957-59 NBC series).

Were you under contract to Warner Bros. when you did House of Wax*?*
Yes...otherwise I would *never* have done it [*laughs*]! The interesting thing is that, with the arrogance of a young actress who thinks she's going to rule the world (and doesn't realize, while she's bitching about *House of Wax*, that *that* will probably be the most memorable thing she does in the movie business), I tried to turn it down. I bitched and moaned and told [Warners executive] Steve Trilling that I was not interested in becoming the Fay Wray of my time. And I was told, "Tough titty. You're under contract, and you'll do what we ask you to do, unless you care to be suspended." I decided I didn't want to be suspended. And he made it perfectly clear that I was insane if I *didn't* do it [*laughs*]! And, incidentally, I went on to have a *lot* of fun making *House of Wax*.

It was just fun—Vincent Price was a divine man, and was a divine actor. As were all the other people, Paul Picerni in particular. He was my "love interest" in *House of Wax*, and he just was a gentle, kind, wonderful person, a dear guy with an *army* of children [*laughs*]! I had a wonderful time doing it.

House of Wax was the first major studio 3-D picture; Picerni said there were good vibes all around, that people at Warners felt the picture was going to be a success, and that he was excited to be in it. What turned you off about it?

I just didn't want to be in a film that I think was using a gimmick. I had already heard about, and *seen* finally, the 3-D picture that preceded us, which was *Bwana Devil* [1952]. And I thought, "I really don't *want* to be in *House of Wax*. It's not *serious*." But, after the film was done, I thought it was quite remarkable.

Do you happen to know who else might have been up for your part?

I have no idea. No one ever told me that anyone else was *ever* up for it.

I think Vera Miles was. And maybe also Joan Weldon.

I don't have any idea. For one thing,

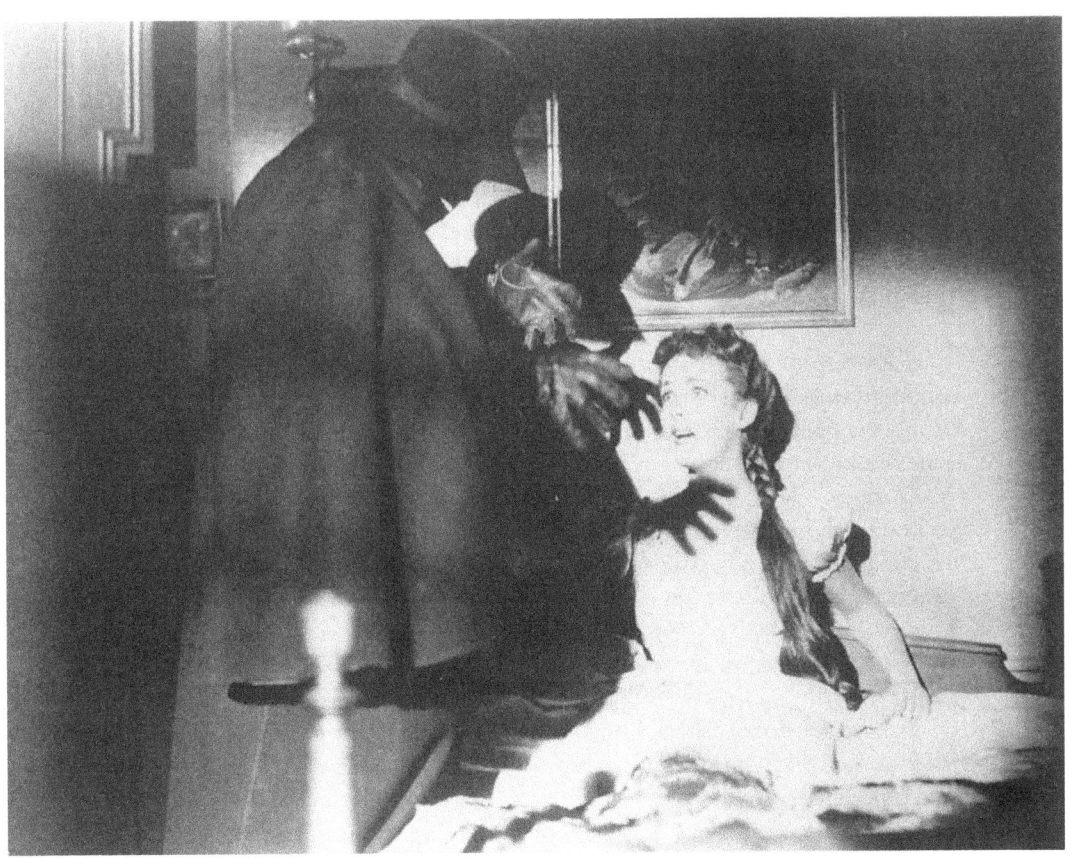

Kirk recoils from the strangling hands of mad artist Vincent Price in this posed *House of Wax* **shot.**

they never tested me. Not that I recall, anyway. But I don't think they did.

Did they show you Mystery of the Wax Museum *[1933]? They did show it to Andre de Toth before he started directing it.*

No, they did not. Now, Andre de Toth was just a remarkable guy. I had worked with him before [on *Thunder Over the Plains*, 1953] and after [*Crime Wave*, 1954]. I admired him and liked him very much. He was really a remarkable director, but he was very unappreciated in Hollywood; he was a director who was much more appreciated in Europe than he was here. In France and in England, and maybe even in Italy, he was considered a *very* imaginative, fine talent. I saw him again not terribly long ago. He's delightful and intelligent—*highly* intelligent. He was a director—and *man*—who knew what he wanted, and saw to it that he got it. I adored him, he was a wonderful guy and I liked him very much.

I don't think Paul Picerni has ever quite forgiven de Toth for insisting that he, Picerni, put his head in the working guillotine in House of Wax.

[*Laughs*] Well, Andre was *tough*, you know. And not given to any bullshit that was going to hold up his film, or *not* be what he wanted it to be.

You were never on the receiving end of any abuse?

No, no, no, no, no. Well, I told you, I had worked with him before. Always good experiences. And of course Charles Bronson—now *there* was a piece of work. His name was not Charles Bronson at the time, it was Charlie Buchinsky. I didn't particularly like him, although in later years I saw that he really was quite a fine actor, he was very worthwhile. (*And*, as with many of us, we get better *as people* as we age.) But I didn't care for him *on that film*. This was the very beginning for him, and he was full of oats and swaggering around and being terribly macho. (It may have had to do with the fact that he wasn't very tall.) I got to know him a bit better later; I didn't work with him again, but I got to know him over the years because of "group things" and charity things. And also, I began to like him much more as an actor.

I had to go to London shortly after *House of Wax* came out, and reporters there would ask me about it. I would just say, "If it's your cup of tea, *drink* it!" [*Laughs*] Anyhow, I felt that it was a well-made, well-directed film. And *scary*! And all those running scenes that I had to do, *I* did. No double worked for me! I loathed all the crap about being made into a wax statue—I mean, that's no *fun*! They pour this stuff all over you to make a mold, and then some genius re-forms the whole thing into wax.

You're talking about the wax head of you that's in the movie.

Well, it was the whole *figure*.

Now that you tell me this, I think I can tell from the expression on the wax head that you didn't have a good time having that mold made!

No, I certainly didn't. I had to go and have my head and shoulders covered with wax, to make the mold. It took a good day for each actor who was having that done to them. Carolyn Jones also had to have the same thing done to *her*. I didn't really know her very well; she was a good actress.

Kirk takes a closer look at one of the *House of Wax* **exhibits (a Joan of Arc statue, modeled on Carolyn Jones) as Vincent Price looks on.**

According to Andre de Toth, Jack Warner ordered him not to wear his eye patch while making House of Wax *because people would make fun of the fact that the movie was directed by someone who had no depth perception. Did de Toth go without it?*

I don't think he ever did. He *may* have, but I don't remember it. But it was my favorite story in London, to point out to everyone that the director of the film Andre de Toth only had one eye and couldn't *see* in three dimensions. Everybody in London thought that was hilarious. But I'm sure nobody at *Warner Bros.* thought it was hilarious that I was saying that!

Did you enjoy making period pictures, wearing costumes of the Gay '90s, etc.?

Well, I did and I didn't. Once I was *in* the costumes and performing, I was fine. But *getting* into the costumes and going through all that rigmarole was a pain [*laughs*]!

The producer, Bryan Foy, had a long and interesting show biz career.

Oh, Brynie Foy—he was just a divine old curmudgeon. That's *exactly* what he was, with a *hellish* reputation for being impossible. I got called to his office before anyone had even told me that I was going to be in that film, and he looked at me long and hard and said, "Wellll, Miss Kirk, we're giving you this part because you're the only intelligent actress I know that I can *stand*." [*Laughs*] All right? That's all I remember!

Did you like the guy?

Well...*yes*. He was a character. I didn't know him intimately, I didn't go to dinner to him, I didn't know his family—I just knew him as a figure in a studio. But I knew a lot *about* him, because he had done some worthwhile things in his career.

And what was Vincent Price like on the set?

Friendly...unselfish...generous, *really* generous as an actor, in terms of working with other actors. I didn't know Vincent intimately, but I knew him as a professional, and I found him incredibly intelligent and with a great sense of humor.

Did you work with him before or after?

No.

Like you, Price didn't want to do the picture. Then de Toth told him his concept of the role—de Toth wanted there to be a vulnerability to the character, he wanted audience sympathy. That won Price over.

I was a fan of Vincent's going into *House of Wax*—right from the days when I saw him first in *The Eve of St. Mark* [1944], where he played a Southern soldier. And *that's* going back. I just thought he was brilliant, and then sort of followed everything he ever did. I got tired after a while of seeing him in horror film after horror film, because he was much *more* than that.

Any memories of Frank Lovejoy?

Oh, well, how could you not have memories of that adorable man? I liked him very much. He was a very kind, warm human being, and fun to work with. He was a *generous* kind of actor, giving and...*dear*, he was a dear man.

What about the final scene, when you're Price's prisoner in the waxing vat?

They had me lying on a table with

a kind of gauzy, flesh-colored sheet over me, to create the illusion that I was nude, or almost nude. Andre kept saying, "Phyllis...pull it *down* a little further." And I said, "Andre...I have *no* bosom. I greatly resemble my *father* in that department, and if I pull it down any further, whatever the 'illusion' is now will be, I promise you, *gone!*" [*Laughs*] I remember that *very* well! I was furious.

How long did that scene take to film?
Oh, I don't know, I can't remember, honey, it was a hundred *years* ago! You're lucky I can remember what I've remembered [*laughs*]!

In one old interview, de Toth tells a funny story about your costume having so much padding in the bust that he once stuck you with a pin, and left it there when you didn't notice.
He stuck me with a *pin*? I probably just thought that he was...you know ...feeling my bosom [*laughs*]! I wouldn't have been able to feel *any*thing, because the padding was...extraordinary! Well, I was even *thinner* than Carolyn Jones, and had practically no bosom at all, so they *had* to do something. Andre's a naughty boy...I don't remember him sticking me with pins, but on the other hand, if he was *distracting* me, and doing it at the same time with the pin, I wouldn't have felt it. What exactly did he say about it?

Quote: "On the first day of shooting, Phyllis Kirk appeared with some Mae West-ish bulges."
Oh, bullshit! He's making all of that up.

"I asked her to shed the kapok. Indignantly she persisted it was all real."
Oh, no. Now, see, that's terrible, that's not true at *all*. I told Andre when we did that [waxing vat] scene that if he wasn't careful, that gauzy sheet would slip, and there wouldn't be anything to *see*! That's the real story, I don't know what *this* crap is.

He said that during rehearsals he stuck the pin in the bulge and you never noticed it. Then, before your first take, "I explained to her and the cast and crew, she had talent, and no kapok was needed to augment it. By the time the first day was over, we were friends and still are."
Well, *that's* true. But it's not *quite* how it happened [*laughs*]!

Jack Warner was reportedly so afraid of production falling behind that he asked some of the key people not to leave the Warners lot!
That was the situation and I was asked, for the duration of the picture, to sleep on the lot, in an actor's...cubicle. No, it wasn't a cubicle, it was perfectly nice, but they resembled apartments. Warners used them for visiting dignitaries and things like that.

Was most of the cast asked to stay?
I think *I* was the only one who *agreed* to do it [*laughs*]. I think I thought at the time, "I have to get up soooo early, and when I leave the studio at the end of the day, I have to drive all the way to Beverly Hills," which is where I was living. I thought, "I might as well just stay here."

Your character is very intelligent—she figures out what Price is up to before anyone else does. But otherwise it's a pretty standard screaming, needs-to-be-rescued female lead.

Well, that was my point. The characters they gave young women in those days were by and large—not *always*, of course, but by and large *dreary*. And so you just did the best you could, right?

At an interview you gave around that time, you said you'd probably always be a spinster because "I'm so strong and I'm so able to look out for myself. Men prefer girls who want to be coddled."

I never felt about my [*House of Wax* character] that she wanted to be coddled.

But I get the impression from your interviews you were a lot more independent than the average young Hollywood actress back then.

I guess that's true. In fact, yes, that *is* true. Still am!

You also worked as an interviewer and writer for an ACLU newspaper, and as a TV interviewer. How did you enjoy that phase of your career?

The ACLU thing happened in the middle of my *acting* career, and it happened mostly because I was hellbent to keep the state of California from executing a guy named Caryl Chessman. Ultimately I had to give an address to the State Assembly about the whole situation; I even went to San Quentin (on three occasions, I think) and talked to Chessman. There's no doubt at all that he did some dastardly things, but he did *not* kill anybody. And it infuriated me because the State Legislature kept going out into the public and saying that his behavior had driven a young girl insane when in point of fact, the young girl had been insane for *years*. It was that kind of thing. And also, I abhor capital punishment, always have and always will. Of course, the William Morris Agency, who represented me at the time, wanted to *kill* me, that I had done *any* of these things. I looked at one of the guys there, I remember, and *very* rudely said, "If it hadn't been for God's kindness, *you* probably would be in prison for the same thing." Well, it was *true*—this particular agent was a great womanizer.

In 1957 you told an interviewer that you wanted to eventually produce and direct. Were you on the level?

Not a director. I would have loved to be a producer, which simply means that you put it all together and tell people what you want and expect them to deliver.

In your interviews, you come across as very feisty, as the type who resented interviewers who didn't do their homework. Was that the real you, or was that just schtick?

Oh, no, that was me! There are a lot of reporters who don't do their homework, and you have to do their homework *for* them. So you wind up interviewing *yourself* [*laughs*]! Other reporters *do* do their research, and they're interesting and fun.

Years and years from now, people in their homes can push a button and see any movie, or any TV episode. Which of your credits would you like them to watch?

I'd like them to watch *The Thin Man*.

Any other "recommendations" for future generations?

Are you putting all of this in a time capsule?

I like to think of my books as "time capsules," yes!

Okay [*laughs*]. There were a couple

The Paramount Theater (New York) "screamiere" of *House of Wax* and celebrity attendees Frank Lovejoy, Vincent Price, "Major" Warner and his wife, Kirk, Mr. and Mrs. Harry Balaban and Paul Picerni.

of live television things I did that I loved doing, and I liked when they were finished. There was a series called *Robert Montgomery Presents* and we did *The Great Gatsby* [1955], and Robert Montgomery played Gatsby and I played the girl. I loved that, I thought they did a wonderful job with it.

There was a lot of speculation way back when as to whether you and Peter Lawford really got along on The Thin Man.

Peter Lawford and I got along *beautifully*, we were good friends, and we continued to be good friends long, long, long after *The Thin Man* was gone.

The rumors that he disliked you, that you two never were friendly—how did they start?

Because that's what [writers] *do*! I mean, how can you *ask* me such a silly question, when every day you pick up a newspaper and read things about actors and actresses that are just…*ludicrous*! Farfetched and *total lies*! They love to write things like that, they think it's "scintillating," and it makes reporters thrilled if they can suggest that there's a feud going on between two people who have to work together every day. That's what it *is*, my friend!

What was it about The Thin Man *that makes it your favorite?*

Well, it was fun, and it was fun to *do*. I loved Dashiell Hammett. Our series was not a carbon copy of the Thin Man books, or the Thin Man [movies] done by Powell and Myrna Loy, because it was television and it was in the '50s. They had us sleeping in separate beds, and you couldn't say even a *mild* expletive—that could *not* be in the script. I just had fun doing it, I *loved* doing it, and I was very fond of Peter.

Rumors circulated that King's TV co-star Peter (*The Thin Man*) Lawford disliked her, but the actress forcefully declares that they "got along *beautifully*."

Do you watch your own movies and TV shows today?

Well, if something comes up on the air I watch it. But I don't have tapes of *any*thing.

I read that you tried to veer away from having show business people as guests on your TV talk show [ABC's The Young Set, *1965].*

No, that's not true, although I *did* do other things, largely. But [guest selection] didn't really have anything to do with *me*, it had to do with the producer, Shirley Bernstein, Leonard Bernstein's sister. We did a lot of interesting things, but not necessarily "show biz guests."

And today?

I'm not doing *any*thing in show business. I've begun over the years having difficulty walking properly, and it isn't because (evidently) of any known illness, it's just...a fact. So I haven't acted for a long time—a *very* long time. Not since the early '70s. And *then* what I did was to find a new career: I went into the public relations business and I worked for a public relations firm for several years, and then I went to CBS as a publicist. Then I went *back* to the original press office that I worked for *before* CBS...because it was time to leave CBS. We had Mr. [Laurence] Tisch galloping around, making weeeeird decisions about all kinds of things. And a whole army of us left because Mr. Tisch considered us "too old." I'm retired now.

Your claim to fame, of course, is House of Wax.

After I left Warners, I went on and did mountains of television, and *The Thin Man* with Peter Lawford, and all of those things are much more memorable in terms of people remembering them than the movies I did. The *movies* I made were [*laughs*]...somewhat obscure, I think you would say. But *House of Wax* was *not* obscure. And I must say, the interest in it over the years, and the comments about it, and the times that they have re-played it, including *with* the 3-D glasses—amazing. Just amazing! And it wasn't a *big* hit originally, was it?

Well, it was on the list of the top grossers of 1953.

It was? Well...what do *I* know? Or...what do I *care* [*laughs*]?!

Phyllis Kirk Filmography

Our Very Own (RKO, 1950)
A Life of Her Own (MGM, 1950)
Two Weeks with Love (MGM, 1950)
Mrs. O'Malley and Mr. Malone (MGM, 1950)
Three Guys Named Mike (MGM, 1951)
About Face (Warners, 1952)
The Iron Mistress (Warners, 1952)
Stop, You're Killing Me (Warners, 1952)
Thunder Over the Plains (Warners, 1953)
House of Wax (Warners, 1953)

Crime Wave (*The City Is Dark*) (Warners, 1954)
River Beat (Lippert, 1954)
Canyon Crossroads (United Artists, 1955)
Johnny Concho (United Artists, 1956)
Back from Eternity (RKO, 1956)
The Sad Sack (Paramount, 1957)
City After Midnight (*That Woman Opposite*) (RKO, 1957)

Suzanna Leigh

Some of the crew [of The Deadly Bees*] looked
like they were came down from space—
they had all sorts of special equipment and walked around
with their hands covered, their necks covered, their faces and
everything. And suddenly you'd hear, "Ow! Ow! Ow!"—a bee would
wriggle up their arms, or wherever, and find a spot!*

English-born beauty Suzanna Leigh's Stateside movie career began with co-starring roles in the frothy *Boeing Boeing* (1965) with Tony Curtis and *Paradise, Hawaiian Style* (1966) with Elvis Presley, establishing her in the sorority of glamour girls decorating Hollywood films of the era. But she became a casualty of a "feud" between American and English actors' guilds, consequently landing up back on her native soil and sharing the screen with deadly bees, vampires, prehistoric monsters and other malevolent movie menaces. The mainstream's loss was horror fans' gain, as Leigh recounted in her 2000 autobiography *Paradise, Suzanna Style*—and in this candid interview.

Born Suzanna Smyth, the daughter of an auto engine manufacturer, she grew up in Belgrave, England, and in convent schools outside London. Leigh began working in movies while still a pre-teen, appearing as an extra in 1958's *tom thumb* (film-debuting in the Dancing Shoes sequence), 1960's *Oscar Wilde* with Robert Morley and other English productions. A few years later, she was the star of the 13-episode French TV series *Trois Etoile*, which every week featured Leigh, her racing car and a different male lead (the "Three Stars" of the series' translated title).

Planning to attend London's Opera Ball costumed as Madame Du Barry, Leigh had a sedan chair made, along with costumes for five footmen who carried it (and her) through the streets of the city. Movie producer Hal B. Wallis saw newspaper photos of Leigh's elaborate stunt and imported the 20-year-old blonde to Hollywood for *Boeing Boeing*. Following her brush with major studio stardom, she resumed her English acting career, showing up on movie screens most regularly in chillers: *The Lost Continent* (1968), *Lust for a Vampire* (1971), the rock-horror *Son of Dracula* with Ringo Starr (1974) and more.

After having starred in mainstream

pictures like Boeing Boeing *and* Paradise, Hawaiian Style, *do you look back on your horror movies as a comedown?*

No, in no way whatsoever. My first, *The Deadly Bees* [1967] was terribly exciting for me because it was a Paramount movie, and it was the first film I was *starring* in. I guess it depends on how you look at things, but I certainly never looked on horror films as a "down" thing. There was a big star in *Deadly Bees*, Frank Finlay, a very serious Shakespearean actor who at the time was *terribly* big in England. That picture was the forerunner of *The Swarm* [1978] and all that sort of thing.

What stories can you tell about working with the bees?

It was shot in Twickenham, and my dressing room was next door to the bees. There were about two million bees—that's a lot of bees [*laughs*]. And, I hasten to add, these bees were big bees—they came from Australia and, I promise you, next to little English bees, they were *massive*, these things! I thought, "Oh, goodness me, I'm going to get really stung here. I better speak to the beekeeper!" So I asked him into my dressing room and I said, "Look, we've got a lot of work to do over the next two or three months. Can you give me some pointers?" He said, "That's fairly easy. With bees, all you really need to do is keep a few things in mind. You don't let fire come near them, they don't like fire at *all*. And another thing is, they *hate* smoke—any smoke really gets them angry. The *third* thing you need to know is: Never hit them, and never *try* to hit them. Just keep these three things in mind and then you're fine."

Well, I was shocked. "Have you read the *script*?" I asked him. "I do *all* of those—and quite *often*!" [*Laughs*] There was fire, smoke, and I was hitting them on a constant basis!

So what advice did he have for you at that point?

He said, "The other thing is, they smell *fear*, and *that* they *really* don't like." I said, "Then *that's* the only thing I've got going for me, because one thing I'm *not* is *afraid* of anything. I'll just have to remember that." And strangely enough, as far as I know I was the only person on that film that never had one bee sting.

What precautions did the people behind-the-camera get to take?

Some of the crew looked like they were came down from space—they had all sorts of special equipment and walked around with their hands covered, their necks covered, their faces and everything. And suddenly you'd hear, "Ow! Ow! Ow!"—a bee would wriggle up their arms, or wherever, and find a spot [*laughs*]! It was so amazing! And there was me, running around in this little slip, whacking these bees (and saying to them, "Sorry! Sorry about that!")—and not getting stung at all!

Were the producers, Max Rosenberg and Milton Subotsky, around for the shooting?

They were around, and I liked them very much, both of them. It was all very exciting in the beginning of the second half of the '60s—there was a lot going on in London, and Max and Milton were around making quite a few movies. Freddie Francis was the director, and he was lovely. He was one of the "hooks" for me to make that movie—I knew I was going to be *seriously* well-photographed, because he was the Oscar-winning cameraman for *Sons and Lovers* [1960] and things like that. *The Deadly Bees* was one of his first directing jobs. His wife Pam had a baby literally *just* after that movie, and they called her Suzanna after me, which was really nice.

How were the bees rounded up at the end of each day?

I don't think there *was* a rounding-up situation; *that* was the reason there were like two million bees there. For each scene where there were a lot of bees involved, we'd use (say) 70,000. And of course, some of them didn't make it [*laughs*]!

You play a pop singer in the movie. Is that you singing?

No, I'm afraid it isn't, but a lot of people seem to think it is. So I did a very good miming job, apparently [*laughs*]!

Your career reportedly hit a snag when the Hollywood and English acting guilds got into a tangle.

That's right, I had a real problem with the Screen Actors Guild. Elvis specifically asked for a movie to be written *for* me—we were both under contract to Hal Wallis—and there were four other applications for me to play in other [Hol-

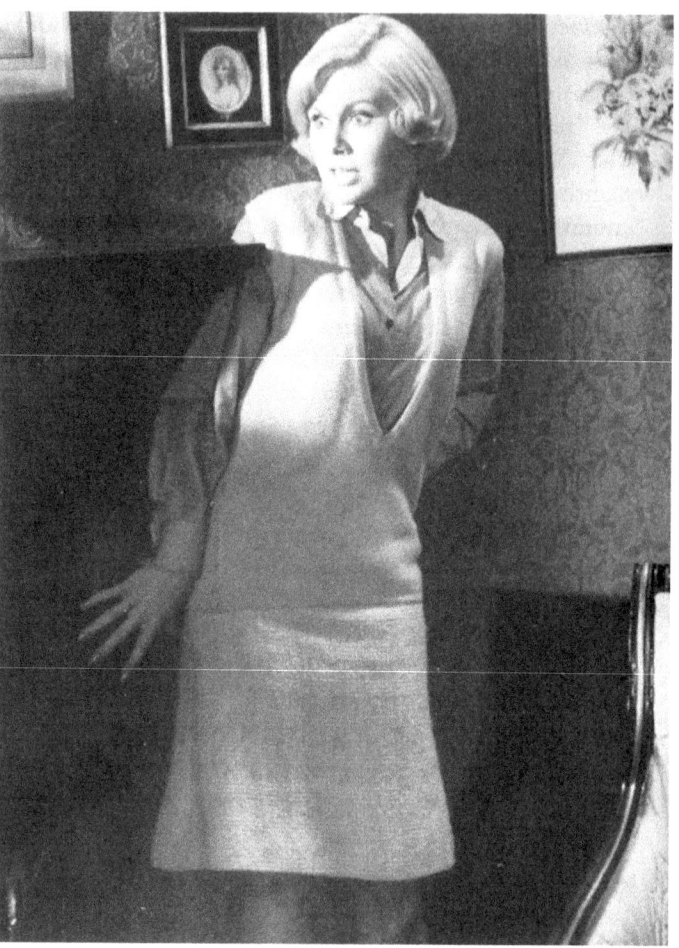

Suzanna Leigh faced the challenge of *acting* fear toward *The Deadly Bees* without showing fear around them.

lywood] films, playing American parts. But just then Charlton Heston was in the middle of making *Khartoum* [1966], playing Gordon of Khartoum in England, and [because of the rules of British Actors' Equity] he had to up and go to Ireland to finish the picture.

And then the Screen Actors Guild in Hollywood "got even" by giving you, and probably a lot of other English actors, a hard time.

I'm afraid so—it was a tit for tat

situation. I kept thinking that, between Elvis and Hal Wallis, they could sort that out. But even they did have the Screen Actors Guild's power!

Did you enjoy getting involved with Hammer and The Lost Continent*?*

I quite liked *The Lost Continent* because my best friend was in it, Tony Beckley, and also another great friend of mine, a New York *serious* actor named "Benny" [Benito] Carruthers who was in a lot of "grown-up movies." *Lost Continent* was based on a Dennis Wheatley book [*Uncharted Seas*]—and Dennis Wheatley wrote some great books! So I was offered this, and I could do what I wanted—design the dresses for it, play it how I wanted and so on. It was fun! It's always nice to work with good people. I think Hammer was great—I made a couple of Hammer pictures, and I'm very proud of them.

Was Dennis Wheatley around when you shot the movie?

Yes, I met him a couple of times, and I liked him very much.

And your director was Michael Carreras.

Not at the beginning it wasn't, no! There was a little bit of a contretemps: The first director's name was Leslie Norman, and then Carreras took over. Norman said something rather unfortunate to somebody who was around, something that was just…unacceptable. (I go into more detail in my book!) So Carreras took over, and he was great. We all sort of "bounced off" each other and it was fine. Carreras was also the producer of the film, and so he said, "Look, we'll give it a try, and if there's a problem, then we can rethink it." But there wasn't a problem at all!

How were all the ocean scenes shot?

The water stuff was all shot in a tank, and it was very wet and it was very *cold*! At the time, that was the biggest tank in Europe—it was quite something. The waves and everything really did take your breath away! Those waves were amazing! They had the fire brigade there, and the fire brigade was just *pouring* tons of water on us. It was *so* serious—your face got really bruised. I saw *Lost Continent* the other night at the Memphis Film Festival, and Warren Stevens [*Forbidden Planet*, 1956] watched it with me. And Warren said, "Early *Titanic*!" And it was true! We shot *Lost Continent* at Elstree.

What do you recall about the scenes where the monster caught you in its tentacles?

That was amazing—there were sort of "pre-Spielberg" special effects in that scene! A lot of money was spent on that [monster], and guys from Disney came over to do that. And everything *worked*, it was *extraordinary*. And it was quite *scary*, actually, once it was moving and puffing and blowing and things like that. It was an expensive movie, actually!

Were there any injuries on Lost Continent*?*

There was a girl in there, Sabrina I think her name was; she's the black girl in the end scene, standing on board ship. And she got *really* badly burned. They were using that phosphorus stuff that really was sort of "sparky," and some got caught on her back and *badly*, badly burned her. I believe that she sued for a *lot* of money. And *successfully*!

Well, *I* nearly got burned to death on *The Deadly Bees*. Here's the [back story] on that: I was talking to Burt

The special effects of *The Lost Continent* may be low-tech by today's standards, but Leigh found them "extraordinary" in 1967.

Lancaster when I was in America, and of course he did *so* much stunt work— he had been a trapeze artist and things like that. I used to ask people their advice on things, and one day I was talking to him and he said, "One thing I can tell you: Try never to work with fire. But if you *do*, *don't* listen to them when they come out with, 'Oh, we've tested it, it's fine.' Because that's…bullshit! At the end of the day, these things go wrong!" He told me that you should *always* have an escape route, even if they tell you, "Oh, no, you don't need all that. It's a waste of money to build escape routes." And then what happened on *The Deadly Bees* was, they couldn't turn the flames off and the whole damn set went up! My clothes were absolutely soaked on the way *into* that scene, because Burt Lancaster told me to do that. All you actually see on screen was a load of fire, but there was an *awful* lot of action going on behind it [*laughs*]! It was unbelievable. And if I *hadn't* had that escape route, there's no question about it, I would have been burned badly, if not…you know…dead. The little tap that turned on the gas stuck, and they couldn't turn it off! The whole set went up, the fire engines were there and all that. Meanwhile, even *with* the soaked outfit I had on, everything was singed. If it wasn't for Burt Lancaster, perhaps I wouldn't still be around!

What are your memories of your other movie for Hammer, Lust for a Vampire*?*

How I got involved was just me phoning up Jimmy Carreras on a Friday and saying, "Hey, Jimmy, I've got a problem. Can you get me in a movie like ...tomorrow?" And he said, "I haven't got any movies tomorrow. Well, I've got one starting on *Monday*—" I said, "That'll do!" The movie was *Lust for a Vampire* and, after much arm-twisting, he offered me a role.

And here I *was thinking that you probably had to be coerced into being in a movie like that!*

Yes, you'd think that they would have had to arm-twist *me* [*laughs*]! But this was an emergency—my mother had just swindled me out of my house! I played a gymnast-boarding school teacher, and it was great fun. And it was funny, because they told me they were making two versions, an English version and a "Swedish version." It was set at a boarding school and one day I walked onto a set to do a scene and there were all these girls with hardly any clothes on—"Oh, my God!", I said! I froze! At lunch, Jimmy Carreras explained to me, "Oh, it's the *Swedish* version!"

Have you ever done a nude scene in a movie?

No, the closest I got was [a love scene] in *The Lost Continent*. By the way, Peter Cushing was supposed to be in *Lust for a Vampire*—I was recently told that by a Hammer fan.

He was replaced by Ralph Bates.

That's right. And Ingrid Pitt was supposed to be in it, too, and *she* was replaced by Yutte Stensgaard. I liked Ralph very much—we got on incredibly well and we became great mates. In fact, we recently did this great big Hammer thing [a Hammer reunion at Bray Studios] for his charity—you know he died of cancer. Mike Raven was in it, too, as Count Karnstein, and I liked him enormously. But [*whispering*]—he was sooo *intense*! Oh, God! And he knew *everything* about the whole occult business and everything! For him, it was *very* serious—there was no tongue-in-cheek *there*!

Bates once said that it was a "tasteless" movie. Would you go along with that?

Well, he was in a different part from me, he was sort of major in it and I was passing by as a gymnast. I was jolly happy to be in it at all 'cause it was a job that happened when I needed it. Then a few years later I did another [vampire movie] called *Son of Dracula*, which was the end of a few people's careers! You've heard about movies that gave people their start? Well, *Son of Dracula* was a movie that gave some people their *stop*! I very quickly realized that this was perhaps the most expensive home movie ever made! It cost a great deal of money. It was with Ringo Starr and Harry Nilsson—Harry was one of the all-time greats as far as writing music and things. And Freddie Francis directing again, which I thought was great. And they were paying *me* a great deal of money. It was all a little "fancy"—you could play *what* you like, *when* you want. Of course, it sounds great when you're all meeting up, but in real life it doesn't *happen* like that, at some point you've got to vaguely sit down and work with scripts and things! It didn't hang together very well.

Who were some of the people whose careers got their stops?

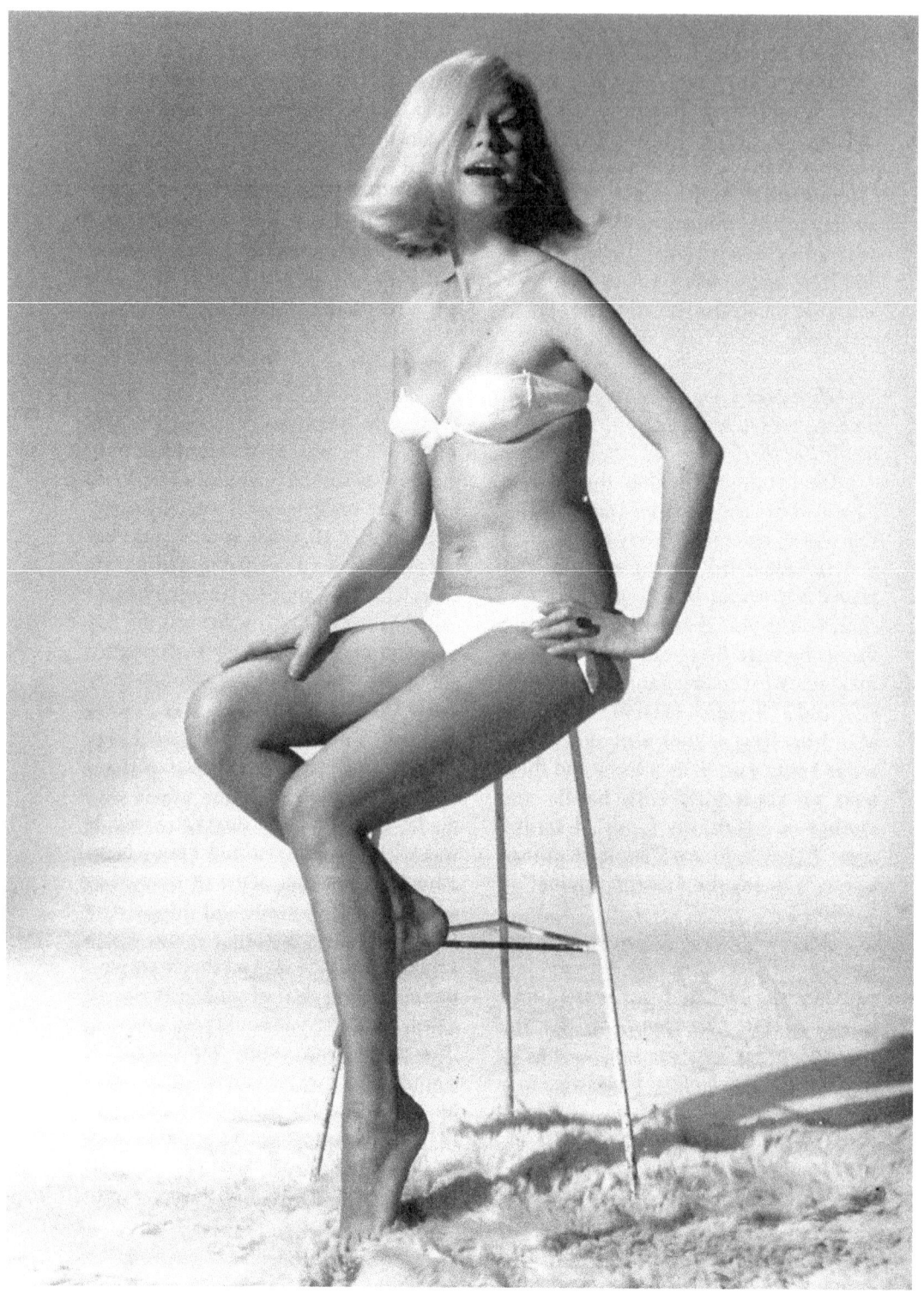

Well, *I* came out of the business after that for quite awhile [*laughs*]! Freddie came out for a long while—he went back to being a cameraman. And also [actor] Dennis Price. I said to Dennis one day, "I can't handle any of this." (You couldn't walk off, because you were committed, but it was becoming…like a nightmare, really!) Dennis said, "Well, it's all right for *you*, darling, you can come of the business. *I've* run out of time!" After *Son of Dracula* was released, the reviews came out in New York and they were apparently the *worst* reviews *in* the world—followed up about ten days later, or *less*, by Dennis killing himself! He obviously took those reviews *far* too seriously [*laughs*]! (That's a cheap joke, that's just me being naughty. In real life, obviously, that was just some terrible timing.)

Ringo Starr also produced it. Why did he want to do the picture?

Because he, like everybody, was a frustrated actor.

Son of Dracula *was written by an actress named Jennifer Jayne, who used a pseudonym.*

I didn't know we *had* any writing [*laughs*]! I must have *missed* that bit!

You've just finished your autobiography—but didn't you also write a novel about a female James Bond?

Well, I was *commissioned* to write [the female Bond novel], but then I had a car crash and I died for a couple of minutes, and that sort of took me out of action for awhile. But getting that [writing assignment] made me feel that I *could* perhaps write. As for my autobiography [*Paradise, Suzanna Style*], a lot of people had asked me to do it, over a period of an awfully long time. It finishes in the late '70s, so it covers all the movies. Over the years, I read so many autobiographies of other people, and I always used to think, "Oh my God, why do they 'stop at the door'?" They write, "Then I made a film at Fox…" and you go, "*Yes!* Tell me what it was like!" But then they jump to the *next* film, or to some domestic situation! And I'm going, "*No!* I want to know what happened at Fox! I want to go in those gates!" So I told myself that, if *I* ever got around to doing that sort of thing, I was gonna go *through* those gates, I was gonna tell people what it was like to have all your dreams come true by the time you're 19—which is what happened to me, and which is not usual. What it's like to go in on the first day and meet everybody, what Hal Wallis had in store for me, what my dressing room was like and *all* those sort of things that I wish somebody else had told *me* about. What it was like to be around in the '60s in London, to get shot at in Beirut and get arrested in Budapest!

Shot at in Beirut?

Well [*laughs*], Europeans *do* things like that!

Opposite: America's loss was England's gain when Leigh traveled back across the pond and made a splash in genre fare.

Suzanna Leigh Filmography

tom thumb (MGM, 1958)
Oscar Wilde (20th Century–Fox, 1960)
Bomb in the High Street (Rank/Hemisphere, 1961)
The Pleasure Girls (Tekli/Compton/Times Film, 1965)
Boeing Boeing (Paramount, 1965)
Paradise, Hawaiian Style (Paramount, 1966)
Deadlier Than the Male (Universal, 1966)
The Deadly Bees (Paramount, 1967)
The Lost Continent (20th Century–Fox, 1968)
Subterfuge (Commonwealth United, 1969)
Lust for a Vampire (*To Love a Vampire*) (American Continental Films, 1971)
Beware My Brethren (*The Fiend*) (Cinerama, 1972)
Son of Dracula (*Young Dracula*) (Apple Films/Cinemation, 1974)

Yvonne Lime

Gosh, [my teenage movies] are nothing compared to what they're doing now. I don't think I'd be in the industry right now—it's changed a lot!

She was a *Teenage Werewolf*'s girlfriend. And a *High School Hellcat* and an *Untamed Youth* and a *Dragstrip Riot*-er. And, a decade later, she retired from acting when she became the wife of successful TV producer Don Fedderson (*The Millionaire, My Three Sons, Family Affair*), to whom she was married until his 1994 death. But, according to Glendale-born blonde beauty Yvonne Lime, one of the most important (and rewarding) parts of her life is her charity work: Beginning in the 1950s, while entertaining U.S. troops in Japan, Lime and her actress-friend Sara O'Meara became concerned with the plight of orphans and took the first steps toward founding International Orphans Inc., an organization that built and maintained four orphanages in Japan, as well as five orphanages, a hospital and a school in Vietnam. Lime and O'Meara later redirected their efforts toward abused and neglected children in the U.S. and changed their organization's name to Childhelp USA.

My mother was a music teacher, and she was *very* into the arts and everything. When I graduated high school, she encouraged me to take up acting. I ended up going to the Pasadena Playhouse and I got into a play on the main stage, *Ah, Wilderness!* with Bobby Driscoll and Will Rogers, Jr. An agent saw me and said, "I'd like to see if I can get you some work." He did; he got me a part on *Father Knows Best*. I worked on that show for four years, playing Dotty Snow, Betty's [Elinor Donahue] girlfriend. That started my career.

In the '50s, it was different than it is now—you used to just work *all* the different shows. I worked on *Father Knows Best* as a running part, but I was free to do other shows, and so I did all the different ones that were on the air at that time. I was very busy, my career just *started*.

You were a regular on The Mickey Mouse Club...

Yes, "The Hardy Boys" was the series I was on. And I did quite a few years on *Burns and Allen*—I played Ron's girlfriend. At the end of each show, I said, "George and Gracie will be right back" and I winked into the camera [laughs]! I did *Ozzie and Harriet*, I did a *lot* of shows. In fact, I worked for my [future] husband Don Fedderson in *The Millionaire*. Then I was on his series *My Three Sons* when we were dating, and he didn't even know that I was cast in the part [laughs]! I did a lot of the "family shows," and I had a lot of running parts on shows like *Bringing Up Buddy* [1960-61] with Frank Aletter and [*Harris Against the World*, 1964-65] with Jack Klugman. I *loved* those kind of parts.

You also had your own series, Happy *[1960-61] with Ronnie Burns.*

That's right. But [starring in a series] is really heavy work, because you not only do the show, but you have to rehearse the *next* show, and you have to do publicity and you have your clothes to figure out—you have a lot of responsibilities when you have your own show. But when you had a *running part* on a show, it was kind of fun 'cause you could come in and do your thing for one day or so, and then be free to do other things in between. It was a lot of fun; I enjoyed my life at that time. I don't think I fully appreciated it until afterwards, when I'd see other people trying to get into the movie industry. I was very fortunate to get into it as easy as I did.

Was your first movie The Rainmaker *[1956]?*

Yes. By then, I was in Glendale College and I was in a play *there*. I had already started my TV work, and so I was in and out of school [laughs]—it was very difficult! But I got into *their* play, *The Man Who Came to Dinner*, then I was tested for *The Rainmaker* and I got *that*. When the *Herald Express* and the *Times* would put out a list of the people who they thought were going to be [Oscar] nominated, they said they thought that I was going to be for *The Rainmaker*—and Paramount was kind of pushing for it. And Hal Wallis, the producer of *The Rainmaker*, brought me back to be in the movie *Loving You* [1957] with Elvis Presley. I had a very minor part in that, really, but Elvis and I became friends and we dated. I got an awful lot of publicity. He was a very, very nice gentleman at that time, when I knew him. It was only his second movie, and he was very kind and very nice.

Then you started doing a lot of teenage movies.

Starting, I believe, with *I Was a Teenage Werewolf* [1957]. It was Michael Landon's first [starring] movie, but I had done a few others before. He was 19, and a *very* nice gentleman. I was very impressed with him. We used to kid him because he was only 19 and married to a woman who was a few years older than he was, and he had a child. And he was very proud of that!

I thought the child was the wife's from another marriage.

That *was* the wife's from another marriage, but he liked to say it was his child.

What did you think of his acting in Teenage Werewolf*?*

For that kind of a movie, for him to make *sense* of that [laughs]—I was very impressed with his acting. I thought he was doing a good job making it believable. And he really *was* the one who made the picture a success, because of the way he interpreted that part. I liked him a lot.

Supposedly Elvis visited the Teenage

Michael Landon made his starring film debut opposite Lime in the exploitation movie milestone *I Was a Teenage Werewolf.*

Director Gene Fowler, Jr., yuks it up with *Teenage Werewolf* leads Landon and Lime.

Werewolf *set. Do you have any memory of that happening?*

No, I really don't.

Do you recall how you got the Teenage Werewolf *part?*

I just went on an interview. At that time, I was quite busy, just going from one thing to another. They'd send me scripts and they'd say, "Would you do it?" At that time, I was really very fortunate, I had a very nice career going. The producer was Herman Cohen, who was *always* very nice. And the director [Gene Fowler, Jr.] was also very nice. We *all* got along well. I loved life and I loved people, and I loved what I was doing. I had a good time all the time! Kenny Miller was in the movie, and also a friend of mine I'd gone to school with, Cindy Robbins. It was a whole group of us, and we just had a real fun time together.

And Michael Landon was fun to know.

He was delightful to work with. A very nice, nice individual. He was very down-to-earth and a lot of fun. I can't remember anything outstanding other than, we all just got along real well, and that he was just a nice person and I felt he did a great job.

Were his ears really as big as everybody likes to say they were?

Well, he had his hair longer, and

his hair went over them. That's why he styled his hair the way he did. I don't know how large they were. (People are very *picky*, aren't they?)

Did you ever see him in his Werewolf makeup?

Oh, sure. I wasn't in any scenes with the Werewolf, but we were all there on the set. It was quite an ordeal for him [*laughs*]—it took a lot of time to get him prepared for that.

Going into a movie with a silly title like I Was a Teenage Werewolf, *did you think to yourself, "What am I getting myself into?"*

Yeah [*laughs*]! Because I kind of did a crazy thing: I did *The Rainmaker*, which was a classy movie, and then I did a lot of teenage movies. But I guess it was the popular thing to do at the time, all those *High School Hellcats* [1958] and the *Beach* movies and *all* those crazy teenage titles. Gosh, they're *nothing* compared to what they're doing now. I don't think I'd be in the industry right now [*laughs*]—it's changed a lot!

Were you still living at home when you made that movie?

I lived at home until the end of '57 or the beginning of '58. That's when I moved in with my friend Sara, and the two of us started our organization. She had played on an *Ozzie and Harriet* and we met each other there, and then she was in one of those teenage movies—we just kept running into each other! I was doing a lot of USO work because I was single at the time. This man named Charlie Watts was an actor—I don't know if you remember him...

Tubby? Kind of balding?

Yes! I met him somehow, in a movie or something, and he was just really nice and we became friends. He used to get groups together to go on weekends to do USO shows, and he asked me if I would like to help him with it. So I organized the younger ones and he organized the older, established actors and actresses, to go on these trips every weekend. I asked Sara to go one time, and we got to know each other and how each other *believed* and *thought* and everything, and so we became friends. She was from Knoxville, Tennessee, and living alone, and she had to move out of the apartment where she lived. We decided to get an apartment together. So I moved out about that time, the end of '57 or beginning of '58.

Then we were selected, out of about 500 actresses, to go overseas to entertain. They sent us into some remote areas that were *way* out, and we had to go by all different kinds of transportation. It was a lot of fun. And it was during this trip that there was a major typhoon in Tokyo, Japan. Of course, we were very young and thought, "Oh, this is fun! Let's go out and see the area that was hit!" [*Laughs*] Little, tiny, silly girls! We took our little dictionaries with us and we started walking along the streets, and these children were huddled together trying to keep warm. We went over to them and said something to them in Japanese. But the minute they looked at us and they said something back, we didn't know what they were saying [*laughs*]! We were *trying* to communicate with them and we kept saying, "Mama-san? Papa-san?"—and they said, "No mama-san. No papa-san." Anyway, we learned that these children were orphans.

We took them back to the man who was in charge of us, Col. Fling, and we said we had found these children. He said, "Oh, my God, there are *so* many orphans because of this typhoon. Just put 'em back on the streets, we can't take care of 'em all." And we said, no way are we going to do that, because these were little children—their little hands were cracked and bleeding from the cold. We said, "We've *got* to find a home for them." So he gave us a list of... Do you want to hear all this?

Yes, I do.

So he gave us a list of orphanages, and the rest of the day we spent looking around. Of course, they were all filled to the brim and they couldn't take these children in. So we sneaked them back upstairs into our room that night, without telling the colonel—we were staying in a hotel where the military stayed. We bribed the maids by giving them cashmere sweaters. We told the maids we found these children on the street, and asked them to help us get blankets and things. They thought it was kind of fun that they were in on this "secret" with us. We all slept huddled together that night, and then the next morning we started out again.

About three or four in the afternoon, we went to this one particular orphanage, and the children began to fuss and hang onto us and cry. Well, we found out that these children had been cast out from this orphanage to make room for pure-blood Japanese children. These children *we* found were mixed blood [Japanese-American]. We were very naive and did *not* know that the American-Japanese child was discriminated against. It was kind of like a "child without a country" because our servicemen would go back home and (in some cases) not *know* that they even *had* a child, and then the Japanese women would give them up. We felt *so* sorry for these Amerasian children. So we went back to the colonel with them, and (of course) he had a *fit*—he said, "You mean you still *have* them? You mean you didn't get *rid* of these kids?" He could have just *died*, 'cause we were always getting into *some*thing when we were over there. He was crazy at first, but then finally he calmed down and he said, "I know a man who is American-Japanese himself, and he runs an orphanage. Maybe he'll be able to help you, 'cause of *all* people, he'd be sympathetic that way." So we went to see *him*, but he said that he was heading back to the States—he stayed there six months of the year. Besides, he was filled to the brim. But then he said, "I know a Japanese lady who's taken in some children off the street. If you want to go see if she'd be willing to take these children, I'll go with you." We went over to see her, and our hearts sank because it was a one-room hut. Her windows were broken, her door needed fixing—the place was in a bad way. And yet when we walked in there, her face was just *filled* with love, you could just *feel* that she would be just wonderful to these children. And we were desperate—we had shows to do, and here we had 11 children!

We said, "We'll make a deal with you: If you take these children in, we'll even help the children you've *already* taken in"—she had about ten others. It was a deal for her because she didn't have any money to take care of the children she had, and it was *fantastic* for us because we didn't know what we were going to do! *Then* we thought, "Oh, my goodness, what have we gotten ourselves into?" Then we thought, "Well, we'll just talk to the men and we'll have them help us." So, every time we'd do a show, afterwards we'd tell the servicemen how much we needed their help. And they were fabulous: They got blankets for us and they would come over and they fixed the building up. Then we built a story on *top* of it, and we ended up with a hundred children in our care before we left there. We did benefit shows for the children and all kinds of things when we were over there.

And this all started in 1959, when you were in your early twenties.

That's right. Then we came back and I had that TV show *Happy*. One day I was sitting on the set telling the producers about the trip and how we found the children overseas. So they did a whole episode around that—they re-enacted the whole thing. They had Sara come on and be herself, and in the story she found orphans. Mickey Rooney directed the show. It was fun. And we got so much publicity on it that the producer said, "Are you incorporated?" and we said no. He got a friend of his, a lawyer, to incorporate us, and we started

Reacting to off-camera carnage, the overage "teenage" co-stars of *Teenage Werewolf*: Tony Marshall, *Playboy* Playmate Dawn Richard, Michael Rougas, Lime, Ken Miller and Cindy Robbins.

International Orphans Inc. We built four orphanages in Japan. In 1966, we went back to Congress to receive an award, and they ended up asking us to work with the Third Marine Amphibious Force in Vietnam, which we did. We build five orphanages and a hospital and a school in Vietnam. And then we arranged for the Baby Lift—remember that from the early '70s? We gathered as many children out of Vietnam and into homes here in America as we possibly could.

Then we started looking around for a new project, because our work was through in Vietnam. We said, "Let's start looking for something to do here in the United States." When Ronald Reagan was running for governor of California, Nancy Reagan told us, "You ought to look into child abuse." We said, "If Ronald gets elected, if he could see to it that we would get a small grant, we would look into the problem and do a feasibility study. If it's as bad as you say, that will be our new project." Well, he *was* elected, we *did* get the money, and we *did* find out that it was the number one killer at that time [the early '70s] of infants. People just didn't want to get involved; it wasn't the popular thing to do. It's a terrible thing to say, but you know how diseases [have vogues]—for instance, fighting AIDS is now [fashionable]? Well, at that time, the attitude was, "They're *your* children, you can treat 'em whatever way you want." It had to get horribly ugly and into the papers before people started wanting to do something about it and say that children cannot be treated this way. We were the first organization to be on television, to talk about the problem, and to try to make people aware of child abuse and to do something about it. Now we're one of the largest non-profit, non-governmental agencies dealing in prevention, treatment and research. That's what we're busy doing now.

Did you stay friendly with Michael Landon after Teenage Werewolf?

In a way we did. We weren't like close buddies or anything like that—I was single and he was married, and he had a different set of friends. But he *did* do things for our charity. We have "villages" where children stay—they're treatment centers where up to 80 children stay, they live there on the grounds. Our first village [Children's Village USA] opened in Beaumont, California, 20 years ago, and Michael came to the dedication. So we remained friends, and I liked him as a person very much.

How many "villages" are there now?

We have Beaumont and an East Coast [Virginia], and then we have two that will be coming up very soon: We're in the process of starting one in Knoxville, Tennessee, and then we're going to have one in Phoenix, Arizona.

Do you watch your own pictures?

I did see them, but I don't see 'em over and over again.

Who were your friends in Hollywood when you were making all these movies?

Kenny Miller and I became friends; Cindy Robbins and I were friends in school. Molly Bee...Kathy Nolan...Connie Stevens...Burt Reynolds—we all kind of grew up together, we all were in the same "era." We all worked together and were friends, and watched each other's careers. And it's helped with our charity work. I'm not as active in Hollywood, but I *married* a TV producer, so

I felt like I never left the industry because *he* was so active and we had a lot of friends in the industry who worked for him and we both knew. It really helped with the charity, because when you know them as friends and you call them and say, "Would you help?", they're very generous with their time. We never have to pay a star to do anything—they've been wonderful.

How did you enjoy making teenage pictures? Were they up your alley?

It was the thing at the time and everyone was doing them. That was the popular trend, like action pictures are now. They wouldn't be particularly my choice, but that was the popular thing, they came my way and I took them and did them.

What kind of roles did you want to play? Around the time you were doing these teenage exploitation pictures, there was a magazine article that said you wanted to be an "intense actress."

Sara O'Meara and Yvonne Lime Fedderson, co-founders of Childhelp USA, one of the largest national non-profit child abuse treatment and prevention organizations.

Yes. And I liked comedy—I played a funny blonde on *Father Knows Best*, and I enjoyed that. I worked pretty much up until the time I got married [March 1969], but when I got married, I never worked after that. I'd had a good 14 years of working and I enjoyed it very, very much, but I never regretted leaving it. As I said before, what with my husband Don *being* in the industry, it was like I was still a part of it.

Do you have a favorite movie, out of the ones you've done?

Maybe *The Rainmaker*. That was my first movie, and Lloyd Bridges was *very*, very kind to me. We knew each other up until he passed away. Earl Holliman was my boyfriend in the show, and we're still friends. He comes to all of our events and is a faithful supporter.

Even though you get co-star billing, you really don't have all that big a part in Teenage Werewolf. *And yet the movie fans who remember you, remember you for* Teenage Werewolf.

That's because I had one of the starring roles, and my name was thrown around. And because Michael became such a big star. Michael being in it kept [*Teenage Werewolf*] alive. It's just like *Loving You*—I didn't have much of a role in that, but because I dated Elvis, I got a lot of publicity. In other things, I had more to do, but they weren't the most popular pictures or TV shows or whatever.

So it's okay with you that your claim to fame with movie fans is Teenage Werewolf.

Well…I don't care [*laughs*]! That's fine! I'd like 'em to also then think about Childhelp. If they could know that my life meant more than just working with the Werewolf! Not that I didn't enjoy that—I *really* enjoyed that at the time, and it's a part of my life that'll always be a part of my memory, a part I'll love. But I love what I'm doing now, and that's helping children. And if whatever I've done in the past can help people be aware of what I'm doing *now*, that they too might join with me in helping the children who are abused and neglected, I'd really appreciate that.

Yvonne Lime Filmography

The Rainmaker (Paramount, 1956)
Loving You (Paramount, 1957)
I Was a Teenage Werewolf (AIP, 1957)
Untamed Youth (Warners, 1957)
Dragstrip Riot (AIP, 1958)
High School Hellcats (AIP, 1958)
Speed Crazy (Allied Artists, 1959)

Norman Lloyd

You recall the scene [in Saboteur*] where I'm falling off the Statue of Liberty? Hitch kept cutting to the seams of my jacket sleeve, connected to the jacket at the shoulder, and the seams start to come undone and finally the sleeve comes off in Robert Cummings' hand and I fall to the base of the Statue. [Writer] Ben Hecht saw it and he said, "He should have had a better* tailor*!"*

Norman Lloyd began his acting career in the theater, first "treading the boards" at Eva Le Gallienne's Civic Repertory Theater in New York. Aspiring to work as a classical repertory player, he gradually shed his "New Yawk" accent and became a busy stage actor in the 1930s; he next joined the original company of the Orson Welles-John Houseman Mercury Theatre.

Lloyd was brought to Hollywood to play a supporting part (albeit the title role) in 1942's *Saboteur* by director Alfred Hitchcock, who later used the actor in *Spellbound* (1945) and, in the 1950s, made him an associate producer and a director on TV's long-running *Alfred Hitchcock Presents* (then in its third year). In the course of his eight years on the series, Lloyd became a co-producer (with Joan Harrison) and then executive producer. He has since directed for other series (including the prestigious *Omnibus*) and for the stage, produced TV's *Tales of the Unexpected* and *Journey to the Unknown*, and played Dr. Auschlander in TV's acclaimed *St. Elsewhere*.

In this interview, Lloyd (now the co-star of UPN's time travel TV series *Seven Days*) takes us back in time Seven Decades, sharing some of the highlights of his remarkable career as well as his thoughts on his current SF assignment.

How did you get the job of co-starring as Dr. Mentnor in Seven Days?

There was a producer on the pilot named David Livingston, and when they were in the stage of casting the show, he suggested that I play this part. They jumped at the idea (if I may say so [*laughs*]), and so David asked me to play it. Now, there is a story behind this: Some 20 years ago, when I was producing *Hollywood Television Theatre* for PBS, I hired David Livingston as a gofer, because his father knew Mel Ferrer and I was directing a show there at the time with Leslie Caron and Mel Ferrer. David's father had come by one day and asked Mel if Mel could do something about putting the boy on, so Mel spoke to me, and I put David on as a go-fer. Subsequently, over the years, as I did work, I hired him as an associate producer and then as a producer, and he went up the ladder and he began to direct and so on, and he has had a very *solid* career as the years have gone by. "Bread cast upon the waters"—there it was, 20 years or so later, he is reminded of this and suggests me for the part in *Seven Days*. It's a nice story!

What kind of character do you play on Seven Days?

[Isaac Mentnor] is what the name sounds like—he's the mentor of the scientific aspect of the whole project. That is to say, much as the Manhattan Project had Oppenheimer—Mentnor's the sort of Oppenheimer. So I am the head of the scientific aspect of the project, as others work on the business end.

An actress named Justina Vail is also in it, playing a Russian scientist named Olga Vukavitch. Are you playing a foreign type?

No, I'm an American. In their "bible" that they write before they shoot [a series], Mentnor was referred to as having worked on the Manhattan Project, on the development of the atomic bomb. So he is older than the other people—most of the people are *much* younger.

You did *work on the Manhattan Project—in the movie* The Beginning or the End *[1947]—correct?*

[*Pause*] Well, you're right, I did. Isn't that amazing? I haven't talked to anyone about that picture since…since I *made* it! You're the first one! And that's 50 years ago!

Livingston wasn't thinking back to Beginning of the End, *was he? That's just a coincidence, right?*

Right, exactly. He wasn't *born* [*laughs*]! Or maybe he was *just about* born. I'm reaching that stage now where I have to check whether the people to whom I am speaking were *born* at the time—*whatever* time! *Beginning of the End* was a picture made at Metro, a sort of "propaganda tribute" to the [Manhattan Project]. It wasn't very *good*, as I recall, but we had a wonderful cast. They used *many* of the people under contract at the studio, and in those days Metro had *the* great contract list in Hollywood. (Of which I was privileged to be a member.) Actors, you name 'em, they were in that thing—it was like an all-star musical, but with atom bombs [*laughs*]!

The basic premise of Seven Days—*do you find it interesting?*

I find it absolutely fascinating. The idea of time travel into space is infinite in the possibilities of subject matter, because it can and does go *any*where, about *any*thing. Also, the idea that you can rectify "bad" things that happen, tragedies that happen. But how do you rectify them? And what do you do when a conflict comes up that is resisting your rectification? So it has that in it. It has what Hitchcock used to call a great "MacGuffin"—this Sphere that can take you *back* seven days and then bring you back again to the present. It's a *great* MacGuffin, so I find it very exciting.

Are they doing justice to the idea with the scripts they're writing?

I must say, I am absolutely delighted and somewhat overwhelmed by the quality of the stuff coming out. I think you'll find the pilot rather spectacular—a terrific job was done by John McPherson, who directed it. It required a man who really knew camera, a man who has a cinematic gift. And McPherson has it. You'll see its evidence in the pilot. The subsequent scripts have been very good; we're coming up to one called "The Doppelganger." Do you know what a doppelganger is?

Yes, I think I do.

[*Sighs*] Well, *that's* a relief, because I was afraid I'd have to *explain* it to you [*laughs*]! Anyway, this is a two-parter in which our leading man, played by Jonathan LaPaglia, gets out there in the Sphere and it's going through space and things happen, and he splits into two. He then has to deal with his good self and his bad self—sort of Jekyll and Hyde. It's a tremendous script, very provocative and very well-written. So, yes, I'm very happy with the scripts, and I'm keeping my fingers crossed, knocking wood and anything *else* I can do to keep up that level—a level I've been very *lucky* with! *St. Elsewhere* and the *Hitchcock* show and the PBS stuff, and the original *Omnibus* years ago—I've been very lucky to have sort of "dropped into" these things. I feel this show has that chance.

Any comments and anecdotes about LaPaglia?

I would give you an anecdote, but I don't *have* it yet—we haven't done that much work together, although we have some coming up on "Doppelganger." However, I'm very much impressed by him. In the first place, this show—for *him*—takes an enormous amount of physical stamina. I mean, he takes a beating, because the Sphere shakes and it shimmies, he goes through steam

Norman Lloyd is currently seen on the UPN sci-fi series *Seven Days*, as scientific genius Isaac Mentnor.

and—*every*thing [*laughs*]. The guy's built like a great light heavyweight, and he does this stuff and I'm very much impressed with it. And I'm also impressed with *him*. He was a doctor, an M.D. in Australia where he comes from. He practiced there, and then he went to the United Kingdom and practiced. Now, in all of these countries he had to pass the medical examinations, which are very tough. Then one day he decided this was not what he wanted to do, he didn't like it. And, since his brother [Anthony LaPaglia] was moving along as an actor, he decided to become an actor!

What would happen in real life if we found out that the government had time travel? Have we reached the point where Americans wouldn't trust its government with time travel?

People would want to know what was going on—"What's been happening to me?" Why'd the stock market go down? Time travel [*laughs*]! I think you'd have an uproar, a furor. Particularly in today's political world—which I don't want to get into, except to say that people are much more knowledgeable about what's going on, in their attitudes and points of view. They're not as passive as they were in the middle of the last century.

The conspiracy theorists would have a wonderful time. Now they could worry not only about what the government did to them in the past, but also what they did to them in the future!

If they found out about time travel, they'd want to know *who* is doing it and *what* are they doing with it and how does it affect *me*?

Any plans to direct for the series?

No, I don't. I daresay, if I raised my hand and said I'd like to [direct], they would be amenable, but…I do not want to direct for 'em. I would direct a feature film or something where I had more time, but in all honesty the pressure on the director on these things is inhuman. *Inhuman*. There are so many things to do, not really just directing actors and staging and the choreography of actors, but involving all the technical things *with* them.

The sets, by the way, are fan-*taaaas*-tic. The major set, where the Sphere sits, is in a hangar. We've moved out to a little suburb called Valencia, and there had been out there one of the Lockheed Martin facilities. (In this facility, I think they developed one of the bombers, maybe the Stealth Bomber. I can't give you that as a fact, but that's the rumor.) There are several buildings out there which we use as stages and offices, the largest of which is a hangar where the Sphere sits. This thing is enormous, it has *steam* and atomic *water* and different colored *lights* and *computers* and *railings* and *ladders* and *heights* and *depths*—and you gotta *stage* all that. Well, that's for a young fella who's full of beans.

But you still want *to direct—*

I would *love* to direct a picture, *but you'd have to have more time*. The pressure on these guys, in regard to time, and in the amount of pages they have to shoot each day, is…abnormal. And they go extraordinary hours: They'll start at (let's say) seven in the morning, and there it is midnight and they're still shooting. It's too much! But they're expected to do that. And so that's why, in answer to your question about directing, I would pass on that.

I always thought that you seemed like a natural part of the Hitchcock circle, because he had a number of British people around him. Now I look you up and see you were born in Jersey City!

That's right!

I always assumed you were English—but now I realize I have no idea what nationality you are.

American! But if you mean descent, on my father's side I'm Hungarian, and on my mother's, Russian.

Do you run into people like me fairly often, people who assume from your Hitchcock connection that you're English?

Virtually *all* people assume that [*laughs*]! Now, the reason for that is as follows: Born in Jersey City and raised in New York City, mostly in Brooklyn, one's speech was not the greatest. I mean, you'd say *kaw*-fee [coffee], *pleece* [police] and so forth. At the age of 17, I went with [actress] Eva Le Gallienne, I became an apprentice at her Civic Repertory Theater. We walked on in the shows and we studied speech and dance and did scenes for her and her teachers there. (Well, they weren't teachers, they were members of the company who would look at our scenes.) And when I went into her company [in 1932], my ambition was to be a classical repertory actor—*not* a big movie star. Le Gallienne said to me one day, "If you really hope to be in *my* company, you're going to have to learn to speak a little better." So I studied speech there with two of the actors, one of whom was very British and the other Canadian. (Le Gallienne herself was English.) As a consequence, in seeking to imitate them and carry out what they were suggesting, my New York speech became tinged with a kind of British tinge. That became known in the theater as "middle Atlantic"—that means you sound British, but an Englishman knows you're *not* British [*laughs*]! It's "theater speech." This enables you to play a lot of the classics which you *couldn't* play if you talked dese, doze and dems. There was a great emphasis on speech which would enable you to play the classics.

Lloyd lost his "New Yawk" accent so completely that many fans have taken him to be English (!).

In the course of human events, I eventually met up with Hitchcock, who was British, and Joan Harrison, who was British, and I heard all this British talk around me for years. John Houseman, who was a dear friend of mine, was also raised in England (although born in Rumania). In my ear, I heard British sounds all the time. Combine this with my studying in Le Gallienne's theater, and people would think I was British instead of just a New York guy! So that's how it came to be. And there have been some encyclopedic books, histories of theater and so forth, that list me as a British actor—and there's no reason they should! I've never said I was born *any*where but in Jersey City, New Jersey!

Your first film for Hitchcock was Saboteur, *in which you take that famous fall off the Statue of Liberty.*

At that time, at the foot of Manhattan Island was a ticket office where you got a ticket to go over on the ferry to Bedloe's Island [now Liberty Island] to see the Statue of Liberty. In one scene, I arrive at the ticket office by taxi—I'm running away, I'm being chased by the cops. I go in, I get a ticket, I get on the boat and go over and find my way to the top of the Statue of Liberty. We were starting to shoot at about eight o'clock in the morning: I arrived at the ticket office, and there were about 35 extras—they were being served coffee and doughnuts. We did my getting out of the cab about four times. Now we start to get on the boat—we do *this* about four or five times. (We're waiting for the sun; the film was not as fast as it is today, and we needed sun.) So we do *that* four or five times, all the 35 extras go on and off the boat four or five times. Now we go out, we're in the middle of the bay, and somebody says, "Will everybody out on the deck take off your coats. It's supposed to be spring, and we're gonna shoot some stuff out here." So the extras get out there on the deck with me, and we do stuff on the deck while I'm looking (supposedly) at Priscilla Lane. (She wasn't there, she was going to be cut in later with a process plate behind her.)

Now, we should mention that you're talking about a second unit shoot here, that you weren't directed by Hitchcock in these scenes.

That's right—it was directed by one of the great [special effects] men, Johnny Fulton. Anyway, we arrive on Bedloe's Island and we go off and on this boat about four or five times, again waiting for the sun. That was the point at which some little old lady says to someone, "Do you have to do this every time you want to see the Statue of Liberty?" Well [*laughs*], she had come up from Virginia and she met with these 35 congenial people, *all* of whom seemed to know each other (they were all extras). And she had coffee and doughnuts with them, and *that* was very nice, and when they said, "Go on and off four or five times," she *went* on and off four or five times! She did this at the end of Manhattan Island, she did this out on the bay and she did this coming off at Bedloe's Island, four or five times [*laughs*]! Now, the great "mystery" is this: The production manager said, "Gee, *I* didn't know that there was a woman in this, up from Virginia! My God, I've got to find her, I've got to get her to sign a release so she doesn't sue the picture for millions of dollars!" Well, he never could find her. And it's *my* theory she jumped in the bay [*laughs*]—I don't know whatever happened to her!

Some of the books that have been written about Hitchcock play up his "dark side" and his supposed kinkiness and so on. Are they at all close to the truth? Did you witness any of this behavior, or has Hitchcock gotten a raw deal?

He's getting a raw, sensationalist deal. For me to say on the one hand "He was just like everybody else" is ridiculous. But on the other hand, if you're speaking about [Donald] Spoto's book—

I am.

This is unspeakable, Spoto's book [*The Dark Side of Genius: The Life of Alfred Hitchcock*]. You can't write that about a guy, [write about] all these relations with

Lloyd dangles from Lady Liberty's torch in the nail-biting finale of *Saboteur* (1942) with Robert Cummings.

his leading ladies and all this stuff that Spoto put in. Yeah, sure, Hitch (like *any* director), he looks at a beautiful leading lady like Grace Kelly or Ingrid Bergman—you're steeped in beautiful women!—and you *appreciate* them. But what the hell's going on [with Spoto], I mean, what is he *talking* about? I don't know what Spoto is *driving* at when he calls the book *The Dark Side of Genius*. Hitch was...like...any...guy...but he was *un*like any guy. He was a unique personality because (first of all) his physical thing of being very heavy, and also whatever was going on in his mind that made these pictures. I'm not saying that he was like every other guy, but I think these books are unjust and unfair and, in many instances, *unspeakable*.

Now, Hitch had this wonderful humor. There's a great story of Tallulah Bankhead in *Lifeboat* [1944], one of my favorite stories about him, one that was typical of his humor. They were doing *Lifeboat*, and in those days they didn't have all the technical effects and special effects that they have today, so the boat was in a tank at Fox. He had eight people in this boat and, in order to make this scene work, rigged around the stage were barrels filled with water. Each barrel had a rope, and on a cue there would be a stagehand, a grip, who would pull this rope and the water would *pour* into the tank and knock the boat every which way. Consequently the people in the boat would go tumbling ass over teakettle. It was all right except for one thing: In this boat was Tallulah Bankhead, who was quite a lady, and it became apparent immediately that she wasn't wearing any drawers [*laughs*]! We're talking about 1943, '44, somewhere in there. *Today* it wouldn't mean anything, everyone would say "So what?", but in *those* days this seemed to be a source of great interest! Particularly to the stagehands, the grips. They quickly spread it around the Fox lot—"Jeez, if you get on that Hitchcock set while he's shooting, you'll see a sight. You'll see Bankhead go ass over teakettle, and there she is to the world!" Well, Hitch began to appreciate that he was getting an audience every time he went into this scene, and this *delighted* him, you see [*laughs*]! He would cue the guys and they'd pull the water—and he would throw in a few *extra* cues so that the people, having come over from other stages, wouldn't be disappointed!

News of this gets upstairs to [production executive] Darryl Zanuck, the information that many man-hours are being lost because these guys were comin' over from other stages to have a little peek at the bottom (and various other parts) of Tallulah Bankhead. When Zanuck gets this news, he summons his assistant Lew Schreiber and he says, "Now listen, Lew, we have this information that this is goin' on on the Hitchcock set. You better go down and talk to Hitchcock and please ask him to have Tallulah Bankhead put on a pair of panties." Lew Schreiber says [*quietly*], "You can't *mean* this, Darryl. I mean, we're grown men, I—" Zanuck says, "You go down there. Your job's at stake." So Schreiber goes down and he walks on the set, and they're not shooting, they're waiting between takes. And there's Hitch, who usually sat sort of like Buddha, sort of staring—you don't know *what's* going on in his mind. (Which is good!) Lew comes up to him and says, "Good morning, Hitch." Hitch says [*Lloyd imitates Hitchcock*], "Good mawww-ning..." Lew says, "There's something I'd like to talk to you about" and he proceeds to talk about the situation and he tells Hitch to ask Bankhead to put on a pair of panties. Hitch says, "I don't know...", and Lew says, "What? What is it you don't know?"

And Hitch says, "I don't know whether this properly belongs in the *makeup...wardrobe...*or *hairdressing* department..." [*Laughs*] Now, that was Hitchcock—*that* was Hitchcock! And if you consider this "the dark side of genius," fine—*I* don't! He was *full* of jokes like that, he would do things to sort of *shock* people. I remember on one of the first pictures, he had a script lady sitting beside him and he saw a little stool near him, so he picked it up and he threw it at her. Just sort of *looped* it—not *cast* it at her—to *surprise* her! These were his little "jokes." He was *in his time*, particularly in England, before he came over here, *known* for the elaborate quality of his practical jokes—he would stage them like small movies! I could go on and on about that, about some of the scenarios that he elaborately worked out just for the joy of seeing human behavior in those situations! I could go on for *weeks* about Hitchcock; I tell you, I loved the man. I *loved* him. He was a wonderful man to me, he did things for me that I could never, ever possibly thank him enough for.

Another one of your early movies was the spooky whodunit The Unseen *[1945], produced by John Houseman.*

I did that with Joel McCrea and Gail Russell and another *marvelous* guy, Herbert Marshall. Gail Russell was one of the leading actresses at Paramount, and she had been in a picture called *The Uninvited* [1944] with Ray Milland. *The Unseen* was a follow-up—and I don't think it was as successful as *The Uninvited*. All I remember is Herbert Marshall, who to me was one of the princes of this business—and one of the best-dressed men, I might add! I finally got to know who his tailor was, and took advantage of that! And Joel McCrea, who was a great guy, a *wonderful* guy. Joel had in *The Unseen* these beautiful suits that he would wear. Then at the end of the day, he would put on a cowboy's outfit and go home! He did the *reverse* of what people do in life! You know, I was fresh out of New York and "full of the city streets," and I said, "What the hell is this guy doing? Is he putting a costume on to go home?" During the day, he was in a business suit! Well, the thing was, Joel was really a cowboy! He owned thousands of acres out in Camarillo—thousands! He had a lot of cattle, and he could ride on a horse all day on his land and never cover all of it. He was a real cowboy and he'd go home and get on his horse!

Houseman, talking about The Unseen, *called director Lewis Allen "rude and ill-mannered."*

I never saw that. By the way, John Houseman is another person that I cannot speak too highly of. I've had wonderful luck in the people I've known: John Houseman, Joan Harrison, of course Hitch, Chaplin, Renoir, Lewis Milestone—I've been so *lucky* in knowing people like that! These were all first-class! John Houseman was like family, I was so close to John, and if he said that [about Lewis Allen], I go along with John. But I never saw it on the set.

I asked Lewis Allen about Houseman's comment. Allen said that Raymond Chandler was writing the Unseen *script, Houseman was interfering, and he, Allen, took Chandler's side. That was Allen's explanation for that comment.*

You provoke some interesting memories. The one time I met Raymond Chandler was in Houseman's office; we went across the street to Oblatt's [restaurant] and had a cup of coffee. He was a rather irascible, sort of *itchy* guy, but *interesting*, of course. Now, whether Chandler disapproved of what Houseman was doing or not, I *question*—and I'm gonna tell you why. John Houseman once wrote for *Harper's* a brilliant piece about how Raymond Chandler finished a script [*The Blue Dahlia*, 1946] for him *at the point of death*. Chandler had a drinking problem, and he was told at this point by his doctor that if he drank, he would die. That's it. It would kill him. So when Houseman called him in to talk about finishing the script [*The Blue Dahlia* was already in production], Chandler said to Houseman, "John, I'd like to help you…" and told him the situation. He was unable and unwilling to continue working on the script at the studio *sober*—but he was confident of his ability to finish it at home, *drunk*. He would be completing the script at the risk of his life. "I have to get drunk in order to write it," he told Houseman, "and it'll kill me, Jack, it'll kill me." But he said he would do it, under certain conditions, and Houseman accepted. There was between Houseman and Chandler this *tie*—I don't think Chandler would have done it, and risked his life, if he didn't have great respect for John.

Speaking of drinkers, Lewis Allen also told me that it was during the making of The Uninvited *that Gail Russell was "introduced" to alcohol. Did she drink during the making of* The Unseen?

I saw no sign of alcohol at that time. I can't give you anything definitive on Gail Russell, because she was rather remote—in a nice way. I spent most of my time between scenes talking to Herbert Marshall and Joel. I was very fond of them, particularly Bart Marshall, whom I got to know very well.

Who do you play in the 1951 M *remake—and why is it the next thing to a lost film these days?*

You know, it is fan-*tas*-tic that you ask that question, and I'm gonna tell you why: This coming Labor Day [1998] weekend, I am supposed to the guest of honor at the Telluride Film Festival, and I have had to tell them that I can't be up there because of *Seven Days*. Now, the reason they asked me is that they are running the remake of *M*, and they wanted me to speak about that. So that's how I came to be invited. Now—truth to tell—I remember little or nothing about it. David Wayne played the Peter Lorre part, and the reason *I* was in the picture is that [director] Joe Losey and I worked together many times in the theater. We did at least four plays together, some of which were very important, like the Living Newspapers for the Federal Theatre—he directed and I played the leads. When he came out here, he did a couple movies and then he got *this* job [*M*] for the Nebenzal brothers. I thought that remaking *M* was a *terrible* idea, because the original is a *masterpiece*—it's one of the all-time great films, I think. But a job's a job. I remember Joe asked me if I would be in it, and I was an old friend of his, and I thought I *should* be in it. The part is *nothing*, I do very little. Of course, Joe's career never took off in this town; it took off when he went to England. Then he did *The Servant*

[1963] and *Accident* [1967] and *King and Country* [1964] and pictures that drew a lot of attention.

Anyway, about *M*, there's nothing I can really tell you; in fact, I don't know *what* I was gonna do in Telluride. I think one of the reasons I turned 'em down is that I was afraid I'd have nothing to say [*laughs*]!

Years ago I interviewed a director named Don Taylor...

Know him very well.

...and we talked about Alfred Hitchcock Presents. He said the way it usually worked was that Hitchcock got the best scripts; Robert Stevens got the next best; and that he and Arthur Hiller were "way down at the bottom."

That Don Taylor should utter such an idiotic judgment is so...pathetic! When I see that sonuvabitch, I'm gonna raise hell with him! (He's a friend of mine, so don't worry about it.) Absolutely untrue! Joan Harrison would pick a story and she'd say, "I want Hitch to do this story." But Robert Stevens would get *equally* good stories. For example, do you remember "Specialty of the House," where they're fattening up Robert Morley? That was Robert Stevens! And Stevens won the Emmy for "The Glass Eye" with Jessica Tandy. I could go on and on like this about Robert Stevens, who had a *brilliant* style particularly suited to the *Hitchcock* show. I myself directed a show with Steve McQueen and Peter Lorre called "Man from the South," and *that's* as great a story as you can *get*!

Arthur Hiller came down from Canada and we were impressed by his work, and he did *brilliantly* on our show. And it moved him along very much towards his movie career. So Don is all wet—and I'm gonna *tell* him so. That's *stupid*, it never was *like* that! *I* directed a show called "The Jar," a Ray Bradbury story that James Bridges [adapted], and *that* was Hitch's favorite show, I think! And *I* directed it! *It didn't matter!* Sometimes Hitch was available, and sometimes he wasn't, and Stevens we *always* tried to get to direct. But there was never any *rank* who got one, two, three or bottom of the list.

I talked to Arthur Hiller just the other day and he made a comment about you—and the more I thought about it, the more I realized it was probably true. And I'd like to see you wiggle out of this one. You ready?

All right.

He said, "Norman Lloyd and Joan Harrison really did that show. I'm not saying Hitchcock wasn't involved at all, but they were the day-to-day people, it was their show." I'd never heard anybody put it that bluntly before.

Well...that is *true*, in the sense that we were on the firing line. But no story was done without Hitch's approval—that is to say, we used to find the stories and then submit them to Hitchcock for approval, rejection or to be put on the "reserve list" in case we ran out of stories. Then Joan and I would develop the story into a screenplay, having selected a writer; and then we would select a director; and then we would cast it. And shoot it. Edit it. And when we had a rough cut, we then would call Hitch and bring it up to him at his bungalow [at Universal] and he would look at it. I don't recall his ever rejecting *any* episode. And even his comments were very modest—he was wonderfully sensitive

Pat Buttram and Collin Wilcox contemplate the contents of "The Jar" in the Norman Lloyd-directed *Hitchcock* episode.

to people's work, and so he just would say, "If you *have* shot a closeup there, you might want to use it." This was very rare. And he never rejected a picture, he would say, "Very good" or "Good"—or "Well, *thank* you" if he *didn't* like it [*laughs*]. He never said, "I didn't like it."

But when all he said was "Thank you," you got the impression he didn't.

Oh, we knew what he meant! You must remember, this was all his company, his money. And retakes cost money [*laughs*].

Then we took the picture back, we did all the post-production on it, found a composer to do the scoring, and the next time Hitch saw the picture was on the air. (He believed you could only judge it when you saw it at nine o'clock on the television set.) But *all* the work that I've described to you, Joan and I *did*, yes. Hitch directed about ten of them* and always the scripts were *delivered* to him, *given* to him. Joan would say, "*This* is a story that Hitch will do" and send it up to him, and he always... [*laughs*] he always accepted what he was told to do!

So, yes, we did the day-to-day foot soldier work, we really developed those shows and put 'em on. But one must remember that we always did it from a Hitchcock point of view. We always had a sense of "This is the way *Hitch* would see it," or "This is the way Hitch would *do* it." And the whole idea of the twist, and the humor, in addition to the suspense, all mixed together with romance if we could get it—although in the half-hours and the hours, there wasn't that *much*, not as much as Hitch would get in the features. But the whole *point of view* of the show was Hitch's, and we were "inoculated," so to speak, having worked with Hitch. Joan had worked with him as a writer on a couple of pictures, and I'd worked with him as an actor, and (I think it's fair to say) we both knew him very well socially. So we knew his point of view. But...what Arthur Hiller said is true!

Now that that series is looked upon as a TV classic, one of the great series in that genre, do you feel you've gotten enough credit? People "in the know" know how much you contributed, but everybody else—obviously—just thinks of Hitchcock. Is that "okay" with you?

Well, *yes*, and I'll tell you why. Hitch was The Star. And without Hitch, it would have been just another show. That is to say, *not* in the sense of quality, the quality would have been the same or very fine, and I'm very proud of that show, I think it's amazing when you look back at some of them. And I did about 260 of them or something—somewhere in that neighborhood, because we used to do 39 a season in the half-hour days and I did five years of that, and then we did the hour shows. What I'm saying is, *he* was the star, and those lead-ins which he appeared in were *very* much part of the draw of the show. So,

---

*Eighteen, actually: "Revenge" (10/2/55), "Breakdown" (11/13/55), "The Case of Mr. Pelham" (12/4/55), "Back for Christmas" (3/4/56), "Wet Saturday" (9/30/56), "Mr. Blanchard's Secret" (12/23/56), "One More Mile to Go" (4/7/57), "The Perfect Crime" (10/20/57), "Lamb to the Slaughter" (4/13/58), "Dip in the Pool" (6/1/58), "Poison" (10/5/58), "Banquo's Chair" (5/3/59), "Arthur" (9/27/59), "The Crystal Trench" (10/4/59), "Mrs. Bixby and the Colonel's Coat" (9/27/60), "The Horseplayer" (3/14/61), "Bang! You're Dead" (10/17/61) and "I Saw the Whole Thing" (10/11/62).

to go back to your question "Am I satisfied?" [*pause*]...it's the nature of the beast. I've done other shows, other series, and they haven't worked as well. I took over the Roald Dahl series *Tales of the Unexpected* at one point, and it was never the same. Roald tried to be a Hitchcock when that series *started*, and he just didn't *have* it. So we have to go back to the Hitchcock show: *Hitch was the star.* And if people think of it as Hitch having done it, what are you gonna *do* about it?

I was looking at a brochure the other day, issued by UCLA. They were going to honor James Bridges the writer-director. Now, James Bridges was a discovery of mine: I found him through a play that he had written and which was being done in Los Angeles, and I assigned him to individual *Hitchcock* shows as a writer. He did 18 for me. Later on, when I was producing *Hollywood Television Theatre*, we did an original work of Jean Renoir's called *Carola* [1973], which Jean was too ill to direct so *I* directed it as well as produced it. With Leslie Caron and Mel Ferrer. I put Jim on to polish the dialogue and make some cuts. In this UCLA brochure, they said that Jim Bridges wrote for Alfred Hitchcock and Jean Renoir. Well [*laughs*], he never met Hitchcock! (At least, I don't *think* he did...*maybe* I took him up to meet Hitch.) I *did* take him to meet Jean. But the point I'm getting at: *He* wrote for *me*! *I* developed those [*Hitchcock*] scripts with Jim, and then they were delivered to Hitch!

By the way, whenever we finally completed a script on the *Hitchcock* show, they were always sent up to him for his reading and approval. There was no formal thing of his calling back and saying, "I approve"—we'd never hear from him except if he had an idea of a *creative* nature. For example, in "An Unlocked Window" [with female impersonator T. C. Jones as a nurse who turns out to be a male

Above and right: **For his TV intros, Alfred Hitchcock would obediently accept any and all outrageous ideas hatched by scripter James Allardice.**

killer], Hitch called back and said, "Make sure, at the end, when the nurse's hat is *ripped* off him, that you also rip his *shirt* so that we see there are no breasts, and we know it's a man." *That* kind of idea he would call down. Or a story which I directed called "The Contest of Aaron Gold," based on a Philip Roth story. It was about a little boy [Barry Gordon] in summer camp, and Hitch had the idea of the kid not putting an arm on a piece of sculpture he was doing. Hitch had the idea that the boy's father walks in at the end and he's missing an arm, and [now the audience understands why] the kid couldn't do this little piece of sculpture and put *both* arms on, because his *father* didn't have an arm. When Hitch had an idea like that, he'd call us, but otherwise, we did the whole shebang.

To get back to what people *think*, they will think in this UCLA retrospective for Jim Bridges that he wrote for Hitchcock and he wrote for Jean. But he didn't, he wrote for me. I have never said anything about that, but you've asked me the question, so why should I pretend it's otherwise?

You mentioned Steve McQueen, who you directed in two Hitchcocks.

The other ["The Human Interest Story"] was a *very* good story about a guy [Arthur Hill] who came down from Mars. But it was a very *naturalistic* story. Steve (with whom I got on very well) and Arthur (whom I *loved* as an actor—he's a wonderful guy) just played the hell out of that, the two of them. They were wonderful.

McQueen was not the headache that a lot of my interviewees describe?

Not for me he wasn't. Later on, when he became a star, maybe there were problems—I don't know. But for *me*, he was a *doll*. He would come down in his car, a Jag that used 18 quarts of oil. Steve loved to race cars; he and Sterling Moss, who was the great English driver at the time, were buddies. They would race up and down Laurel Canyon. (I'm glad I never met 'em going the other way!) But, boy, would they go! And Steve would come in in his prototype Jag convertible. Eighteen quarts of oil! Wow, he was great.

The lady at the end of "Man from the South" whose hand is missing some fingers—did that actress really have missing fingers?

No, we made a glove to fit that. Katherine Squire, a very good actress, played the part and we made a glove like that and she thrust her hand into it. Also in "Man from the South" was Peter Lorre, one of *the* great actors—it's tragic what happened to him. He was charming, brilliant, a great conversationalist...but by the time he came to us, he felt that his career was sort of over. He wasn't doing the features any more, and he was rather...sad about it, I thought. But he was wonderful—marvelous.

Then there was a Bradbury story I loved directing, "The Life Work of Juan Diaz." That was an *Alfred Hitchcock Hour* with Alejandro Rey and that *great* Mexican actress Pina Pellicer, who had been with Brando in *One-Eyed Jacks* [1961].

And who committed suicide not too long afterwards.

Right. And also Frank Silvera, one of the *best* American actors, who died trying to fix a plug—he got his finger in the plug and was electrocuted. This show, which Bradbury wrote himself from his own story, was about a man who earned more money dead than alive. His body was put into a catacombs, but it happened to be in an area that preserved the bodies. The tourists would come through to look at these dead people, who were dressed up and standing there! So the guy's wife and the young son steal his body and put it back in *their* house, which is on the *way* to the catacombs, so that people stop off there *first*. So he earned much more dead than alive. *Wonderful* story! And Bernard Herrmann did the score—a wonderful score. Ray Bradbury said that someone tried to make an opera out of that story, but I don't think they succeeded.

It seems like practically every time Bradbury worked on Hitchcock, it was an episode you either directed or acted in.

I did many, many shows with Ray. You may think I'm a bore because I say everybody's wonderful—

We'll get to somebody who's not.

Oh, I have a *list* here—as a matter of fact, I *prepared* it just before you called [*laughs*]! But Ray is...*great*. First of all, he looks like one of the characters from his Martian stories. Ray *looks like a Martian*—and if anyone *is* a Martian, it's Ray! He's constantly creative, constantly dreaming up ideas, constantly promoting his ideas. I'm proud to say that he said this once at a tribute lunch given to me by the Pacific Pioneers radio people: We had the *most wonderful collaboration* between him and Joan Harrison and myself. So I can only sing his praises. And the *material* that I got from Ray, some of which I've already mentioned to you and others that I haven't, was just wonderful. He adapted a story for me once, somebody else's, but for the most part they were all his stories. There again, to go back to Don Taylor... If I were John Houseman talking to you, I'd say, "To go back to that *rat* Don Taylor..."—that's the way Houseman would talk! The thing about Houseman, by the way, was...your phone would ring no later than seven o'clock in the morning, you'd answer, and he'd go [*gruffly*], "Hel-*lo*, you! What are you doing a-*sleep*?! What are you doing?! What's up? What's going on?" Houseman on the telephone was science fiction itself [*laughs*]!

Now, go back to "that rat Don Taylor."

What he said bears *no* relation to the truth *whatsoever*. And when I *see* that dumb lug, I'm gonna tell him! He's a friend, Don Taylor—I directed him in the theater and he's worked for me as a director. But he shouldn't *say* that—I mean, that's, that's *stupid*. I'll straighten *him* out [*laughs*]! [Actor-director Taylor died in December 1998, shortly after this interview was conducted.]

I'll bet when people talk to you about Alfred Hitchcock Presents, *you're often asked about guest stars who later made it big. I want to bounce six or seven names off you and get your comments on people you're probably asked about a lot less. Starting with Claude Rains.*

Oh, well, Claude Rains...now you're talking about one of the greats. He was wonderful. He came on...he was about 70 years old then, I think...and he played this wonderful priest [in "The Horseplayer"]. He was an old Hitchcock *star*—I mean, he is so marvelous in

Notorious [1946], which by the way Hitch always called "*No......torious.*"

With the long pause in there?
Right! Written by Ben Hecht. Ben Hecht said when he saw me in *Saboteur*—you recall the scene where I'm falling off the Statue of Liberty? Hitch kept cutting to the seams of my jacket sleeve, connected to the jacket at the shoulder, and the seams start to come undone and finally the sleeve comes off in Robert Cummings' hand and I fall to the base of the Statue. Do you remember that?

How could anybody ever forget it?
Ben Hecht saw it and he said, "He should have had a better *tailor*!" [*Laughs*] Anyway, Claude Rains...a doll, just wonderful, a marvelous actor. I was an admirer of Claude Rains ever since I saw him in the theater [in the Theatre Guild production *They Shall Not Die*] playing Sam Liebowitz, the lawyer who defended the Scottsboro Boys.* He was wonderful. When he came on to do this *Hitchcock*, it was just a delight. That show was about a priest [Rains] who bet the church funds on a horse race so he could repair the roof of the church.

Here's an actor I'm certain no one has ever asked you about, but he was so terrific on Hitchcock—Pat Buttram.
[*Excitedly*] Oh! God! Wwwwonderful! I don't think that, until I put him in "The Jar," Pat Buttram had *ever* done a straight play or straight dialogue, he'd always been a stand-up performer. We were noted, if I may say so, for the excellence of our casting—in those days, we used to bring people out from New York. But not Pat, Pat was right here. And I think I had Slim Pickens in it, too, didn't I? Oh, these guys were marvelous. Pat, *he* was so wonderful in "The Jar" that I didn't know where the part started and he left off, or vice versa! In one scene when he got into bed with Collin Wilcox (who was a tasty dip), he'd say [*imitating Buttram*], "Mmmmm ...my Albert is misbehaving!" [*Laughs*] Collin was, shall I say, a very sophisticated lady, and she handled it very well. But, oh, Pat was a *funny* man, oh, God! And he *loved* doing legitimate work, because it gave work to his Albert, I guess [*laughs*]! He was just so wonderful in it that I put him in another one with Teresa Wright.

You've segued into an episode with the very next actor I was going to ask you about ["Lonely Place"]—it featured one of the best Hitchcock *villains, Bruce Dern.*
Oh, he was superb! Making "Lonely Place," I had a marvelous time with Pat, he was so funny, he had me laughing all the time. But Bruce Dern—very remote. A superb actor, and wonderful in the *Hitchcock*s, but he was rather remote, and one *respected* that. He sort of had his own "machinery" in his head, the way he worked, and one just hoped to have that flower and to aid and abet whatever he needed. He's a very interesting actor, and excellent to work with. We *never* had any contrary people. Never.

Never?

---

*The Scottsboro Boys—nine black Alabama youths—were accused of a criminal assault on two white girl millhands. In a court case that because a national cause célèbre, *they were defended by New York attorney Sam Liebowitz, whose counterpart ("Nathan G. Rubin") was played by Rains in* They Shall Not Die.

Well, there was *one* actress, who I think was as fine an actress as there was in America: Joan Hackett. She had a [hang-up] about people *seeing* her while she worked. So we used to have to encase the show in flats, so that people walking onto the stage from outside wouldn't walk right into the scene, so to speak—they wouldn't be able to walk onto the stage and see her work. We had to protect her against that. That was purely her own..."psyche," so to speak—she was an extraordinarily sensitive person. Brilliant, brilliant actress. And a very attractive lady. But she had this "thing," and so we just went *with* it.

Robert Stevens, who was our *superb* director and did extraordinary shows for us, was also was quite eccentric. He was very nervous, so he was easily upset. He had Robert Morley in "Specialty of the House," and one day Morley was approached on the set by the Screen Actors Guild representative and told that he'd better cough up 65 bucks because he hadn't paid his Screen Actors dues. (He was a Brit, you see—from England.) He was a true eccentric, too, old Morley: He went over to Robert Stevens and he said, "Can you give me $65 so I can pay this man?" Well... Stevens *flipped* [*laughs*]! Stopped shooting...came up to us in the office...and said [*babbling*], "You know what he did?? He wanted $65!!" But Bob Stevens was *brilliant* in that episode. He won the only Emmy the show ever won [for his direction of "The Glass Eye"]. We never won an Emmy other than that one Emmy, and I think history has shown that *Hitchcock* is one of the great shows. People tell me even now that, when they run on TV Land, these stories absolutely are marvelous. And what actors! I mean, my God, we got the cream!

Sometimes it seems like this actor was in every other episode...John Williams.

In some ways, I think it's fair to say he was Hitchcock's favorite actor. I really always had that sneaking suspicion. Hitch had him in *every*thing—and big parts, I don't mean just a good luck charm. He's in *Dial M for Murder* [1954], as the inspector, and he was the *perfect* English inspector. And he was that way on-screen and off-screen—you couldn't tell the difference with these guys! He had charm and style and a very objective way of approaching everything. *Very* English, but attractively so. Whenever we had an inspector [in an episode], the first one we'd go to was old John, and if he was free, he'd do it. I don't know *how* many he did! Then he retired to La Jolla, and now he's not with us any more. But he was the *definitive* Hitchcock actor, *every*thing in his style served Hitchcock's purposes: The underplaying, the subtle humor, the indirect approach that he had.

Two more English actors: Sir Cedric Hardwicke?

He was a great friend of Hitch's and a most amusing man. What I just said about John Williams, Cedric also had. But Cedric *as a person* was more open and, I think, socially very much a friend of Hitch's. He was a very funny man. My two favorite stories about Cedric Hardwicke: He knew Bernard Shaw, who I *think* wrote the play *The Apple Cart* for him. Cedric was talking to Bernard Shaw one day, and Shaw said to him suddenly, "You know, you're my fourth favorite actor in the world." And Hardwicke said, "Thank you very much, sir. May I ask who the first three are?" And Shaw said, "The three Marx Brothers!" [*Laughs*]

At the end of his life, Cedric finally was doing a play in New York. He was *well* along in years *and* divorced—a couple of times, I think. He was doing this play and a friend went backstage to see him after the show. And sitting there very comfortably in the room, obviously waiting for Cedric to finish taking off his makeup and get dressed, was a *very* beautiful young lady. The friend was able to get Cedric aside and he asked, "Is this your semi-annual?" And Cedric said, "No, dear boy, it's my annual 'semi'!" [*Laughs*] He was a *most* amusing fellow and, in the *right* part, very effective.

Christopher Lee?
Oh, Christopher—what a riot he is [*laughs*]! In addition to working with him on *Hitchcock*, years later I also acted with him in a movie in Yugoslavia [*Journey of Honor*, 1992]—maybe we brought the whole civil war on [*laughs*]! The thing about Christopher was, he was a true eccentric (as I've said about a couple of other guys). I cast him in this part and I became fascinated with him: First of all, he knew the name of every English executioner from the fifteenth or sixteenth century on. Now, that is the *weirdest* hobby I have ever encountered—but it absolutely fit him like a skintight suit! There was an actor I knew back when I was in the Mercury with Orson, Martin Gabel, and he knew the name of every winner of the Kentucky Derby since the first Kentucky Derby—he rattled 'em off. Christopher could do that with the executioners of England! You see, this is why one loves the profession—you don't *find* that in the grocery store [*laughs*]!

Christopher also collected swords—great big swords—and also instruments of execution. And I believe he lived in an old brewery! (He was married to a Tuborg beer heiress.) *Very* strange man. He was not imaginative casting in the pictures that he made—I mean, he *was* Dracula! And therefore when we were in Yugoslavia and acting, I was surprised to see him with health food grains and oats and corn flakes and stuff that he carried from England into Yugoslavia in little packets, so he could have them every morning with his breakfast. It all seemed so healthy and normal, I thought it was out of character! He was very amusing and a very nice man...but there was something very *dark* about him too.

And the last of the performers I want to hear about—Vera Miles. What was the Hitchcock-Vera Miles relationship like in the 1960s?
Vera is someone I was very fond of, but I haven't her seen in many, many years. It's interesting you bring her up, because in relation to the hundredth anniversary of Hitchcock's birth, all sorts of people are participating [in various activities], including myself and anyone else who's alive. But not Vera. This is all sort of second-hand, but I think what happened with Vera is that she just wanted to resist the control that Hitch liked to exercise over people who worked for him. I remember that when I was working for him, Sam Spiegel was making a picture in England and wanted Hitch to let me go for a period to produce the picture for him. Hitch said *no* [*laughs*]—Hitch just wouldn't brook anything like that.

There was another actress, Joanna Moore, who did brilliant work on the *Hitchcock* shows. She was a *marvelous* actress. Hitch put her under contract... and he then wanted to change her hairdo and things of that nature. As soon as that happened, Joanna Moore *quit*. I think this was the same thing that happened with Vera—I think Vera had her own life and she wanted to be in control of that. So she just resisted. And as soon as the resistance appeared, Hitch was no longer [interested], because you just couldn't *do* that with Hitch. You had to fit into his "operation," so to speak. I was very fond of Vera, and we used to hire her on the half-hour show. But she seems to have remained aloof from all the celebrations.

The way I've heard it, Hitchcock wanted Vera Miles to star in Vertigo *[1958] —and she may have "rebelled" by getting pregnant.*

I don't know that story that you're telling. But I *do* know that story in relation to Audrey Hepburn! Hitch had a property called *No Bail for the Judge* by Henry Cecil, a *very* good writer who I think *had* been a judge or a barrister. Hitch was going to do it with Audrey Hepburn. The story was of a beautiful young lady who was the daughter of a judge, and this judge was [arrested] for having murdered a prostitute he picked up on the street. The daughter didn't believe he was guilty—and he was *not*, actually. So she posed as a prostitute and walked the streets, hoping to find the murderer. This was the nature of the story.

Hitch had this property and he was going to do it with Hepburn. Hepburn became pregnant by Mel Ferrer, and they then had to postpone. In the meanwhile, during that postponement, the English passed a law saying prostitutes could no longer ply their wares on the street, that they had to sit behind windows and knock on the window as you walked by, to attract the attention of fellows who were looking for prostitutes. They would have signals, or whatever, and the guy would come in the building. This absolutely destroyed Hitch's concept of the work—it *had* to be on the streets, he couldn't see himself shooting people knocking on windows [*laughs*]! So he dropped the property and blamed Mel Ferrer for ruining his picture! Mel is a dear friend of mine, and I never bring it up because I think it's a very sensitive point with him!

You mentioned a ways back that "The Jar" may have been Hitchcock's favorite episode.

He was shooting *Marnie* [1964] at the time, and I called him and said, "If you have time, I'd love to run it for you." Even when he was doing pictures, he would stop for an hour or so to look at the rough cut that we had to bring him, because we had to get 'em on the air. (We would never *dare* go on the air without his approval.) So you'd call him and he'd find time in the course of shooting that day, perhaps in his lunch hour or whatever. I remember running "The Jar" with him and then going back on the set of *Marnie* with him, and he was telling people, "I have just seen a *wonderful* picture"—which I thought was rare for Hitch. I don't think he ever came out and said, "This is *the* best," but I know he always really liked "The Jar."

What was in "The Jar"?

Literally, what did we put in it? A couple of bedsprings; some foam rubber; we made a head for Collin Wilcox and a ribbon with her name on it, a silly sort of "Maisie Sue" name. But the original jar, before Collin Wilcox was beheaded and her head put in it, just had foam rubber, bedsprings...and there was another element in it, something that floated. It *could* have been a piece of fruit [*laughs*]!

And filled with water, also.
Oh, yes, that's right. But, you see, it was just *nothingness*, and that was what was so wonderful about it—because everybody saw his *life* in it.

What were your favorite two or three Hitchcock episodes?
"Lamb to the Slaughter" of Hitch's, certainly, and Bob Stevens' "Specialty of the House." And, I think, "Man from the South." Then, later on, "The Jar" perhaps, or "Juan Diaz." Oh—*whoa!*—do you remember one Joe Cotten did, called "Breakdown"? The one that ends with the tear coming down Joe's face? *Wow*, how could I forget that? Magnificent!

James Allardice, who wrote Hitchcock's intros and exits—what was he like?
James Allardice, in one word, was *a genius*. (Did I use two words there, "a genius"?) He...was...*remarkable*. He was a little fellow, he was built and looked a little like Woody Allen, and he had the greatest humor. And anything he wrote, Hitch would do. Jimmy would put Hitch inside a bottle; he would put Hitch on with a lion; he would put Hitch in knickers, as a golfer; Hitch would play his own brother, Arthur Hitchcock, or whatever his name was—Allardice would write these things, and Hitch spoke *every word he ever wrote*, and never questioned a word. He did that for every show for ten years. *Plus*, when *Psycho* [1960] was a big hit and audiences had to line up outside the theater, there was a tape of Hitch talking to them, a tape that would be playing for the line waiting to get in. Jimmy wrote *that*, too. He was *great*. He came from Yale; he had the show *At War With the Army* on Broadway, and that was a hit; and then turned it into a script for Martin and Lewis [for the 1950 movie version], which was also a hit. Then he wrote on the first year of *The George Gobel Show*, which was *another* hit. MCA represented him, and they took him *off* that and put him with Hitch. Whoever thought of that deserves a few million dollars [*laughs*]! I *cannot* speak highly enough about Jimmy Allardice.

And a nice guy, on top of all this?
Oh, a *dream*. By the way, we'd shoot about six stories, and we would then send the synopses over to Jimmy and ask him to write for Hitch. We'd send them to him about ten days to two weeks ahead of time. And we'd wait. Then we'd call him in about a week: "How are things going, Jimmy?" "Oh, I haven't started yet...I'll get around to it..." And then, a few days later, we'd call again: "Oh, yeah, yeah," he'd say, "I haven't got anything yet, but..." *Now* it was (let's say) the Friday before the Monday when we were going to shoot these things, and he'd say, "I'll get 'em done over the weekend." And that's how he wrote—he had to write right up against the deadline. He couldn't write unless it was gonna be shot tomorrow [*laughs*]! *That* [deadline pressure] would give Jimmy "the electric shock," and he would take off and do this work, which I think had genius in it. They were *brilliant*—so creative and marvelous. Just wonderful!

I just found an old TV Guide *article that featured a tidbit I'd never read before—it said that Hitchcock would come in and do his opening and closing scenes in English, and then he would do 'em in French and German. Is there any truth to that?*

I never remember his doing them in French and German. It is *possible* that they were done without my knowing about it, at another time, but the only ones I know about were the ones he did in English. Now, he was very proud of the show doing so well in Japan, and he used to describe how the Japanese wrote [the translated dialogue] perpendicularly along the side of the film, he thought that was great! The show played in France and Germany but I don't recall his ever doing [his opening and closing comments] in French and German. Way, way back, he *started* in Germany, in a way, so maybe he *was* able to do the German; then, during the War, he did a documentary in French. So it's possible he worked in those languages. But I was never aware of it.

I read somewhere that Allardice's passing was a factor in Hitchcock deciding not to continue with the show.

That was a theory advanced by others. The real reason was that Hitch didn't want to do it any more. He felt ten years was enough, and he had a lot of other things to do.

You also had Robert Bloch working on the series.

Robert Bloch was a favorite of mine, a darling, darling man. Some writers who write that kind of stuff *look* like the stuff they write—you say, "Oh, he's capable of murder, no question." Robert Bloch didn't *at all*—he was a very nice man. He wrote the one show we never were able to release because of censorship, the one ["The Sorcerer's Apprentice"] where Diana Dors was sawed in half. She was in a carnival act where she was "sawed in half" by her magician-husband [David J. Stewart]. And Brandon de Wilde [playing a retarded boy] saw this and thought he could do it— and he *really* sawed her in half! We couldn't release that one—and that was a Bob Bloch story. I don't have an anecdote about Bob, except to say that he was a wonderful writer of that kind of material.

After Bob Bloch wrote the book *Psycho*, Hitch gave that book, strangely enough, *not* to Bob to dramatize but to another writer who had done *outstandingly* fine work for us on the *Hitchcock* show. He had done such good work that his reward was to do *Psycho*. But when it came to the moment in the book when Norman Bates moves a picture on the wall and reveals a peephole and looks through it into the shower, this writer *eliminated* that. And it was *precisely* at that point that Hitchcock put down the script and said, "There's no need for me to read any more. He doesn't understand the story." That was when Hitch hired Joseph Stefano [to write the *Psycho* screenplay]. What is interesting from the Bob Bloch point of view is [the fact that] this was in Bloch's book. How *strong* his visual elements were, that Hitch brought to the screen.

How strong Bloch's visual elements were.

Yes, his suggestions, which were done so brilliantly by Hitch. By the way, Mrs. Hitchcock [Alma Reville] was so important in Hitch's entire career— Hitch never released a film before he ran it alone with her. When she saw *Psycho*, all ready to be shipped, she said, "You can't ship it." (It was in a composite print already.) She said, "You can't ship it" and he asked, "Why not?" Remember the scene after Janet Leigh's death, where the camera pulls back from her open eye? She said, "When the camera pulled back from Janet Leigh, *she swallowed once.*" Now what is interesting about that is that *Psycho* went through the hands of cutters, of sound cutters, of music cutters; had been run and run and run; and nobody spotted it but Mrs. Hitchcock! That was one reason that his faith in her was limitless—her opinion meant more to him than anybody else's.

Is the swallow still in the movie?
No. They had to go to the composite print and take out one frame.

When you'd hire old-time directors for Hitchcock—people like John Brahm and Robert Florey, guys who were used to making movies—did they shoot fast enough for TV?
Absolutely. Brahm was a wiz—as a matter of fact, he adapted in such a way that it was almost a *model*, the way he shot. Actually, Robert Stevens was our most brilliant director—exclusive of Hitch—but Brahm was terrific, because he figured out a way of shooting that fitted television very well. He was absolutely on the button. And Robert Florey too, in a more gentle way, in a more remote way, in a less *energetic* way. But his own cinematic style. They adapted very well indeed, yes.

John Brahm was a good friend of mine. He had come out of the theater in Europe and he was highly considered, he had a big hit in *The Lodger* [1944] with Laird Cregar, he had been married to a movie star (Dolly Haas, who later divorced him and married Al Hirschfeld the cartoonist). John was a man of culture, he knew theater, he knew good actors *from* the theater, he knew "the traditions"—all of which have disappeared today, by the way. He was an admirable fellow and a delight to work with.

Did you ever run across a story that you would have loved to do on Hitchcock...*but realized that, no matter how much you monkeyed with it, the censors wouldn't permit it?*
I honestly cannot say I remember one. My favorite story about that is the *reverse*: Sometimes Hitch would like a story and we would discuss it, and one day we were discussing a story which *I* didn't think was very good. But Hitch wanted to do it. In the story, a bomb was the gimmick. I told Hitch that I really didn't think very highly of the story—and Hitch said to me [*imitating Hitchcock again*], "Nawwwm...a bomb is *always* a good thing." [*Laughs*] In other words, he was saying, "*Do* the story, because the bomb'll save it!"

In a picture called *Sabotage* [1936] with Sylvia Sidney and Oscar Homolka, Hitch had one of his most extraordinary sequences with a kid carrying the bomb and not knowing it. The kid gets on a bus and the bus gets frozen in traffic, and Hitch kept intercutting that with a clock which was moving up to 12 o'clock—and the audience knows the bomb's gonna go *off* at 12. And it *did* go off, and it blew up the bus, the kid and everybody else. But Hitch always said, "I never should have blown up that boy." It was a brilliant sequence, but he had no solution, you see.

Back in the Alfred Hitchcock Presents *days, you often had to worry about the censors. And now, today, when censors wouldn't be a problem, the TV "powers-*

that-be" probably wouldn't want this kind of sophisticated material! Is that a source of frustration?

It was in those days *to a degree*. What'll amuse you is this: Whenever I got into a discussion about censorship of a particular story with Broadcast Standards [the network censors], I would finally fall back on Shakespeare. I'd say, "Now, look—in *King Lear*, they stamp out the guy's *eyes*! 'Out, out, vile jelly!' Now, are you gonna tell me I can't cut Diana Dors in half?!" After a while, the guy would say, "You *cannot* saw Diana Dors in half—*and don't quote Shakespeare!*" [*Laughs*]

The biggest problems were always solved by Jimmy Allardice, with Hitch's [closing comments]. There was at that time the requirement of *retribution*—in a program, if a person killed somebody or committed a theft or did *any*thing unlawful, you had to have some form of retribution. So *we* used to do it by having *Hitch* do it—which, obviously, the audience never believed! For example, in "Lamb to the Slaughter," Barbara Bel Geddes kills her husband with a frozen leg of lamb. Then she puts it in the oven, cooks it and serves it to the police —who of course can never find the evidence, and she goes off scot-free. *Now* comes retribution: We don't do it *in the story*, but *Hitch* comes on and says, "She remarried, and she got very upset with this new husband and decided to do away with him too. So she hit him over the head with the leg of lamb...but the freezer had gone on the blink and it hadn't *frozen* quite. It was a *soft* leg of lamb, and she was caught." Who believed *that*? We'd *done* the story. That's the way we'd get away with it.

They say that imitation is the sincerest form of flattery; I'm not sure that it is. Do you happen to know what Hitchcock thought of the people who imitated him? People like William Castle, for instance.

He was *impervious* to that. He was like a great mountain [*laughs*], letting the wind go by. They're remaking *every*thing of his now—*Psycho*, *Rear Window* [1954] and quite a few others. And they'll never "capture" it. Like the new [1998] *Psycho*—they're going to shoot it with the original script, shot by shot. They'll *never* get it the way he got it. They'll never get *anything* the way he got it. Because what he had was something "between the lines," so to speak. It was an overtone. It was something in the way he saw things. And his pictures were done with great *simplicity* at times. Not only did he have a great cinematic gift, a great visual gift, but he had a gift of simplicity. Today with their lenses and booms and all the different cameras and so on—you can't capture it that way!

Nothing antagonizes me more than when a director yanks you out of the story with some show-offy camera flourish. Even Spielberg can't seem to understand this!

Oh, it's *true*! It's absolutely true!

You talked about Hitchcock's practical jokes before. Were you ever the "victim" of one of them?

No. I tried to *perform* a couple, all of which fell flat. I tried to make them in such a way that Hitch would be involved, but I always laid an egg [*laughs*]! I once made up in blackface when he was at the St. Regis [Hotel] in New York—I thought it'd be great. I knew he was due to take a plane, and I was going to go over and have a drink with him or a cup of tea or something. But on the way over, I bought some Stein's Blackface

Makeup and a mirror in Walgreen's Drug Store, where all the actors bought everything, and I went over to the hotel. I got upstairs—he was on the fourteenth floor, I remember—and in the hallway, I made up. (I realize, now that I look back on this, I could have been easily arrested as a blackface *thief* caught in the St. Regis! But fortunately I got away with it!) I knocked on the door of his suite and Alma opened it, and I quickly took my hat off and showed my full head of red hair and said, "Alma, it's Norman, it's Norman." And I told her I wanted to sort of see how Hitch would react. She said, "He's downstairs in the King Cole Bar!"—*she* went with the joke right away. She said, "Let's have him come up, and see what happens!" So I put the hat back on and she phoned down to Hitch and she said, "It's getting time to go." Then she told me, "*You* open the door." And I did—there I was in blackface with the hat pulled over my red hair and the collar up; I thought he might jump a foot or two. He looked ...and he said, "Nawwwm...we'll be late for the plane..." [*Laughs*] *That* was my "practical joke"!

Oh, I loved Hitch, and I loved Alma. The story I just told you I really told for the benefit of Alma, because she was just a wonderful, wonderful person. And she went with it right away! Once I brought Richard Conte over to meet Alma or something—Hitch was coming in from New York on a plane—and I said, "Alma, suppose we get dressed up as cops?" (You know about Hitchcock's fear of the police.) I asked, "Suppose we get dressed up as cops and meet him at the plane and say we have a warrant for him, as he gets off?" Alma said, "Oh, that's great! Oh, that's a *wonderful* idea!" But Dick Conte and I ran out of guts, we were afraid to do it [*laughs*]. I cite it only because Alma would go along with it if *we* would have *done* it!

Did you have any contact with Rod Serling when you were in the Night Gallery *episode "A Feast of Blood"?*

None—he wasn't around at all. My leading lady was the very beautiful Sondra Locke, and [in the story] I was madly in love with her and gave her a pin which grew and grew and grew until it devoured her [*laughs*]! It was directed by a short fellow named Jeannot Szwarc —I don't know what's happened to him!—and the producer was Jack Laird, a good producer with a very good story sense.

Were you involved with Roald Dahl's TV series Tales of the Unexpected *right from the beginning?*

I knew Roald Dahl because I had directed Patricia Neal in a production of *The Cocktail Party* at La Jolla. Eventually she came to New York and started going with Roald Dahl, whom she eventually married, and I met Dahl through Patricia Neal. Dahl sold us several stories for the *Hitchcock* show—I think we did almost all of Dahl that we could *do* on the *Hitchcock* show, including the great Hitch one, "Lamb to the Slaughter." Then time passed; the *Hitchcock* show was over; and Dahl in the course of human events began to catch on as a writer. These wonderful short stories he wrote were not giving him much of a living, and he eventually hit on this gold mine of children's stories— which has made his estate worth millions.

Dahl told [English producer] John Wolf that the rights to all his old short stories came back to him, and sold him

Roald Dahl's Tales of the Unexpected.
Roald did the lead-ins like Hitch did. Then at the beginning of the second or third year, they ran out of Roald Dahl stories and he gradually lost interest in it. They were making all these stories in England, and at that point they decided to make a number in the United States. And so they called me and asked me if I would produce them, under the aegis of [advertising agency] J. Walter Thompson. I produced and directed a couple of 'em over here, and Wolf kept doing them over there in England—in fact, he did *most* of them over there. I would do about half a dozen a year over here. But he had people like Gielgud and Wendy Hiller—Gielgud did about five of them!

Were you pleased with the work you were able to do on Tales of the Unexpected?

Oh, yes, very much so. And I got some good people—Arthur Hill and Sharon Gless and people like that. But not the movie stars who we got on *Hitchcock.*

And the TV series Journey to the Unknown—*what was the story on that?*

Journey to the Unknown was produced in England. I was asked to produce the series by Fox, and at precisely the same time I got an offer to direct a film in Italy. So I suggested to Fox (and they took the suggestion) that Joan Harrison do it. Well, she said she would do it, but on a limited basis because she had married Eric Ambler, the great thriller writer, and she didn't want to devote her life to a series. So she started it, shooting in England, while meanwhile I went to Italy to do my picture, which like *alllll* the Italian pictures I've ever done was never made [*laughs*]! The Italians, I *love* them, I just think they're the most wonderful people in the world, but if you want a frustrating time, get involved in a deal trying to make a movie with them!

I found myself in Rome after nine weeks of no movie, when I heard suddenly from Joan that she had done four or five of these and she really wanted to devote more time to Eric. So I came over and took over on *Journey to the Unknown.* In those instances, we used to import the lead from America—we brought over Patty Duke and Roddy McDowall and Chad Everett and so forth, well-known actors.

Around that same time, you had a small part in Robert Wise's reincarnation drama Audrey Rose *[1977].*

I thought right from the beginning "This picture will not be successful" because you can't end it with the death of a child. I just couldn't understand the [thought processes of] these *very* smart people—this wonderful guy Robert Wise, one of the gents of our business, and Anthony Hopkins was in it, and the author [Frank DeFelitta] was around. I played that great last scene—not that *I* was great, but it was a great scene—of bringing this child back [from a previous life]...that finally killed her! I said, "I appreciate the scene, gents, but...can't we work out something else? I mean, the audience will never go to *see* this!"—and they didn't! And the book had been a runaway best-seller, which proves people will take something, sitting in the armchair reading, that they won't take when they see it up on the screen. That's what happened there. But I enjoyed working with Bob Wise, and the child [Susan Swift] was a very good actress, and Hopkins, of course, was first-rate.

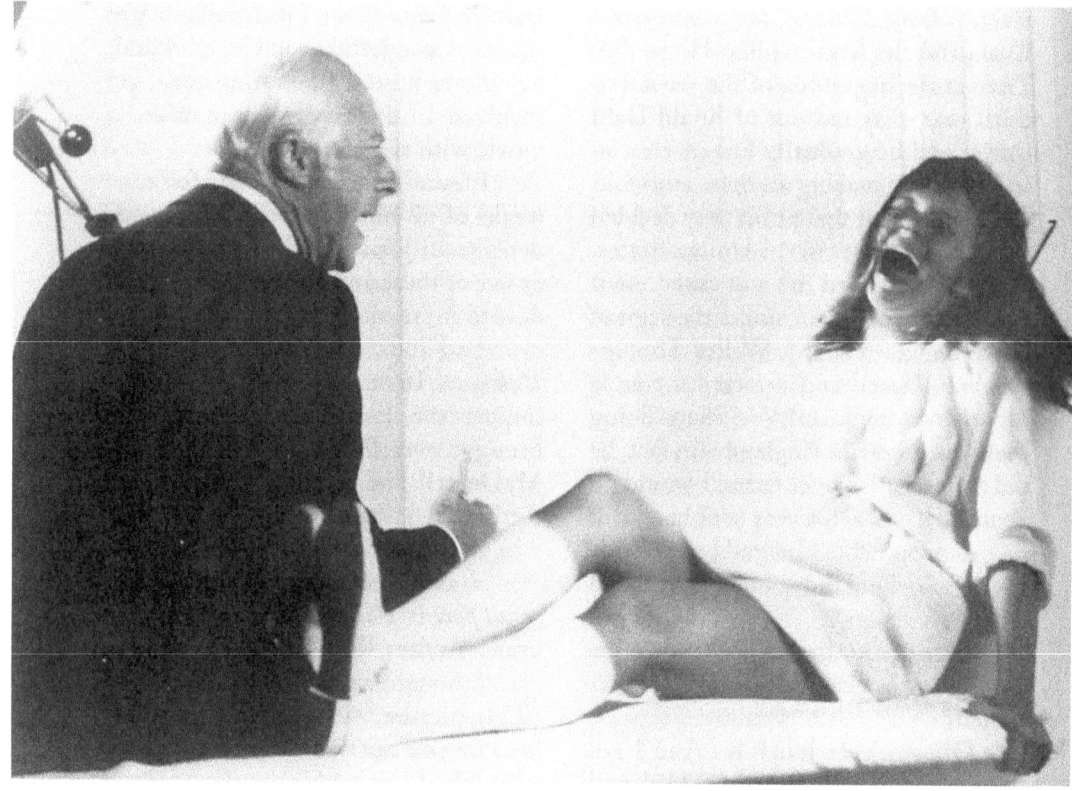

Lloyd knew right from the outset that *Audrey Rose* would flop, because it ended with the death of a child (Susan Swift, right).

It's just that that story was too depressing.

Did you have any association with the Alfred Hitchcock revival series in the mid-1980s?

I wouldn't go *near* it. I was against the whole idea. They did them in color, which defeated it right away—and then took Hitch's lead-ins, put them in color and used *those*! Disgusting...destructive... terrible! Terrible idea!

You said you wouldn't go near them—but were you offered a chance to go near them?

I don't think so—I do not recall an offer, and I'm almost certain I wasn't. And I think with good reason—they may have heard that I was shooting my mouth off around town about the *stupidity* of doing it. Which I am now saying about the stupidity of doing his pictures over again.

You've done so many suspense and "thriller" movies, often in creepy parts. Do you feel an attraction to these parts, or are you typecast?

I think people think of me as a *strange type* [*laughs*]—and therefore say, "*He's* strange, let's put him in!" Although, on *St. Elsewhere*, I played a most compassionate and sympathetic and *humanistic* doctor. For six years! So that was quite different from the genre you're talking about. And when I was with Orson Welles [in the Mercury Theatre], it was in Shakespeare and Elizabethan drama. So, with Welles, it was more of a humanistic theater too.

But you are sometimes associated with this macabre stuff, and I was wondering what the plusses and minuses were.

I don't think there's anything one way or another—I don't think people say, "Oh, he was in (whatever), so we must get him because this is sci-fi." For instance, *Seven Days*—getting this job had nothing to do with my [screen image], it just had to do with the fact that I gave a guy a job as a go-fer 20 years ago [*laughs*]!

Norman Lloyd Filmography

Saboteur (Universal, 1942)
The Unseen (Paramount, 1945)
The Southerner (United Artists, 1945)
Within These Walls (20th Century–Fox, 1945)
Spellbound (United Artists, 1945)
A Letter for Evie (MGM, 1945)
A Walk in the Sun (*Salerno Beachhead*) (20th Century–Fox, 1945)
Young Widow (United Artists, 1946)
The Green Years (MGM, 1946)
The Beginning or the End (MGM, 1947)
No Minor Vices (MGM, 1948)
Scene of the Crime (MGM, 1949)
Reign of Terror (*The Black Book*) (Eagle-Lion, 1949)
Calamity Jane and Sam Bass (Universal, 1949)
Buccaneer's Girl (Universal, 1950)
The Flame and the Arrow (Warners, 1950)
The Light Touch (MGM, 1951)
M (Columbia, 1951)
He Ran All the Way (United Artists, 1951)
Flame of Stamboul (Columbia, 1951)
Limelight (United Artists, 1952)
Dark Intruder (voice only; Universal, 1965)
Audrey Rose (United Artists, 1977)
FM (Universal, 1978)
The Nude Bomb (*The Return of Maxwell Smart*) (Universal, 1980)
Jaws of Satan (*King Cobra*) (United Artists, 1984)
Dead Poets Society (Touchstone/Buena Vista, 1989)
Journey of Honor (*Shogun Mayeda*) (Rocket Pictures, 1992)
The Age of Innocence (Columbia, 1993)
The Adventures of Rocky & Bullwinkle (Universal, 2000)

Maureen O'Sullivan

*There was a period when I got so sick of all they
would ask me about Tarzan, as though I had done nothing else.
...I changed my mind when my oldest son said to me
he was very proud that I was Tarzan's mate.*

Ask a Tarzan movie fan to name his favorite Tarzan, and any one of a half-dozen names is liable to be offered up. Favorite *Jane*—there's a much more shallow pool of nominees in *that* category, partly because there have been less Janes than Tarzans, but primarily because Maureen O'Sullivan, who played the scandalously clad role in a half-dozen of the MGM Johnny Weissmuller jungle adventures, has become such an iconoclastic screen figure that her successors pale by comparison.

Before teaching the niceties of civilization to her "King of the Jungle" mate, O'Sullivan was Irish-born and convent-educated; she never studied acting prior to her 1930 screen bow. The pretty ingenue made her Tarzan debut in 1932's *Tarzan the Ape Man* and reprised the role in five follow-ups (*Tarzan and His Mate*, 1934, *Tarzan Escapes*, 1936, *Tarzan Finds a Son!*, 1939, *Tarzan's Secret Treasure*, 1941, and *Tarzan's New York Adventure*, 1942) before retiring from fulltime filmmaking in 1942 to bring up her children (a total of seven). The elegant actress made occasional movie appearances during the ensuing two decades, sometimes in films by her director-husband John Farrow, then Broadway-debuted in 1962 and began an active career on the Great White Way. But despite her refined roles in many movie and stage classics, O'Sullivan remains permanently linked with the jungle yodeler, both in the minds of fans and on Hollywood Boulevard, where her Walk of Fame star is beside Johnny Weissmuller's. O'Sullivan died at Arizona's Scottsdale Memorial Hospital in 1998. [**Interview by Tom Weaver and Ray Nielsen.**]

Tom Weaver: The screen test for your Tarzan movies was directed by Felix Feist. What did you do in it?

I don't remember exactly, to tell you the honest truth, but it was like a scene out of a Tarzan. It was not jumping around or anything like that, but it was probably an energetic scene for a girl, or energetic *talking*, you know. In other words, something that would show her character, that she wasn't just a simp wandering around the jungle. Whatever it was, it came out well, I guess; I never did see it. But it *must* have come out well, or I wouldn't have got the part.

TW: Was there a Tarzan in the test with you, or were you alone?

I think I was alone, but I could be wrong. I know there was not a Tarzan; there might have been a father or some other character. But I truly can't remember.

TW: At the time, you were 19 and behind in your rent, so you were probably very anxious to land the part.

I was the kind of girl who didn't worry very much about anything. I'd got to Hollywood quite by accident, really, and I figured, if I got the part, fine, if I didn't, there'd be something else. I wasn't a bit dreary about anything, or worried, *really*, except I *was* $150 behind in my rent, which was one month's rent at the Garden of Allah where I was staying.

TW: Tarzan director "Woody" Van Dyke had somebody else in mind for the part of Jane.

Yes, it seems there *was* another girl—whose name I've forgotten. But

The King of the Jungle and his beautiful Queen: Johnny Weissmuller and Maureen O'Sullivan (from *Tarzan Finds a Son!*).

she *was* up for the part, and "Woody" Van Dyke apparently wanted her. And the producer wanted *me*. Anyway, I got the part. "Woody" used to say this about *every*thing I was in: "Honey, I didn't want you in this, but now that you're *in* it, I think you're wonderful." I don't know what *that* was supposed to mean [*laughs*]!

Ray Nielsen: I remember talking to you ten years ago and we sort of touched on Tarzan, and you weren't too keen on it. You were weary of all the Tarzan talk. I

Johnny Sheffield (Boy) flanked by his "jungle mother and father," during the making of *Tarzan's New York Adventure*.

understand you've gone through some sort of a metamorphosis.

It does sound that way, doesn't it? Yes, I have. After all, by now Tarzan has gone into history.

RN: It's so enduring.

Yes, it's quite remarkable, and I think I've really changed. Well, I was doing stage work, a *lot* of stage work, and other films, and, well, there *was* a period when I got so sick of all they would ask me about Tarzan, as though I had done nothing else. Whereas I had been around a long time. So I suppose that was what I meant. Anyway, I changed my mind when my oldest son said to me he was very proud that I was Tarzan's mate. And then I did feel differently about the whole thing. I felt, well, if this next generation, *his* generation, is that proud of me, that's very wonderful, you know?

RN: How did a young colleen from Roscommon County, Ireland, get to Hollywood in the first place?

Well, that was sort of one of those freak things. It was through a film [*Song o' My Heart*, 1930] with John McCormack, the great Irish tenor, the one film that he made, or the one *big* one. They were shooting it in Ireland, and I happened to meet the director, Frank Borzage. I was at a dance, and he sent his card over to the table, very polite in those days, asking if I was interested in being in films and would I come to his office the next day at 11 o'clock.

RN: And were you interested? Was acting something you'd thought about?

Well, I'd never, no, I'd never really thought about that at all. As a matter of fact, there were several very beautiful

Sheffield, O'Sullivan and Weissmuller in *Tarzan's Secret Treasure.*

girls in Dublin, and it was in all the papers about the film, and I had sent some of my friends to be interviewed by him. I said, "Well, look, you are Dublin's most beautiful girls, you should go." Well, it seems that he didn't want Dublin's most beautiful girls. He wanted somebody that was Irish and round-faced with freckles like me. And so, anyway, to make a very long story short, I got the part and came to Hollywood with my mother, and here we were. And then later, the studio, Fox Films, fired me and said I was poison at the box office.

RN: Some pretty good actresses have had that said about them, Katharine Hepburn, for one.

Yes, but they hadn't at that time. Anyway, I was fired, and then Johnny Considine [movie producer John W. Considine, Jr.] got me an agent, one of his relatives, and he got me a test. I only had $150 in my entire fortune, and I was living at the Garden of Allah. That was $150-a-month's rent, which was all I had. Fox had fired me, and I had $150. So Johnny Considine, who was being kind to me, said, "You should have some wonderful photographs taken. I'll send my cousin over to represent you." So a very nice man called Tom Conlon, I'll never forget him, took me across the street, and I had these smashing photographs taken which cost $150 so I couldn't pay the rent. Then he took them out to MGM, and they decided to give me a test.

RN: You met Edgar Rice Burroughs on the set of the first Tarzan movie.

Yes, I did. When I signed my contract at MGM, I was taken on a tour of the sets—somebody from the publicity department took me around all the sets, and showed me the back lot and where we would be shooting and showed me the different stages and projection and so on. Then whoever was showing me around took me on a set, and Edgar Rice Burroughs was there watching a test they were shooting of Johnny—that was how we met. Johnny was standing with just that loin cloth, and he was holding a spear in his hand, and he had his foot on a lion that was supposedly dead. It was probably a prop, I don't know. Anyway, he was supposed to spear this lion. It was very effective, and he raised his arm, and he had the golden makeup on—I had never seen anybody look so terrific. So, then Mr. Rice Burroughs took me over to the director, and the director introduced me [to Weissmuller], he said, "Johnny, here's your Jane." So that was the way I started.

TW: Was that the only time you met Edgar Rice Burroughs?

Yes, until we started the film, and then I met him quite a lot. We became nice friends, Edgar Rice Burroughs and I, and I liked him, and I guess *he* liked *me*. He would invite me to his place in Tarzana and I met Mrs. Burroughs, and they had a dog called Tarzan. It was nice; I used to go there on Sundays sometimes.

I was always strangely truthful, which I don't know is a good idea or not. He asked me if I knew about Tarzan. Well, I didn't. I had read Rider Haggard, so I knew a little bit about the jungles, but I never *had* read any Tarzan books. So he said, "Well, I'll send you some." So he sent me one copy of every Tarzan book that he'd written, each of them inscribed in a different way to me. By the time he'd reached his last one—I forget how many there are, ten or some-

Even though Edgar Rice Burroughs gave O'Sullivan copies of every Tarzan book, "I'd *played* them, so why *read* them?" (Photograph from *Tarzan and His Mate*.)

thing—in the last one he wrote, "By now your education in Tarzan should be complete." It was very nice, and I do treasure those books.

TW: Did you read them all?
[*Pause*] Noooooo.

TW: Did you read any *of them?*
I'd *played* them, so why *read* them? [*Laughs*]

TW: In the earliest Tarzan movies, your wardrobe is very skimpy. Did that make you self-conscious at all?
I didn't think it was so skimpy. What was it now, I've forgotten...the outfit torn up the side? No, I thought it was appropriate for where I was. It *wouldn't* have been appropriate to wear at Buckingham Palace, or to church or something [*laughs*], but it was appropriate for what I was doing. So, no, it didn't worry me at all—*until* I started getting mail about it. And I thought, "Well, people are crazy. They have to write about *some*thing." If they didn't write about that, then they wrote about they liked me—it was one thing or the other. I did get a lot of mail on my costume and I thought, "Do people really have nothing to do except write to strangers?" [*Laughs*]

TW: In the movies, Tarzan's jungle looks like a paradise. What was the MGM back lot really like?

The back lot was "in pieces"—short bits here and bits there. We did have a lake on the back lot, and then we had a nice jungle built out at Lake Sherwood, toward Santa Barbara. They had a lake there and they had a forest there—whether they built it or whether it was natural, I've forgotten. So that was "natural" to work in. Pick-up shots, closeups and so on, if necessary, we did on the back lot.

TW: You have a stunt double in all your movies, but I was wondering if you were ever asked to do anything you would have preferred not doing.

I *was* asked to do something: In the second Tarzan [*Tarzan and His Mate*], they were trying to outdo the first Tarzan, so they were trying to be very experimental and very daring. I remember them asking me to stand nude behind the tents, and they would put a light behind me so you could see my nude shadow. I objected to that—and I forget what happened! But I did object to that because I thought it was...you know, cheap. And not necessary, it had nothing to do with the story anyway. That was the only thing I ever objected to. [Stunt-wise], no, they never asked me to do anything to do anything dangerous. I mean, they would ask me if I wanted to do such-and-such a shot, which any normal 20-year-old girl would do, you know, jump from here to there. I mean, not that I was an athlete, I *wasn't*, but, you know, at that age you're not too careful. But they wouldn't let you do anything where you would endanger yourself, *naturally*, not only because of yourself but because of endangering the film.

RN: Cedric Gibbons started out directing Tarzan and His Mate. *He had been an art director before, and this was his first time directing a film. And about midway through, he was pulled off.*

Not even midway, right in the beginning. It was strange. Cedric Gibbons was the art director at MGM and very important and did all those beautiful sets for which MGM is remembered. But he wasn't a motion picture director. So, I don't suppose he really knew too much about actors and cutting.

RN: I wonder why they gave him that shot in the first place.

I think the reason behind that would be that he did such beautiful things with his sets, and telling people what to shoot. If you remember those sets of those times, they were extraordinary even for the B pictures and smaller pictures. They were wonderful, and I think they felt that the sheer beauty and the talent that he had, he could bring off any kind of very beautiful film. Which, of course, he couldn't do because you have to know the technique, and you have to know the actors, and the sound man, and the prop man, and all these pedestrian things. So, he wasn't a director.

TW: In Esther Williams' autobiography, she writes about swimming—and being groped underwater—by Johnny Weissmuller at aquacades.

Really? I never heard anything like that about Johnny—never. *ever*. This is all news to me. Well, I suppose *she* appealed to him, and I didn't [*laughs*]. Oh, Johnny was wonderful, I really loved Johnny like a brother. There was never any romance or anything like that—well, there *couldn't* have been anyway, he was always married to somebody else during the run of these Tarzan films. We were like brother and sister, and we had *fun* together. But long working hours and trying to do our best—there's an awful lot of waiting on any film, and particularly a Tarzan one. In those days they didn't use quite so many doubles and special effects, and so we had to wait for the animals to do whatever they were supposed to do. Sometimes it took a long time. So there was a lot of sitting around on those Tarzans, believe it or not, so Johnny and I got to know each other...to the point of boredom, actually! (Not really, but you know what I mean.) And there certainly was no romance. The studio tried to "engineer" a romance—they had Johnny take me out one night to the Trocadero. Johnny was late to pick me up; *I* fell asleep waiting for him—I'd seen him all day anyway [*laughs*]! And that was the end of that, they never asked us again!

He was wonderful, Johnny was. He was a big kid. He was fun. He was just what he looked like. He loved to laugh. He had no pretensions whatever about being champion swimmer or any of those awards that he had won—national and worldwide awards. He had no feeling about that. He was just like anybody else, like a prop man or like one of the electricians. He was just a real nice guy. And a good friend. I was very fond of Johnny.

TW: You were in so many really terrific MGM movies like Anna Karenina *and* David Copperfield *[both 1935]. After you'd gotten a taste of movies like those, and now you're trudging back to make yet another Tarzan movie, were you still enjoying that experience?*

Well, probably not. People usually ask me that question in a different way, they say, "How was it you 'grew' in your acting, to be able to *do The Barretts of Wimpole Street* (let's say) when you

O'Sullivan and friend on the set of 1936's *Tarzan Escapes.*

O'Sullivan's revealing jungle costume raised eyebrows—and the ire of some audience members—during the actress' "Jane" phase.

started out in *Tarzan*?" What they don't realize is, I probably was shooting a Tarzan in the morning, and then I would have to change my costume and go on to another film, 'cause we were contract players. I remember doing as many as three films a day, three *different* films. That's the way we shot them; I don't know if it's still that way or not. I didn't *like* it very much—you have to get all that body makeup off, and then get into a crinoline. But I don't see any

O'Sullivan says there was never any real-life romance with Johnny Weissmuller. Maybe it was the lack of privacy.

progression in my acting or anything like that, I think it was always the same. Same person, you know.

TW: By the time you were making your last Tarzan movie, had your feelings about working in the series changed?

The last one was *Tarzan's New York Adventure*, and I never saw that film. I didn't enjoy doing it. I'd already told the studio I was leaving—I really had *had* it, after all those years.

TW: You'd had it with Tarzan, or you'd had it with MGM?

It was the same thing! The first shot I ever did at MGM was a Tarzan and the *last* shot I did at MGM was a Tarzan—there was *always* a Tarzan, in the morning, or in the afternoon, or in the evening. It was one continual Tarzan. And the scripts weren't as good, and I didn't like the idea much of Tarzan in New York, no. I didn't care for that film, I didn't care much for the script. I missed our old jungle days.

TW: What other Tarzan actors have impressed you?

I never saw [the other Tarzans].

O'Sullivan eventually tired of the Tarzan rut—and who could blame her?

People find this hard to understand, but as a matter of fact it was a looong time before I saw *my* first Tarzan. Because we didn't have *time*! They didn't run the films for us (I don't know if they do now or not), so unless we caught a preview out of town, say Riverside or somewhere where they previewed the pictures, we didn't get to see our films for maybe *ages*. There was nowhere to see them if you were working all day—*and* we worked in the evenings, because this was before the Guild [Screen Actors Guild guidelines], a lot of it. So we didn't have time to take makeup off and get dressed and go down Hollywood Boulevard looking for a movie. A lot of the movies, to tell you the truth, I didn't see. Didn't see *to this day,* unless I saw them on TV.

TW: You were pregnant when you did Tarzan Finds a Son!—

Yes, I was.

TW: And according to one book, MGM thought about replacing you.

Did they? They probably did.

TW: Would that have broken your heart?

No. I think I might have been *insulted* slightly, but I wouldn't have grieved, no.

TW: There's a script of Tarzan Finds a Son! *where Jane is hit in the back with a spear and dies. In the movie, she's hit with a spear and survives. There's a question as to whether the death scene was filmed or not.*

Yes, it *was* filmed. It was also coincidentally my last day of shooting. I had already said that if I was condemned to Tarzan *always*, I didn't want to continue any more. I was getting older (what the hell was I?, 20-something), I was married, I was having a baby, my husband was successful, and I thought, "Do I want

On the opening night of the play *The Subject Was Roses* (1966), O'Sullivan is greeted by her newlywed daughter Mia Farrow Sinatra.

to keep on doing this until people are *sick* of me?" So I had already handed in my notice.* So, yes, that's true, they shot that. But MGM had to check everything very carefully with the Rice Burroughs office, and they found that Tarzan could not be killed, according to contract, and Jane couldn't either. So after they shot the film, they had to shoot a new scene and say that Jane was only wounded, or something like that. At any rate, she wasn't dead, 'cause that was against their contract.

RN: Johnny Sheffield, who played Boy, told me in very emotional terms about the kind of family you had there on the set, the things that he learned from playing Boy and having the good parental relationship there.

Well, I suppose he was of that age, impressionable. We were on the set and we worked long hours. We'd be there, on the set, we'd be ready by seven in the morning to catch the light, and then we'd work until dark. And, you know, that takes the place of a day in an ordinary life, and I suppose it all became very real to Johnny that we were his jungle mother and jungle father. It must have been very real to a little boy.

RN: Yes, it was. He's told me so.

He's a nice guy now. It was a happy time, really. We had a very happy time then.

TW: What do you do to keep busy today?

Well...I *don't* keep very busy [*laughs*]! I feel I'm entitled to my laziness. I try and cope with fan mail—believe it or not, I get an *awful* lot of fan mail. I can imagine what's gonna happen when the [American Movie Classics Tarzan] festival comes along. I can't really keep up with it, it's just staggering.

I just enjoy life...I have friends, and I'm not doing anything in particular. I've thought of writing a memoir, but I think Mia [actress daughter Mia Farrow] has done such a good job on that, her youth. Have you read her book? Oh, you must read it, you'll like it very much! *What Falls Away* [1997], it's called. You don't have to read about Woody Allen, you can read the beginning part [*laughs*]! It's a lovely, very well-written book and I'm very proud of her. So I started writing and then I thought, no, I won't, I'll leave it at that.

Maureen O'Sullivan Filmography

Song o' My Heart (Fox, 1930)
So This Is London (Fox, 1930)
Just Imagine (Fox, 1930)
Princess and the Plumber (Fox, 1930)
A Connecticut Yankee (Fox, 1931)
Skyline (Fox, 1931)
The Big Shot (RKO, 1931)
The Silver Lining (United Artists, 1931)
Okay America (Universal, 1932)
Fast Companions (*Information Kid*) (Universal, 1932)
Tarzan the Ape Man (MGM, 1932)

O'Sullivan appeared in two more Tarzans after Tarzan Finds a Son!: Tarzan's Secret Treasure *and* Tarzan's New York Adventure.

Strange Interlude (MGM, 1932)
Skyscraper Souls (MGM, 1932)
Payment Deferred (MGM, 1932)
Robber's Roost (Fox, 1933)
The Cohens and Kellys in Trouble (Universal, 1933)
Tugboat Annie (MGM, 1933)
Stage Mother (MGM, 1933)
Tarzan and His Mate (MGM, 1934)
The Thin Man (MGM, 1934)
The Barretts of Wimpole Street (*Forbidden Alliance*) (MGM, 1934)
Hide-Out (MGM, 1934)
West Point of the Air (MGM, 1935)
David Copperfield (MGM, 1935)
Cardinal Richelieu (United Artists, 1935)
The Flame Within (MGM, 1935)
Anna Karenina (MGM, 1935)
Woman Wanted (MGM, 1935)
The Bishop Misbehaves (MGM, 1935)
Tarzan Escapes (MGM, 1936)
The Voice of Bugle Ann (MGM, 1936)
The Devil-Doll (MGM, 1936)
A Day at the Races (MGM, 1937)
Between Two Women (*Surrounded by Women*) (MGM, 1937)
The Emperor's Candlesticks (MGM, 1937)
My Dear Miss Aldrich (MGM, 1937)
A Yank at Oxford (MGM, 1938)
Hold That Kiss (MGM, 1938)
The Crowd Roars (MGM, 1938)
Port of Seven Seas (MGM, 1938)
Spring Madness (MGM, 1938)
Let Us Live (Columbia, 1939)
Tarzan Finds a Son! (MGM, 1939)
Pride and Prejudice (MGM, 1940)
Sporting Blood (*Sterling Metal*) (MGM, 1940)
Maisie Was a Lady (MGM, 1941)
Tarzan's Secret Treasure (MGM, 1941)
Tarzan's New York Adventure (MGM, 1942)
The Big Clock (Paramount, 1948)
Where Danger Lives (RKO, 1950)
Bonzo Goes to College (Universal, 1952)
All I Desire (Universal, 1953)
Mission Over Korea (Columbia, 1953)
Duffy of San Quentin (Warners, 1954)
The Steel Cage (United Artists, 1954)
The Tall T (Columbia, 1957)
Wild Heritage (Universal, 1958)
Never Too Late (Warners, 1965)
The Phynx (Cinema Organization/Warners, 1970)
Too Scared to Scream (The Movie Store, 1985)
Hannah and Her Sisters (Orion, 1986)
Peggy Sue Got Married (Tri-Star, 1986)
Stranded (New Line Cinema, 1987)
Good Ole Boy: A Delta Boyhood (*The River Pirates*) (Vidmark Entertainment, 1988)
The Habitation of Dragons (Turner Home Entertainment, 1991)

Paul Picerni on *House of Wax*

> *Believe it or not, [House of Wax] was made for like a million dollars, and it grossed like 20,000,000. I think the cost vs. the gross was bigger than* Titanic. *Percentage-wise,* House of Wax *made a bigger profit.*

3-D may have been a passing fad, but the first major-studio movie made in that process remains popular nearly half a century later: *House of Wax* (1953). The color/3-D/stereophonic thriller not only made Vincent Price a top horror star, it earned millions of dollars for Warner Bros. during that tumultuous time in Hollywood history when the movie and TV industries first competed for the number one spot in the entertainment world.

In the Andre de Toth–directed chiller, Price played the mad sculptor coating corpses in wax; Phyllis Kirk was the mandatory damsel in distress; and featured as the romantic male lead was Paul Picerni. Born on Long Island, New York, Picerni had aspirations to become an attorney until he acted in an eighth grade play and later learned that the school principal liked his performance and called him "a born actor." He next appeared in little theater productions, then (after World War II and Air Force service) on the stage at Loyola University. Picerni was acting in a play in Hollywood when he was spotted by Solly Biano, head of talent at Warner Bros.; brought out to the studio, the young actor was given a role in *Breakthrough* (1950). This WWII actioner turned out to be aptly named, as it led to a Warners contract for Picerni and a long succession of roles at that studio. Best-known for his second banana role on the TV classic *The Untouchables* with Robert Stack, Picerni today is the father of eight and grandfather of ten.

How did you land your co-starring role in House of Wax?

Brynie Foy was the producer and a fellow named Joe Breen was the associate producer. They were preparing *House of Wax*, and it was a big thing because this was the first time a major studio was doing a movie in 3-D. Just prior to that,

A wax John Wilkes Booth gets the drop on fellow *House of Wax* player Picerni.

I was tested for a part, kind of the second lead, in a picture called *The Eddie Cantor Story* [1953] with Keefe Brasselle. I tested for the part of this doctor, along with about 15 or 20 other actors. Finally Sid Skolsky, the producer, called me into his office and he said, "Paul, I've got some bad news for you. We've decided to go with Arthur Franz in the part of the doctor, because Arthur has light hair and you have dark hair. Keefe has dark hair, and we want a little contrast between Keefe and his best friend the doctor." I was *very* disappointed—I was *shattered*, because I was really hoping to get that part.

Right across the street from Warner Bros. was a little drug store, and I walked over there with a friend of mine, a fellow named George O'Hanlon, a comedian who was in a series called *Behind the Eight Ball*. We were sitting there having a cup of coffee, and George was consoling me. All of a sudden, Joe Breen walked in. He had been the associate producer on *Breakthrough*, and I had become friendly with him. He said, "What the hell are you so down about, Picerni?" I told him that I had just lost the part in *The Eddie Cantor Story*, and he said, "Well, when you're down like that, there's only one way to go and that's *up*. I just found out that you're gonna play the romantic lead in *House of Wax*." That's the way I found out about getting that part. It was kind of a lesson that I always remembered, that when you're really down in the dumps, there's only one way to go and that's up! And that was *way* up for me, getting a lead in a picture like that. That's how it started.

So everybody felt, going into House of Wax, *that it was going to be a "big" movie.*

I knew it was going to be a big movie because at that time, all the major studios were trying all different techniques of photography, to get the people back to the theaters, away from their TV sets. TV was coming in very strong; as a matter of fact, if you had a living room set in a movie, Jack Warner wouldn't allow a TV on the set! They *hated* TV! So we knew *House of Wax* was going to be big, because CinemaScope was new then, and now they were going to try this 3-D thing which they thought might bring the people back in the theaters.

In January 1953, before House of Wax *started shooting, you did 3-D tests with Vera Miles.*

I wanted her to get that part *so* badly. I tested with Vera, I assisted her on her test, and I just *adored* her—she was so gorgeous and such a nice girl. I didn't know Phyllis Kirk at that time, so I really was rooting for Vera to get the part. Phyllis ended up getting it, and she was fine, of course.

Do you remember what other actresses might have tested for the female lead?

I just remember Vera—I don't remember the others. But I did a *lot* of tests at Warner Bros. through the years. I tested with Jayne Mansfield and Mari Aldon and Mari Blanchard—a *lot* of actresses. I never did play a love scene in a movie, only in the tests [*laughs*]!

I just interviewed Joan Weldon, who was acting at Warners at the same time you were, and she said that Warners always kept their actors hopping—"God forbid you should have a day off!"

Warners signed me in June of '50— my first picture as a contractee was *Operation Pacific* [1951]. A seven-year contract, and you usually work 40 weeks out of 52 a year, and 12 weeks you're laid off. Well, I never was laid off a *week* [*laughs*]. Joan is right, they worked you all the time you were there. They would even put you in the looping room. I remember once, I looped a whole picture that Errol Flynn made in Spain, and played about ten different characters. It was kind of a buccaneer-type picture [*The Master of Ballantrae*, 1953], and I was doing all these different voices of the sailors.

In one scene in *Breakthrough*, I'm one of the soldiers sitting on the deck of this ship and we're making the invasion of Normandy Beach. All of a sudden a voice comes over the loudspeaker: "Gentlemen, a message from our commanding chief, General Dwight D. Eisenhower." Then over the loudspeaker comes *my* voice, doing Dwight D. Eisenhower [*laughs*]! "Men, you're making a great contribution to your country—"

And you're sitting there as a soldier, listening to your own voice!

That's right!

When you were preparing for House

of Wax, *did they bother to show you the old movie it was a remake of?*

No, they never did. But I finally saw *Mystery of the Wax Museum* [1933] just a couple of months ago—a friend of mine brought a copy over to my house, and I looked at it. It was so *old* that I thought the Vincent Price version was a much better movie.

What was your impression of Price?

Oh, Vince was just an angel—one of the most delightful people to work with, a very artistic man and very generous. Just a wonderful guy. I loved working with Vincent, and unfortunately that's the only time I ever had the opportunity.

Andre de Toth told me he thought there was something "missing" about Price as an actor. He said Price had a "feminine" quality that kept him from achieving his potential.

I wouldn't say a "feminine" quality; he had an artistic, *gentle* quality. You've met people in your life like that; they're just not De Niros, they're not ballsy kind of people, because of their background. A lot of Englishmen have that quality, and there were also actors who were brought up years ago in New England or in Main Line Philadelphia who had that quality that would almost give an impression of being effeminate.

According to the film's publicity, Price's makeup was so gruesome that he was banished from the studio commissary.

Well, *I* don't recall him ever being in the commissary with that makeup on, so that's probably true. By the way, Gordon Bau was the head of makeup at Warner Bros. and Gordon got billing on all the movies 'cause he was the head of the department, but his brother George did Vincent Price's makeup. George is the guy who did all of the work on Vincent.

Memories of Phyllis Kirk, your leading lady?

Phyllis was lovely. Later, when we were in New York helping to promote the picture, Phyllis and I traveled all over to do publicity pictures, in hansom cabs in Central Park and on the steps of St. Patrick's Cathedral and all that.

Frank Lovejoy, who plays the police lieutenant in House of Wax, *was a good actor, but to me he seemed like a very unlikely type to get to be a star. What was he like?*

I first worked with Frank on *Breakthrough*. I was a young actor; as a matter of fact, the day I started *Breakthrough* was the day I graduated from Loyola University. My first scene on the picture was with Frank and a couple of other actors. We went through the rehearsal, and I had several big speeches in the scene. And Frank looked at me with a straight face and he said, "Is that the way you're gonna play it?" A thing went through my whole body saying, "Oh, my God...I've *failed*!"

From that moment on, I never liked Frank. What a terrible thing to say to a young actor, "Is that the way you're gonna play it?" Now to this *day* I don't know if Frank was serious or if he was kidding—that's like a standard joke with actors, "Is that the way you're gonna play it?" But he said it so convincingly that I believed he really *meant* it! And for years, while we were both under contract to Warner Bros., I never liked Frank. Then later on, when he did a TV series called *Meet McGraw*, I was

"If you don't watch your (wax) figure, no one else will!"—Picerni and "Little Egypt" between takes on *House of Wax*.

enough to have *me* go get them, and not the assistant director or somebody else. But up until then, I always had this "thing" about him, ever since that opening remark.

I'll tell you one funny story about Frank—well, it's not really funny, it's kind of sad. Frank was moving up the ladder and finally he was cast as Joan Crawford's leading man [in *Goodbye, My Fancy*, 1951]. In those days, we always had big premieres for these pictures at the Warner Bros. Theater on Hollywood Boulevard; at this premiere, my wife and I and [actor] Dick Wesson and *his* wife were greeted by Gordon MacRae, who was on a little dais there, introducing the actors as they arrived. And now, finally, up pulls this limousine, and in the limousine is Joan Crawford, Frank Lovejoy and Frank's wife Joan Banks, who was a radio actress. The limousine pulls up and Gordon MacRae says, "And now, ladies and gentlemen, the stars of the film, Frank Lovejoy and Joan Crawford!" Frank gets out of the back door first; he reaches in and he says, "Joan..."; and his wife, Joan Banks, puts her hand in his. And he *casts* it aside and says, "*Joan...*",

cast in a guest part. We were on the set one day, and he made a face and he sat down and he said [*in an out-of-breath voice*], "Paul...do me a favor, will you? In my dressing room...on top of my dresser...you'll find a little bottle of nitroglycerin pills. Go get 'em for me, will ya?" I looked at his face, and I could see that he was in pain, and so I rushed and got the nitroglycerin. He took a couple of tablets and he said, "Thanks a lot...thanks..." And at that moment, I suddenly *liked* Frank, I said to myself, "He's okay," because he trusted me and he pulls out Joan *Crawford* [*laughs*]! He's basking in the applause, in the limelight of the moment with Joan Crawford his leading lady, and he just leaves his wife Joan sitting there in the car! She climbs out by herself and she comes over to where Dick Wesson and I are standing with our wives and she says to us, "That son of a bitch, I'll *kill* him when we get home!" [*Laughs*] Frank was so dazzled by the glare of the lights and the "big moment" that he just neglected his wife!

I watched House of Wax *again last night, trying to dream up questions to ask you, and one thing I noticed about every scene with Frank Lovejoy is that it was stolen by Dabbs Greer [playing Lovejoy's sidekick]!*

Dabbs *is* good, isn't he? I noticed that, too—he was *very* good in that picture!

I've never seen him play a bigger or better part in a movie.

Dabbs was a fine actor, a *brilliant* actor—I agree with you about that! Well, Frank Lovejoy wasn't happy with that part, he really wasn't. It wasn't that good a part; like I said, Frank was playing parts with Joan Crawford and so on, and all of a sudden they stuck him in something like *House of Wax*. Another guy who was in that picture was Ned Young [as Price's boozy assistant Leon]. Poor Ned, he was mixed up in that [HUAC] Communist thing, and that kind of ended his career. I *liked* Ned; we weren't great friends, but I liked him very much.

I've got a cute little sidelight story about Charlie Buchinsky [Bronson], who's also in the picture, playing Vincent Price's deaf-mute henchman. As you recall, Buchinsky when he first started had a crew haircut, and he was built like a weightlifter—oh, a *tremendous* build. I think he got that from working in the coal mines in Pennsylvania. He wasn't very attractive—sunken cheekbones and all—so, for the part of this grotesque deaf-mute character, he was perfect! One day we were having lunch, just Charlie and I, in the Green Room, the Warner Bros. commissary. On the walls in the Green Room, they had pictures of all the contract players—Humphrey Bogart, Bette Davis, John Garfield and so on. Well, Charlie looked up at Garfield's picture. *You* remember John Garfield—he was a fine actor and a romantic lead, although he was offbeat looking. And Buchinsky said to me, in a very quiet tone, "Someday *I* will play romantic leads like John Garfield." And I said to myself, "This guy's *kidding* himself! How the hell is he gonna play romantic leads with a face like that?" Well [*laughs*], I learned a lesson: He did become a leading man and did play romantic leads!

I had that happen to me once again in my career, when I was doing a soap opera called *The Young Marrieds*. I had the lead in it with Peggy McCay, and we had different actors come in and out. There was a young actor who came in there and played a minor role in several episodes. We had lunch a few days and I *liked* him, I liked him very much—he was very bright and very clever. And I said to him one day, being the "older actor" handing out free advice (that wasn't wanted, sometimes!), I said, "You know, Chuck, you should think about writing and producing. You have a great mind and you seem to have a good talent as a writer. But as far as being an actor…I think you oughta forget about it. Just think about directing and producing and writing." Do you know who the actor turned out to be? Charles Grodin [*laughs*]! I never *dreamed* that he would become as big as he did in films!

Several years ago I tried to do an in-person interview with Andre de Toth, but at the restaurant he told me not to turn on my tape recorder. He said, "Just talk to me, and then later you write down your impressions of me and your impressions of what I said. That will be more interesting!"
You know he's still *alive*? He's must be *90*!

He was an interesting old buzzard, but he wouldn't let me record our conversation!
Oh, he's a devil—a *devil* [*laughs*]! He was an *average* director, I thought, or a *good* director, but...he was kind of a sadistic individual. He loved to see people in *danger*, you know? I remember they were shooting the fire sequence, and he had Vincent Price walking through the flames rather dangerously, rather than use a double.

Even though you weren't in the fire scene, you stopped by to watch it being filmed?
Oh, yeah, because they were gonna burn down that little wax museum, and it was right there on the sound stage. Bob Morgan doubled Vincent in the big fight sequence in the cellar; he was married to Yvonne DeCarlo. He also doubled Vincent in a scene where he swings on a rope, from one building to another, into Phyllis Kirk's bedroom. Wherever it looks like a stunt, that would be Bob Morgan. But Vincent did most of the fire sequence himself. I still remember the end of that scene, where Vincent runs through a doorway and the burning beams fall down behind him. Vincent did that himself—Andre de Toth *enjoyed* [watching the actors] doin' stuff like that! Now we come to the big fight sequence with me and Charlie Buchinsky...

That is such a great, scrappy, realistic fight. I just love it.
Right! And I guess that's what Andre *wanted*. He comes to us prior to the fight and he says [*Picerni speaks with a Hungarian accent*], "Now at this point we have a big fight. But the depth of focus of the thrrree-D camerrra is so grrreat that we cannot use stunt doubles. You and Charrrlie must do the fight yourrrselves." I'm a young contract player, Charlie is a young, powerfully built guy, and we're both pretty handy, so we agree: "Okay, sure, we'll do it." And we start this fight: We're throwing axes at each other that go into the camera and we're throwing chairs, and finally Charlie lifts me up over his head and he *slams* me down on the floor of the museum. Oh, I landed on my tailbone, and the pain went through my back like you can't believe—I just laid there. So they took me to the hospital and X-rayed me, but everything was fine. I took the rest of the day off, and then we went back and continued the fight. Now Andre proceeds to have Charlie bouncing my head off the floor! I said, "Charlie...you know...kind of *fake* it a little bit!" But Charlie was like Jack Palance at the time, he was sort of really *living* the part, and he was bangin' my head on the floor!
I'm now rendered "unconscious," I'm a mess. Andre says, "Now, Charrrlie, you pick up Paul, and you carrry him

over to the guillotine." It was a real, workable guillotine that they had borrowed from a French museum or some place, and it had a razor-sharp blade and a 35-pound block of wood attached above the blade to give it impetus as it came down. Andre says, "Charlie, you carrry Paul over to the guillotine and you put his head in place and you put a block of wood over the back of his neck." I go over and I check the guillotine, and they have two big spikes on each side of the blade to hold it in place so it won't fall. That was okay. We shoot that, and I'm in the guillotine now, "unconscious," and a block of wood is over the back of my neck. Andre says to Frank Lovejoy, "For the next shot, Frrrank, *you* come in with the other policemen. You see Buchinsky! He's got Paul in the guillotine! You rrrush over, you grrrab Buchinsky, you fight, you fight, you subdue Buchinsky, the cops take Buchinsky. Now you see Paul! You go over! You lift up the block of wood, you pull out Paul and, *zoooom*!, down come the blade! *That's* the next shot! Light it!"

I say, "Andre...excuse me. You're gonna shoot this in separate cuts, aren't you?" He says, "No, no, no! We do it in *one* take, *one* cut! Frrrank pulls you out, *zoooom*!, down come the blade!" Now, bear in mind I'm a young actor under contract. I say, "Andre, I don't wanna intercede on your job as director, but how do you propose to do it in one take?" He indicates Red Turner, the prop man—Red was a little short guy, always had a little black stogie in his mouth and he always wore his hat 'cause he was bald. A cute little guy—I loved Red. Andre says, "Red Turner will sit on top of the guillotine; he will hold the block of wood between his legs; when Frank pull you out, Red will release the blade. And we see it all in one take!" I say, "Andre...supposing Red drops the blade *prematurely*?" He says, "Only hurt for a second. Now don't t'ink about it, [it'll] make you nervous." And he walks away!

I go over to the assistant director Jimmy McMahon and I ask him, "Jimmy, is this a *gag*?" He says, "No, this is no gag. I just called Charlie Greenlaw in the production office and told him about it." I go out to Pev Marley, who was our cameraman, and I said, "Pev, is this a gag? Come on, level with me." He says, "No, no. That's the way he plans to shoot it." Oh, God...

I walk over to Andre, who is over on the side, and I tell him, "Andre, look, this isn't a case of getting *hurt*. This is a case of being *beheaded* if something goes wrong. Supposing Red Turner has a heart attack. Supposing there's an earthquake. Supposing *some*thing happens and he drops the blade prematurely." Again Andre says, "Only hurt you for a second. Don't worry about it, make yourself nervous." I say, "Andre, we *can't* do it like this—", and says [*angrily*], "We *do* it like this! Now, don't talk about it! Go 'way!"

So I go to my little portable dressing room on the set, which is 30, 40 feet away from the guillotine, and I'm thinking about it. Charlie Horvath, a stuntman, is on the set, and I ask *him*, "Charlie, would *you* do this thing like he's outlined it?" He says, "No way." "Would you do it *at all*?" I ask him. He says, "The only way I would do it—and I would think about it 100 times—is if I had control over the release of the blade. But I wouldn't do it if I were you."

I go to several other people—Frank Lovejoy is there, and he says, "Don't do it, kid." Finally the set is lit and everybody is ready, and Andre says, "Places, everybody!" Everybody takes their places, Buchinsky takes his place by the guillotine, Frank Lovejoy and the cops take *their* places. There's kind of a silence on the set, because…they *know* things aren't quite right [*laughs*]! And I just stand there on the steps of my little portable dressing room, and I don't move—I don't know what the hell to do. I had four kids, one on the way, and I don't want to disobey the director, lose my contract—

But you don't want to lose your head either!

No, no! So Andre says, "Come *on*, Paul! Put your head in the guillotine!" I just stand there. And finally I say, "I'm not gonna do it, Andre." He bellows, "Put your head in the guillotine, you *cowarrrd*!"—he *screams* it out. There's a silence on the set. The hair stood up on the back of my neck—just…*stood up!*—and I said, very *quietly*, almost like a Marlon Brando delivery, "If you call me a coward again, Andre…I'll fucking *kill* you." The Corona Italian came out in me [*laughs*]! And I *meant* it!

How far away are you two from each other?

Picerni feels he came uncomfortably close to *literally* losing his head on the *House of Wax* museum set.

We're maybe 60 feet. And he *screams*, "This man is *finished* in this film! Send him home, McMahon! Send him home! Get rid of him! I don't want to see his face on this set again!" And...that's it. Jimmy McMahon tells me, "I guess you better go home, Paul," so I go home. Now I sit home for like three *days*, and I don't know *what* the hell's gonna happen—I've still got some major scenes left in the film!

Including being rescued from the guillotine.

Right. In the meantime, Charlie Greenlaw comes down on the set, Eric Stacey [the head of props] comes down, and they see the setup and they agree that it's kind of a dangerous situation. Jack Warner hears about it, and he tells Andre, "You go back and shoot that scene and shoot it properly, without endangering anybody's life or limb." Joe Breen comes to my house and he says, "Paul, Andre sent me here. He wants you to come back to work tomorrow, and he wants you to *request* that he shoot the scene exactly as he had it planned." I said, "*What*??" [*Laughs*] I ask him, "What do *you* think I should do, Joe?" He says, "I think you should say, 'Up your ass, Andre!'" "Well, *that's* my answer—not 'Up your ass,' but just say *no*, I won't do it that way."

Then the next thing that happens is, I get word from Solly Biano, the head of talent: "Paul, we've got everything squared away with Andre. He's gonna shoot the scene properly, without endangering your life. You go back to work tomorrow morning and do it." So I go back the next day and it's a very silent set—a *very* silent set!—and there's the guillotine set up and all the people in place. I look up, and now there's a parallel platform built next to the guillotine, out of camera range, and Eric Stacey is standing on the platform. He had drilled a hole in the side of the guillotine under the blade, with an iron bar holding the blade up. At the crucial moment, when Frank pulled me out of the guillotine, Eric would pull the bar out and the blade would come down. Basically, it was still one shot—what Andre wanted!—but it was *still* dangerous, because I had to depend on Eric Stacey pulling the iron bar out at the proper moment [*laughs*]. If *his* timing was off, my *head* was off! Anyhow, that's the way we shot it; I figured, "I can't say no again," because there *was* a considerable change from the original plan of Red Turner sitting on the top, holding the blade between his legs! So that's the way we did it, and when you see the movie, you'll see that it was in one take!

Were all the wax figures in the museum scenes wax, or were there real people mixed in?

There was one person, a very muscular guy—he looked like the Hulk!—and he was standing by a rack, stretching a girl. He was the only one who was real, everything else was wax.

Was Jack Warner on the set much?

Jack rarely came on the set of *any* film. The only time you would see Jack—at least, the only time *I* would see him—is, he would be walking down the main street of Warner Bros., usually with Steve Trilling, Bill Orr and Solly Biano. They were all his "henchmen," you might say, and they would be walking down to their private dining room, smoking big cigars. Bill Orr was a young kid at the time, but he eventually became the head of TV there; he was married to Jack's daughter. He was a talented guy, and I liked Bill—but every time my option came up for the next year, he would say, "Paul, we like your work, we'd like to keep you, but we can't give you the raise." I always had a baby coming and my agent would say, "What do you want to do, Paul?" I'd say, "Well, I wanna get the raise." The agent would say, "You're gonna have to take a chance—they may *drop* you!" And I'd say, "Okay, forget it!" [*Laughs*] I started working there at 250 a week, and I think when I left I was making 350 a week—they finally gave me a raise after *Mara Maru* [1952], the picture I did with Errol Flynn. There's a guy I really loved—oh, God, I loved that guy. He was fabulous. If you ever want any Errol Flynn stories, I got some *great* ones!

You were in New York for the House of Wax *premiere.*

I went to New York with Vincent Price, Frank Lovejoy and Phyllis Kirk for the opening at the Paramount Theater. And the Paramount Theater was *packed*—5000 people. But I think a thousand of them were my *relatives* [*laughs*]—my mother, my aunts, my uncles, my cousins, 'cause I *came* from New York. It was a big opening: Major Warner, who ran the New York office, was there, along with all the executives, and Mort Blumenstock [the head of publicity] was backstage. Eddie Fisher had a big band in those days, and they performed preceding the movie. In his opening remarks, Eddie Fisher said, "Ladies and gentlemen, I'd like to dedicate my show tonight to the man who discovered me and helped get me started in show business, Mr. Eddie Cantor." Then he did his show, and after that he introduced Vincent Price, and the audience went crazy. Vince said a few words, Frank Lovejoy goes on, Phyllis Kirk goes on, and finally he says, "Here's the young romantic lead in the picture, Paul Picerni." I came on stage, and the audience *erupted* in applause, because—you know—it's all my relatives [*laughs*]! They went crazy! And I was really full of emotion, it was *such* a big moment in my career. "Ladies and gentlemen," I said, "at the beginning of the show tonight, Eddie Fisher dedicated his performance to a gentleman who helped him a great deal in his career, Mr. Eddie Cantor. Well, a lot of people helped get me to this point, and I feel this is quite a step in my career, being on stage here at the world-famous Paramount Theater and opening in a picture like *House of Wax*, which is the first major studio production in 3-D. A *lot* of people helped me get to this point, but I want to pay tribute to one person tonight."

And I said, "Ma...take a bow!"—and my mother stood up. *I* was crying...*she* was crying....the audience was crying...Eddie Fisher was crying... *every*body was crying, and it was just a great moment. A *great* moment. I came off stage and Mort Blumenstock, a great, big, jovial, wonderful guy—*he's* crying, he's got a handkerchief to his eyes. He says [*sobbing*], "Paul...oh, my *God*, Paul, that was *wonderful*, that was *beautiful*!

"But, listen, Paul: Can your mother come back for the second show??" [*Laughs*] Isn't that something? I'll *never* forget that!

How long were you in New York?

For like ten days, for the whole early run of the picture. One night Vincent Price and I and Vincent's wife Mary (a lovely woman) went to Sardi's. We

Picerni and Vincent Price arrive in New York for the April 1953 *House of Wax* **world premiere.**

On one of the stops in his whirlwind 25-city *House of Wax* public appearance tour, Picerni (right) pauses to pose with the picture's impressive 24-sheet.

were upstairs having a late supper, and there were a lot of familiar faces in the room, all the actors who'd come off the stage and come up there for *their* late snacks. Vincent said, "You know, it's always so embarrassing when you see the familiar faces of these actors and you can't remember their *names*. But I found a solution to that." I said, "What is it, Vincent?" He said, "As soon as I see an actor approaching me, I stand up...I extend my hand...and I say, 'Vincent Price.' And inevitably they will say, 'Joe Blow,' or whatever *their* name is, and shake hands." I said, "Boy, that's great."

At that precise moment—at that *precise moment*, like it was written in a script—this actor starts walking toward Vincent. And I see this blank stare come over Vincent's face! So, to get himself off the hook, he goes into his bit: He stands up and he sticks out his hand and he says, "Vincent Price." And the actor says, "*You* don't have to tell me your *name*, Vince! I *killed* ya in three movies!" I'll never forget that—oh, God!

Did you ever figure out who it was?
No! I don't know to this day!

Many of the people I've asked about Price talk about his mischievous sense of humor and even sometimes being a practical joker. Did you see any of that during the making of the movie?

No, I don't recall any of that, to tell you the truth. I was more concerned with Andre [*laughs*]!

Did you make any other personal appearances in connection with House of Wax*?*

After that opening in New York, they sent me on the road for *ten weeks*—I went to Dayton, I went to Akron, I went to Milwaukee, I went *all* over. At the point when I'd been on the road for eight or nine weeks, they had Gordon MacRae meet me in Chicago. I'm really tired now—I haven't seen my wife, I haven't seen my kids. I'm at the Ambassador Hotel with Gordon MacRae and his wife Sheila, who eventually became an actress and did some of *The Honeymooners*. We're at the Ambassador and I get a phone call from the head of publicity at Warner Bros....

You're traveling around alone? None of the other House of Wax *players are with you any more?*

Right, I was going around alone. But every stop I made, the box office went up five, six thousand dollars. I was supposed to go home after the Chicago opening with Gordon MacRae—they sent him in to help me in Chicago, because it was a big site there. Anyhow, I got a phone call from the head of publicity at Warners and he said, "Paul, instead of coming home after Chicago, we want you to go straight to San Francisco, and then up to Seattle, Tacoma and Portland." I said, "Marvin, I haven't seen my wife in eight *weeks*. I'd like to go home now." He said, "You *can't*. The opening is night after tomorrow, you gotta be in San Francisco. You're doing so well, the picture's doing so great!" I said, "I guess I *have* to, but I don't *want* to..." And Gordon overhears the conversation; at that time, Gordon was a much bigger star at the studio. He says, "Gimme the phone."

Gordon gets on the phone and he says, "Marvin, Paul is not going *anywhere* after Chicago, he's going straight home. Do you understand this man's been on the road for eight weeks, he hasn't seen his wife and kids—" Marvin says, "He's *gotta* go to San Francisco, Mr. Warner *wants* it." Gordon says, "All right: He'll go to San Francisco if you fly up his wife and kids and meet him at the hotel in San Francisco." Gordon *said* that! And Marvin said, "Okay! Agreed!" [*Laughs*] So I'll always love Gordon for that moment. They sent my wife and two of my four kids (the other two were too little at the time), and they met me in San Francisco and we had three or four days there, and then I went on to all the northern cities. I was on the road for ten weeks.

Helping make House of Wax *an even bigger success.*

Believe it or not, that picture was made for like a million dollars, and it grossed like 20,000,000. I think the cost vs. the gross was bigger than *Titanic* [1998]. Percentage-wise, *House of Wax* made a bigger profit.

Now I come back to Warner Bros. and I'm a hero 'cause every town I was in, the grosses far exceeded the towns I *wasn't* in. I got all sorts of letters that went to Warner Bros. and the publicity people gave 'em to me, letters saying what a great guy I was and how I did all these radio spots in each town. I'm feeling pretty good about the whole thing when I get a call from Solly Biano, the head of talent. Solly says, "Paul, I'm sending you a script, a Randy Scott movie, *Riding Shotgun* [1954]. There's a part in there for you." I said, "Oh, great. Who's directing it?", and he says, "Andre de Toth." I said, "You're kidding!" and he says, "Andre *requested* you." Andre *requested* me...?!

I get the script, and Randolph Scott is riding shotgun on a stagecoach and they come into this way station. Randy gets off the wagon, he comes in the way station and he says, "How *are* you, Jeff?" I'm Jeff. He says, "Jeff, listen, can you do me a favor? Can you take the stage into Dodge City?" I say, "Yeah, I'd be glad to." So I get on the stage and we ride out of town; there are a couple of montage shots of the stage going; and all of a sudden we're attacked by Indians. And on page three of the script, Jeff is shot with an arrow and falls off the wagon and is killed [*laughs*]!

So I call up Solly and I say, "Solly, what the hell *is* this? I just had star billing in the biggest hit of the year, *House of Wax*, and now you put me in a picture like *Riding Shotgun* and I get killed on page three!" He said, "You're killed on page three? You're *kidding*! Jeez, I thought it was a big part!" He hadn't read the script; all he knew was that Andre requested me. Solly said, "Paul, I'm sorry. I don't know what to tell you. We have nothing else going on the lot. I guess we'll just have to put you on layoff, because there's nothing else happening unless you wanna *do* this stupid thing and stay on salary 'til something comes up." Well, like I did many times in my stupid career, I did the movie—I did *Riding Shotgun* with Andre de Toth, and I guess he got a semblance of revenge [*laughs*]!

Have you seen him since?
Fifteen years ago, they reissued *House of Wax* in 3-D on Wilshire Boulevard and they called me to come down to make an appearance. I go down to this theater and it's *packed* with people; I brought a couple of my *grand*children to see it, 'cause they had never seen 3-D. And who is there but Andre de Toth and Vincent Price, and I had a wonderful reunion with Vincent. And Andre [*in a sweet voice*]: "*Paul!* How *are* you, sweetheart? I haven't seen you in *years!* So good to *see* you!" Like a true Hungarian, he embraced me and kissed me on both cheeks—and that was the last time I saw Andre [*laughs*]!

What did you think of House of Wax *back then—and now?*
It still holds up today. I went to Chicago for an autograph session and met with a fellow named Frank Partapillo, a camera buff, has a beautiful theater built in his basement. He has all the 3-D equipment, and while I was in Chicago he had a "special evening" and invited about 30 people and showed *House of Wax* in 3-D. I got up before the movie and told some of my stories, and I saw it in 3-D for the first time in maybe 15 years. And the audience *loved* it: All these young kids were there, and older people, and they all had the 3-D glasses on, and they marveled at the movie! It was a great evening. So it still holds up.

I think you do a great job in the few movies where I've seen you play "good guys," and you're great on The Untouchables; *but you're also excellent every time you play a villain or a mobster. And I can't decide whether I like you better as a hero or a villain. Which do you prefer?*

Well, one of my favorite roles is the one in *Mara Maru*, in which I played kind of a villain-good guy. Errol Flynn is the good guy, Raymond Burr is the bad guy, and we're searching for this buried treasure in the ocean off the Philippine Islands. When it looks like Errol's gonna win, I go with Errol. When it looks like *Raymond's* gonna win, I go with *Raymond*. It was a wonderful part—it was like the Italian nation, going with Germany and then going back to America [*laughs*]! And at the end of *Mara Maru*, I go with Errol—and, of course, Raymond Burr shoots me! It was one of my favorite parts, because I was good *and* bad.

Paul Picerni Filmography

Story of Amos (1948)
Beyond Glory (*The Long Grey Line*) (Paramount, 1948)
Twelve O'Clock High (20th Century–Fox, 1949)
When Willie Comes Marching Home (20th Century–Fox, 1950)
Where the Sidewalk Ends (20th Century–Fox, 1950)
Three Secrets (Warners, 1950)
Prisoners in Petticoats (Republic, 1950)
The Secret Fury (RKO, 1950)
A Lady Without Passport (MGM, 1950)
Dial 1119 (MGM, 1950)
I'll Get By (20th Century–Fox, 1950)
The Killer That Stalked New York (Columbia, 1950)
Saddle Tramp (Universal, 1950)
Breakthrough (Warners, 1950)
Operation Pacific (Warners, 1951)
Jim Thorpe—All American (Warners, 1951)
Inside the Walls of Folsom Prison (Warners, 1951)
Force of Arms (*A Girl for Joe*) (Warners, 1951)
Fort Worth (Warners, 1951)
I Was a Communist for the FBI (Warners, 1951)
The Tanks Are Coming (Warners, 1951)
Mara Maru (Warners, 1952)
The Miracle of Our Lady of Fatima (Warners, 1952)
Cattle Town (Warners, 1952)
Operation Secret (Warners, 1952)
The Desert Song (Warners, 1953)
She's Back on Broadway (Warners, 1953)
The Master of Ballantrae (voice only; Warners, 1953)
The System (Warners, 1953)
His Majesty O'Keefe (Warners, 1953)
House of Wax (Warners, 1953)
Riding Shotgun (Warners, 1954)
The Bounty Hunter (Warners, 1954)
The Shanghai Story (Republic, 1954)
Pushover (Columbia, 1954)
The Adventures of Hajji Baba (20th Century–Fox, 1954)
Drive a Crooked Road (Columbia, 1954)
Bobby Ware Is Missing (Allied Artists, 1955)
Hell's Island (*South Sea Fury*) (Paramount, 1955)
Lord of the Jungle (Allied Artists, 1955)
To Hell and Back (Universal, 1955)
Dial Red O (Allied Artists, 1955)
Miracle in the Rain (Warners, 1956)
The Come On (Allied Artists, 1956)
Flight to Hong Kong (United Artists, 1956)
Wiretapper (Great Commission Films/ Continental, 1956)

Omar Khayyam (Paramount, 1957)
The Shadow on the Window (Columbia, 1957)
Operation Mad Ball (Columbia, 1957)
The Big Caper (United Artists, 1957)
The Brothers Rico (Columbia, 1957)
The Night Heaven Fell (voice only; Kingsley International, 1958)
The Deep Six (Warners, 1958)
Marjorie Morningstar (Warners, 1958)
Return to Warbow (Columbia, 1958)
The Man Who Died Twice (Republic, 1958)
Torpedo Run (MGM, 1958)
The Young Philadelphians (*The City Jungle*) (Warners, 1959)
Strangers When We Meet (Columbia, 1960)
The Scarface Mob (Cari Releasing Corp., 1962)
The Scalphunters (United Artists, 1968)
Land Raiders (*Day of the Landgrabber*) (Columbia, 1970)
Che! (20th Century–Fox, 1969)
Airport (Universal, 1970)
Kotch (Cinerama, 1971)
Capricorn One (Warners, 1978)
Beyond the Poseidon Adventure (Warners, 1979)
Escape to Athena (Associated Film Distribution, 1979)
Fearmaker (*House of Fear, Violent Rage*) (Prism Entertainment, 1987)
Enemy of the State (Touchstone/Buena Vista, 1998)

Picerni also appeared as an extra in several 1940s Bowery Boys comedies (*Live Wires, In Fast Company*, possibly *News Hounds*) and in footage cut from *Jet Pilot* (shot in 1950, released by Universal in 1957).

Anthony M. Taylor

*Incubus really was too crazy—certainly too crazy
to go into a mainstream theater.
There were just too many things in it
that were too strange for the time.*

In the mid-1960s, commodities trader Anthony Taylor carved a niche for himself in horror movie history by producing the first (and still only) film in the "universal language" of Esperanto: Writer-director Leslie Stevens' *Incubus* (1965), starring William Shatner. The film that aspired to be truly universal found only one country willing to adopt it—France, where it opened briefly to ecstatic reviews. Then *Incubus* vanished from the world stage, almost *literally*. In 1993, Taylor discovered that his 35mm print materials and negative, stored in a vault at Consolidated Film Industries in Hollywood, had disappeared! Fortunately, Taylor had one remaining hope of recovering the only picture he ever produced. It had been sufficiently admired in France to become part of the permanent collection at the Cinémathèque Française. But, as Taylor explains, being the film's producer did not give him any rights to this last surviving print.

The story of *Incubus* encompasses craziness, bankruptcy, even murder and suicide, but it has a happy ending: Taylor eventually rescued his film, restored it to excellent condition, and is now making it available to a new generation of admirers in VHS and DVD through mail order and via a website (www.incubusthefilm.com). His story makes entertaining, and *cautionary*, reading for anyone interested in motion picture production. [Introduction written by Tim Lucas, editor of *Video Watchdog* magazine.]

Was an interest in motion pictures and TV inevitable for you, growing up near Hollywood?

I guess so, being born in Los Angeles and living in Brentwood. Pat O'Brien lived on our corner, Dore Schary lived across the street and Tyrone Power lived down the block. My best friend in high school had a father who was a screenwriter, and the son of [director] Allan Dwan was in my class. And I worked as an extra in movies [*That's My Boy*, 1951, *Pat and Mike*, 1952, *Stalag 17*, 1953] when I was going to college. So I've been around it most of my life, and most of the people I knew worked in it. Also, I served as a Photo-Radar Intelligence Officer in the Strategic Air Command of the U.S. Air Force and I produced films used to train B-52 crews about the targets they'd bomb in the event of war. So I did have lots of expertise in film production prior to *Incubus*.

How did you happen to get acquainted with Leslie Stevens?

I was dating a girl named Mona Skager, who later went on to be Francis Coppola's assistant and associate producer on some *Godfather* movies. She was then Leslie's assistant, and through that I got to know Leslie. Of course, I knew him by reputation, by his TV series—*Outer Limits* and *Stoney Burke* and some other things. *Outer Limits* was still on the air then.

And eventually you and Stevens started talking about making a movie.

At that point in the '60s, the idea of movies for television was just starting up. We had the idea that movies were something that television would have a voracious appetite for, and that TV was going to need some more current ones. Leslie and I talked about doing something—Leslie had done a movie before this, *Private Property* [1960], which had gotten reviewed in *Time* magazine and shown at various festivals. (Sad to say, it now is lost.) I had the money, and finally one day I said, "Let's see if we can do an independent film." The difficulty was that in those days, you did not have home video; even to this *day* it is very difficult for independent films to get into theaters. Art theaters seemed more accessible–at least to us [*laughs*]. So the idea of doing an art film occurred to us.

Whose idea was it to make a supernatural "art film"? Stevens'?

Well, there are only so many genres that you can [work in] when you're gonna make an independent movie, *I* felt. Horror certainly being one of them. I certainly would say that, yes, it was Leslie's idea, *Incubus* and the script and every aspect of it.

Did either of you speak Esperanto?

Actually, neither of us did, although Leslie had more of an interest in it than I did. Sometimes decisions that you make in your life seem rather simple, but as time goes on they seem to loom a lot larger than they did at the time. I don't know that we really spelled this out, or sat down and did a point-by-point analysis, but basically we wanted *Incubus* in a foreign language because it "put us in a different place," and we thought that it *might* help in getting into art houses, the one place where subtitles *were*. We were doing it for the *uniqueness* of it. And, to the extent that Esperanto *is* another language and really *does* put you "in a different place," it *worked* to a certain degree. The idea was pretty extraordinary, but somehow when you're just sitting there talking about it and there's only a couple of people, it doesn't seem nearly as extraordinary as it does in retrospect.

My guess had been that part of the reason Incubus *was made was to promote Esperanto.*

That *would* be a logical assumption. You can't imagine that people would do it who *didn't* want to promote Esperanto!

It makes better sense to me now that I've heard the reasoning behind it. Doing the movie in Esperanto just seemed to me so limiting...

From an artistic standpoint, I think

it works to a certain degree, but I don't know whether I would do it *again* [*laughs*]! Also, we really didn't think *Incubus* was going to be like the only [movie] we ever did in our *lifetime*—at least, *I* didn't. As soon as we got through with making it, the other people went on to other stuff, and I had to take *Incubus* around and show it to people back in New York. That's when I realized how extremely difficult the selling of it would be.

I had a feeling, between the Esperanto and the scenes that were way ahead of their time, like the rape scene, that Incubus *would have been an awfully "hard sell."*

It really was too much for people. The Esperanto, coupled with the fact that Milos Milos, who played the Incubus, had just gotten a *lot* of publicity for murdering Mickey Rooney's wife [and then killing himself]! And Ann Atmar, the girl who played William Shatner's sister, *she* committed suicide. And most of the people I showed it to were aware of all this!

Conrad Hall, who photographed Incubus, *said in an old interview, "Leslie Stevens is a madman."*

The concept of doing a movie in Esperanto was, I think, what Conrad was driving at. I'm sure it was meant in a loving vein.

His photography also sets Incubus *apart from other movies of that sort that were being made at that time.*

In the last conversation I had with Leslie, right soon before he died, we mentioned that—we said *Incubus* was the only film that had *two* Academy Award-winning cinematographers. Conrad Hall photographed most of it, and Bill Fraker did one of the last scenes, the one with Allyson Ames and the goat.

How funny that you should say that—I had the feeling that last scene might have been shot by someone else. It's…well, it's not nearly as good as the rest of the movie.

You picked up on that last scene being different, or not quite as good as the other ones? That's interesting. It's really apparent to *me*, although other people normally don't comment on it, but it was obviously apparent to you. Anyway, the best thing in the film, really, is the cinematography—I notice that now, because people have not really seen good black-and-white cinematography. Even with the difficulties we had, I still think it looks pretty good.

How did you like working with Hall?

Oh, great. He's a really humorous, intelligent person. Gave a very light touch to everything. I don't know how he is now, but he *wasn't* like some serious, heavy-handed person. It was not an easy location shoot—we weren't using Arriflexes, we had big giant cameras and things. In moving really fast, a guy *could* be pissed off all the time, but he wasn't at all, he was very light-hearted and everything. I talked to him several months ago, after I'd restored *Incubus* and sent it to him, and he really recalled the whole film shot by shot, and we discussed it at great length. It was interesting to me how vividly he recalled every bit of it, and he still remembers it as a fun thing. I think he's *still* sorry that, as we were finishing up *Incubus*, he had to go to do a Paul Newman movie [*Harper*, 1966]—that's why he couldn't shoot the end of our film.

Both Conrad and Fraker were students of Ted McCord, an old-time cinematographer, and they had both done *Outer Limits*. Conrad was a good friend of Leslie's, he saw Leslie a lot; when we last talked, Conrad said he and Leslie had lunch certainly once a month, usually more than that. So they remained friends. Conrad's father was James Norman Hall, who wrote *Mutiny on the Bounty*. In fact, Conrad was born in Tahiti and didn't come to the States 'til about '40 or '41 to go to Cate, a prep school down outside of Santa Barbara.

You shot Incubus *mostly at Big Sur.*
The principal photography was done at Big Sur. Then we went from Big Sur over to near King City, where Mission San Antonio is. The full name is Mission San Antonio de Padua and it's one of the original California missions, founded by Junipero Serra. It was on Hunter Liggett Military Reservation—which is not a military reservation now, it's been deactivated since then. The military base surrounded the locale of the Mission and we shot there. We shot in the Mission and we utilized the officer's club to eat our meals and do one thing and another. That officer's club had been Randolph Hearst's hunting lodge, designed by the same woman who did the San Simeon Castle. (Now they've converted it into a luxurious hotel of some sort.) There weren't any accommodations there, so we stayed in motels in King City, which was close by. For the underwater scenes, we went over to Catalina Island on a Sunday—we flew over to the Isthmus and shot those.

Who was your underwater camera operator?
I don't recall his name, and it isn't in the credits. He was quite experienced—he brought his own equipment and used an aqualung. [Actor] Bob Fortier had a friend with a 40-foot catamaran which we used all day around the Isthmus, and then we sailed to Avalon to catch a seaplane back to Long Beach. It was the same day that Steve Cochran's death was reported under strange circumstances involving a boat.* Leslie, Allyson, the cameraman and I flew back.

Where did you stay while you were shooting in and around Big Sur? A hotel?
There *were* no hotels there. Those little buildings that you see at the beginning of the film, with the monks outside—we stayed in *those*. That was a "lodge" sort of place that had been there since the '30s. Now there are luxurious places to stay there, but in 1965 those didn't exist. The various people that are in that scene, the monks who turn the

---

According to a chapter on movie tough guy Cochran in Hollywood Players: The Forties *(Arlington House, 1976), "In 1965, Cochran placed an advertisement in the trade paper* Variety *for a six-girl crew to accompany him on a boat trip. The girls he hired left him in Acapulco. He then placed another ad, this time in a Mexican paper, stating that he would pay the girls 70 pesos (about $5.83) a day. He received 180 applications but he took only three because there were 'no real lookers.' The trio of girls were 21, 19 and 14 years of age. The vessel left Acapulco on June 3, but encountered a hurricane off the coast of Oaxaca. The boat was badly damaged and Steve was forced to remain at the helm for two days and nights combating the storm. Completely exhausted and in considerable pain, he collapsed and died on June 15, 1965, at the age of 48. The girls were not rescued until June 21, by which time they were in a state of total hysteria at being adrift with a decomposing corpse."*

cross around and do various things—well, one of those is the prop man, Ted Mossman, and another one is the guy who did the sound, Jay Ashworth. They were actually members of the crew.

And the robed guys on the beach? Crew members again?

Yes. That was up at Big Sur.

Are you in it?

No. It's bad enough being the producer!

How did the makers of a rather lurid supernatural horror movie get permission to shoot in a mission?

Leslie wrote a complete *other* script which disguised the movie as a documentary! It was called *Religious Legends of Old Monterey*. We had to get permission to shoot at Big Sur, 'cause that's a state park, and also from the Franciscan Order and the Archdiocese to shoot in the mission where we were for several days. So, because of our subject matter, Leslie wrote this phony script, which is like a series of episodes, one of them being "The Legend of the Deer Well." Now [*laughs*], you warned me that you were going to ask me exactly what a "deer well" was, and I'm *still* not certain. I even went to the *library* to try to research that [*laughs*]! I can't see a deer lowering down a little bucket or anything like that! It must just be something that deer drink out of, something that I assume has a well-like appearance.

So you misrepresented your movie to get permission to shoot in a couple different places.

Yes, particularly the mission. I had gone to a parochial high school, so I was familiar with the Catholic Church, but

Incubus' Robert Fortier is punished (severely!) for drinking from the deer well.

Eloise Hardt taunts Ann Atmar, struck blind by a solar eclipse, in *Incubus*.

I wasn't aware that this mission was where the Franciscan Order sent all their sort of offbeat priests who were *weird*. Most of the other missions are like in Santa Barbara and Los Angeles and Monterey and big tourist spots, whereas *this* mission was way off the beaten path. But none of us was molested by them or anything [*laughs*]!

The scene of Allyson Ames and the goat—where was that done?
We went out to the San Fernando Valley and photographed it in like a vacant lot, with Fraker. The goat's name, oddly enough, was Billy, as a matter of fact.

Did you also have a phony goat head for some of the shots in that scene?
Yes. I think we shot that the same day. By the way, I recall vividly Leslie calling me afterwards and asking me what I thought of the goat licking its chops, asking whether that was in bad taste, if we'd gone too far [*laughs*]! I said, "God, the whole *idea* may be going too far!"

On a day-to-day basis, what did your work entail?
Aside from being present—and not interfering too much [*laughs*]—I don't know really what one would say. We were all staying together in the same place, so we naturally talked about what we did every day and how things were going and the various scheduling.

How much of the shooting were you there for?

I was there for every bit of it. I was pretty much a line, hands-on producer. When you're away from Hollywood and off on your own, there are always a lot of things to be done, and you seem to keep busy all day! Elaine Michea was the associate producer, and she right after that went on to *Bonnie and Clyde* [1967]. She was exceptionally good.

How many days to shoot?
It was about two and a half weeks in Big Sur and then over to the Mission.

And how much did the picture cost?
Low six figures or something like that. *Very* low [*laughs*]!

What about the scene of Ann Atmar being raped? Any worries, or were you confident it would "play" in the art houses?
Actually, her breast being exposed caused more of a furor than the rape scene did, frankly—I don't know why! They didn't have ratings then, so that wasn't particularly difficult. Ann committed suicide soon after the conclusion. I don't know why she killed herself; I didn't really know her. She was a good friend of Allyson's, and she had appeared in several other movies and on some TV. She was not *terribly* well-known, but she had worked and everything.

Who cast the movie? Leslie Stevens?
Both of us did. Probably the casting decision of a lifetime would be putting Milos Milos as the Incubus—who then proceeded to *murder* someone [*laughs*]! I probably got to know him better than other people did, just due to the fact that I had a lot of friends who were Serbians. My father was in the construction bond business, and many contractors were of Serbian descent, so many of his clients were Serbians. It was always part of our "thing" to go to Serbians' Christmas, which is celebrated at a different time, and I knew some of their language and one thing and another. In general, people didn't *know* anything about Serbia back then—they didn't until we started *attacking* them recently [*laughs*]! I remember talking to Milos about Dragoljub Mihajlovic, who was supposed to be a big Chetnik, and Milos was just really amazed that anybody even knew who Mihajlovic was in the Second World War. (Of course, it was quite vivid to Milos.) Milos had a strange look to him, and spoke a foreign language, and yet he didn't seem that outlandish, really. He was rather an interesting guy, actually, but a "stranger in a strange land"—he was here trying to be an actor, but there just were no countrymen, *no*body around that he could identify with. And I guess he was a lot crazier than we thought he was: He had a relationship with Mickey Rooney's wife, and obviously that meant so much to him that when she probably said "It's all over"...he killed her.*

William Shatner?
Bill and I became really good friends after that. He's just a thoroughgoing professional, and he has always been nice up to the current day, highly cooperative. People think that he had really not worked much before *Incubus*, but he *was* really a pretty big deal then—he'd starred [on TV] and starred on the

---

*In January 1966, Milos (a.k.a. Milos Milosevic) shot Barbara Ann Thomason Rooney in the jaw, and then shot himself in the temple, in the Rooneys' Brentwood home.

Broadway stage and everything. I remember driving from King City back to Los Angeles in my car; everybody else took buses up there and back, but I took my car. And while Bill and Mona Skager and I were driving back in my car, Bill was saying that he had never really been *treated* like that—we'd treated him just like one of the *people* rather than having any special thing. Which he rather *enjoyed*—he just became part of the operation, more than he had been in other things where he had special chairs and special things around. We just recently spoke about *Incubus*, and he had (of course) not seen it in some time. I think he does a good job. I think he's a lot "looser" in this than he has come to be known as Captain Kirk.

I like him in most everything pre–Star Trek—and in not too much afterwards!

He sort of "stiffened up" [in *Star Trek*], I don't really know why. But, really, he does have quite a sense of humor. And in retrospect, where are all of the people who were TV stars then? Most of 'em have sunk without a trace. But I've noticed just in the last three weeks that Bill's got a movie coming out and two new books and various other things—man, this guy's all over the place [*laughs*]!

Allyson Ames?

She married Leslie Stevens soon after *Incubus*, although at the time they were an "item" or living together or however you want to phrase it. (Then they divorced, which was *another* disaster!) She was strange, in a way. Certainly very good-looking. I think her abilities as an actress are sort of a toss-up, but she had a great *look* to her. When she and Leslie divorced, she married an *incredibly* wealthy guy named Rothchild—which is not a bad name. I sort of lost track of her. When I sued Consolidated Film Industries for destroying *Incubus*, she was deposed, and she gave an entirely different story about the movie than *I* remember [*laughs*]! Like everybody taking dope—but *I* don't recall that! And if they did, nobody was offering it to me!

What in the world would people smoking dope while you were making the movie have to do with CFI destroying the prints?

It had *nothing* to do with it, she was just like rattling on.

How many of the cast members spoke Esperanto?

Taking a break from speaking phonetic Esperanto, Allyson Ames and William Shatner share a romantic moment in *Incubus.*

Nobody spoke it! It's amazing to me, 'cause it's difficult enough to do a low-budget film and *go* some place when they're all speaking English! We had rehearsals beforehand, for ten days or something like that, where they sat down and learned it phonetically. Those rehearsals took place at Daystar's offices on Sunset Boulevard. The fact that it's even *intelligible* to Esperanto people is—

Is amazing!

It is to *me*! Forrest Ackerman speaks Esperanto, and he really thought it was perfectly good, and I took *his* word—just by virtue of the fact that he's been around a long time! He thinks it's fine. *Other* Esperanto people were *not* that happy, because some of the pronunciation is not perfect. But nobody knows that except them! Obviously we had to have somebody translate the script into Esperanto for us, so we *had* worked with the people, but at the San Francisco International Film Festival these Esperanto people came and just caused all sorts of excitement, and even to this day I can sometimes feel *resentment* from these people. They're basically highly intelligent, professional people, and I guess I haven't delved into it quite enough to see what goes on in the minds of these people, who are so nice on the surface. But I can't believe that they *really* think Esperanto is gonna take over. *Now* they've been very nice and a lot different than they were then.

Did you have any of the Esperanto people with you during the filming?

No. They translated it for us, and also did one thing or another, but they were not there for the filming. Frankly, I don't know that we made a conscious decision about that, or if it was just a case of no one being prepared to take off from work and go some place with us.

Where did you see Incubus *for the first time?*

Well, I saw it all along—we did everything, from putting the sound in and everything. So I saw it reels at a time as it was being completed.

But where did everybody sit down and see it from beginning to end for the very first time?

Probably in Nosseck's projection room, on Sunset Boulevard.

And was everybody pleased?

Oh, yeah, no question about it. See, we didn't see any dailies when we were shooting up there, none of those people had. Most of them had seen *nothing*. Which was a pretty gutsy thing, 'cause we didn't really know whether we *had* anything 'til we got back to Los Angeles!

What kind of a ruckus did the Esperanto people kick up at the San Francisco opening?

Well, several things happened. This was for the premiere, 1966—we were the American entry in the San Francisco Film Festival, and everybody from Shirley Temple to I-don't-know-who was there. I had ordered a new print, and it was going to be shown in a very large Masonic auditorium that seats about 6000 people. First, right before the screening of *Incubus*, they had quite a dinner for us at the Fairmont Hotel that involved me and my date and about 20 other people, including Sharon Tate and her husband Roman Polanski. Then they took us in limousines over to this large auditorium. They gave me an award and I talked a little about the film and everybody clapped. But it went downhill from there—it was like your worst nightmare: The print started rolling, and there was no sound. I thought, "Well, the projectionist hasn't turned the sound up yet," but then *more* time goes by and there's *still* no sound. So I ran out to try to go upstairs and find the projectionist, which was like four floors up or something. I went up there and I'm saying, "Turn up the sound!", and the guy said, "There isn't a soundtrack on this print." So then I had to get the head of the festival, and he had to make an announcement. I had another print that I was using in a projection room, to show to critics and various people, so we could send somebody for *that*...but in the meantime we had these 5000 people who'd come to see a film, and suddenly there *was* no film [*laughs*]! And they're just like screaming and hollering. The announcement was made and they showed some short subject, and then we showed *Incubus* over again.

Then there was the incident with the Esperanto people. Prior to this, the Esperanto people were very excited about *Incubus*. I had just moved into a home in the Hollywood Hills and they all *insisted* they come and visit me, and they were all enthusiastic about *Incubus*. Then when they all got together to go to the San Francisco showing, they sat together, about 50 or 100 of 'em, all in one spot. And any time they thought things were not pronounced correctly, they screamed and laughed and carried on like *maniacs*, and no one else could understand *why*. Everyone else thought it was just some unruly group up there, yet when you looked at them, these were not kids or hippies, they were a bunch of guys in suits, very schoolteacher-looking, making raucous sounds! I thought they'd be some calm group of people; perhaps *wrongly*, I didn't ever think of Esperanto people as being some madhouse group. But *today* they can't even seem to *find* the parts that are mispronounced and they're very happy and want to show it at their conventions and do all sorts of things!

Talk about trying to find a distributor.

After the film was completed, everybody went about their business while I would show it to people in New York, in the screening rooms. Joe Levine wanted to open it in New York and he wanted me to split the costs! But *he* was the sort of person that we'd show this thing to. They'd be sitting there smoking cigars and watching it, and they'd be really amazed, particularly when they got to the end of the film with the *goat* and everything—it was just like almost too much! You'd be sitting in a room with like three guys, and they'd look at you really strangely and go, "Well, thank you" and walk out—and there you'd be, just sitting there! But I don't really *blame* them, because it *was* strange and offbeat, and they didn't have a whole lot to *gain* by [releasing it]. They didn't know what to do with it [*laughs*]! Artie Shaw was another one that was gonna do something with it, and I wasted like six months with him.

Artie Shaw the bandleader?

Right. He went into film distribution; in fact, *Séance on a Wet Afternoon* [1964], a big foreign film back then, was one of his. He was quite an interesting guy: He actually wrote several short stories that were published and he was a distributor ...aside from marrying all these great-looking babes! *I wanted to learn from Artie how he did that,* and he said, "Well, nobody else ever *asked* them!" He was married to Ava Gardner and Lana Turner and all sorts of people.

How much release did Incubus *eventually get in the U.S.?*

Zero. France is the one and only place where I'm certain it was released theatrically.

Tony Taylor, producer of *Incubus*, had rescued and restored the movie and is now releasing it on home video.

From the press materials you sent me, I see that Incubus *got some great reviews in France.*

It opened big in France, as far as business, and *certainly* from a critical standpoint. I mean, you can't do much better than reviews that say, "It's better than *Nosferatu*," better than Murnau and Dreyer! They really *loved* it, as you can see from those reviews. Which was quite a surprise to me. I thought that that would translate into a lot more than it did—it didn't translate into *anything*, frankly! I think some people almost *resented* [the French reviews]—they said, "Oh, the French like Jerry Lewis!" [*Laughs*] But, had *Incubus* not gotten those reviews, and had the Cinémathèque Française not put it in their collection, it wouldn't exist now.

Francis Coppola says he once saw a "nudie" version of Incubus. *Do you know what he's talking about?*

I do know what that was about. As I told you, Francis Coppola's assistant Mona Skager was a friend of mine, and she was Leslie Stevens' assistant prior to that. At some point in 1968, Leslie and I talked and we had an idea that perhaps, inasmuch as not much had transpired with *Incubus*, we'd cut in some new things and make it something different. We shot with some girl who I hired, doubling for Allyson in the nude, in color. Dick Brummer, who recently worked on the reconstruction with me, also worked with me on this, he and I were basically the ones who did it, because I had the time and Leslie was working full-time at Universal [on the TV series *It Takes a Thief*].

Was Allyson Ames still married to Stevens at this point? Did you try to get her to do the nude scenes?

Allyson had remarried Harry Rothchild by this time, so no thought was given to having her do it. I did speak with her and tell her what I was doing. She thought it was quite humorous and had no objection.

Where did you find the nude girl you used in those scenes?

I called someone at a casting office and told him what I wanted to use the actress for, and about the fact she would be naked in parts of the shoot. This was not easy, but he knew me and Leslie and he sent me some pictures. I chose one who looked a lot like Allyson—she was a topless dancer working in Pasadena. I thought it would be best if she went out to Universal and met Leslie and me in Leslie's office, just to prove we were legit. ("Are you sure David O. Selznick started like this?" I asked Leslie.) We shot north of Zuma Beach, where Bob Fortier knew an L.A. County lifeguard lieutenant who for a small consideration used his key to let us gain access to a secluded beach that was private. We were there for two days, shooting in color and without sound. The girl rolled around in the surf, ran on the beach, beckoned Bob Fortier into the water. At first the girl wore Allyson's costume, and then later she was topless with a thong. Fortier wore the same costume he did in the original. I was the director, and the photographer was the "legendary" Ray Steckler—"legendary" in underground circles, anyway. And Steckler's wife [Carolyn Brandt] did makeup. He was certainly an interesting guy—he and his wife *directed* films, *shot* films, and they both acted in that *Mixed-Up Zombies* thing [*The Incredibly Strange Creatures Who Stopped Living and Became Mixed-Up Zombies*, 1963]. They were very enthusiastic film people.

Then, I believe on a weekend, I directed some more footage with the girl in the backyard of my home in the Hollywood Hills. I can't remember what went on in those scenes; it's possible Fortier was there too. We did a bunch of outdoor shots, to match some of the Big Sur locale. Naturally we shot in front of trees and used closeups because my backyard did *not* resemble Big Sur! Those scenes were photographed by a guy who was then working on *It Takes a Thief* and who, if I'm remembering right, was up for an Emmy for his work on that show. In a screening room at Universal I showed Leslie the footage I shot, and he said laughingly that only Tony Taylor would be working with Ray Steckler and an Emmy nominee in the same week!

By the way, we also had the idea of perhaps losing the Esperanto and having Shatner do a narration. (And Shatner *did* do portions of the new narration, *again* as a favor to me, *while* he was doing *Star Trek*. I bring that up just to show *again* that the guy has been *so* cooperative about doing things that people just ordinarily wouldn't do.) Verna Fields helped me edit the new color footage into *Incubus*—I worked with her in her tiny pool house in the Valley. Her assistants who hung around a lot were George Lucas and his soon-to-be wife. Verna became very close to George and to Steven Spielberg, and she later ended up a vice-president of Universal due to them.

Then what did you do with this new "nudie" version?

Nothing was really ever done with it. I just don't think it would have worked, and we didn't expend any great amount of money on it. It wasn't the greatest idea in the world, but then again, when you're sitting with some film that went absolutely nowhere, you think of all sorts of things! [The nudie version] was never shown publicly, but Francis Coppola happened to see it because of the connection with Mona Skager. He may have been the only person who did.

The nudie stuff you shot that weekend—was that material lost by CFI also?

Yes, it was all together there at CFI. They lost *all* the parts, it's gone forever.

When did you find out that CFI had destroyed your prints?

In May of 1993, I called the vault custodian at CFI, where the negative and prints were stored. But after lots of probing, I was told that they could not be found. CFI's nickname is "Can't Find It," so I wasn't surprised. We got numerous different stories: First CFI said they couldn't find it, then they said it was out at UCLA, on and on. We never did really establish what happened to it. (You know, when people talk about film vaults, you think that your movie is better off there than in the trunk of your car, you think that they treat things fairly well.) Later I found they had been destroyed in an accident or in error. I contacted my attorney and we filed suit. In November 1994, I settled the case against CFI for a certain amount. I thought that was the end of *Incubus*.

What was the attitude of the people at CFI once they had to admit they'd lost your movie?

CFI tried to establish the fact that it was like worthless property and that they didn't owe any money. The implication was that, if they destroyed it, they were actually doing everybody a *favor* [*laughs*]! Then, finally when they settled, they said, "Of course, if you *find Incubus*, we wanna be in for some of the dough." But there was a time limit which expired prior to my finding it.

I don't honestly understand how they could have destroyed *every*thing that was there, because there were so many [different elements]. Subtitles in Italian from the Venice Film Festival, we had it in French, we had it in English, Allyson's husband had a 16mm print—there were just so many things in different places, I still don't understand it.

And then you did find a print in France.

On the 27th of November 1996, there was a message from my longtime friend and agent Howard Rubin that he had discovered a print in the permanent collection of the Cinémathèque Française in Paris. Naturally I was overjoyed and thought a Fax to Paris would get me the print. Boy, was I wrong! The Cinémathèque is a member of the FIAF [Federation Internationale des Archives du Film], the international association of film archives, and they won't even negotiate with an individual. One must contact an archive in his area who will vouch for him. Again I thought I was home free: The Academy of Motion Picture Arts and Sciences, the American Film Institute and UCLA were my contacts. Howard Rubin was a member of the Academy; Conrad Hall, my friend and *Incubus*' cinematographer, had won an Academy Award; and the American Film Institute is dedicated to the preservation of the moving image. Well, not *my* moving image! All I was asking was for someone to Fax Paris to discover the condition of the film and to ask how I, the copyright owner, could obtain access to it. Michael Friend, head of the Academy archives, reacted to my phone call as if I had asked for access to the archives for a cigar-smoking orgy—he told me how busy he was, etc. And the American Film Institute archivist stated to me they had no facilities for handling film [*laughs*]! Bottom line, they both refused to be involved, and it took months. As a last resort, I made a cold call to UCLA—I'm a graduate of crosstown rival USC, so I didn't expect much cooperation. But the archivist, Charles Hopkins, said "no problem" and that he would Fax the Cinémathèque Française right away. He briefly described the film, said that they [UCLA] supported my efforts and they hoped the Cinémathèque Française would give my request to borrow the sole surviving print every consideration. The next day, Bernard Maitland of the Cinémathèque Française Faxed UCLA back, saying, "Leslie Stevens is a great director and *Incubus* is a strange and interesting film that is to be protected." He confirmed they held a print in good condition (it turned out to be in *terrible* condition!) and they would choose a French lab who would do the work and directly invoice me. I ended up negotiating with several labs before deciding on Centrimage in Paris.

Now the fun begins. I don't speak French, so the task of restoring and copying a 30-year-old print that Cinémathèque had been running to packed houses for years was daunting, both financially and every *other* way. First I thought I'd ask for a digital tape copy, but this was impossible because the print was in such poor condition. The lab guy looked at it and said it was in such bad shape that it couldn't possibly be run through the machine. Of course, he didn't speak English and I didn't speak French, so we sent Faxes back and forth. He said the only way we were going to be able to do it was to make a frame-by-frame optical negative and a separate soundtrack. Then the French customs authorities refused to let the stuff I'd paid for out of the country as they considered it a national treasure—along with Jerry Lewis' *The Bellboy*, I guess! When FedEx showed up at my doorstep with a giant box of negatives and soundtracks, I could hardly believe it. The suspense on my drive to L.A., where I could actually see what I had, was painful to say the least. Now began work with a Rank telecine which allowed us to digitally correct and erase scratches—a long and expensive project. We also remastered the sound track. Dick Brummer and his partner Gary Adelman did the work restoring *Incubus* and are credited on-screen *and* on the new one-sheet as "Restoration Consultants." Dick Brummer has been an editor since the 1950s—he did most of Russ Meyer's films and many horror and "underground" films. He also worked with me on the "girlie" *Incubus*. Gary Adelman has been a production manager and associate producer on many independent movies. They did the new subtitles, telecine work and are very familiar with all the new technology that made restoring *Incubus* possible.

At the time you shot Incubus, *were you still making your living as a stockbroker?*

No, I had sold that, and pretty much was going to produce films.

Was Incubus *your only producing credit?*

I certainly *attempted* to do many more, with everybody from John Ford on down. Ford was going to do a script I had that Joe Stefano had written, a Western. I was just re-reading it and it's pretty good, as a matter of fact!

So Incubus *is your only producing credit.*

Yes. This movie really almost had a curse on it. Leslie, who had really been a very big deal, having done *Outer Limits* and all—his career didn't exactly take off after this, he went into bankruptcy and various things.

But not *as a result of* Incubus*!*

No, nothing to do with this. But you just don't normally don't get an actor murdering someone and a suicide and various other things so soon after the conclusion of a picture. (But *I'm* still here!) I also recall that Eloise Hardt's daughter was murdered. [Actress Hardt plays Allyson Ames' "sister succubus" in *Incubus*.] Eloise was at one time married to Hans Habe, a well-known European novelist, and they had a daughter named Marina Habe. One night when Marina was about 16, she was at Doug Weston's Troubadour [nightclub] and returned home late in the evening, and she was kidnapped by hippies in a van in Eloise's driveway. Her body was discovered in the Hollywood Hills several weeks later. This was around the time of the "Manson family" murders, and they were suspected, as I recall.

Tying in with what Connie [Conrad Hall] said about Leslie Stevens [that he was "a madman"], *Incubus* really *was* too crazy—certainly too crazy to go into a mainstream theater. There were just too many things in it that were too strange for the time. Any *one* of them might have been all right, but we had a combination of the language and rapes and *goats* [*laughs*]—it was just a little much! The whole thing about exhibiting films is not taking too much of a *risk*, and nobody wanted to get involved with something like this. Because if they *do*, a lot of people will come to them and say, "My God, you must have been *nuts*. Why would you ever distribute a film that had *blank*, *blank*, *blank* and *blank*?" If it works, great, but if it doesn't work, your ass is out in the street. But I'm very happy that I did it, and to have been associated with such a very nice group of people. And seeing it again recently, and realizing that we *would* be able to [restore it], was really more exciting than seeing it the first time!

Incubus (1965)

Daystar/Contempo III; Associate Producer: Elaine Michea; Produced by Anthony M. Taylor; Written & Directed by Leslie Stevens; Photography: Conrad L. Hall & (uncredited) William Fraker; Music: Dominic Frontiere; Editor: Richard Brockway; Makeup: Fred B. Phillips; Assistant Director: Maurice Vaccarino; Location Sound: Jay Ashworth; Continuity: Mary Chaffee; Main Title: Wayne Fitzgerald; Transportation: Richard Margrave; Electrician: Norman McCloy; Property Master: Ted Mossman; Assistant to Mr.

Stevens: Mona Skager; Wardrobe: Forrest T. Butler; Sound Editor: Arthur J. [Jack] Cornall; Assistant Cameraman: Charles Rosher; Music Editor: John Caper, Jr.; Chief Grip: John W. Jackson; 78 Minutes.

William Shatner (*Marc*), Allyson Ames (*Kia*), Eloise Hardt (*Amael*), Robert Fortier (*Olin*), Ann Atmar (*Arndis*), Milos Milos (*The Incubus*), Paolo Cossa (*Narrator*), Ted Mossman, Jay Ashworth, Forest T. Butler (*Monks*).

Shirley Ulmer

[Edgar G. Ulmer] started me out on a tremendous journey which was 40-odd years of marriage with him before he died.

Behind every great man, the old saying goes, there's a woman. In the case of legendary director Edgar G. Ulmer, "the Miracle Man of Poverty Row," the woman was his devoted wife Shirley, who script-supervised all his movies from the mid–1930s on—and who married Ulmer even though it meant years of major-studio blacklisting for both of them. In this interview, Shirley Ulmer talks candidly about her "tremendous journey" (her 35-year marriage to Ulmer), the experience of working with him in the margins of Hollywood, and some of the many cult films they made on small budgets, in 16-hour days, and against all odds.

Born June 12, 1914, in New York City, teenager Shirley came out to the movie capital for the first time in the early 1930s, after her banker-father was wiped out in the Crash. While her dad tried to make a new start in California, Shirley met picture people and began working as a script supervisor. She was married to independent producer Max Alexander when she met and instantly fell in love with Edgar Ulmer, eventually divorcing Alexander—nephew of Universal president Carl Laemmle. Hollywood outcasts, Ulmer and Shirley were subsequently forced to work in the East, on Poverty Row and at other small indie studios, where the indomitable Ulmer forged a remarkable career as a master of minimalism with memorable movies like *Bluebeard*, *Detour*, *Strange Illusion*, *The Man from Planet X* and others. Shirley is also a writer of screenplays, teleplays (*The Lone Ranger*, *Batman*, *S.W.A.T.*, *CHiPs*, more) and the book *The Role of Script Supervision in Film and Television*; in more recent years, she and her daughter Arianné maintained a high profile keeping alive the memory of Ulmer and his highly personal films. They were collaborating on the documentary *The Edgar G. Ulmer Story* when Shirley's health began to fail. She died in 2000.

Your father came out to Hollywood to make a new start as a banker or in the picture business?

In *anything* [*laughs*]! He didn't have any idea about the picture business, and banking was a no-no at that time. My grandmother (that's on my mother's side) knew a lady who was Willie Wyler's mother. I remember that Wyler's mother was very annoyed that the Hillcrest County Club was anti-Semitic then. She was the one who introduced me to [MGM production executive Irving G.] Thalberg and so forth, and that's how I got to be a script supervisor, thanks to her and my grandmother and a lady by the name of Moree Herring, a script supervisor at Metro. Thalberg was very kind to me, he said, "If you want to be a writer and you want to be on sets and learn something about the business, being a script clerk is a good way for a woman." That was what really got me started in the business.

Were you already Mrs. Max Alexander at that point?

No, not yet. I wrote a little play that Pasadena Playhouse put on and I played a small, autobiographical kind of part in it. After the show, Junior Laemmle and Max Alexander came backstage. So we went out, Junior and Max and another girl, I think her name was Betty.

On a double-date.

Yes. I picked Max, who was Uncle Carl Laemmle's nephew, and then I sort of saw him exclusively during that entire summer. When the big [Long Beach] earthquake happened [in 1933], my mother said, "I've had it out here, let's go back to New York." We did, my mother and father and I landed up in Brooklyn, Kings Highway. I was very unhappy that they brought me back to New York. Max began telephoning me long distance, because he wanted to marry me. Finally I said yes, because I was very unhappy about living at home with my mother, who didn't like the idea of me going around meeting producers and trying to sell my scripts [*laughs*]! He sent me a train ticket and a thousand dollars to come out to California. I cashed the train ticket in and I bought myself a boat trip, a two-week trip on the Grace Line, a boat that went through the Panama Canal and stopped off in all these different ports along the northern part of South America. It was very exciting 'cause I had a little flirtation on the trip [*laughs*]—I was quite a gal, I didn't realize it! I wasn't scared, I was going to marry Max Alexander, but I met [actor] Dane Clark on the boat. We had a little romantic thing going, but nothing serious. We didn't go to bed, but we did spend a lot of time together. Then I got out to California and I married Max.

Did you marry him because you loved him or to get away from home?

I married him to get away from home. I *was* very fond of him, he was a nice guy, but a very simple man. When we were first married, we went to Hawaii on our honeymoon, then we came back and lived in Uncle Carl's big house. Then we took a little apartment on Stanley in Hollywood. Uncle Carl helped us with furniture and all kinds of lovely gifts, and he was very happy with the marriage.

How did you meet Edgar Ulmer?

Max was hiring Edgar to work [as a second unit director] on *I Can't Escape* [1934] and he invited him to dinner at our apartment on Stanley. I was in the kitchen making a pot roast when I heard this man's voice that was so *exciting* to me—not just the accent, the *timbre* of his voice. I thought, "Oh, what a crazy, exciting man, what a beautiful voice!" I went in the living room and Max introduced me, and that's how I met Edgar.

Throughout nearly his entire directing career, Edgar G. Ulmer, "The Miracle Man of Poverty Row," had his script supervisor wife Shirley at his side.

Then after we had dinner, Max made the mistake of saying he was very tired and he had a headache, and that *I* would entertain Edgar, go out to the movies or something with him. Well, I entertained Edgar...and that was the beginning of the end of Max [*laughs*]!

Where did you and Ulmer go that night?
We went driving out to the beach. I had never met anyone like him, his knowledge was...incredible! He made me feel *stupid*, really. I talked about the book that I was writing [*Sinners in Sight*] and he talked about his experiences as an orphan after the War, when he had been sent to Sweden, and all the people he knew were famous—amazing brains. And *he* had an amazing brain. It was a very exciting evening. He started me out on a tremendous journey which was 40-odd years of marriage with him before he died. It wasn't always *easy*—he was not faithful, I had to watch out for that! He even had a daughter out of wedlock while we were married.

Subsequent "dates" with Ulmer took place behind Max Alexander's back, correct?
Yes.

What was it like, being part of the Laemmle clan?
It was *horrible*. That marriage only lasted a *year*, dear. Sundays were a disaster—on Sundays you sat around the table with the whole family at Uncle Carl's house, and everybody who was a top person at the studio was invited. That was a big deal, to be invited. Uncle Carl (unfortunately!) liked me very much [*laughs*] and he had me seated there and he had me giving my opinions. I remember one opinion I gave, I told him how I had seen Margaret Sullavan in a play in New York, I've forgotten which one, and I thought she was a great actress. He turned to Junior and he said, "You hear what Shirley said? Find out more about Margaret Sullavan!" And he later hired her! So *that* was my contribution to the industry! Uncle Carl had a tremendous estate—it got broken up into five or six estates. It was a huge hunk of land with *many* houses on it. He sold it when he sold the studio.

When you say that Uncle Carl "unfortunately" liked you, does that mean that you didn't particularly like him?
Oh, I didn't *dis*like him, he was a *funny* old man. But he was deaf, and you had to scream for him to hear you. He wouldn't use his hearing aid. He had very old-fashioned ideas, and he *never* forgave Edgar for taking me away from his nephew Max.

Was James Whale at the Sunday luncheons?
Yes, he was at the luncheons very often. He was nice. My memory doesn't tell me too much, only that he was a nice, comfortable man.

What was Junior like?
Junior was...weird. He was such a hypochondriac—he was always fighting some illness, some of them real and some of them, I think, imaginary. He wore Kotex to keep from catching cold on his penis—*that* I remember! By the way, there was once an article which said I was having an affair with the old man [*laughs*]. That was not true—that made me *mad*!

Did Junior live at home with his father?

Yes, he did.

If Max Alexander was part of the Laemmle family, why wasn't he making Universal pictures? Why was he making independents?

He had his own company, Beacon Productions, because he wanted to show that he could do something on his own. He owned a little studio on Santa Monica Boulevard. But he was on good terms with his Uncle Carl and he took care of Uncle Carl's business things. Uncle Carl owned that whole block on the corner—Melody Lane was a restaurant where *everybody* went, there on the corner of Hollywood and Vine. Uncle Carl owned that and the rest of that whole square block. Max used to collect rents and things like that—

In addition to running his own motion picture company.

Right. Max's other two uncles (on his mother's side) were the Stern brothers—they made the *Our Gang* comedies, and they were very famous and very wealthy.

The first movie you worked on was Max Alexander's I Can't Escape?

Yes, with Lila Lee. In those days, when you got divorced, you had to wait a year to get it finalized, and when I met Edgar, he was just finished with that year of waiting and he was celebrating. He had been married to a girl by the name of Joan Warner, whose name he used sometimes as a director [Ulmer did some early directing under the name John Warner]. She was a society girl and she had a relative, I think an uncle, who was a vice-president of the United States. Edgar and Joan Warner had a little girl, but after the divorce, Edgar never saw the child. I sent a check of $80 every month, as the court had decreed. We never saw her until she was grown-up and we were doing *Carnegie Hall* [1947]. She came and saw Edgar and borrowed $10,000 from him—she was sick and she needed an operation or

Autographed shot of Edgar G. Ulmer, 1920s. The inscription reads, "my dear Mother from a town between desert and pacific ocean far away from european culture with thanks and best wishes—Edgar—Hollywood"

something. Then we never heard from her again. I don't blame her. She didn't have the advantage of knowing her father.

What are some of your memories of the making of The Black Cat?

The Black Cat would never have been made if "Uncle Carl" had not gone to Europe, that I *know*. Junior was a very psycho, mixed-up young man, and Edgar was playing psychiatrist for him or something [*laughs*]! And so Junior had a real *crush* on Edgar, they were very close. It was Junior who got Edgar to do *The Black Cat*. When the old man came back from Europe, he didn't even want to *release The Black Cat*, because it had classical music in it. He didn't like that, he said, "The public can't take classical music, *I* can't take it! It's no good!" [*Laughs*] So it was a very strange thing that *Black Cat* became successful.

What impressions did you get of Karloff and Lugosi?

Boris was an intellectual, a very nice, easy guy to work with. Bela was a *clown*. Bela told jokes, he told crazy stories that he was a *hangman*. On the set, he did all kinds of funny things to get attention. He was showing off.

That's funny, because from everything I've heard and read, Lugosi usually kept to himself on the sets of his pictures.

Why he acted that way, I don't know. He invited Edgar and me to his home, which I understood at that time was a big deal. He treated his wife [Lillian] like she was a servant maid—that was *my* impression [*laughs*]. I didn't like him for that, but I never said anything. He seemed to be very fond of Edgar and took direction nicely.

Was your visit to Lugosi's house during the making of The Black Cat?

No, *much* later, after the movie was made, after I started living with Edgar. (We weren't married legally yet, but I was living with him.) Lugosi invited us to his home, and I recall that in the foyer of the house, right where we came in, was a huge painting of him in *Dracula*. And, again, I remember him forcing his little wife around very harshly. I felt sorry for her.

Several film historians have written that Ulmer's "dark side" manifested itself on The Black Cat. *Is that true, or is that just modern writers trying to be dramatic?*

I've heard that, too. Maybe it did; I can't say whether it did or not. That early on, I didn't know he *had* a dark side—I just knew that he got *difficult* at times [*laughs*]!

Were you romantically involved with him when he was making The Black Cat?

Not until afterwards.

So it was just a coincidence that you were assigned to The Black Cat *as script supervisor.*

I wasn't *assigned* to be the script supervisor, I just wangled my way in there because I wanted to *watch* Moree Herring the script supervisor, I wanted to learn more from her. So I wound up doing all her notes. I didn't get any credit, but in those days, you *never* got any credit. It was mostly an occupation for men, believe it or not. At Metro, there was only one girl [script supervisor]—everybody else was male. They changed that when they found that these males, like Mervyn LeRoy and a lot of others who started there as script supervisors, would leave and become directors, and the girls would *stay*.

What was Peter Ruric, the writer of The Black Cat, *like?*

He was brilliant, really, but *cuckoo* [*laughs*]. He wasn't like any *ordinary* person I'd ever met. But very, very brilliant—Edgar adored him, and they were very close. He was one who used to show up for the Sunday luncheons at Uncle Carl's.

Black Cat *was made very cheaply and very fast. Obviously you worked long hours.*

Oh, and *how*! Not only on *The Black Cat* but on *all* Ulmer films, it was usually a 16-hour day. You'd get to work at six in the morning and you were lucky if you got home before midnight. The cameraman on *The Black Cat* [John Mescall] was very, very good. He was already recognized as a top cameraman.

And Ulmer got along well with him?

Very good. He always got along with the heads of the departments. He didn't get along with anybody that was a four-flusher or anything, but he got along with all of his crews. His crews always loved him, and he tried very hard all the way through his life to get the same people again and again.

And you didn't *get the impression that Karloff and Lugosi were close friends.*

They weren't close friends if they were friends *at all*, they just were sort of polite to each other. But you could feel a certain amount of jealousy or *tension*, I should say, going on between them.

Even emanating from Karloff?

Oh, yes. He had a certain contempt, because Lugosi *did* act like a clown, he acted silly. I don't think Karloff, any more than Edgar or I, believed these stupid stories Lugosi told us!

Did Lugosi tell people his stories one-on-one, or did he hold court?

He would hold court. He was reserved on his other pictures—at least that's what everybody tells me. But not with *us*! But I thought he was excellent in the picture.

Who was better in the picture, Karloff or Lugosi?

They were both good, they were both right for their parts. Karloff didn't want to make the picture, he didn't want to be known as a horror actor. He didn't want to do this film, but when Edgar showed him his sketches and the sketch of the costume he [Karloff] would wear, he weakened and said okay. Jacqueline Wells [Julie Bishop] was a pretty girl and she did a fine job, and David Manners was good, too. Edgar was a very interesting director—he directed with a baton. He *timed* their speeches. He drove Hedy Lamarr [star of Ulmer's *The Strange Woman*, 1946] crazy because he timed the way she spoke with the baton, and would slap her on the ankles with the baton if she goofed [*laughs*]!

Was he using the baton as early as The Black Cat?

Yes. Once Edgar told Peter Bogdanovich that he was a frustrated conductor—Edgar was *very* knowledgeable. He read music and he always had scores around the house, and one year he taught a course at the Curtis Institute in Philadelphia [on music theory and history]. So maybe he felt he was conducting! For Father's Day every year, our daughter Arianné always gave him a new baton, because he broke them all the time. He would go crazy on a good Beethoven's Ninth or things like that, "conducting" in the living room while he was listening to the music.

Right in the middle of The Black Cat, *and then later, in the middle of* Bluebeard, *Ulmer includes a scene of comic relief.*
He usually did that on purpose, because he was worried about being considered too serious. He felt people needed comic relief and he tried to do comedy whenever he could. But he was not known for being a good comedy director.

Supposedly Karloff's Satanist character was based on several real-life people—one of them Fritz Lang.
Well, Fritz Lang was one of the few people that Edgar did not get along with, so I don't know. They spoke badly about each other [*laughs*]!

In the Bogdanovich interview, Ulmer said that Fritz Lang was sadistic and he couldn't get along with him. Then, a few pages later, he said Erich von Stroheim was sadistic and that he loved *him! What was the difference between those two sadists?*
There was quite a difference. Von Stroheim was very intelligent and a much more knowledgeable man [than Lang]. Edgar liked someone he could *admire*.

What were some of his cost-cutting methods on a movie like Black Cat?
He always got to a point where he would suddenly say, "Well, it's getting towards the end of the day. I'm gonna *cheat*—and you're gonna cheat along *with* me. We're gonna go *fast*, we're gonna do one take." They would call him "One-Take" Ulmer—the actors would get scared [*laughs*]!

That's one way to hurry things up! Peter Bogdanovich asked Ulmer, "How in the world do you do 80 setups a day?" and Ulmer said, "Ask my wife." Well, 30 years later, I'm asking.
How did we do 80 setups a day? Well, because he would do these one-take things. He used the dolly like nobody had ever used it before; he would make five-minute, ten-minute shots. He was always unhappy that they didn't make film reels longer [*laughs*]!

Are you in any of his movies?
I was in *Natalka Poltavka* [1937]; it was a case where a girl didn't show up at work one day and Edgar said, "Go get in her costume." But I was Edgar's script supervisor on everything after *The Black Cat*, from 1934 on.

Is he in any of his movies?
No. He didn't have the acting bug.

Even though he started out as an actor?
Well, he was a different kind of actor, he was a stage actor.

One of the most striking scenes in Black Cat *is the one where Karloff prowls through the basement where he has all his dead wives in the upright glass coffins.*
[*Laughs*] I *loved* that scene. *All* of his sets were to me incredible, *always*. On his preparation for every film, he spent a lot of time and energy on creating sets that were unusual. In those days, his use of Plexiglas and glass and all the other crazy things he did was completely modernistic. He made wonderful sets.

An actress named Lucille Lund, who played Karloff's wife in The Black Cat, *says that Ulmer treated her nicely until he started* to flirt with her and she turned him down. After that, she said, he wasn't very nice at all!

Oh, that's very likely [*laughs*]—I believe her! Edgar did not have much carrying-on with actresses, his playing-around was not with people in the business. Hedy Lamarr, who he knew from school days, was probably the only one he *may* have had an affair with, but I'm even inclined to doubt that it was for very long. 'Cause he really didn't like her. But he got a performance out of her in *The Strange Woman* that nobody else ever got. Also in *Loves of Three Queens* [1953], which we made in Italy.*

Did the Laemmles ever come onto the sets of any of these movies?

Just Junior. Like I said, we were lucky that *Black Cat* even got released because the old man was furious. When he came back, he was so angry at his son, who had allowed Ulmer to go so crazy and use classical music and crazy sets and all of this. He didn't like the film at *all*.

Next Ulmer directed Thunder Over Texas *[1934], which I've never seen. Was there anything about it that set it apart from other Westerns?*

Yeah, it was accused of being another *Little Miss Marker*, it was the same kind of story. I wrote that film [using the pseudonym Shirle Castle].

Did Ulmer seem out-of-place directing a Western?

Shirley substituted for a no-show actress and played a small part in Edgar's *Natalka Poltavka* (1937).

---

*The three-part film (a.k.a. L'Amante di Paride *and* The Face That Launched a Thousand Ships*) is comprised of the stories of Genevieve of Brabant, Empress Josephine and Helen of Troy. After Ulmer directed the Genevieve of Brabant story, he and Hedy Lamarr had a fight (Lamarr had "bought out" the producers and started giving Ulmer instructions). For the first and only time, Ulmer walked off a picture. Lamarr engaged director Marc Allegret to direct the other two segments.*

No, he *liked* the idea. He wasn't too good at it, but he did it and he liked it [*laughs*]! He was fascinated because that was part of America that he knew nothing about. He used the name "John Warner" on that film—later, when I got annoyed, he stopped using it. I got annoyed because I thought maybe Edgar still cared for her [Joan Warner]. She had left him, and in their divorce she said he had slapped her. He never hit me, he was not violent in that way. He screamed like crazy, but he never touched me [*laughs*]!

Do you think he slapped her?
Maybe...if she made him *mad* enough.

Were you still married to Max Alexander when you did Thunder Over Texas?
Yes. Then I started living with Edgar without being able to marry him because I had to wait that whole year, and we didn't get married until '35. I legally married Edgar a few months before my twenty-first birthday. Before that, I lived with him for almost a year, which was unheard-of in those days, too! We were living in the Christie Hotel on Hollywood Boulevard.

When you did fall in love with Ulmer and decided to marry him, do you remember breaking the news to Max Alexander?
Well, he thought I was nuts [*laughs*] —*everybody* did! My own parents didn't talk to me for a couple of *years*.

And Laemmle-wise, what were the repercussions?
Oh, we were told that we'd never work in Hollywood again. He couldn't get a job—that's why we went back to New York.

He was told by who that he would never work again?
By everyone he called.

So there was no face-to-face confrontation with any of the Laemmles.
No, no, no. But [Hollywood] just didn't want him around.

Were things touch-and-go financially throughout all your years with Edgar?
Well, until we made *Carnegie Hall*, yes. I think [*Carnegie Hall* producer] Boris Morros saw to it that we had dough.

After living and working in the East for several years, you and Ulmer came back to Hollywood and started working at PRC.
Edgar met [PRC producer] Leon Fromkess, who was an accountant of sorts—a businessman—and a real movie buff. Edgar and he struck up quite a friendship. He was very nice, he *and* his wife Rita—she was a bit of a pain in the neck, because she was always around on the set and Edgar was always shooing her away! But a nice lady. Both of them were devout Christian Scientists. At PRC I was very busy looking up scripts for them and writing little cards with synopses of what the basic stories were about.

What memories of Bluebeard?
The script was written by Pierre Gendron—he was a sick man in that he was, I guess, a semi-alcoholic. That made it a little difficult to work with him. But he could write like a dream and he got along with Edgar beautifully. He had a wife whose first name was Mary and she assisted him, especially when he couldn't show up or was too far gone in the cups [*laughs*]!

Back in Ulmer's Universal days, right after The Black Cat, *he was going to make a movie about Bluebeard, so it must have been something that was in his mind even—*

It *was* very much in his mind right along, yeah. He had a lot to do with the writing, and Pierre and his wife put it down on paper properly. He was an educated guy, this Pierre, very well-versed in literature. I might tell you that Edgar was terribly self-conscious because English was a second language to him. He could write wonderfully, but he didn't trust himself, he always wanted [help from] somebody who was knowledgeable in the English language. Pierre was a fine writer, but a difficult man.

How was working at PRC different from working at one of the bigger studios?

Edgar had complete charge. *N*obody else had a word to say. Fromkess was a very quiet man…his wife gave Edgar a little problem now and then, but Fromkess and Edgar got along very, very well. Or they *did* until *The Strange Woman* came about. Hedy Lamarr wanted Edgar to direct her, and so Fromkess made a deal and loaned Edgar out to [*Strange Woman* producer] Hunt Stromberg. I've forgotten what Stromberg paid but it was a very large sum. Edgar had been earning $200 a week on his contract with Fromkess, and Fromkess never gave him a penny of the extra

Early glamour shot of Shirley Ulmer.

money that he made by lending Edgar out to do *The Strange Woman*. That's when Edgar decided *enough is enough*, and *very* shortly thereafter, when his contract came due, he refused to work there any more.

In what way was Mrs. Fromkess a pain in the neck? What was she trying to do by hanging out on the sets?

Well, she was a frustrated moviemaker, I guess [laughs]. She was a good woman, and they had a daughter who died of cancer. Mrs. Fromkess also died at an early age.

Did Edgar Ulmer have input in the music of these PRC movies?

He had *all* the input! Everybody, Fromkess included, thought that he was crazy to want to do an operatic thing, the *Faust* [marionette show], in *Bluebeard*, but he insisted on doing it. And it *was* noted; in fact, *The Hollywood Reporter* gave us a very fine critique on it.

What do you remember about composer Leo Erdody and cinematographer Eugene Schüfftan, who collaborated with Ulmer at PRC?

Erdody and Edgar were bosom pals. Erdody was a fine musician. Erdody died very suddenly and it was a tragedy for Edgar—he didn't really get over it *ever*. He loved Leo Erdody. Erdody's father was a conductor in Hungary, and Liszt left Erdody's father his baton. The father gave the baton to Erdody, Erdody gave the baton to Edgar and Edgar used that baton when he was directing. That baton still exists.

Schüfftan was a big help. Schüfftan couldn't join the union [the American Society of Cinematographers], they wouldn't let him in, but he was *very* much around and in charge of the camera. He was a darling man. He was Edgar's favorite cameraman, and he and Edgar were very close friends. But Schüfftan couldn't learn English properly. Every sentence had words from five different languages [*laughs*], he had all these languages mixed up. And he made us laugh very much and he would get very hurt, but we couldn't *help* laughing. It was very strange and very funny. He was a man of many languages—all at once!

Talking to Bogdanovich, Ulmer called Bluebeard "a very lovely picture." What were some of the parts of it that he particularly enjoyed?

He enjoyed very much being able to do the *Faust* aria. Sonia Sorel, John Carradine's girlfriend, was good in that, too. Edgar *didn't* want her in it because he didn't like hiring someone just because she was John's girlfriend, but she surprised him and gave a very fine performance. As did all of them. Edgar felt that Carradine did one of his finest jobs in *Bluebeard*. And Carradine kind of agreed with him [*laughs*]!

Your daughter Arianné tells funny stories about Ulmer losing his patience and getting tough with actors who weren't giving him what he wanted. In all your years of working with Ulmer, what actor got it the worst? Who got it with both barrels?

Offhand, I think it might have been John Saxon [on *The Cavern*, 1966]— Edgar treated him pretty bad! But he got along with his women fine. He was known for pinching their ankles sometimes during a closeup, to get an expression [*laughs*], but none of them seemed to mind. They all got along with him.

How about behind-the-camera people? Did he ever get tough with any of them?

No. He got along beautifully with *every* crew. They were hand-picked and they were all wonderful.

I like the flashback scenes in Bluebeard, *with the distorted sets and imaginative camerawork.*

Beautiful camerawork, yes. Those were the kind of touches that Edgar relied on Schüfftan for.

What more can you tell me about Carradine?

He was the Man Who Came to Dinner [*laughs*]! He and his son, who calls himself David Carradine, a funny little youngster. They had been living at the Garden of Allah, which was a very well-known place, an outdoor hotel with bungalows all around the pool area. It was very popular with the stars at that time. John brought his boy to dinner and he told us a sad story about this wife whom he was divorcing, the mother of David. She was trying to get John for back alimony, and he had to hide out from her. So he asked if he could stay with *us* awhile. So we always laugh—he was the Man Who Came to Dinner, but he stayed with us for *months* [*laughs*]!

So you got to know him quite well.

Of course, and also David, who was a *wild* boy who took our daughter Arianné to play with him. He called himself Captain Midnight and they would run all over the roofs of the buildings! It was so dangerous, it scared the hell out of me—I was always chasing him and scolding him [*laughs*]!

Did you ever regret letting Carradine move in?

Oh, no, he was *fun*. He could have been a professor of literature, really, and Edgar admired anyone who was that knowledgeable. When Carradine and David were staying with us, they stayed in Edgar's bedroom and Edgar moved back in with me.

You and Ulmer had separate bedrooms?

We had separate bedrooms but we usually slept in my bedroom. Edgar's room was always a mess—he had his drawing board there and all of his stuff, and he wouldn't allow anybody to come in and clean up [*laughs*]. That was Edgar's "bedroom." He'd go back and forth—he would spend part of the night in my bedroom and then go into the second bedroom. He was an insomniac and he would get up in the middle of the night and work. This second bedroom attached to Arianné's bedroom, with a bathroom between them. If Arianné was up late at night or if she went into the bathroom and the light was showing beneath the door, she could go in there and talk to him. Most of the time Arianné talked to him was in the middle of the night.

If Ulmer and Carradine were such great friends, why wasn't Carradine in more of Ulmer's movies?

Because Carradine got more money—he went on to become a *name*. When we used him, he was *not*.

What was Sonia like?

[*Pause*] I didn't like her too much, but she *was* a good little actress. We went to their wedding—my daughter was the flower girl and David Carradine was the ring bearer. It was in the Episcopalian church on Wilshire Boulevard and they dressed in Shakespearean costumes. It caused a little publicity, and people talked about it. Arianné and David scattered the rosebuds.

John Carradine in more than one interview mentioned directing one scene in Bluebeard. *Do you know what he's talking about?*

No. And I don't think he'd say that if Edgar were alive!

What do you think of Bluebeard? *Do you think it's one of Ulmer's better pictures?*

I certainly do. It's hard to name my favorites, I can't pick *one*, but I can say offhand quickly *Ruthless* [1948], *The Cavern* and *Detour* [1945]. And *The Naked Dawn* [1955] *definitely*. Those would be the ones that I would name off the top of my head.

Even though it's certainly not a horror or science-fiction movie, I want to hear some of the great stories you have about The Pirates of Capri *[1949].*

During the bad period in the U.S. [the HUAC period], Edgar and I were off to Europe. We were never really bothered at all, although the FBI did come see us before we went off—two gentlemen came to the house on King's Road and asked questions about certain friends of ours. I remember in particular they were interested at that moment in Gale Sondergaard. We didn't know anything about where she joined [the Communist party] or what she did, so I don't think we helped them! Then they gave Edgar an envelope with a special address on it, and said when we were in Europe and we were meeting all these

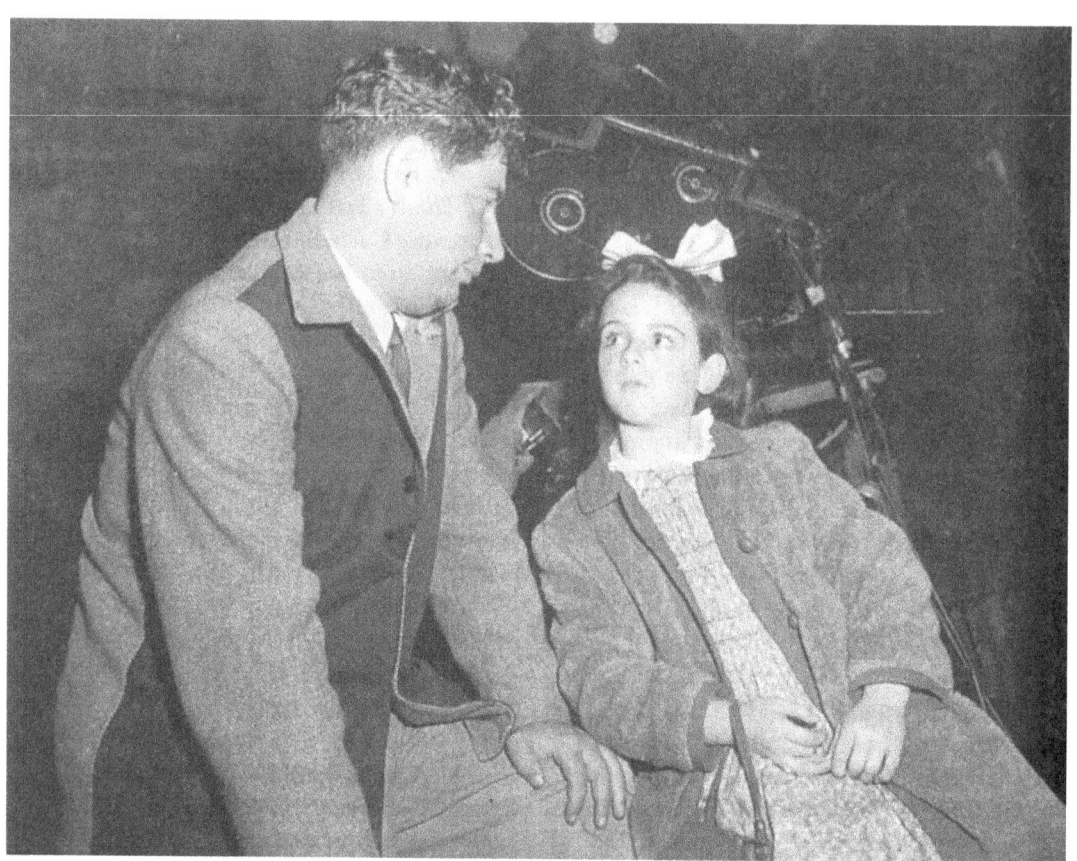

Arianné Ulmer, Edgar and Shirley Ulmer's daughter, visits the set of one of their 1943 PRC productions.

people that were suspect, Edgar could [write it all down and] mail it back to them. And he said he'd be delighted.

So now we were off to Europe [to make *The Pirates of Capri*] with a producer by the name of Victor Pahlen, who was quite a character. I think they did that movie *The Bad and the Beautiful* [1952] about him. He had a lot of charm, he charmed everybody to death, but he was a bit on the crooked side [*laughs*]! He had gotten a deal together with a lady from Egypt to do this *Pirates of Capri* in Italy. Edgar had gone on first, to get everything arranged, and then he sent me a lot of telegrams and lists of things he was going to need.

I arrived in Italy with Arianné, who was a little girl—oh, she couldn't have been more than 11 or 12 years old. We arrived at Ciampino Airport near Ostia. (Everything was bombed out pretty bad, from the War.) We got out of the plane and I had all these toys and books and things for Arianné. And some little Italian children started running after us. With all these bundles and everything, and trying to keep hold of the child, I was having a little problem! And these children were running after me, making me very nervous, yelling, "Jew! Jew!" And I thought, "Oh, my God, you mean they're anti-Semitic over here too?" So I was frightened. I later found out they were yelling at me "Giu! Giu!" meaning "Down! Down!" because I was schlepping all of these huge suitcases and wouldn't let go of them. They wanted to help me [*laughs*]! I didn't know a word of Italian beyond *arrivederci*!

I got into a little building there on the airfield and they opened up my suitcases and they immediately took away my cigarettes—I had a couple of cartons in there. They took *them* away. And there was no one there to meet us—I was looking for Edgar. Finally a lady came and she said she was sorry she was late, she was delayed. She had promised Edgar she would meet us. We could come to the hotel and rest a little and have a little something to eat, but then we had to catch a midnight train down to the location, which was in Taranto. I thought of *Canada*, that's the only Toronto *I* knew! "What are we doing in Toronto?" [*Laughs*]

This was probably October-November and we had been told that sunny Italy was *warm*, so I didn't have heavy clothes with me. Not for the child and not for me. We rushed to that train and we made it all right, and, my golly, it was *freezing*. One of my memories is that I couldn't put my head down on the pillow. We had a private train compartment and it was lovely, but it was so cold that the pillow felt like a block of ice [*laughs*]. There was no stop in Taranto, we got off the train at a little village close by, and there we were met by a car and chauffeur and driven down to Taranto. Now, Taranto had been bombed to the ground by the English. There wasn't a building with [an unbroken] window in it any more. We were taken to the best-looking building of them all, which had some boarded-up windows. We got in there, into a great big sort of lobby, round, with a very unattractive lady sitting in the center at a raised dais or desk. We called her "The Animale" later—"The Animal." She was a very unattractive and ugly-*acting* person. And there were a lot of *very* pretty young women running around, most of them with just towels wrapped around them. Nothing ever dawned on me [*laughs*]—I led a very sheltered life! We

Shirley, Edgar and Arianné.

were shown to our room, which was stone-walled and no windows, but at least it sheltered us a little from the cold. It had a great big double bed and there was a little single bed for Arianné over in the corner. It wasn't until maybe the second night that I realized where I was, because finally I asked questions. Edgar told me, "Look, I couldn't find any better accommodations. This is a whorehouse!" A legal, government-licensed Italian naval whorehouse. Later on, Edgar would tell this story—he said, "I'll bet you I'm the only man who took my wife and daughter to a whorehouse!"

And what happened to the envelope that the FBI asked you to bring along on the trip?

Oh, we destroyed it right away [*laughs*]!

What can you remember about the making of The Man from Planet X?

Last night I put on my goggles and I watched my *Man from Planet X* tape all over again, and I thought it was a *very* respectable, *nice* picture. It was made in 1950 at the Hal Roach Studios, produced by Jack Pollexfen, who was a rather shy man. We all almost died because of the use of Nu Gel to make the fog you see in the picture. It was a ghastly experience and we all got sick. When we made *Man from Planet X*, we were in a *terrible* rush, because we had a job coming up that would take us to Spain.

Planet X was one of the few Hollywood-made movies that you did around that time. Which did you enjoy more, making movies in Hollywood or abroad?

I don't know whether the right word is "enjoy"—they were hard work!

Both at home and *abroad.*

Yes. The experiences in Europe, of course, were much more exciting in those years, because *they* didn't know Americans like *we* didn't know *them*. We were strangers to each other.

Man from Planet X *was the first time working with Robert Clarke. How did you like him?*

Easygoing guy—*very* nice person. I can't say enough nice things about him. Margaret Field was the mother of Sally, and Margaret gave up her career and put all her efforts behind that little girl of hers. (It paid off!) Margaret was a very simple, pleasant, nice personality.

And the guy who played X?

I think he was okay —*very* okay, actually. But he was a bit of a complainer! He'd complain about the gear. He didn't complain *bitterly*, but he wasn't too happy. Edgar called that [mask] a "douche bag"!

Robert Clarke talks about making $210 for starring in that movie.

Well, Edgar got about 300, so Robert Clarke didn't do so bad! *Man from Planet X* was made in a very fast and tense schedule. As I said, Nu Gel was the product that caused the fog, and it caused us all to get sick. It was *horrible* to breathe. We didn't know any other way, Edgar couldn't get the effect if he didn't use the Nu Gel. So somehow or other, sick or not, we got through. We *couldn't* have a delay because Harry and Eddie Danziger [producers of Ulmer's earlier *St. Benny the Dip*, 1951] had promised us that we were going to make a picture in Spain. We had to get going.

Shirley with Louis Hayward on the set of *Ruthless* **(1948), one of her favorite Ulmer movies.**

Did you get the sense that Edgar liked the way Man from Planet X *came out?*

He wasn't that impressed, but he liked having done it, 'cause he *wanted* to do a science-fiction of that sort. But we were in such a rush to get it done because that crazy couple was cabling us all the time, the Danzigers. We went to Europe on a ship called the *Liberte*, and it was absolutely magnificent—I had a wonderful trip. We arrived in France and from there we took a car or a train into Paris and met the Danzigers, who proceeded to give Edgar all kinds of scripts and ideas. The Danzigers were a couple of Americans who became very successful...became English citizens...owned the Mayfair and other hotels in London...and now they were producing movies. They were nice, they were pleasant, but they just drove us *crazy* because they'd give Edgar ideas of pictures that they were going to make, and Edgar would prepare them. He spent six months, after rushing to get there, before finally they got the deal set to make *Babes in Bagdad* [1952] in Spain.

When we got into Spain, there was a problem: I used to be like the go-fer, and [before leaving the U.S.] I had packed all the film and everything we'd need and sent it to Paris, where the Danzigers were waiting for us. Then, when I heard we were gonna be actually shooting in Spain, I transferred it all to Spain. When we were in Spain and ready to go, we couldn't get all this stuff out of customs. You see, Arianné was a junior high school student, and Edgar and I arranged for her studies to be sent from her junior high so she wouldn't fall behind. Unfortunately, amongst the many books that were sent in that shipment was a book called *For Whom the Bell Tolls*.

[Laughs] *Oh, Franco's "favorite"!*

Here's the way we got our stuff: We had in that film Paulette Goddard, who was married at that time to Erich Maria Remarque, the author of *All Quiet on the Western Front*. Remarque had a beautiful home in Switzerland, and Paulette had come over and stolen him away from Marlene Dietrich [*laughs*]! Now Goddard was working for us in *Babes in Bagdad*. She had a lot of clout in Europe, and she went down to Franco. Edgar didn't dare let Franco even know his *name*, because Edgar had once been interviewed and called Franco "the butcher of Europe." It got a lot of publicity in Europe, and Edgar was worried that Franco would find out that it was him! Fortunately he didn't. Goddard went down there and fooled around with all these big shots of Franco's, and she got a special permit to get the stuff off the ship! I remember that, because we were going crazy waiting!

The other problem that Edgar had was, the girls they had gotten together for him were supposed to be harem girls, beautiful girls—and they *were*. But most of them had hair on their chests! And long hair under their arms and all over their legs. And they were infuriated when Edgar made them shave [*laughs*]! They thought they'd lost all their sex appeal—back then, men *liked* the hairy girls over there!

Why did Ulmer become involved on Beyond the Time Barrier *and* The Amazing Transparent Man, *the two science-fiction movies he made in Texas?*

They were done for dough. We shot *Beyond the Time Barrier* at an Air Force base, and that's interesting in my memory banks because we had to wear special badges and we were body-searched going and coming from work at the base. Remember the old saying, "If you don't like the weather in Texas, wait a half-hour, it'll change"? It was always on and off and weather-permitting calls —you never knew what the weather would be. We had a lot of terrible storms. Both of them [*Time Barrier* and *The Amazing Transparent Man*] were made quickly.

There was a rumor that Ulmer did not direct all of Amazing Transparent Man.

He directed the whole thing. In fact, he stayed on in Texas longer than I did—he sent *me* and Arianné home and he stayed on there, because he did his first cut down there. Douglas Kennedy, who played the invisible man in that, was a gentleman and Marguerite Chapman was a very nice, simple lady.

What do you remember about shooting L'Atlantide *[1961] in Italy?*

When we started, Frank Borzage was supposed to direct it, Edgar was a producer and Nat Wachsberger was the money man—he was a big producer in Europe, a Frenchman. (Actually, he was a Belgian, but he liked to be called a Frenchman!) Wachsberger and his wife Yvette [Lebon], a well-known actress, were quite interesting people. We started the picture and we were either one or two days in when we realized Borzage was so sick, he could hardly hold his head up. I was helping him the best I could, but I didn't know what to do about it—he was really in terrible shape. When Wachsberger came to visit us on the set, he saw what we were up against and he had a conversation with Mrs. Borzage and she agreed, and Frank Borzage retired. He never did another thing, he died shortly after. It was very sad—it was *awful*.

How much of the picture had he directed?

There was nothing in the camera, really—a couple of long shots done on the beach. We were just marking time until Wachsberger came and did something about it. Anyhow, we did it, and it was interesting. It was a tough picture to make, but it was interesting.

Why tough?

Under the circumstances, we were all pretty shook up about Borzage. But I think Edgar did a very good job, a *splendid* job on that picture. I remember Arianné [the movie's dialogue coach] teaching Jean-Louis Trintignant the dialogue phonetically—he didn't speak English. But he was awfully good-looking [*laughs*]!

What happened to Borzage got hushed up. The trade papers said he couldn't direct L'Atlantide *because of the "language barrier."*

Well, his wife didn't want that publicity, because he wouldn't get any more work. Which he *didn't* and *shouldn't* have gotten—he was a sick man.

Ulmer's last feature was The Cavern, *which he made in Europe.*

We had a good cast in *The Cavern*. Brian Aherne was in it and he was *really* excellent, and if you ever read his autobiography, he talks a little bit about *The Cavern*. He gives his sympathy to Edgar —and me, too!—because we were really having a very rough time. In our cast we had Aherne and Larry Hagman, who was a very *amusing* young man who kept me going—who kept *all* of us

Shirley Ulmer in 1986.

going. It was so cold on the location there, and Larry was a drinker at the time, and he had his little flask going. He brought along some instant soup tablets—bouillon—and he made cups of bouillon for all of us, and then he would put something in from his flask [*laughs*]! It was a Yugoslavian liquor called Slivovitz, plum brandy, and it was probably 100 proof, because we *felt* it. And it did warm us up [*laughs*]! So we were grateful to him! He was always carrying on with funny jokes. We also had Peter Marshall, God *bless* him—he was the steadying influence, a *wonderful*, wonderful, decent human being. And John Saxon, who was a nuisance, and who doesn't like Edgar very much because Edgar didn't pay much attention to him [*laughs*]!

When we all got over there, we met in Rome and we were told, "Everything is set, the dough is in the bank in Yugoslavia. We're off to Belgrade!" We took off from Rome and got onto the train. But we didn't see our luggage—we had taken two or three taxis [to the train station] and one taxi had all our luggage, and none of us had seen that luggage arrive. I was seated with Edgar and Larry and Peter, and I remember Peter was upset because Edgar had rushed us so and he didn't have a toothbrush [*laughs*]! We had *nothing* with us but the clothes on our back. And we were all pretty hysterical and angry at Edgar about this! We arrived in Belgrade and, my God, there's no luggage. So here we are in a strange country with*out* luggage, with just what we had on our backs.

The Hotel Metropole in Belgrade was a very beautiful hotel, but not quite finished off good. In the bathrooms there were no toilets, there was just a hole in the beautiful marble floor [*laughs*]! The first activity I recall there was going shopping with Larry Hagman, looking for big tubs that we could put down on the floor and make ourselves some kind of a quasi-wash place. All the store windows had things *in* them, but when you'd go inside the store, there *wasn't* anything. We were pretty upset. We only found one tub, which became a community tub, going from room to room. And it was winter, the snow was *way* up, up almost to my waist in spots, and very, very cold, and Hagman's booze was very welcome! In the hotel we had a woman who sat in uniform in the lobby, and if we wanted to receive or make phone calls, we had to do them down there on her phone.

And when we went even onto location, there were two Yugoslavian officers assigned to us. It was *very* Communistic. We had a maid who had paper in her one pair of shoes because they had holes in them, and she wouldn't take another pair because she would be arrested. Horrible. The people were *lovely*...but frightened. There was great fear in the air.

Like I told you, the Hotel Metropole had marble floors, and Larry Hagman made a bonfire on the floor in his room [*laughs*]! He had his family with him—he had two little girls and his wife. A charming, lovely family. (He *is* a family man, as you can see—they've stayed together all these years.) Anyhow, he was gonna feed his family, and somehow or other he'd gotten hold of some sausages and he wasn't gonna take them outside, so he just made a bonfire in the hotel!

We shot for I would say three, four days, maybe a week on the location, which wasn't far from the main city of Belgrade. And all of a sudden, when Edgar went to the bank, he discovered that the money had been confiscated. And we got the news from others around us, from the [Yugoslavian] crew, that the country had a new minister, the old guy had been booted out, and there had been a lot of changes. And we better get the hell out of there!

Which you did.
They got us onto a workman's train that left in the middle of the night. We left like thieves in the night. And on that train, Edgar had the first signs of what he got later—a small stroke. He kind of half-passed out, he was not feeling good, and Peter Marshall was his "doctor" who was helping him and was so kind. I'm always grateful, Peter *really* helped him—he kept everybody from bothering Edgar while on the train.

The original plan was to shoot it all in Yugoslavia?
Yeah. And we were *stuck* now. Everybody was so good about it except John Saxon—of course. He was suspicious 'cause he didn't believe us that we *would* get financed again. We didn't have money there for a week or so, and everybody just said, "Don't worry, we're not gonna stop filming." Only John Saxon gave trouble.

You resumed shooting in Italy.
Yes. Edgar was in terrible shape, and now he had to try and find a cave, which he did, in the city of Trieste. As I can tell you, it was a very nerve-wracking experience. I thought that Larry Hagman gave the finest performance, not only of *his* life, but of anybody playing a drunken person who's out of control. He was really awfully good, and I thought Brian Aherne was lovely. The girl was Rosanna Schiaffino, and she was very pretty and very nice. Nothing spectacular—she never got anywhere, not like Loren and Gina Lollobrigida. But we thought she might, so we used her. It was all quite an experience!

In the mid-60s, Ulmer finally tried to branch out into television.
That's right, that's why we came home from Europe. And also because I thought Edgar needed doctoring—I didn't know what was wrong with him. He was getting *terrible* migraines.

Edgar wrote 13 scripts for *The Doris Day Show*, for which they didn't *pay* him. Doris Day's husband Marty Melcher took over, and then Melcher got a stroke and Doris Day's son said he didn't know anything about [the money Ulmer was owed] and he didn't pay him. We had to sue Doris Day and the suit went on for four, five years. Edgar was dead by the time I settled the suit with her for $3000. I couldn't afford the lawyers.

The scripts he wrote were produced?
Yes. But no credit. The son said Edgar never wrote them, but he never met Edgar, he didn't know him.

What was Doris Day like to work for?
Edgar got along with her fine. She was friendly, but with a little ice, *always*. She had a *cold* nature. But she was pleasant always and on time and very professional.

At that same time I was still working as a script supervisor, for Jacques Demy and a lot of different directors here. I was working at Columbia on a film directed by Demy [*The Model Shop*, 1969] and I didn't finish that film, because I came home late one night and found Edgar on the floor. He'd had his big stroke. Unfortunately, Edgar had a *very* rough ending: For four years, one stroke after the other. He was unable to move, unable to talk. We communicated by my giving him an ink pad and holding his hand, and he would scrawl with the little movement he had in the hand—*very* little. He couldn't even raise his head, he had to be fed intravenously. It was four years of this agony. And he didn't like being in the hospital—he was at Cedars, and when the insurance people cut us off, I didn't know what to do. I went to the Motion Picture Home, and they said they would take him in for $400 a month if I would sign off all my belongings—car, jewelry, clothing, *everything* you have to sign off. I had to do it. We got him set up in a nice private room and they were very good to him and took care of him. I took him home every weekend—they arranged for the ambulance and... [*chokes up*]. Excuse me—this is horrible stuff, it was a horrible time. It was the toughest four years of my life.

You said you had to sign away everything. How did you still have a house to bring him home to on weekends?
The house was *gone*, I had taken an apartment. I had *nothing*, dear—really nothing! But I was lucky to be a good script supervisor, so I got work. Not steady—I worked sporadically. I made commercials, I made a lot of money doing commercials. There was a man by the name of John Hazard who took pity on me—he knew Edgar, and he kept me very busy, at least two, three commercials a month, and in those days they were paying 200, 300 dollars a day. That got me on my feet again.

Are you surprised that, 25 years after your husband's passing, there's still so much interest in him and his movies?
[*Laughs*] I am *shocked* [*laughs*]—of course! I am *not* surprised at a *few*, because even before he died he had quite a little fan club going. Young people flocked around Edgar, and he loved it, and he told wonderful stories, and I wish I could tell them like he did.

Ulmer enjoyed the freedom to make his movies the way he wanted to make them—that's part of the reason he worked at all these small studios. But would it have really broken your heart if he had been taken in by a big studio and went to work every day and made "bigger" movies, just maybe not exactly his way. Would that steady employment really have been a bad thing?

I think it *would* have been, yeah. He wouldn't have made those particular movies that *he* picked. Let's face it, no studio would have okayed the kind of films he made.

So even with all the financial ups and downs—

I have no regrets. *None.* It was a man who gave me a wonderful journey [*laughs*] —an exciting journey, an instructive journey. He broadened my horizons like no university could.

Ray Walston

Lugosi said something [complimentary] to me...
"You are the best Renfield I've ever had!"

Long before his Tony Award-winning performance as the Devil in Broadway's *Damn Yankees*, before he became a household name via television's *My Favorite Martian*, and before his two Emmys for TV's *Picket Fences*, a young Ray Walston "paid his dues" in the acting profession working at summer theaters and repertory companies. He recalls three early encounters with horror star Bela Lugosi in this exclusive interview.

Born in New Orleans, Walston started his acting career as a spear carrier with a local stock company. When the family moved to Houston, Walston's father wanted to teach him the oil business, but Walston instead joined a traveling repertory company (selling tickets as well as acting). He went on to associate with Margo Jones at the Houston Civic Theater for six years, then spent three seasons with the Cleveland Playhouse before arriving in New York in 1945. It was on the East Coast that Walston worked with Lugosi: In the 1947 play *Three Indelicate Ladies* (which opened in New Haven, Connecticut, moved to Boston but never made it to New York), in a 1947 East Hampton, Long Island, production of *Dracula* (with Lugosi in the title role and Walston as Renfield) and in a 1949 episode of TV's *Suspense* (a modernized version of "The Cask of Amontillado").

You worked with Bela Lugosi on several different occasions in the late 1940s. Did you get to like him?

I learned to like him very much. He and I became very good friends. When we were doing *Dracula*, we used to go out every night, around that little East Hampton, New York, where the theater was we were working in. And drink. And smoke cigars. I liked cigars, too, so we'd sit there smokin' cigars and this and that. Now and then, his wife Lillian would be with him. The first time we went out, I learned something from him that I used for the rest of the time I was on the stage: He drank Scotch, and he would order a drink and they would bring it. And then he would reach in his inside pocket and pull out a bottle, a specimen bottle that had about—oh, I don't know how many ounces of Scotch in it. He would bring this extra Scotch and he would pour it on top of the drink they gave him. I asked, "Why do you *do* that?" He said, "Well, it's so *weak*, what they give me." I said, "Why don't you order a *double*?" He said, "What?! That's too *expensive*." Well [*laughs*], I incorporated that into my *own* drinking habits!

Where would you and Lugosi go? To a restaurant? To a bar?

Oh, a bar...or a restaurant-bar...or a bar...or *another* bar...or another restaurant-bar [*laughs*]! Up and down the avenue!

Lugosi obviously knew Dracula *backwards and forwards by this point. Did he actually rehearse with the rest of you?*

Oh, sure. Oh, he *loved* that—he *lived* that part! He was there all the time. And sitting out in front when he wasn't in the *scene*!

Would the director [Jerome Coray] make suggestions to people like Lugosi, the stars who the theater "imported," or just let them "do their thing"?

They learned that they'd better be careful about making suggestions to Lugosi about that show, because *Dracula* was "his" show. It was "his" show from the first time he did it, when he was hired to do it in New York some time in '27. Nedda Harrigan, who was in [the original Broadway production of] *Dracula*, told me this: They fired him after two days. Were you aware of that? No? Well, they fired Bela Lugosi after two days of rehearsals. Then they had another guy in there for three or four days, and they fired *him* and then brought Lugosi back. And, of course, history was made.

Any other memories of rehearsing with Lugosi?

On the rehearsals, Elaine Stritch [playing Lucy Seward] was perturbed about the fact that Lugosi, who smoked cigars—big, black cigars [*laughs*]—had tobacco juice running down the sides of his mouth a little bit. And he liked the girls, you know—he *really* liked the girls. He would grab her in his arms—there were a couple of times in the play where they kissed—and he'd bend her over and slobber all over her. And she was beside herself with that!

There was also an actor in it named Pat McVey, playing the attendant in the asylum. He was supposed to come on stage and open his hand, and there in his palm were two white mice. His line was, "Look at this! Look what I caught Renfield doing! He was gonna eat these mice!" Well, McVey came out in rehearsal and Lugosi, who was sitting in front with the director watching every move that everyone made, said, "What is that in your hand?" Pat McVey said, "Well, it's...uh...it's...uh...it's..." Lugosi said, "What *is* it? What *is* it?" And McVey said, "Well, it's *cotton*. I rubbed 'em up and turned 'em and twisted 'em to look like little mice." And Lugosi said, "No, no, no, no, no. No, no, no, no, no. Uhn-uh. That won't work. That's not gonna work as well as it would with *real* mice." McVey said, "Well, you know, I'm kind of *skittish* about those things crawling around my hand like that. I, I, I, I, I don't think that I... This *bothers* me..." Lugosi said, "Well, I tell you what: Whoever plays that part *has* to work with *real* mice!" And Pat McVey said as he walked off the stage, "Well, okay! Okay! Get *Clyde Beatty*!" [*Laughs*] The famous animal trainer!

When you played Renfield, had you ever seen the movie Dracula *[1931]?*

In the early days of his long career, Ray Walston played Renfield to Bela Lugosi's Dracula in a Long Island stage production of Bram Stoker's spooky tale.

I had seen *Dracula* when it first came out, when Dwight Frye played Renfield. Lugosi said something [complimentary] to me; I think he was swayed by the applause that I got on opening night. (I was a popular figure in that theater; I'd done quite a lot of things up there and they *liked* me.) I think he was impressed by [the applause] because his remark was, "You are the best Renfield I've ever had!"

Did you think Renfield was a good part?
Oh, yeah! From the time I saw the movie, oh, I *loved* it. I thought that guy in the movie, Dwight Frye, was *very* good.

The stars that the East Hampton theater imported—where would they stay?
They stayed in rooming houses. There were no hotels to speak of, as I recall—not in East Hampton proper. So people who had houses would rent out a couple of rooms, or *a* room, and that's where we stayed. I remember my first encounter with Lugosi: I went to one of these houses to check out a room, and I'm walking up some stairs in this eerie, dark place. All of a sudden I was aware of black shoes, two legs. I looked up and there was this guy with a coat and a derby on. It was Lugosi—*leering* down at me [*laughs*]! He *loved* to play that stuff!

When you went out with him socially, what would you talk about?
We'd talk about the theater. You know, he was *supposedly* a very active Shakespearean actor on the Budapest stage. He played a lot of classic things, according to *him*, and to his *wife*. Whether or not that's true, I don't know.

Any other memories of Mrs. Lugosi?
One night he gave a big party at his apartment, and his wife (naturally) cooked Hungarian goulash. She was *devoted* to this man and his career. She would be talking about how good he was in *this* and how good he was in *that* and so forth, and at one point she said, "Well, you know, he was the John Barrymore of the Budapest stage!" And with that, Lugosi spoke up in *alllll* seriousness and said, "No, *no*. I was the Clark Gable of the Budapest stage!" [*Laughs*]

By the way, everyone there at the party, with the exception of Lugosi and his wife, had a *terrible* sunburn [from hitting the beaches]. Oh! *Oh!* I remember the one *I* had was absolutely *violent*. And have I been paying for it the last 25 years!

Did you ever meet Lugosi's son?
No, I don't think the son was ever up there. In fact, when I first learned that he had a son, I was rather surprised.

I've read that Lugosi told Elaine Stritch, "If it hadn't been for Boris Karloff, I'd have cornered the horror movie market!"
I think he made a mistake when he turned down the Monster in *Frankenstein* [1931]. He told me that it was in his contract that he *had* to do it—that unless Universal could find somebody else who was [right for it], *he* would have to do it. Lugosi told me that he actually went out scouting around by himself and that he found a *truck driver* named Boris Karloff. Are any of these stories familiar to you?

That is not *how Boris Karloff got the part in* Frankenstein, *so it's very interesting to hear that that's Lugosi's version.*
I guess that was Lugosi *hedging* [*laughs*]!

How about Lugosi getting in and out of the coffin in Dracula? *Did he have any trouble with that?*
Oh, no, he managed that. But there were bats flying around the theater—*real* bats! And he was concerned about that. When we did plays in that theater, we learned you just had to put up with it. These bats would come *zooming* down through there. For *Dracula*, there also were big *fake* bats on the stage—they'd come out of the proscenium, they'd come from out of the ceiling and swoop down and out. But these *real* bats—they troubled Lugosi a little bit! But he got used to it.

What other anecdotes can you recall about Dracula?
An incident that happened on one of the performances. Toward the end of the play, when Dracula is staked, you didn't actually *see* Dracula lying there and somebody driving a stake in his heart, but you could *hear* the thuds. All the audience could see was a shadow—a shadow on the wall of a reclining figure, lying on its back, a stake at its breast, and this big, huge, hammer-like thing coming down on top of the stake. It was like the sound of someone knockin' a spike down with a sledgehammer or something. Each time it happened, Lugosi (who was on the other side of the stage) would let out some kind of a rrrrrrrr-oooooooo-owwwwwww [*groaning noises*]. Well, they hit it, he let out one or two; they hit it, they hit it, they hit it, and he let out one or two more. And then there was no more hitting, but he kept going with the *rrrrrrrr-oooooo-oo-owwwwwww*. And so Elaine Stritch screamed, "Hit him again, Bram, and hit him *hard*!" [*Laughs*]

When you'd go bar-hopping with Lugosi, did he ever get out of hand?
[*Laughs*] Well, I don't know what your meaning of "get out of hand" is. But he *would* leer at the ladies and make remarks and so on. *Today*, they would put him in jail! But he got away with all of that—they *laughed*. In those days, the women *laughed*. He did a lot of flirting.

He would grab 'em as they went by the table and put 'em on his lap and hold his arm around 'em and not let 'em go. He would hold onto them!

Did Lugosi's wife turn a blind eye to all of this?
Oh, she'd be there smiling and laughing.

You also worked with Lugosi in a play called Three Indelicate Ladies.
I did *three* things with him. About the same time as the production of *Dracula*, I did *Three Indelicate Ladies*— that was produced by Hunt Stromberg, Jr., and Elaine Stritch was in *that*, too. It closed in Boston. And then Lugosi and I were both in a TV show that CBS did, a half-hour show [Lugosi's *Suspense* episode "The Cask of Amontillado," 10/11/49]. A *live* show, which was so *bad* because he couldn't remember his lines. He was bad about that, it was hard for him to remember his lines. He had a hard time on that half-hour show.

It was directed by Robert Stevens.
A very nervous man. A man who was in the wrong place at the wrong time [*laughs*]! Also in it was an actor named Romney Brent, who had also been in [the play] *Joan of Lorraine* [1946] which Margo Jones directed; Brent played the Dauphin. Interesting man. He had had a terrific background in acting, and he was somewhat of an intellectual. I found talking with him rather interesting, and I inquired about his early career and things like that.

When you would encounter Lugosi time after time, would he remember you?
Oh, *sure*. Oh! "Ray! Rrrrray!"

When you knew him, were you aware of his drug problems?
I was absolutely *shocked* when I learned of his dope problems later on, after he came back to Hollywood. There was a photograph of him in the newspaper: All that dark black hair had turned to white, and he was in a hospital on a drug treatment. I had no idea, and I don't think anyone in the *company* had any idea that he was on drugs of any kind—*hard* drugs. We didn't know that.

Did you know that he had painful back problems?
No. But that reminds me that at one point, during the rehearsals for *Three Indelicate Ladies*, one afternoon he was lying down on a bench, stretched out with his eyes closed. One of us in the group, I don't know which one it was, said, "Quick! Quick! Get a stake!" [*Laughs*] But, no, I was not aware of his back problems. Maybe that had something to do with the dope.

Three Indelicate Ladies *was directed by Jessie Royce Landis. How did you like having a lady director?*
I liked her—I liked her very much. In fact, later on I was doing a show in London and she was, too, and we saw quite a lot of each other. Lugosi somehow did not get around to [flirting with] Jessie…!

Any other comments on Lugosi?
He was a charming man. A couple of years ago, I was given a star on the Hollywood Walk of Fame, and I dug up a lot of memories of Hollywood Boulevard and presented 'em to the people at a luncheon at the Roosevelt Hotel. And *two* of the things were about Bela Lugosi.

No funeral processions were allowed to travel on Hollywood Boulevard, but they made a special exception with Lugosi: *His* funeral thing went up the street. Now, that's what I was *told*; whether or not it's true, I don't know. But this one happens to be *very* true: He came out here in the early '20s, but he didn't make *Dracula* until 1930. And in between, he had a torrid romance with Clara Bow. That surprised me.

You knew Lugosi when he was heading into the final lap of his career. What "image" did he have of himself?

Well, I think that the impression that *he* gave when he said he was the Clark Gable of the Budapest stage [is the] answer to that question. It was not conceit. He was part of the "lore" of that play *Dracula*, from the time he did it in New York and then came out to Hollywood and did it. I think that he felt he "owned" it, that no one else could play it. And he may very well have been right.

Ray Walston Filmography

Kiss Them for Me (20th Century–Fox, 1957)
Damn Yankees (*What Lola Wants*) (Warners, 1958)
South Pacific (Magna Theatre Corp./20th Century–Fox, 1958)
Say One for Me (20th Century–Fox, 1959)
Tall Story (Warners, 1960)
Portrait in Black (Universal, 1960)
The Apartment (United Artists, 1960)
Convicts 4 (*Reprieve*) (Allied Artists, 1962)
Who's Minding the Store? (Paramount, 1963)
Wives and Lovers (Paramount, 1963)
Kiss Me, Stupid (Lopert/United Artists, 1964)
Caprice (20th Century–Fox, 1967)
Paint Your Wagon (Paramount, 1969)
The Sting (Universal, 1973)
Silver Streak (20th Century–Fox, 1976)
The Happy Hooker Goes to Washington (Cannon, 1977)
Popeye (Paramount, 1980)
The Fall of the House of Usher (Sunn Classic, 1980)
Galaxy of Terror (*Mindwarp: An Infinity of Terror*; *Planet of Horrors*) (New World, 1981)
Fast Times at Ridgemont High (Universal, 1982)
O'Hara's Wife (Davis-Panzer, 1982)
Private School (Universal, 1983)
Johnny Dangerously (20th Century–Fox, 1984)
Rad (Tri-Star, 1986)
O.C. & Stiggs (MGM, 1987)
Blood Relations (Sutton Entertainment/New Line, 1987)
From the Hip (De Laurentiis, 1987)
Paramedics (Vestron, 1987)
Saturday the 14th Strikes Back (Concorde, 1988)
Blood Salvage (Paragon Arts, 1990)
Ski Patrol (Triumph Releasing, 1990)
Popcorn (Studio Three Film Corp., 1991)
Of Mice and Men (MGM/Pathe Communications, 1992)

The Player (Fine Line Features, 1992)
House Arrest (Rysher Entertainment/ MGM, 1996)
My Favorite Martian (Disney, 1998)

Walston also appeared in many made-for-TV movies and direct-to-video features. He died on New Year's Day 2001.

Joan Weldon

[Them!] would have been terrible in color. The ants would have been very attractive, because they had very pretty eyes...

Filmdom's fairest exterminator, Joan Weldon followed an unlikely route to her career in giant-pest control: The blue-eyed, chestnut-haired beauty trained to be a singer, and made her professional debut as a member of the San Francisco Opera Company. While appearing with the Los Angeles Civic Light Opera Company, she came to the attention of Warner Bros., who took her out of grand opera and put her in horse operas (*The Command*, *Riding Shotgun*), a crime drama (*The System*) and—most famously—the biggest and best of the "Big Bug" movies, 1954's *Them!*

Between movie roles—all of them dramatic, non-singing parts—Weldon sang at the Hollywood Bowl, on her TV series *This Is Your Music* and in *The Music Man* (on tour for three years as the repressed Marian the Librarian). But, as so often happened to actresses in the 1950s, Weldon has found that the most lasting impression she made was on cult movie lovers, battling the horde of humongous ants in *Them!*

What were your hopes for your movie career when you were signed by Warners?

I was a singer, that was my first love, and I needed a job to *support* myself. I was offered 250 a week by Warners. Well, everybody at Universal, including (I think) Rock Hudson, had all started at like $85 a week, and I think he was up to something like a hundred and a quarter, a hundred fifty. So 250 a week? I thought [*gasps*], "Ter-*rif*-ic!" At the time that I was signed, I knew nothing of the studio system. *Nothing*. My background was singing and opera—not even musical comedy. Movies were just totally foreign to me.

Was Warners the first studio you screen-tested for?

No, I did a screen test with Carl Betz for 20th Century-Fox, but they weren't signing singers, they were signing dancers.

How did you get that screen test?

I had been seen in a [stage] musical by Stanley Rubin, who was a producer for 20th Century-Fox, and Lilli Palmer; what Rubin and Lilli Palmer used to do was, they'd go to the theater and they'd pick out one person who they thought bounced over the footlights. Later that same evening I had a date, and after the theater my date took me to the Bantam Cock—the same restaurant that *they* were having dinner at. Stanley Rubin sent a note over stating that he was very interested, and would I consider contacting the drama coach at 20th Century–Fox, Helene Sorrell. So I did—I went over and I worked with her on a screen test in which Carl Betz played opposite me. But 20th wasn't interested.

Before I got the notification that they were *not* interested, I was invited to a big benefit-type party; I was going to go with my friend Alain Bernheim, who was a literary agent. When Alain came to pick me up to go to this party, he said, "I hope you don't mind, but a friend of mine doesn't have a date, and he would like to go with us." I said, "By all means!"—having no idea who it was. And then we picked up Peter Lawford! So I had *two* dates that night...which was *divine*! (I was gaga over Peter Lawford when I was a kid—I mean, who wasn't?) At that party was Bill Orr, an executive at Warner Bros.—

And he was Jack Warner's son-in-law.

That's right! He wanted to know who I was, what I was doing there. (He was probably impressed that I had two dates, a literary agent and Peter Lawford!) Alain proceeded to tell him all about me, and said that I had done a screen test at 20th. Bill Orr said, "If 20th isn't interested, *we are*." So when 20th wasn't interested, I went over to see Warner Bros. I sang everything from soup to nuts [*laughs*]—from opera down to a love song. They were interested, but they said that they were signing people just for *specific pictures* and they had nothing for me then. I guess it was three weeks later that I decided I was going to go to New York, and I was supposed to leave on a Friday. My agent Lily Messenger was over at Warner Bros. and she proceeded to mention to somebody that I was heading for New York. And they said, "Oh, please, tell her not to go. We'll find a picture for her!" And they did—*The System* [1953, starring Frank Lovejoy]. I went over and I saw Frank Lovejoy and I did a screen test with him, a scene from *The System*. And then Warners said I had the picture and they would like to put me under contract. And this was at a time when the studios weren't really putting people under contract any longer, they were going to more or less "go independent." Just prior to my being signed, Warners had let their drama coach go, so I had to scrounge around and get my own. I had a neighbor, his name was Bert Freed, a very fine actor, and he gave me my first drama lesson for movies. I worked with him during *The System*, and then eventually I found another drama coach for other roles. That's how I got into movies.

By the way, when I signed with Warners, I had to sign a paper saying that I was not and never had been a Communist. "What *is* this paper?" I was a *kid*, I was *very* young, and my background was not politics. I *knew* something about what was going on in Washington, but to have this paper presented to me to *sign* was the shock of my life. "What does this *mean*? What am I *signing*?" I've always been told, "Never sign anything unless you read it thoroughly. And read between the lines." *That's* when my ears perked up about the Un-American Activities Committee in Washington, about the McCarthy era.

Opera singer Weldon could hit the high notes for theater audiences, but couldn't get out a scream for *Them!*'s giant ants.

(Which was disgusting—as we all know.) That extra piece of paper in my Warner Bros. contract was something which I really didn't want to sign, because I thought that it was unnecessary. But it was either sign or lose the contract. I remember that I *really* resented *having* to sign it, because America *was* supposedly a free society, and I felt this took my choices away. I felt that the Communist Party at that time was *not* gonna overthrow the government, and they were not gonna make little bombs and throw them at Washington [*laughs*]!

What did you expect to get out of appearing in the movies?

I wasn't expecting much from movies, but I thought it gave me a chance to learn to *act*. That was *not* my background—doing musicals on the stage is a *little* different than acting in movies. It was all sort of like a training ground.

What did you do to fill out your days at Warners?

I did six pictures within a year. Six pictures...within a year. So I think *that* answers your question [*laughs*]! Especially when you're the female lead. I remember I was supposed to have one or two days off, and I stopped in at Bill Orr's office to do something. He asked, "What are you doing? Aren't you working today?" I said no, I had a day off. He said, "You've got a day off? That's what *you* think. Go to wardrobe." I said, "What do you mean, 'Go to wardrobe?'" They were doing a picture with Will Rogers, Jr., called *The Boy from Oklahoma* [1954], and I went to Costumes, got into one, and I was queen of the B-girls in that movie. But that was Warner Bros.—Warner Bros. was six days a week. And working six days a week, even at *my* age (I think I was 20), was too much. Every day, six days a week, I was in the wardrobe and makeup at six.

To show you how penny-pinching Warner Bros. could be in those days: They didn't have a picture for me for a month, or two months, and they gave me two months off without salary. So I got another picture, *The Stranger Wore a Gun* [1953] with Randolph Scott at Columbia. And the minute I got that picture, Warners wanted to put me *back* on salary—Warners said, "She's under contract to *us*. *We* will take the money [from Columbia], and she will get her usual salary." To which my agent said, "*No way*. It doesn't work that way. *You* put her on suspension for x-number of weeks, and she *stays* on suspension." She *fought* and she *won*, and I got the full money, which was very, *very* nice! But [Warners] wanted every penny!

I found some behind-the-scenes paperwork on House of Wax *that indicates that, during pre-production, you might have worked one day.*

The only thing I might have done is tested for it. God forbid you should have a day off! They didn't *believe* in that. They really utilized you, whether you were right or wrong for a part [*laughs*]! I remember I screen-tested for *King Richard and the Crusaders* [1954] only because I had a day off! And, if my name is connected with *House of Wax*, then I probably tested for *that*, too. They kept you hoppin'—which was *fine*. It was hard *then*, but in retrospect, you got a lot of experience.

What was your reaction when you got assigned to Them!*? Be honest!*

[*Laughs*] Well...not a lot! Number one, I *hated* science fiction pictures—I just *really* didn't like them. And they *still* aren't my tastes, I *still* don't go to them. I *loved* in those days the English movies, the English *mysteries*, and intrigue and things like that. I didn't think much of *Them!* when I read the script; I just knew that my character was a scientist, and I was hoping that *some*where along the line there would be some romance or love interest. But [director] Gordon Douglas didn't want a thing—not a *thing*—to refer to any kind of romance whatsoever. It was totally devoid of any interplays with *any*body. The ants were supposed to be the stars. Of course, the major thing was [the message] that, when you disrupt the world with the *kinds* of bombs that we were releasing, it's only going to do more destruction to the Earth. Basically *Them!* was an anti-war, anti-nuclear message.

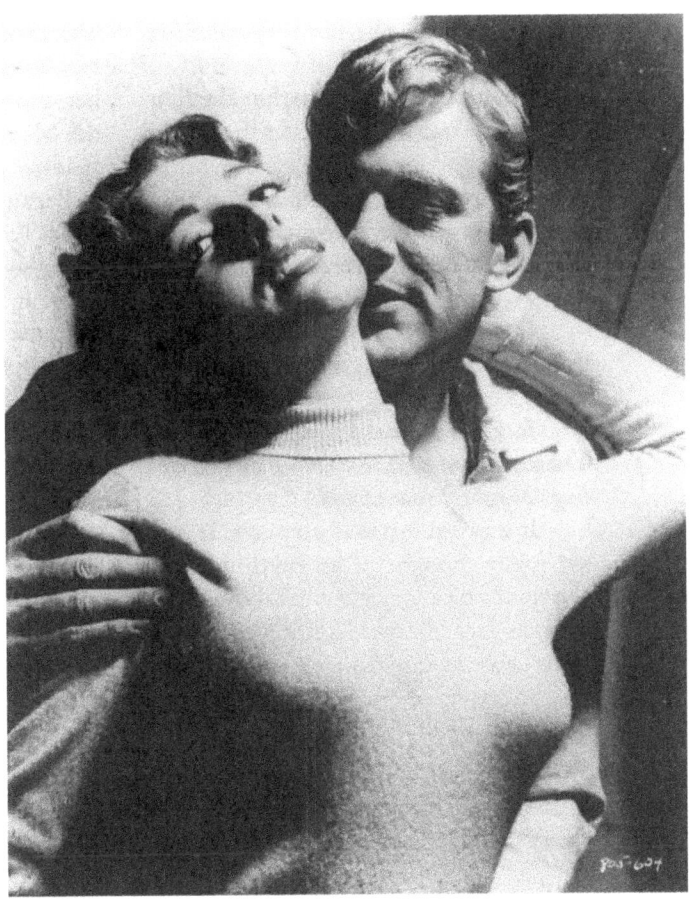

No romantic byplay could be found in the movie, so Weldon and James Arness played catch-up in the photo shoot.

Was that message in the movie intentionally?

Oh, that was *very* intentional.

So how did you "ease into" making the movie?

For starters, I went to Wardrobe and saw Moss Mabry—very good-looking, and a really nice man. He said, "I've got this idea for a beautiful wool suit. This is the material..." And high heels! I said, "In the *desert*? A wool suit? And a hat?" He said, "Well, you're coming from Washington and you're supposed to be very much a *scientist*." I said [*sighs*], "All rightee..." [*Laughs*] To me that was ludicrous, but there was nothing I could do about it. *Them!* was my sixth picture—I'd done four at Warner Bros. and one at Columbia.

There were umpteen versions of the script, all very different from each other.

Was the script you received very much like the movie?

I don't remember whether the first script I read was the final draft or not.

In one draft, the conclusion takes place in an amusement park, and your character is chased by the ants through a tunnel of love, through a funhouse—

Oh, no, no, no. My recollection is that the script that I got was the movie.

Jack Warner was unenthusiastic about Them!, *and an executive named Steve Trilling thought it was stupid.*

It was *new*—it was *very* new. It was *not* really thought of as anything that was gonna be a major picture. Not at *all*, as far as Jack Warner and Steve Trilling were concerned. And even Bill Orr. It was just another picture. Ted Sherdeman was one of the writers at the studio, and he had always wanted to do this kind of a movie. He decided that he was gonna write this, basically an anti-war movie about how these kind of warheads were going to discombobulate the Earth, discombobulate *nature*, in a major way. It was a terribly anti-nuclear picture, and if you're going to be anti-nuclear, you're going to be anti-war [*laughs*]!

While making the movie, did you think you were doing something new and exciting, or did you think to yourself, "What the heck have I gotten myself into here?"

I knew that it had to be made and I knew that I was under contract and I couldn't choose the pictures I wanted. It was a job, and I had made a commitment, and I would never try to release myself from a commitment. There was nothing I could do. At that time, *Them!* was just another picture—and a very *tough* picture to make, because of the heavy wool suit that I wore. We were in the Mojave Desert and it was 110 in the shade. I guess the men also had to feel it, because they had lots of clothes on. Poor "Teddy" Gwenn [Edmund Gwenn, who played her scientist-father], he had a suit and a tie and a hat, and I had the hat and the high heels and the hose [*laughs*]. And, in those days, you wore girdles, and *they* were heavy! The hose and the high heels and the hat and the wool suit, with a little light blouse underneath the wool suit, and it's 110. In the *shade*.

And the blowing sand?

Oh, that was "wonderful" [*laughs*]! Ab-so-lute-ly wonderful. Every grain of it that was blown onto your face. When you were through at the end of the day, it was like, stay under the shower as long as you can, and get all that stuff out of your hair! We were in an area where I think the best restaurant they had was a diner or a coffee shop. This was up near Palmdale, and back then Palmdale was a "jumping-off" place. Palmdale? You didn't go to *Palmdale*...!

According to Warner Bros. publicity, when the cast and crew did go into Palmdale, they were instructed not to converse with locals about the movie, because the studio wanted to keep the ants a secret.

I would venture to say that that was true, because I remember that we did stick pretty much to ourselves. In Palmdale, we stayed at a motel—not very fancy. They put us all in the same place and, if I'm not mistaken, they had dinner brought in. When we finished shooting, we'd go back to the motel and eat and go to bed! We sat around after dinner and chitchatted at the table, but after that, people were too tired to do anything but maybe look over the next day's dialogue and go to sleep. I remember there weren't any locks on the doors at that motel, because I would have locked my door if there *was* a lock. One night I was sound asleep, and in Onslow Stevens walked. He opened the door and there was light behind him from the hallway. I must have said something like, "What are you *doing*? What do you want? Is everything okay?" That's when I realized he was still asleep, and *sleepwalking*! I took my arm and pointed it and said [*in a commanding voice*], "*Go back to your room...!*" I still remember that gesture! He just turned around and walked back to his room, and I went and closed *his* door and *my* door! It was funny when I realized that he was sound asleep. That was the first time I had ever come in contact with that!

Stevens had a career that went way back. Was he a nice guy?
  Oh! He was *such* a lovely man! A *sweet*, lovely gentleman. More recently I saw some very old, old movies that he was in, and he was quite a good-looking man and a fine actor.

Weldon, James Arness and Sean McClory (left) take to the skies to locate the desert lair of *Them!*

Sean McClory is another actor who was in Them! *His recollection of Onslow Stevens was that Stevens said he was a nudist and he wanted McClory to try it!*

Oh, that's a *hoot*! Okay, then I shall 'fess up: When he was sleepwalking, he didn't have any *clothes* on [*laughs*]! I just thought he didn't have clothes on because he was very hot—they didn't have any air conditioning! I forgot to tell you he was naked—I mean, I *didn't* forget to tell you, I just didn't think it was appropriate! When I realized he was asleep and he was stark naked, that's when I used my arm as if I was on an opera stage—"Go back to your room!" I felt like a Valkyrie [*laughs*]! Afterwards, I thought it was just so funny, I was hysterical—I don't think I slept the rest of the night!

Then—from the ridiculous to the "sublime"!—we spent several nights down in the Los Angeles storm drains. That was terribly, terribly cold. Very cold and *very* damp. We worked at night—all night long—and I'm a day person! The hours never bothered me, being at the studio at six A.M., but it was working all night that bothered me. I'll never forget those drains, it was chilling to the bone, it was *so* cold in there.

The Los Angeles riverbed was dry when you made the movie, and Warner Bros. had to pump the water into the drains.

I remember that. But the water was all pumped in before we got there, it wasn't pumped in while we were there.

Gordon Douglas was someone else who didn't take Them! *seriously when he was first assigned to it—he said at one point that they should get Martin and Lewis to star in the thing!*

He wasn't quite sure what he was doing—I mean, *no*body really did! Gordon Douglas was all right, he was fine, no problems, but he related better, I think, to the *men*, he was really a man's director. (He was always "playing Jimmy Cagney"—he *loved* to imitate Jimmy Cagney. And he was very *good* at it!) James Whitmore and James Arness were both very nice, very pleasant, very professional. *Every*body was pleasant! Edmund Gwenn was a doll—an absolute lovely man. *Very* private...and he was in great pain. He was riddled with arthritis. But when they said, "Camera! Action!", you'd never know that there was a thing wrong with him. He was just *right there*, and he'd *move*, and the moment they said, "Cut!", he'd just crumble. His manservant Ernest would come in on the set and help him off.

William Schallert, who's also in Them!, *told me that Gwenn came out of retirement in the '50s only because he needed the money for arthritis treatment.*

That probably is true. Although Edmund Gwenn was quite elderly at that time, maybe he did not have enough for retirement also. He was a lovable man, a *very* nice man, but a man who was in great pain and discomfort most of the time.

When I spoke to Sean McClory, he was a little...disparaging about your acting abilities.

Well, I didn't come from the East, I wasn't an actor. I had come from music. I sang and danced, and then acted. Acting in a musical *can* be a wee bit different! Sean McClory and I were very good friends on the movie, and at one point he tried to teach me Gaelic. Well [*laughs*], *that* fizzled out! Coming from the opera,

Fess Parker (in bathrobe) won his star-making role as TV's Davy Crockett as a result of his comic vignette in *Them!*

I have knowledge of French and Italian, and I was interested in languages, but Gaelic was a total loss! Talk about a foreign language—*that's* a foreign language! It was like looking at Chinese on paper!

You were also in the one scene Fess Parker had.

[*Laughs*] Oh, *yes*! He was very funny; I liked his portrayal. When Disney saw *Them!*, he said, "I'd like to see that young man [Parker] about playing Davy Crockett," and that's how Fess Parker got *Davy Crockett* [the Disney TV series].

Early on, there was talk of Them! *being in color and maybe even 3-D, but then a memo went around that said,* "Them! *will now definitely be black-and-white and no 3-D, and we want to cut every corner to bring down costs."*

That's saying it exactly the way it was. I remember that they talked about 3-D, but the color I don't remember. It would have been terrible in color. The *ants* would have been very attractive, because they had very pretty eyes—they were colorful. And their bodies were brown—brown hair. They were *not* that ghastly to look at [*laughs*]! But in *black-*

and-white they are. This is the reason why I am totally against colorization, because they'd spend *hours* lighting a scene, they'd take pains to set up *one* shot that was perhaps 60 seconds. That is the beauty of black-and-white. And to change it, to put it into color—*fake* color—is ludicrous.

The ants themselves—how were they operated?

It's very funny, everybody has their own recollection. *My* recollection is that they were on wires, like large marionettes. They were very hairy; they were very big, probably like six feet high and six feet wide. That doesn't include the legs that dangled out here and there.

Did you think, when you saw them in operation, that they'd be effective on screen?

Ummmm...not really! But they certainly *were*.

You weren't too many years out of your teens when you did Them! *Did you think you'd be "up" to the part of a no-nonsense lady scientist at that age?*

Well, when they sent me the script for my screen test, the description of my character was, "Thirty-one-year-old divorcee." And I thought, "Thirty-one years old? How am I gonna make *that?* I'm 20!" But, the way they dressed me, all of a sudden it worked. I *always* looked older. But, strangely enough, today I don't look my age, as opposed to *then*! If you ever see *Them!* back-to-back with a picture I did with Fred MacMurray at Universal, *Day of the Bad Man* [1958], those are two different people. In the *later* picture, I look much younger [than in *Them!*]. The way I looked in *Day of the Bad Man*, the way I played her, and the way I played Pat Medford in *Them!*—there's two different people there.

Is it true that you weren't able to scream in Them! *the way they needed?*

That's right, I couldn't scream. At the same time I was doing a concert at the Hollywood Bowl and I could hit a high C for you, but I couldn't scream [*laughs*]! Years later, I found out I *could* scream—I went to visit a friend about ten years ago, in the Hollywood Hills, and I opened the screen door and I thought, "What's that little black thing down there?" So I went in the house and I said, "Dick, come here. What's that?" He said [*casually*], "Oh! A tarantula." A tarantula! I screamed bloody murder! I went into the kitchen, and I kept screaming!

Them! *was put together pretty quickly, and I believe part of the reason was that Warners wanted to get it out before Paramount put out* The Naked Jungle *[1954], another "ant movie."*

I don't remember anything about *The Naked Jungle*, but I know that there was no kidding around when we were making *Them!*—this was all business. I've never been on any project that was so *totally* business!

When Them! *was released, did you make any promotional appearances?*

No, none of us did. 'Cause [Warners] really weren't thinking much of it. They didn't want to put any money into it—they really didn't do much. It never had a premiere, like *The Command* [1954] did. The premiere of *The Command* was at the Pantages, I think, and I went with Barbara Warner, Jack Warner's daughter, and we all dressed appropriately, in cowboy dress and everything. But *Them!* was shown in a movie house, and that was *it*. They really didn't [hold out much hope] for it.

And it turned out to be a big hit.

Right. In fact, I was told that when Warner Bros. released *Them!* in Europe, it made more money than any other Warner Bros. picture that was released that year. Which was a surprise to me. At that time, we thought it was just science fiction, and…what is science fiction? They were just weird pictures.

Where did you see it for the first time? What did you think?

I want you to know that I *really* didn't like making the movie. They had some screenings here and some screenings there, and I heard that Jimmy Arness had seen it and Whitmore had seen it and blah-blah-blah had seen it, and I thought, "Well, I guess I'd better go see it." I think I was one of the last people to see it and, honestly, I don't remember what I thought of it. Recently I saw it in New Jersey, on a large screen, and both my husband and I were *both* very impressed with it. It was a joy not to see it on a little screen, on television. It really is a picture that holds up today.

And your performance?

Eeeyyyuuuhhh…

[Laughs] How do I spell that?

I'm not quite sure! There's a couple of lines that I wish to God I could do over. Actually, it's my last line of the picture—if I had my druthers, I would read it differently. But, then again, I think if it was read differently, the way I would *want* to read it, it would dilute "Teddy" Gwenn's closing speech. It was appropriate for the daughter, it was appropriate for the moment, but I would *love* to have that last line read over.

By the way, I've always not cared for myself on film; I think *every*body has that feeling. And I remember that they really didn't want any femininity in the picture. I had a low speaking voice, and there's a scene where they brought my voice *down* a fraction—gave it more of a bass quality. I found that *very* disconcerting.

They did it themselves?

Yes, in the mixing. It was mixed down, because they really wanted it *sterile*, if that's the word. It wasn't, shall we say, *Dragnet* [*laughs*]—it wasn't Jack Webb directing—but that sort of acting was more or less what they wanted. "Just the facts, ma'am."

Why did you leave Warners?

My contract was up—which, knock on wood, I was very happy about. I had signed a seven-year contract, like everybody does, and they did not renew it. And I was very happy.

Because the work load was just too heavy.

Oh, yes. Six days a week! It was *such* a work load. And, when I am extremely unhappy and nervous, I gain weight. I gained 20 pounds during my time at Warners, and you can see it in *Them!* My contract was up December 31st [1954], and on December 26 I went to Acapulco with a whole bunch of people. And Warners was gonna *sue* me for it! I was still under contract until the 31st of December! How 'bout that?

Sounds like it was a good place to get away from!

I went to them and I said, "This is ludicrous. You're not picking up my con-

Meeting famous people was one of the primary perks of her Hollywood career, says Joan Weldon (seen here in a current shot).

tract; what am I going to do? I'll do *any*thing you want when I come back. If you want these four days, I'll give them to you on the other end, when I get back." Well, I went to Acapulco for two weeks or three weeks, and I lost the 20 pounds! It was from *nerves*. I came back 20 pounds lighter, and I was never sick a *minute*.

Did you ever sing in any picture?
Yes. Then, of course, I ended up on the cutting room floor! It was at MGM, *Deep in My Heart* [1954], the story of Sigmund Romberg [played by Jose Ferrer]. Roger Edens was the producer, and I sang "One Kiss," up on a hill — I was waiting for Tony Martin's fishing boat. He comes in and I'm still up on the mountain, waiting for him, and he comes and he sings "Lover Come Back To Me." At which point I run *down* the hill and into his arms and I sing the last eight bars of "Lover Come Back To Me." But, since I was the only [co-star of the movie] *not* under contract to MGM, that ended up on the cutting room floor. But I want you to know that the billing was fabulous — the whole screen was one name at a time, and they couldn't cut my name out!

Looking back at your show biz career, what are a couple of your favorite memories?

I feel that I've been very lucky, though I worked very hard. I never wore a watch when I was working: I would leave home to go to work, and when I was finished working, I would come home. I just never wore a watch until I finally got one when I went into *The Music Man*. I was never a clock watcher because I loved what I was doing. There was great stress in it, but it was the only thing I ever could do! I always said, from the time when I was 16 and I worked at the telephone company, that if I had to work in an office, I'd be in the poor house [*laughs*], because I just didn't have any talent for it! But I had a *collective* talent, and had a little bit of everything going for me, and I worked very hard. But you also have to have a little bit of luck with you, especially in show business. And I think I *did* have a wee bit of Lady Luck with me.

Another thing that was wonderful about show business is that I met such wonderful people — people that I had (as a child) "grown up with." I met people like Robert Taylor and Merle Oberon and so many more. I remember going to a dinner party at Jack Warner's, and they had food in one room but desserts in another. I went to get a little more dessert and I was in there and I thought, "I can't believe I'm in this room with Artur Rubinstein...!" *Ohhhhh*! I want you to know, *that* was a thrilling moment —*truly*, a thrilling moment. And to have him talk to me—actually *talk*! Being in show business afforded me some wonderful moments of meeting people like that, people I admired—I remembered my father taking me to Rubinstein's concerts in San Francisco, like Mussorgsky's "Pictures at an Exhibition." So that's one thing that the theater has given me: Memorable moments of meeting great people.

Joan Weldon Filmography

The System (Warners, 1953)
So This Is Love (Warners, 1953)
The Stranger Wore a Gun (Columbia, 1953)
The Command (Warners, 1954)
Riding Shotgun (Warners, 1954)
The Boy from Oklahoma (Warners, 1954)
Them! (Warners, 1954)
Deep in My Heart (MGM, 1954)
Gunsight Ridge (United Artists, 1957)
Day of the Bad Man (Universal, 1958)
Home Before Dark (Warners, 1958)

June Wilkinson

A lot of the people who worked on [Macumba Love], in the crew, believed in voodooism. So there was a lot of tension there.

The 1950s were the Hollywood heyday of the blonde bombshell, epitomized by Marilyn Monroe and also represented by sultry sirens like Mamie Van Doren, Jayne Mansfield and Joi Lansing. From the English stage came teenage June Wilkinson, a typically top-heavy temptress whose formidable physique graced the pages of *Playboy* (unclad) and was seen in movies ranging from the Western *Thunder in the Sun* to the exploitative *The Private Lives of Adam and Eve* and *The Playgirls and the Bellboy* (in added scenes directed by Francis Ford Coppola).

The succession of sexy (but low-quality) film romps soon soured Wilkinson on the movies; since the early 1960s, she has worked much more regularly on the stage than in pictures, most notably in numerous productions of *Pajama Tops* over an almost-40 year period. But before beginning to drift away from movie work, Wilkinson had her best-remembered screen role in director Douglas Fowley's 1959 horror-adventure *Macumba Love*, the Brazilian-made tale of voodoo rites and deadly wrongs co-starring Walter Reed and Ziva Rodann.

After working on the stage in England, when and why did you decide to move to the U.S.?

When I was in England, I got a contract to come over to the States for four weeks. The deal was made with a plastics company out of Boston that wanted me to help them advertise their kitchenware. Part of my deal was that I had to be in Chicago for a big convention. In return, they put a gentleman by the name of Jimmy McCullough in charge of me over here, and he got me on *The Today Show*. The day before I was to appear on *The Today Show*, he had me go over to [fashion mogul] Oleg Cassini's factory to get a dress to wear on the show; Oleg was doing outfits that weren't the sack dress which was popular then. When he saw me, he said, "If you wear one of my dresses at a function I'm going to, I will give you four originals." I thought that was a pretty good deal! At the function, which was in New York, he introduced me to Ray Stark and Eliot Hyman from Seven Arts. They asked, "What do you do?" and—being 17—I said, "I'm an actress." They said, "Oh! Would you like to be under contract?" and I said, "Yes." They said [attorney] Greg Bautzer would have a contract made up for me the next day.

I then went to Chicago and, after I did the first day of the convention for the company that brought me over here, we were all going out to dinner. They showed me *Playboy* magazine, and I looked at it. It just amazes me how cocky you are, your attitude when you're 17: I just looked at it and I said [*scoffing*], "Oh! *My* body's as good as anybody's in there." And I called up Hugh Hefner that night when I got back to the hotel, which was real late. He answered the phone himself, which he *never* would have done if it had been the daytime—he was the only one in the office. He had already *seen* me; I don't know if he knew of me in England or if he had seen *The Today Show*, but he was already familiar with me. He said, "Sure, we'd love to have you in the magazine. When can we shoot?" When I told him I was leaving town the next day, after the convention, he said, "Come on over now. I'll get the photographers out of bed." And that's what he did!

I went back to England to fulfill a contract, then I came back to America under contract to Seven Arts. By then, I'd had my eighteenth birthday. So that's how I got to America.

And you went out to Hollywood.
Right. At first they put me up at the Hollywood Studio Club, a huge old mansion off of Lexington Avenue in Hollywood. It was all aspiring actresses. At the time, my roommates were Shirley Knight and Jo Anne Worley; a lot of famous people had previously lived there, Kim Novak for one. It was just a really cheap place to live that was "protected" and for people who were interested in show business. Girls only.

Did you ever make a movie for Seven Arts?
I was under contract to them for a year, which gave me...not a lot of money, but at least *survival* money. And they put me in a movie with Jeff Chandler and Susan Hayward called *Thunder in the Sun* [1959]. I think I had two lines in it. That was my first movie.

Followed by The Immoral Mr. Teas *[1959] for Russ Meyer.*
Now, let me just tell you about that: I was under contract to Seven Arts and not allowed to be in a Russ Meyer movie, of course, because it was not the kind of movie a company like Seven Arts would want you to *be* in. After *Playboy* came out, Seven Arts was horrified, because at that time *Playboy* and nudity were [disreputable]. This was at a time when most movies had two versions, the European and the American; European versions had nudity and American versions didn't. When I came out nude in *Playboy*, Seven Arts were a little aghast. But they decided that, well, since I did it, they would make me the most photographed nude in the world! They hired Russ Meyer, and Russ Meyer took *masses* of photographs of me, some of which appeared in other layouts in *Playboy*. They appeared *every*-where. Russ was making his first movie, *The Immoral Mr. Teas*, which of course I could not be in. But, as a favor to him, and just for a lark, I *was*. There was one short scene where a gentleman looks up at a window and there's a naked lady whose head you do not see—you just see her breasts. For one quick moment. Then she closes the shade. Those breasts were mine. But it didn't go unnoticed, because breasts are like fingerprints, there's no two alike [*laughs*]! Everybody

An ad for *Macumba Love*.

recognized my breasts immediately! So much for doing something incognito!

I went to acting lessons, which Seven Arts paid for, and got my check every week. Then I auditioned for Spike Jones' band. I was a lady who was used to working, not sitting around doing nothing—I wasn't used to this idle scene of Hollywood. So I called up Seven Arts and I said, "Listen, I auditioned for Spike Jones' band and I got the job. Is it all right if I do it?" And they said, "Well...hang on a minute." Nobody knew who I was! It took them a *day* to figure out who I was and all the rest of it, and they said, "Yeah, go ahead, do it!"—*they* didn't care [*laughs*]! It just boggles my mind when I think about it now. I probably should have been more aggressive and calling them up regularly, but they were doing *The World of Suzie Wong* [1960] at the time and there wasn't a part for me in it. I think that involved everybody's attention for at least a year.

How did you happen to hook up with the people making Macumba Love?

After my contract was up, after the year, they never renewed it, and that was the end of Seven Arts. I was going to acting school, but I didn't drive at that time and I didn't have a car. But Bill Wellman, Jr., was in my acting class, and he was always very sweet and he would pick me up and take me to the class and drop me off. One day he was waiting in the lobby of the Hollywood Studio Club for me to come down the stairs (men are not allowed beyond the lobby), and Doug Fowley was waiting for his date. He and Bill started talking, and Doug asked, "Who are you waiting for?" Bill said, "I'm waiting for a girl called June Wilkinson. We're going to acting school." And when I came down the stairs, Bill introduced me to Doug Fowley. Then we went off on our merry way. Later, Doug called Bill Wellman up and he said, "You know, you two looked good together. I've got this part of a husband and wife in a movie we're shooting in Brazil. Would you two like it?" *Sure* [*laughs*]! It happened *that* easy.

You were still a teenager at the time.

I was 18 years of age, and I had my nineteenth birthday while I was in Brazil making *Macumba Love*. We stayed at a hotel in São Paulo, and then we moved to a little island off of the coast of Santos (which was *great*) to film some of the rest of it. I remember being in *love* with Brazil—I thought it was wonderful, and I had a great time. I loved the people, I loved the tropics. I was from England [*laughs*]—I thought the tropics were a strange and wonderful place. And I loved the music, all that Brazilian music and the steel drums and stuff. It was just great.

What scenes were shot on the island?

We shot jungle-type scenes there. It was just off the coast of Santos, a little tiny, tiny island where the mega-rich went for their summer vacations.

Even though Macumba Love *was your third movie, this was your first time doing any real acting in a movie.*

Yes, it was.

On a small-budgeted movie like that, you had to get it right on the first take or else. Did you feel any pressure, a greater sense of responsibility?

Of course not! When you're a teenager, you don't *have* any sense of responsibility [*laughs*]. Well, that's not *really*

June Wilkinson brought a touch of scantily-clad glamour to the va-va-va-voodoo thriller *Macumba Love*.

true. All my life, being a professional and being in show business, I had the discipline. I was always in theater, and when you grow up in theater, you *have* to be there on time, you *have* to make your cues, you *have* to know your lines. I was a very *disciplined* actress, but I knew no fear as a teenager. Now, in my 50s, I know *lots* of fear, and if it was the same situation, I would be *very* nervous! But not then.

Was it generally one-take?
Of course!

And you did get the impression that they didn't have much money, correct?

Oh, they didn't have a lot of money —of *course* they didn't. This is how the movie got started: Mike Ripps, who was the producer, was a drive-in double-screen theater operator and owner from Mobile, Alabama. He kept on watching movies, and he said, "Well, I may not be able to do much better than these movies they keep giving me to show in my theater, but I sure can't do worse. I think I'm gonna go produce a movie!" So that's how *Macumba Love* got started.

Where were some of the places you shot?
Different locations. In people's houses, and on the beaches, and in the

jungles of Brazil. We also shot in a nightclub.

Do you recall how much you were paid?

I don't remember. I'm sure it wasn't a huge amount, because my contract with Seven Arts at the time was only $150 a week. That was probably the equivalent of, what?, 750 today.

Memories of your co-stars?

I *loved* Walter Reed; in fact, Walter didn't have a copy of *Macumba Love* so I sent him a copy just recently. He was helpful and very sweet and supportive, a very pleasant man. Our paths didn't cross again for a long while, not until years later, when I was getting married to [football star] Dan Pastorini. Walter and his wife lived out in Northern California and I was getting married in Carmel, and I got a little note from Walter saying, "We hear you're getting married and we would love to see you and attend your wedding." And I sent back a note saying, "*Absolutely* you can. And please come to my reception, too."

Wilkinson was on hand (along with director Douglas Fowley) for *Macumba Love***'s Detroit opening.**

Wilkinson flaunts her 44-20-36 uber-figure.

Ziva Rodann actually kept away from me quite a bit. I don't know if she felt I was "competition" or what, but I never had a close rapport with Ziva. She never socialized with me; she tried *not* to take pictures with me, other than once when she was forced to.

Was she friendly with everybody else but you, or was she stand-offish in general?

I don't know. I know that the producer was not very happy with her. It was funny: I didn't even know who the producer was, but I kept on seeing this slightly heavyset man smokin' a cigar, an American, at poolside at the hotel all the time. I had no idea who he was. One day about a week later, I hear him cursing about Ziva Rodann. I just thought it was somebody at the pool and so I said, "*Excuse me, sir?*" He said, "I'm the producer of the movie. My name is Mike Ripps." And he was obviously mad at Ziva for *some*thing! And later, when we were going around promoting the movie, Mike never had *Ziva* go around promoting. So I guess he was pretty angry at her, for whatever it was.

If Ziva Rodann was such a pill, why did you pipe up when you heard Ripps complaining about her?

It wasn't like a defense, I just said, "*Excuse me?* Is there some problem?" I was just inquiring—I had a curiosity about what was going on. When you interviewed Walter Reed, he said *he* [argued with Rodann], but I avoided fights. She just never associated with me and she wasn't that friendly towards me. I never went to lunch or dinner with her—not that *I* had any objections. But she didn't seem to want to be anywhere that I was.

You had a nude swimming scene with William Wellman, Jr., correct?

It is *so* interesting: We shot the American version, which was me frolicking in the ocean with a one-piece swimsuit on. A *very* conservative swimsuit—I mean, I could put a skirt on that swimsuit and go to *church* in that top, that's how conservative it was. Only maybe a quarter of an inch of cleavage showed, it was so high-cut. In the European version, they had me frolicking in the ocean, and the ocean was supposed to have made my swimsuit top come off. And, *foronebriefsecond*, I came out of the water with no top on. It was *that* fast.

And it didn't take any "persuasion" to get you to do things like that, right?

No, 'cause nudity was nothing to me. There was another scene of me which did show in some theaters and didn't show in others, depending on the theater and how nervous they got about it. I had on a strapless full skirt, which came down to my mid-calf. It was not tight, it was flared-out. Wearing that dress, I did a little dance for Bill Wellman that was *very* tame. But with my having a large bosom, the dance was a little much for a lot of theaters; people weren't quite as used to large bosoms as they are today. Of course, a large bosom in those days was not like it is today. Today, if you want a large bust, you take a break at lunch and go get a large bosom. But back in [the '50s], it was before the bust jobs. So my bust was large and a little controversial in those days. The dance was absolutely in the European version, but [in America] some theaters *did* and some theaters *didn't* allow it.

Hugh Hefner named me "The Bosom"; I think if I went to *Playboy today* and he met me and I was taking shots for the magazine, I *definitely*

This Russ Meyer photo of Wilkinson was used in *Macumba Love* ads.

wouldn't be called "The Bosom" because there are certainly larger bosoms than mine in *Playboy*.

You just said "nudity was nothing to me." To what do you attribute that attitude?

Because I was brought up in Europe. And I also worked at the Windmill Theatre in London before I came to America, and the Windmill Theatre was like the equivalent of the Ziegfeld Follies over here—there was nudity. I was their lead dancer, and one of the things I used to do as the lead dancer was a fan dance. Now, the "rule" in England on nudity is that you could not *move* if you were naked. Obviously, I did the fan dance naked, but the whole idea was that you had to keep yourself covered. [The appeal] was the *illusion* of being able to *maybe* see something. Always, when you did the fan dance, there were about six girls dancing with you; they were dressed, and they each had *a* plume or a couple of smaller fans which they held in front of you. Then at the very end, you would station yourself in one position and everybody would have their fans *over* you, and the finale was everybody taking one fan away, another fan away, another fan away. And then the spotlight would be on you, motionless, naked. And then a blackout. So I was used to doing *that* from the time I was 15.

And what did your parents think of this?

Nothing! Incidentally, I was a virgin at the time; and when I was in *Playboy* the first time, I was a virgin. So being naked and your virginity were two *totally* separate issues [*laughs*]!

I hereby crown you empress of the world, and you make all the laws. At what age can a girl legally appear nude in front of an audience?

I think it depends on what the arena is. *I* like nude paintings and *I* like nude statues—*I* find a nude body beautiful. But I do not like pornography. I find a nude with legs spread wide open *gross*. If you're talking something of beauty, and something that's not rude, crude and lewd, then I don't have a problem with it. But I have a problem *any* time if I look at it and I find it rude, crude and lewd. I have a picture of me in a fan dance at 15, and I think it's a beautiful picture. There's a fine line. Some people can look at a *baby's* picture and find it sexual [*laughs*]!

What was Douglas Fowley like as a director?

Doug was extremely nice, extremely sweet. He didn't really socialize with me too much, but he was very pleasant. I liked Doug. At the time, he was on a TV series called [*The Life and Legend of*] *Wyatt Earp* with Hugh O'Brian. After the end of the movie, about a month later, Doug called me up and he said, "June, you gotta do me a favor. Hugh O'Brian found out that I did the movie with you, and you gotta go out on a date with him. I have to live with him 'cause I'm doing this show. I *beg* you!" I said okay. So I had a blind date with Hugh O'Brian because Doug was doing the series with him [*laughs*]!

Walter Reed complained about the snakes in the jungle scenes. Did you have any contact with them?

Oh, yes, yes. Snakes have always been something that have given me the creeps. They had these huge, *biiig* snakes, and you'd always look and you'd think they were slimy. The keeper of the snakes, a Brazilian, made me touch one and they're *not* slimy, they're like velvet! But to this day I do not like snakes.

Reed also mentioned that there were real "voodoo people" around.
Yes, and they were very unhappy about us making the movie because it was like somebody degrading their religion. There was a lot of worry about that—Fowley was worried, and I'm sure that everybody involved in producing was, too. And a lot of the people who *worked* on the movie, in the *crew*, *believed* in voodooism. So there was a lot of tension there.

Did you learn to speak any Portuguese while you were there?
Just a *little*. One of the things that makes you lazy as an English-speaking person is the fact that, almost anywhere you go in the world, people speak English.

What did you do with yourself in Brazil when you had time off?
Went around and looked at stuff and looked at scenery and looked at the shops and had breakfasts, lunches, dinners—I had a *great* time. I was in the swing of the social life, and it was wonderful. And I fell in love madly and passionately with a Brazilian.

Was he part of the movie?
No, he was on the island. His family vacationed on the island every summer (I think they owned a telephone company in Brazil). In the evening, after we finished shooting, everybody used to go into a patio-pool area at the hotel; there'd be music there, and we would all have dinner outside. Carlos came over and asked me to dance, and I said sure. And he just romanced me like Brazilians do—they're *very* romantic, they send flowers and cards and stuff. He was extremely sweet, and I just fell madly in love with him. And, when I was back in the United States, the phone calls started coming. In fact, he came to visit me, he was going to surprise me. But I was doing [the play] *Fanny* with Walter Slezak in San Diego. My roommate said, "You take the Santa Ana to San Diego," and he ended up in Santa Ana! He was in town for a week tryin' to get in touch with me, but we never saw each other. Then he went back to Brazil and I never saw him again. "*Next!*" [*Laughs*]

What was your reaction to Macumba Love *when you saw it?*
I remember one reaction: There was one moment when I stepped out of a car and leaned forward, and I said, "*Oh!*"—I could not believe my breasts took up the entire screen [*laughs*]! That was one thing I thought was like…"too much"! Overall, I think it's a very innocent picture, and it just amazes me that it got the reaction that it did!

Douglas Fowley recently told a friend of mine that it was "a piece of junk."
Well, let's face it: You have to look at things as they were for the time, at that moment. *Macumba Love* was a *perfect* summer drive-in movie.

It was also very profitable.
It did *unbelievable* business. When the movie came out, we opened it up at a drive-in in Phoenix, Arizona. Bob Steuer, who was in charge of me going around promoting the movie, did such a good job, you could not get into that drive-in theater for love or money. Opening

night, there was a traffic jam that you wouldn't believe! He got me on television, and they gave away free love potions—I remember everybody lining up, wanting the love potion. It was just unbelievable.

What was in the love potions?

Oh, who knows? But some people swore it worked [*laughs*]! They flew me into lots of towns where *Macumba Love* was opening up. It's all a blur; Detroit, I think, was one of them, and New Orleans, I think, was another.

A fan comes up to you and says he's never seen any of your movies. Which one do you tell him to look for?

The movie that I loved the most, that I thought was the best was a movie I did in Spanish in Mexico City called *La Rabia* [*The Rage*]. I thought this was a *wonderful* movie, and if you ever can get a copy of that, I would be forever grateful to have it. It was about a bank robbery; I played a gringo stripper that had this macho boyfriend [Armando Silvestre] who was not very nice; he got me to seduce the bank clerk, to get him involved in the robbery. It was a really good little movie. That was 1962. I had done *Pajama Tops* at the Seattle World's Fair [opposite John Agar] and I was doing a national tour which was *very* successful. But when I got offered this movie, I left the tour to do it.

As you started doing exploitation movies and doing nudity in movies, did you know that any hopes you might have had for a conventional movie career were going out the window?

No, 'cause I was too stupid to realize that at the time. If I could turn back the clock and I was to do it again, when I had my contract with Seven Arts I wouldn't have done any of the *Playboy* stuff. (I could have done that later.) I would have been at the studio every day, *bugging* them for parts in their movies, instead of just taking my money and going to acting class and saying, "Isn't this great?"

Lately I've been working on a TV pilot called *Absolutely Glamorous*. Julie Newmar is in my pilot, and it has to do with all things glamorous; the theme is to have a guest star in each one who's over 50 and who still looks really good. I still am involved in theater, and I *like* working a lot—I don't think I would ever be a lady who would stop working. I never did the memorabilia shows until a few years ago, and those are a lot of fun. I'm finding that meeting all the people is fun, and I'm having a good time with that too.

June Wilkinson Filmography

Thunder in the Sun (Paramount, 1959)
The Immoral Mr. Teas (Pad-Ram Enterprises, 1959)
Career Girl (Astor, 1960)
Macumba Love (United Artists, 1960)
The Private Lives of Adam and Eve (Universal, 1960)
Twist All Night (*The Continental Twist*) (AIP, 1961)
Too Late Blues (Paramount, 1962)
Who's Got the Action? (Paramount, 1962)
The Playgirls and the Bellboy (*The Bellboy and the Playgirls*) (Rapid/United Producers Releasing, 1962)

The Rage (*La Rabia*; *The Rage Within*) (Cronos, 1963)
The Candidate (Atlantic, 1964)
The Florida Connection (*Weed*) (Unicorn Video, 1974)
Frankenstein's Great Aunt Tillie (Video City Productions, 1984)
Sno-Line (*Death Line*) (Vandom International, 1986)
Vasectomy: A Delicate Matter (Vandom International, 1986)
Talking Walls (*Motel Vacancy*) (New World Entertainment, 1987)

William Read Woodfield on *The Hypnotic Eye*

*Once you've talked to a few hypnotists,
you realize that they are basically masturbators
who have a way of getting their rocks off without
having charm or anything! They are really strange people!*

A beautiful young woman sets her own hair ablaze in the stove-top flame of a gas range. Another girl pours sulfuric acid into her bathroom sink and proceeds to wash her face. Police investigators visit with women who (respectively) drank lye, stuck her face into the blades of an electric fan and burned out her eyes. The plot sounds like something out of a modern gorefest, but these horrific self-inflicted mutilations are actually part of the misogynistic storyline of 1960's *The Hypnotic Eye*, an ahead-of-its-time shocker that sprang from the mind of William Read Woodfield.

At the time he hatched the idea that became *The Hypnotic Eye*, Woodfield was one of the top photographers covering the Hollywood personality beat. The six-foot, 260-pound Woodfield had already tried his hand at television writing when he concocted the Jacques Bergerac-Allison Hayes chiller; to give the movie even more offbeat appeal, he assembled a campy cast of supporting players (including real-life beatniks and "The Great Impostor") and inserted a gimmicky, William Castle-esque passage in which Bergerac, playing a stage hypnotist, attempts to place the movie audience under his mesmeric control.

After this one-of-a-kind movie experience, Woodfield became one of the legends of the television industry. He has scripted *Columbo* episodes, the *Perry Mason* telefilms and, with writing partner Allan Balter, he has utilized his love of con games and chicanery to fill the plots of TV's *Mission: Impossible* with dizzying, elaborate cons—and make it a ratings smash hit. This same "scam artist" mentality also spawned the lovably lurid *The Hypnotic Eye*, as Woodfield explains...

The Hypnotic Eye *is "a Bloch-Woodfield Production."*

Star Jacques Bergerac displays *The Hypnotic Eye.*

Charlie Bloch was my agent—I was a magazine photographer at the time. You want to know the history of this story? It's hilarious. I was a photographer who, sort of on a dare, had written some television shows—a couple of *Sea Hunt*s and a *Death Valley Days*—but it never occurred to me that anybody made a *living* as a writer in television. Charles Bloch was with Globe Photos and he was my photo agent. I was up shooting *Spartacus* [1960] in Death Valley, staying at the Furnace Creek Inn, and I drove to Las Vegas to see Frank Sinatra, who was an old friend.

You were one of the still photographers on Spartacus.

One of the *magazine* photographers. They had still men on the picture, but four or five of us were [also] hired to shoot pictures. We got all of our expenses, we owned the pictures, and then we sold them to the various magazines around the world.

After Las Vegas, I was driving back to Death Valley to continue work with *Spartacus*—it was the pre-dawn, early morning hours. I should mention that I'd been a magician in my youth—a prodigy magician, as a matter of fact—and was publishing at the time a magic magazine which I started when I was about 20. So I'm driving along and I'm seeing the white line on the road. I look at the white line and I say to myself,

"You know, you could make a *movie* about this...!" People would come into the theater...the picture would start ...and it's just a white line, like the one on the road. A voice would say, "All right, everybody—just relax. Keep your eye on the white line." And we would *hypnotize the audience*. And, once we'd done that, we'd say, "Now we're going to give everybody a test, and everybody who doesn't pass the test will get their money back. The *others* can stay for the greatest movie you've ever seen in your life." We would then *tell* the ones who passed the test a story while they were under, and we'd keep getting them under deeper and deeper hypnosis. Ultimately we'd tell them it was the greatest movie they ever saw in their life and to tell all their friends. Goodbye! The post-hypnotic suggestion would be, "Talk it up!"

We were only in Death Valley on *Spartacus* for, oh, five or six days, and then Kirk Douglas fired the director, Tony Mann. When I got back [to Hollywood], I was telling Charlie Bloch about my idea—"What a way to make a

William Read Woodfield (second from right, with glasses) cracks the Caryl Chessman case.

movie! It'll cost *nothing*!" I told it as sort of a whimsicality to Bloch, but he said, "Mmmm. We may be able to *sell* that." So he went over and he told it to Allied Artists, and they said, "We *love* it!"—they thought the idea was terrific. But they had one little problem: They really wanted a *movie*. They thought that the idea of what I called HypnoVision was terrific, but they said, "You can't really *do* that [make a movie that's nothing but a white line], you gotta give 'em a movie."

What a shame! Your "white line" movie would have been a great experiment.

It *could* be a fun movie, because the imagination is *so* powerful. If you put somebody into a trance and tell 'em a tale and make 'em think they really saw it—at least in theory, it seemed to me like a rather interesting entertainment. But Allied Artists wouldn't go for that—they gave me x-number of weeks to write a movie, and they paid me 30 or 40,000 dollars. I sat down and I banged out this turkey story; *The Screaming Sleep* was what I [initially] named it.

Ben Schwalb, who made a lot of movies at Allied Artists, got an executive producer credit.

He was there to watch us, but he didn't really have anything to do with the movie. Ben was the studio's line producer, and a very nice fellow. He let us do what we wanted—I mean, he was not gonna get into *this* [*laughs*], he didn't *understand* hypnosis. But he wanted to make sure that we were being frugal and not wasting the company's money, and make sure we didn't do anything too tasteless. So it was a very pleasant relationship. Truly, it's hard to believe, in this era today of everybody getting into everything, and then the studio having a final cut, that none of that happened. Nobody said, "Change the script. Do this. Do that." Nobody went in for final cuts. And therefore I must tell you that all the faults in that picture, I take full responsibility for [*laughs*]! I really had as much control as I wanted. They wouldn't let me direct it, but they brought in a director [George Blair] who I could just tell what to do next! I'm not proud of that, because it wasn't a very good *movie*. It's an interesting *idea*.

Was Jacques Bergerac your first choice for the evil hypnotist?

My idea of casting was a man named Pedro Armendariz; I thought he would have been wonderful as the hypnotist. Somebody got the idea of Jacques Bergerac, and Bergerac was available and Armendariz wasn't, and Armendariz had language problems that were too much. But Armendariz to me had the *look*. No one has ever accused Bergerac of being a very good actor.

You being a photographer, did you collaborate with Archie Dalzell, the movie's cinematographer? There are a number of innovative shots in the movie.

Well, *I* was the photographer. I was a very good photographer—really, I say in all modesty, I made several million dollars as a magazine photographer in that period and photographed the biggest stars in the world and worked on the biggest movies that were made, with the best cameramen and directors. I did things like *The Manchurian Candidate* [1962] and all of Frankenheimer's pictures, and Billy Wilder's. So you *do* pick up stuff! When you're a magazine photographer, you really have absolute control over the stars and the set *when you are doing your pictures*. In other words, they shoot the film, and then *you* get to re-stage it and re-light it—you can do anything you want with it. And you have the stars. So you really have a great sense of power! On *The Hypnotic Eye*, I would sort of tell [Dalzell] generally how I wanted it to look and he'd say, "Fine." It was all just play—I mean, nobody took all this very seriously.

I like the stove's-eye view of the girl putting her hair in the flames, and the sink's-eye view of the girl washing her face with acid.
Filmically, shots like that—for instance, shooting from behind the fireplace *out*—became the subject of dissertations, about that being absolutely bad film form and so forth. At the time, it seemed like a good idea [*laughs*], but no really good director did that.

How about that effective poster of Jacques Bergerac outside the theater?
That big poster where only half of his face is showing, and there's a dot in the eye? That was something that I did, and had blown up.

I thought the beatnik scenes disrupted the mood of the movie.
Yes, no question about it. The beatniks in the picture, Lawrence Lipton and Eric "Big Daddy" Nord—that was an attempt just to get publicity and to "bring something to the game." Fred Demara*, too, "The Great Imposter"—he's in it, playing a doctor, and that got us on the [Jack] Paar show.

What was "The Great Imposter" like?
"The Great Imposter" was like 6'3" and 300 and some-odd pounds, and a heavy drinker. Very pleasant. A great storyteller. He could get a little "hot" every so often; he almost took the head off a guy named Fred Otash, who was a *very* sleazy private detective in Los Angeles. Demara and I became friends; as a matter of fact, I wrote "The Further Adventures of the Great Imposter" for *Argosy* magazine. (Which we *totally* made up—they were just absolutely fiction.) I also remember that Fred visited my parents, who lived in San Francisco, and my mother or father asked him if he'd like a drink and he said yes. "What would you like?"; "What do you got?" And they went to the liquor closet and he looked in and he saw a bottle of absinthe, which my mother somehow or other, when they went to Europe, smuggled back in the country. And he drank the whole bottle of absinthe [*laughs*]! But he would drink everything in the house.

Around that same time, William Castle was using a lot of audience participation gimmicks in his horror pictures. Did the things he was doing give you any of your ideas?
I don't think so. What gave me the idea was, I realized I had to write x-number of pages, and what do you do when you're [writing about] hypnosis? As I discovered later, as I wrote a lot of television stuff, you have to entertain the people, you have to show them some stuff that surprises them. I mean, what do you *do, how* does a hypnotist kill people? He doesn't *strangle* them, he uses hypnosis!
Hypnotists...basically, they all used

Ferdinand Waldo Demara, Jr., had no more than two years of high school but was able to successfully masquerade as a college professor of psychology, a penologist who reformed hardened criminals, a Trappist monk and a Navy surgeon. Tony Curtis played Demara in the 1961 biopic The Great Impostor.

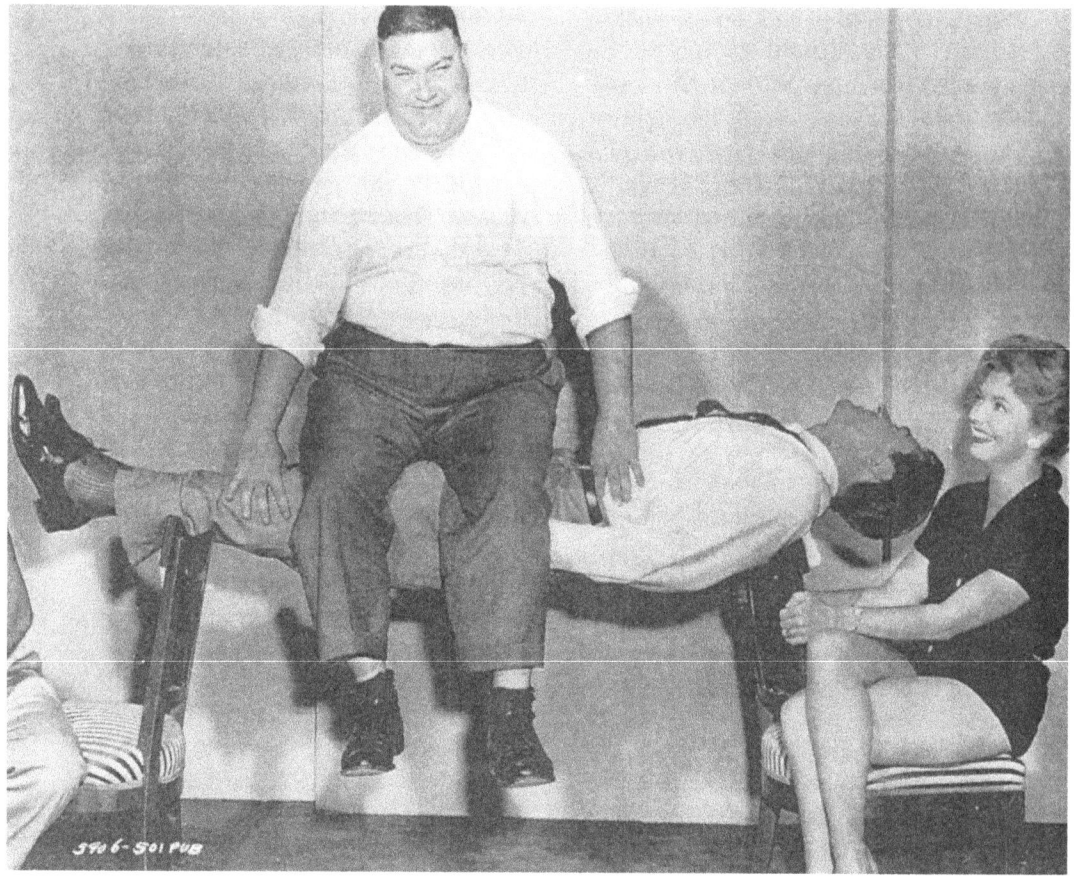

Fred Demara defies the laws of gravity (as Merry Anders looks on) behind-the-scenes on *The Hypnotic Eye*.

to walk around with a couple of girls, and those girls they would put into a trance *instantly*. Most hypnotists—if you ever get talking to them—tell you that the reason they got into hypnosis was to be able to control *women*. That's the fact of it. So once you *know* that, and once you've *talked* to a few hypnotists, you realize that they are basically masturbators who have a way of getting their rocks off without having charm or *any*thing! They are really strange people!

Your "Hypnotic Technical Advisor" on the picture was somebody named Gil Boyne.

Gil Boyne ran a hypnotic school; I think he's now the head of the American Hypnotic Society and all that sort of thing. He's a big macher in the hypnotic world. He was serious and he had academic credits and all that sort of thing. I'm mindful of him taking (I think) Merry Anders and putting her between two chairs and having Fred Demara *stand* on her. And as I remember, she said, "Get *off* me, I'm gonna *fall*!", and he hopped off and they gracefully saved the day.

There really are a lot of very cruel

touches in the script. As a horror film, The Hypnotic Eye *was ahead of its time a bit.*

Frankly, I don't remember that. Look, in a movie, you try to get conflict in every scene, try to get something that makes people remember. Stop 'em and hold their attention.

How many days did you have to shoot it?

I think we did it in 12 days, something like that. It cost 365,000 bucks—that's it! That included the 30 or 40 or whatever the hell it was I got. It was a delightful experience.

Where did you premiere the picture?

We opened *The Hypnotic Eye* with [hypnotist] Gil Boyne on the stage at the Golden Gate Theater in San Francisco, a large first-run theater that used to be a big vaudeville house, on the corner of Taylor and Market. We had a little press screening the night before the opening, in a projection room some place. A very good friend of mine, George Davis, was [convicted felon] Caryl Chessman's* lawyer; I invited George to see the movie, and he came and he enjoyed it. Chessman at that time was getting *enormous* amounts of publicity because he was on his eighth stay of execution; there was a worldwide clamor about Chessman. His execution was coming up, and I said to George, "You're getting all of my publicity. How can we tie in Chessman to *The Hypnotic Eye*?" He said, "I don't know."

We had Gil Boyne with us, the hypnotist who (between pictures) was doing the stage show, bringing people up. (Gil did a week's personal appearances at the Golden Gate Theater, three or four shows a day.) I said to George, "How 'bout this: You take Gil over to Chessman; he hypnotizes Chessman, and gives him a post-hypnotic suggestion; and then *you* file a lawsuit saying that you didn't realize that this hypnotist from *The Hypnotic Eye* hypnotized your guy, and they can't send a man who's under hypnosis to the gas chamber." George said, "I *like* that!" I said, "Will Chessman do it?", and George said, "Why the fuck not?"

By the way, in your opinion, was Chessman guilty?

I *asked* George, I asked, "Is he guilty?" And he said, "Yeah. And he's a real *prick*!"

Did he then ask Chessman to get involved with this?

George did ask him, and then he came back to me and said, "Chess'll do it." Almost at that exact moment, the governor gave Chessman a stay of execution at the State Department's request. Actually, a White House request—they wanted to take the "heat" off of this trip Nixon was about to take to South America, or wherever the hell it was. So we lost *that*. Oh, and I remember I did say to George, "Listen, if it doesn't work and he dies, can we have the body and we'll put it in a glass case and put it in the theater?" "Billy," he said to me, "I think that's going a little too far!" [*Laughs*] It's funny but it's true.

Now, the interesting thing about it is, shortly thereafter, I got a call from

---

Sentenced to die for the crime of kidnapping, Caryl Chessman wrote three books that made him the symbol of the controversy over capital punishment. One book, Cell 2455, Death Row *(1954), was made into a movie the following year, with William Campbell as Chessman.*

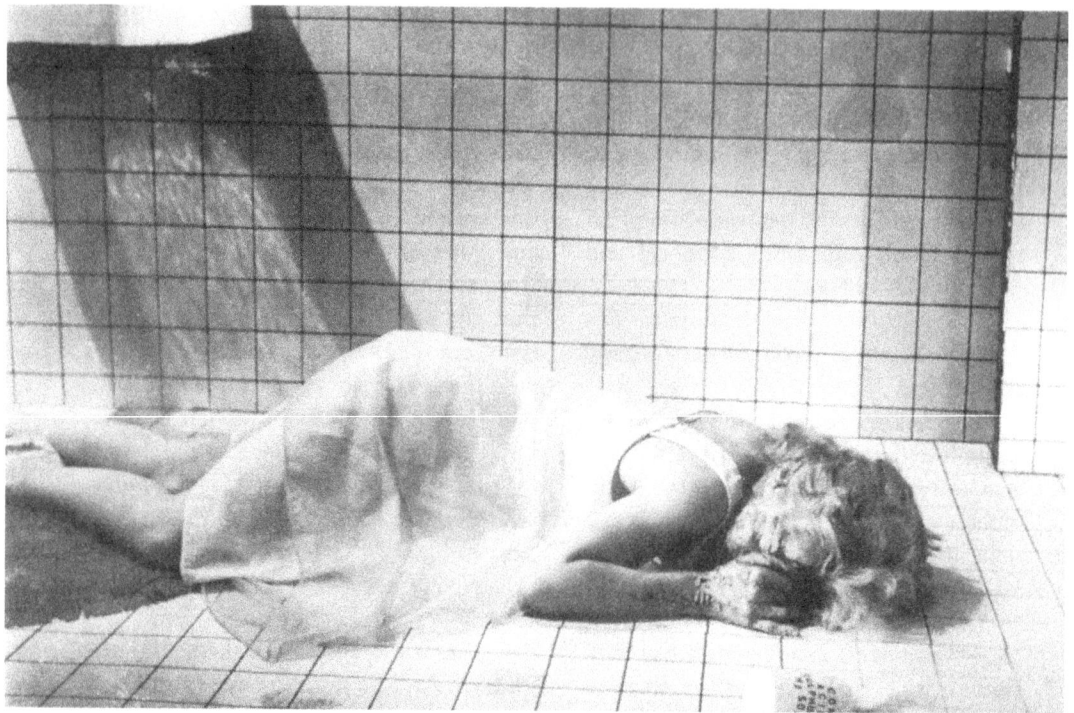
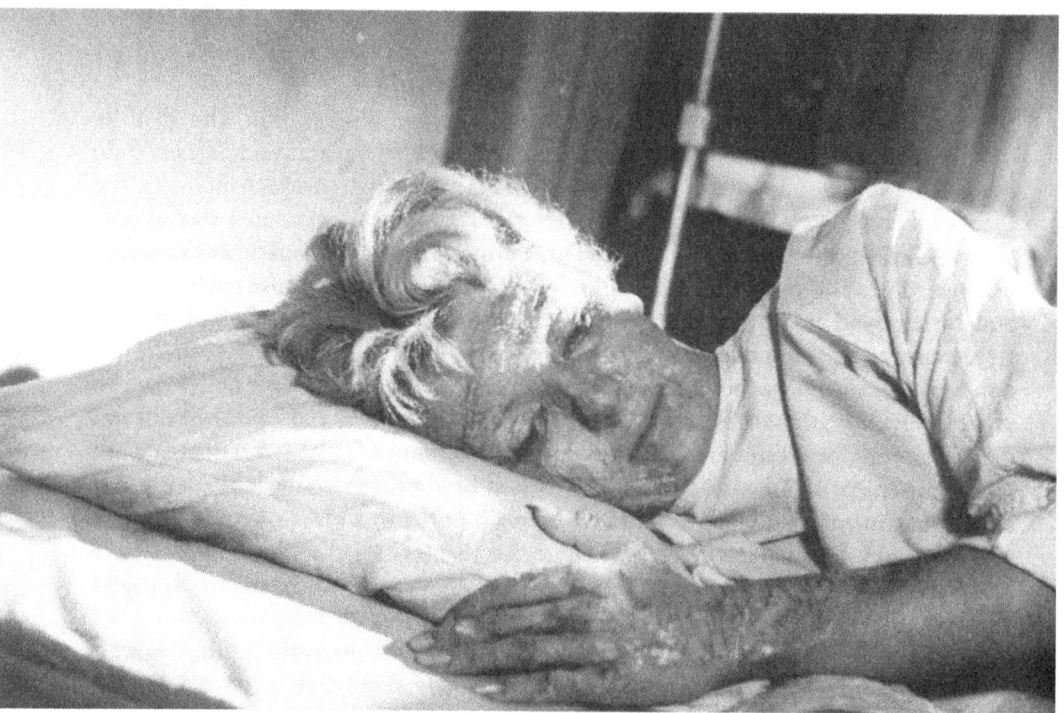

Washing her face with acid lands a mesmerized Merry Anders in the hospital in *The Hypnotic Eye*. (Notice in top shot the shadow of the clear-bottomed—and pipe-less, drain-less—sink.)

Argosy, with whom I was working on the Demara piece "The Further Adventures of the Great Imposter." Milt Machlin, the editor, said, "Do you know anything about Caryl Chessman?" I said, "Sure. What do you want to know?" He said, "We want a story about him—we'd like his confession." I go and I meet Chessman in Death Row, and this man is rather extraordinary—he just had an amazing bearing, a great deal of dignity. And we *bond*. I told him I would like his confession, and he said, "Well, I unfortunately didn't do it." I said, "Look, nobody believes you. Is there any way to prove it?" He said, "Yes. I have a private detective who's been working with me for the last five years. I have instructed him to give you everything, to take you down to the courthouse, go through all the files, give you all my notes, give you everything. And you write whatever you want. If you find that I have at *any* time lied, you may consider that a confession. If you catch me in a lie, I'll sign a confession. That's our deal."

I went immediately to the courthouse, and there were all the boxes there and the guns and all the stuff. Being a photographer, I photographed it all. And I photographed all the documents. Then I came back to Los Angeles and had 'em all developed and I'm laying it all out and looking at it, and I see some things. I said, "Shit...this guy might not have done it." So I phoned George Davis and I said, "George, get on an airplane and come down. I wanna show you something." I laid it out for George, and George said [*softly*], "He didn't *do* it..." I said, "No...I don't think he did either." Now we call Machlin in New York, and Machlin flies out, sees Chess and gets the same feeling about it. And now Machlin and I decide that we will try to save him from the gas chamber. And indeed, in that period of time, we gathered a lot of evidence, including we burglarized the arresting cop, who was on [gangster] Mickey Cohen's payroll. We named Charles Terranova, a guy who the D.A. was saying did not exist— we named him [as the actual guilty party], we had his F.B.I. rap sheet, his m.o., etc., etc. Bottom line is, at the very last minute we got a judge to agree to give Chessman another stay of execution based on this evidence, Chessman's ninth stay. But in the judge's office, a secretary misdialed the phone number— and Chessman was executed in that five minutes that it took. This became the essence of the *Argosy* pieces and a book which we did called *Ninth Life* [1961] that is available in your library.

It's strange how things [develop]. This all started with a silly idea about making a movie that's nothing but a line. And then, "No, you gotta make a movie." Then, "You've made the movie, and you've gotta sell the movie." And then, through that, you get involved in a thing like this Chessman thing, which ultimately altered my entire life. The Chessman thing is one of the things I'm most proud of. It was done for *allll* the wrong reasons, but the character changed and became a good guy from being a cynical prick. So, *The Hypnotic Eye* was very interesting for me!

How did Hypnotic Eye *do box office-wise at the Golden Gate Theater?*

We did something like $15,000 the first couple of *days*. Then business went to hell [*laughs*], and we all realized that we had gotten all the hypno-nuts—hypnotic nuts—in the world; that was everybody who was there. After that, there was no further audience! In other words, the audience was limited. But it ran it all over the country and it did well. I never saw any of the net points that we had, but no one else has ever seen it either—better people than *I* haven't seen it!

What do you think of the movie today?
Look, I *told* you the history [*laughs*] —I had an idea, a wacko idea about the line, then instead of making a film for 45 bucks with a line in a loop and a voice-over, we're into 365,000 bucks. It was cast badly, and it wasn't a very good movie by any stretch of the imagination. I went on to do better things. This was an early, quick effort. I must tell you, I never took it very seriously, it was all just sort of a *lark*. The funny part is that a little magazine called *Films in Review*, a publication of the National Board of Review, listed at the end of each year the Best Films of the Year on the back page. And among the best films that year was *The Hypnotic Eye* [*laughs*]—I couldn't fuckin' believe it! That and *Ben-Hur*! I *can't* figure that out. *You* check! In general, it got very mixed reviews. A lot of people said it was trashy but fun…but it wasn't *intended* to be serious.

Some of the reviewers thought the highlight of the movie was the part where the theaters would turn up the house lights and Jacques Bergerac would try to hypnotize the actual theater audience.
There was a little book called *Hypno Tricks*, about 10 pages or so, that I had when I was a boy magician. It told you how to simulate hypnosis. Those were the tricks that I used in the movie. All of those tests—*if you go along with them*—work. They're old stage hypnotists' tricks, they're foolproof. Put your feet forward so you can see the tips of your toes, and cross your arms, and you cannot rise out of the chair. You just can't *do* it. Those things *work*, and so that became part of the picture.

I'm not ashamed of *The Hypnotic Eye*. I'm not *proud* of it either. But I want to tell you something: Most people *never* make a movie. And *this* came out of probably the most wacko [idea for] making a movie in the world: "We're gonna photograph a *line* and hypnotize the audience." *The Hypnotic Eye* was an interesting interlude…one that I had almost forgotten.

The Hypnotic Eye
(Allied Artists, 1960)

Allied Artists; A Bloch-Woodfield Production; Executive Producer: Ben Schwalb; Produced by Charles B. Bloch; Directed by George Blair; Screenplay: Gitta & William Read Woodfield; Photography: Archie Dalzell; Music: Marlin Skiles; Art Director: David Milton; Editor: William Austin; Production Manager: Edward Morey, Jr.; Assistant Director: Ray Gosnell, Jr.; Music Editor: Eve Newman; Sound Editor: Marty Greco; Set Decorator: Frank Wade; Set Continuity: Virginia Barth; Recording Engineer: Ralph Butler; Special Effects: Milt Olsen; Wardrobe: Roger J. Weinberg; Makeup: Emile LaVigne; Construction Supervisor: James West; Property: Arden Cripe; Hypnotic Technical

Advisor: Gil Boyne; Hairstyles: Carmen Dirigo; 77 minutes

Jacques Bergerac (Desmond), Merry Anders (Dodie Wilson), Marcia Henderson (Marcia Blane), Allison Hayes (Justine), Joe Patridge (Detective Sgt. Dave Kennedy), Fred Demara (Hospital Doctor), Lawrence Lipton (Beatnik Poet), Eric "Big Daddy" Nord (Bongo Player), Guy Prescott (Dr. Philip Hecht), James Lydon (Emergency Doctor), Carol Thurston (Doris Scott), Eva Lynd, Carey Calvert, Gloria Moreland (Ladies), Evan MacNeil (Miss Thompson), Phyllis Cole (Mrs. McNear), Holly Harris (Mrs. Stevens), Mary Foran (June Mayes), Cosmo Sardo (Ticket Taker), William Janssen (Man), Norman Nazarr (Cab Driver), Marlyn Gladstone (Screaming Woman), Jim Healy (Radio Voice)

Dana Wynter

One man was writing a thesis on Invasion of the Body Snatchers *for his degree, and he measured—he measured!— the distance from one corner to the other in the town where we shot. ...I thought to myself, "These people are out of their minds!"*

"I hate the idea of a double," Dana Wynter once told a *TV Guide* interviewer, adding that she always refused to allow herself to be doubled in her movies. She was referring, of course, to the standard use of stunt doubles and stand-ins during picturemaking, but for fans of *Invasion of the Body Snatchers* the comment has a coincidental "double" meaning: It vividly recalls her co-starring role as Becky Driscoll, the chic divorcee romantically pursued by Kevin McCarthy—then stalked and ultimately duplicated by the extra-terrestrial pod people—in the 1956 science-fiction classic.

The daughter of a noted surgeon, she was born Dagmar Winter in Berlin, Germany, and grew up in England. When she was 16, her father went to Morocco to operate on a woman who wouldn't allow anyone else to attend her; he visited friends in Southern Rhodesia, fell in love with it and brought his daughter and her stepmother to live with him there. Wynter later enrolled as a pre-med student at Rhodes University (the only girl in a class of 150 boys) and also dabbled in theatrics, playing the blind girl in a school production of *Through a Glass Darkly* in which she says she was "terrible." After a year-plus of studies, Wynter returned to England and shifted gears, dropping her medical studies and turning to an acting career. She was appearing in a play in Hammersmith when an American agent told her he wanted to represent her. She left for New York on November 5, 1953— "Guy Fawkes Day," a holiday commemorating a 1605 attempt to blow up the Parliament building. "There were all sorts of fireworks going off," Wynter later told an interviewer, "and I couldn't help thinking it was a fitting send-off for my departure to the New World."

Wynter had more success in New York than in London, acting on TV (*Robert Montgomery Presents*, *Suspense*, *Studio One*) and the stage before "going Hollywood" a short time later. The willowy, dark-eyed actress appeared in over a dozen films, worked in "Golden Age" television (*Playhouse 90*) and even co-starred in her own short-lived TV series, the globe-trotting *The Man Who Never Was*. Married and divorced from hotshot Hollywood lawyer Greg Bautzer, Dana Wynter, once called Hollywood's "oasis of elegance," now lives in happy retirement in the County of Wicklow, Ireland.

When you first arrived in New York from England in 1953, things must have been touch-and-go for a while.

Yes, I was living on doughnuts, living on...absolutely nothing! The English only allowed you to take £500 out of the country—that was *it*. Then you were on your own, you had to make your own way. But I was very lucky, I was great friends with [composer] Richard Rodgers from England, and when I got my first TV show, *Robert Montgomery Presents* or *Suspense* or whatever it was, he had quite a few people watching it. I had the lead in the show—Eva Gabor fell out, and they pushed *me* in. It was one of those miraculous things that happens in America, one of those wonderful, crazy, no-reason things. (By the way, on that first show, I thought to myself, "How *kind* the Americans are, they employ deaf veterans." Well, I didn't realize all the floor managers had things on their ears so they could talk to the control room! I was *that* naive!) But Richard Rodgers had everybody watch, [TV producer] Martin Manulis and people like that. And after that, I was very lucky, all the rest of the live TV stuff *happened*. My life has really been *blessed*, it's all been quite magical.

You also acted in a play in New York, a comedy called Black-Eyed Susan *with Vincent Price.*

Vincent was the *most* enchanting man, a most *civilized* man, having taught art and being tremendously well educated. *Such* a lovely person! I had never done comedy before, and so of course I was falling into everybody's laughs and I wasn't getting my *own*—it was rather awful. We got to Boston, where Elliot Norton was really *the* critic at the time—if you got a decent notice from him you were okay for New York, and if you didn't you might as well fold up. I got lucky, he said I was the best thing in the play. (Which wasn't saying much!) We opened in New York just before Christmas [1954], and—imagine!—in the audience there were five people, all relatives of people in the play [*laughs*]! We closed in three days! It was quite an experience, I'll tell you—a baptism by fire!*

The best days—the *best* days were the *Playhouse 90* days. Oh, they were magic! I did three of those, two with [director] Johnny Frankenheimer, and I'll tell you, that was a golden time in American theater-drama-live television. The excitement of that will never be duplicated. Think of the writers who came through, and the directors, and with John Houseman and Martin Manulis guiding the whole thing—it was just so *civilized*, you know?

I found a 1958 interview where you exclaimed, "I hate movies!" and talked about how much you liked live TV.

"[Black-Eyed Susan] is a farce," wrote a New York Daily News *critic. "It also is a fiasco. Moreover, it is shoddy, sleazy, leering, vulgar, blatant, ill-mannered, coarse, witless, feckless, insulting, discouraging and unfunny." According to the headline of the* New York Times *review, "All Goes Well in* Black-Eyed Susan *Until First Actor Steps on Stage."*

Born in Germany and raised in England and Rhodesia(!), Dana Wynter began her starring film career with the science fiction milestone *Invasion of the Body Snatchers*.

Yes. Quite right. I like the preparation, I *love* the rehearsal—it was absolutely intense, it was sort of total *immersion*, those rehearsals. The actors used to sit around and, if there was a problem with *any*body's lines or *any*body's speech or *any*thing, *every*body tried to fix it and make it better. It was an *intense* experience! And then the *excitement* of playing. When we did "Wings of the Dove" [on *Playhouse 90*], in the cast was Isabel Jeans, the lovely, lovely actress who played the aunt in *Gigi* [1958]. She kind of looked at me on the first day of rehearsal and she said [*haugh-tily*], "What do *you* play, dear?" And I was playing the lead, you know [*laughs*]! Well, after about three days, we became great friends, and one day she turned to me and said, "I've never *done* live television before, dear. How many people do you suppose *watch* this program?" This is *Playhouse 90*! I said, "Well, I don't know. On a *bad* night, I guess 20,000,000. On a *good* night, 40,000,000." "Forty million people...? *Forty million people*??!!" Well, after that she was just pacing the corridors, gripping her script and muttering, "Forty million people..." [*Laughs*] We were on the air, in the middle of this scene in a conservatory in our lovely costumes and hats, and suddenly I saw "Forty million people" go across her eyes [*laughs*]! I thought, "That's it! She's going to go up!" And we were only halfway through it. But I saw the old lady pull herself together...take a very deep breath...and go on. And she was just wonderful. But I'll never forget that silent moment of panic that just *struck* her in the middle of this production, because she knew that 40,000,000 people were looking at her. *That* was the excitement! When you heard the *Playhouse 90* theme come up and they were counting down, "Ten, nine, eight, seven, six"—I can't *begin* to describe the adrenaline rush, the extraordinary kind of excitement. Because there was jeopardy—I mean, if anything went wrong, there were all those people looking in.

When I did "The Violent Heart," a Daphne du Maurier show with Ben Gazzara, we were playing a scene and all of a sudden, out of the corner of my eye, I saw something go down and I heard a bit of a thud. Turned out to be the cameraman! We had four cameramen on this live show, and an electrician had been standing next to one with a klieg light. The electrician leaned on him or something, and the light shorted through his camera. The guy got a very sharp electric shock and fell off his camera. A cameraman from another set had just wandered onto ours, because whenever Johnny Frankenheimer was working, everybody would come and watch because the crew absolutely *worshipped* him. This other cameraman climbed on the camera and he said over his microphone to the control booth, "Johnny, I don't know this show, but I'll *try* if you want to talk me through it." It was tremendously difficult, but Johnny called all the shots, all the lens sizes and the moves, and we got through the show and nobody knew that one of four cameras had almost been lost. The original guy climbed back on his camera for the last of the six acts. Now, *that* kind of thing never happened in film—I mean, it was all so *dull* by comparison.

You started your Hollywood movie career under contract to 20th Century–Fox.

I was offered [contracts by] Metro and Fox, and I signed with Fox. [Studio boss] Darryl F. Zanuck later told me that he wasn't very lucky with his last few women contract players, and he hoped that he'd get lucky with me.

But before you appeared in a single Fox movie, you co-starred in Invasion of the Body Snatchers. *Why did producer Walter Wanger think of you?*

Some time prior to that, I was in the William Morris Agency in New York. They weren't my agents, so I don't know why I was there; I was probably there with a friend or something like that. Walter Wanger happened to be there and he saw me and he asked somebody who I was. I didn't meet him at the time, I didn't know *any* of this.

But he thought of you when he went to do Body Snatchers.

Apparently Vera Miles had been penciled in by Allied Artists for *Invasion of the Body Snatchers,* and Walter Wanger said, "No, I want that new girl. The English one." That's when they found out that I was under contract to Fox, and Fox allowed me to push the [start of the] contract a few days backward so that I could do this picture. *Invasion of the Body Snatchers* was my first movie.

No, you were in some English movies—

No, no, don't, don't, I really wasn't *in* them, you know. I was sort of trying to make a living doing whatever I could while I was studying.

So Body Snatchers *was the first movie you had a sizable role in.*

Oh, yeah.

Any "first-picture jitters" on Body Snatchers, *or had you had enough experience on TV to walk right in and go to work?*

Not jitters, no, because everybody was awfully nice. Well, *most* people were. From live TV to *this*, it was a *dawdle*, you know what I mean? You could kind of gather yourself together. Also, I was quite young and inexperienced, and…well, "fools rush in," you know [*laughs*]! And the cameraman was very kind to me, too, Ellsworth Fredericks. Just terribly concerned and kind of "there" and friendly and helpful. People gathered 'round and the crew gathered 'round—I think it was probably my English accent, they probably thought I was an orphan!

"Most people" were nice, you just said. Who wasn't nice?

I must say I learned a lot from her, but Carolyn Jones was…strangely unfriendly and un-helpful. But I learned a lot from *that*, too, because I learned that if there's somebody in your cast who's kind of new and hasn't been around much, you gather 'round and you try and help them through. That was the only…"strange" event.

You had to have a plaster cast made of your body for the pod scenes. What was that experience like?

[*Laughs*] Well, worse for Carolyn, because she had claustrophobia. For me, it wasn't bad, except they were "funny," the guys who made the thing. I was in this thing while it hardened, and of course it got rather warm! I was breathing through straws or something quite bizarre, and the rest of me was encased, it was like a sarcophagus. The guys who were making it tapped on the back of the thing and said, "Dana, listen, we won't be long, we're just off for lunch!" [*Laughs*] In the end, we had to be covered except for just the nostrils and I think a little aperture for the mouth.

One article said it got to be 120 degrees inside that thing.

Yes, that plaster heated up all right!

I never quite understood why you and the others had to go through all that, why these dummies had to be made. Why couldn't the actors themselves just lie inside the pods in the scenes where they opened up?

Probably because the special effects people hadn't decided *how* it was going to work, and if they *had* these [dummies], they could experiment. They weren't that advanced in special effects, I suppose. I only saw that picture once, and that was a very long, long, long, long time ago, and I really don't remember the scene with the pods opening.

Did you read the short story that the movie was based on?

Yes. This may sound stupid, but I really can't remember what I thought of it. I'll tell you something: Once something is *done*, I sort of put it behind me. I suppose one remembers the very important things in one's life and not the minutiae, you know. [My career] *wasn't* my passion, and that's why I left. Because I think you *have* to [have a passion for it] to devote your life to it. Kevin McCarthy, for instance, is a very fine actor and the theater is his passion. For *me*, I do things out of sort of intellectual curiosity very often. I once wrote for a year or more for *The Manchester Guardian*, the newspaper Alistair Cooke wrote for. It's one of the oldest English newspapers, and I had a series of my own, every fortnight. The fact that they took me on on that basis and that I had my series, that was lovely. But once I *did* it—it's like flying. Once you fly solo, *that's* the thrill; after that, it's on to something else. That's terrible, it's a very flibbertigibbet way of going about one's life, but it's great fun!

Walter Wanger—how did you like knowing him?

Walter was an *extraordinary* man. Tremendously civilized. I have nothing to say about him that everybody else doesn't say. He was highly educated and had beautiful manners and was well-read and had good taste. I don't know how he *survived* in that community.

Was he on the set a lot?

"I really don't care for actors very much," says Wynter—but she's made an exception for *Body Snatchers* co-star Kevin McCarthy.

He was quite a bit, yeah.

He called you "a brunette Grace Kelly with the zest of Ava Gardner. My best discovery since Hedy Lamarr."
Oooh, how lovely [*laughs*]! A great compliment!

In interviews, Don Siegel sometimes told a farout-sounding story that he once broke into your house and put a pod under your bed.
That *is* a bit farout. Actually, he left it on my doorstep. He had a girlfriend who lived next door to me—I lived on Santa Monica Boulevard near the Mormon Temple in an enclave of five little cottages. Don Siegel was courting this girl, and he would pass my cottage all the time. And one night he just left it on the doorstep!

And you found it—
Yes, I did, leaving at five-thirty or six in the morning, and there it was!

Did it have the desired effect?
Yes, I nearly broke my neck, because when you open your front door to go to your car, you don't expect to find something large on your doorstep [*laughs*]!

What was Siegel like as a director?
Very interesting. He had so much *fizz*, he had that kind of New York buzz, fizz, energy. Enthusiasm and drive and

sort of a wry sense of humor. It was all good. And then Sam Peckinpah was the dialogue coach.

Peckinpah used to give interviews in which he claimed to have re-written the script of Body Snatchers. *Finally the real writer got fed up and threatened to sue, and Peckinpah never told that lie again.*

That's very interesting. I must tell you, he was a very nice man but I had no memory of him later. Even now, if he were alive, and I ran him over in the street, I wouldn't know him [*laughs*]!

According to one of the trade papers, Body Snatchers *was mostly shot on actual locales, and only four out of the 24 days was shot in the studio.*

That could be right. Bronson Canyon was where the final chase took place took place. Also in Bronson Canyon is the tunnel where Miles goes off and leaves Becky. They dug a trench and put planks over it and had the camera looking down at us. You know, people write theses about *Invasion of the Body Snatchers*; it's the most extraordinary thing about this film! One man was writing a thesis on this film for his degree, and he measured—he *measured!*—the distance from one corner to the other in the town where we shot. He said to me, "Dana, the line when you say, 'I'm here, Miles,' when Kevin McCarthy comes back to the cave. It's a tri-tonal line—you go from B-flat to E to G. Now *that* was brilliant. How did you decide upon that tri-tonal thing?" And I thought to myself, "These people are out of their *minds!*" [*Laughs*]

Have I given you the impression that I'm out of my mind yet?

[*Laughs*] *You* sound absolutely wonderful!

Did you have a stunt double at any point in those strenuous scenes?

No, and poor Kevin—p-o-o-r Kevin—had to carry me! I was quite chunky at the time [*laughs*], and all his good breeding came out. He didn't huff or puff or pull a face or anything, he was *terrific,* 'cause he had to run in and out of this muddy canyon carrying ol' Dana!

It really looks like a very grueling chase. Was there enough time between shots for everybody to catch their breath, or was it a real hard day?

The picture was shot in, what?, three weeks, and there were a lot of setups. So there *wasn't* much time in between, I seem to remember! They really got a move on, which was quite good.

After you and Kevin McCarthy hide yourselves beneath the floorboards of the cave, the townspeople swarm in searching for you. At the very end of the shot, one guy steps between the boards and starts to fall forward. Did he fall on top of the two of you?

I don't remember. I just remember an awful lot of bits of stones and things falling down on us [*laughs*]!

Was the scene on the giant staircase a hassle?

Yes. But it all went very well, the people were tremendously professional. That was one of the impressive things about that picture, that Wanger and Siegel were professionals and they got a crew together which was also very professional. And I think the actors were mostly theater people, so there was no waffling about and not knowing the lines. Also, there wasn't a lot of discussion about motivation and all this kind of stuff. Performances were thought through [by the actors themselves] and performed.

What's the key to playing in a farout movie like Body Snatchers? *Or didn't your mind work that way?*

Well, you see, *on the surface* nothing was said about it being farout. It was just supposed to be a plain, thrilling kind of picture. That was what Allied Artists thought they were making. By the way, we realized—Walter and Kevin and people who *can* think about things—that we were making an anti-"ism" picture. Anti-"ism"—fascism, Communism, all that kind of thing. *We* took it for granted that's what we were making, *but* it wasn't spoken about openly on the set or anything like that. They were delicate times, and I think if Allied Artists had had the slightest idea that there was anything deeper to this film, that would have quickly been stopped!

I don't know if Don Siegel ever owned up to it being an anti-Communist movie. I think he always sort of ducked the subject.

Well, maybe it was just one of these things that one *thought*. I mean, there's no point in talking about it, because the story was what it was, and it works. So there was no point in saying, "Well, now, look here, what we're really doing is *this*..." I took it for granted that that's what it was, and I'm sure Kevin did too. Now, Kevin has stories about the humor in the film that was knocked out by Allied—"We don't want any *laughs* in here!" Oh, they were *something*, those people, they *really* were something. I tell you, it took some getting used to, going into that town [Hollywood] and being part of it when you come from a completely different culture. Quite extraordinary! I remember being in Walter Mirisch's house—terribly nice people—and there were some extraordinary paintings. It was the usual thing: Dinner (quickly!) and then right into the projection room and watch the latest movie from the studio. Out of the corner of my eye I saw what I thought was a very precious painting—a Matisse or a Renoir or something—plummeting. I cried out, "Watch it!" and everybody turned around. Well, they had had this painting fixed to the ports of the projection room—the projectionist had pressed a button to let the panels go down so that the glass aperture was revealed, the window the film was shown through. But the panels had precious paintings on them, and when I saw this painting falling, I didn't realize it was *nailed* to a panel that was going down! Everybody looked at me thinking, "What a fool *she* is," "What on earth is the matter with her?" [*Laughs*]

You just mentioned that the humor was cut out of the movie by Allied Artists. Walter Wanger didn't have enough pull to keep that from happening?

I don't know *what* his position was in the studio system at that time. I thought he seemed to have lost quite a lot. I mean, he was making *very* serious pictures at one time. He'd either lost his grip *or*, as Billy Wilder says, "You don't lose your talent in this business, you just become unfashionable." (That's pretty good, isn't it?) Anyway, I don't know what happened to Walter; I don't know whether the shooting of Jennings Lang* kind of made him into a bit of a laughingstock in that

---

*In 1951, Wanger, the husband of actress Joan Bennett, discovered that Bennett and her agent Jennings Lang were having an affair, and he shot and wounded Lang in an office building parking lot. Wanger served a short prison sentence.

Don Siegel consults with *Body Snatchers* stars Wynter and Kevin McCarthy before burying them beneath the floorboards of Bronson Cavern.

town. Maybe he was just too good for them, he was a bit too sophisticated, too highly educated. Maybe he made them feel a little uncomfortable. That's understandable, isn't it?

Your impressions of Kevin McCarthy?
You feel there's not a *shadow* on Kevin: He doesn't speak badly of people, he's full of praise, he's full of enthusiasm, you feel that he's decent through

and through and through and through. *Apart* from being so charming. And he doesn't *have* that "actor thing"—I really don't care for actors very much! I've had no actor-friends, I can't bear "actor talk" [*laughs*]!

And you felt that way about him in 1955, as you were making the movie?

In 1955, I hadn't been exposed to many actors. I mean, I'd done a couple of plays and things, but I hadn't been exposed to that whole genus of "*ac*-tor." Actors always try to enlist you against *other* actors if you're in a play or something; they kind of gang up on each other and talk about each other. I can't bear it! But Kevin had such a *masculine* thing—there was nothing petty about him. Well, look at where he comes from—he and his sister [writer Mary McCarthy] are serious people. An absolute joy.

In your early publicity, the first movie you made for Fox, The View from Pompey's Head *[1955], got all the attention. If* Body Snatchers *was mentioned at all, it was referred to as a quickie, as something that had to be gotten out of the way before you could start your* real *movie career.*

That's because all that was done through the Fox publicity machine, and of course they weren't interested in doing anything for *Body Snatchers*. Also, remember that *Body Snatchers* was a B picture from the start—at the time, it was never considered to be anything other than a B picture, because that's what Allied Artists made. So Fox wasn't interested in that, the "push" was behind the new girl at the studio. By the way, one movie I made at Fox, *D-Day, the Sixth of June*, was just on here—every year they play it here in Ireland. *That* was my favorite, I *really* enjoyed that.

Your favorite movie to make, or the best movie you're in?

It was the one I really *enjoyed*, because it was with Robert Taylor and Richard Todd. We were great pals before the picture, and it just so happened we made it all together at Fox. That was kind of marvelous.

Honestly, this *Invasion of the Body Snatchers* thing—looking back on it, I'm not really mad about thinking about it. I was sort of new and looked kind of young and…boring. And my acting—I was boring *in* it. There was no edge. If you're lucky, you develop a bit of that as you get older. And you develop a bit of humor. In your first picture, you're so terrified that you're going to do the wrong thing that you just play everything *straight*. So it's nothing I'm *proud* of. Now, I was happy to be in it, especially because of Kevin and because of Don, and it was a fun thing to do. But I'd just as soon forget it.

Did you feel, by making a B picture, a science fiction picture, that you were starting off in Hollywood on the wrong foot?

Oh, no, it was very much the *right* foot for me. I was happy to be doing it because I liked Walter very much. Your first picture, you're delighted *whatever* it is. Mind you, I've always said that I was terribly embarrassed by that title. I *begged* Walter, I said, "Walter, you can't [call it *Invasion of the Body Snatchers*]! I mean, my *parents*! How can I admit to my parents that I'm doing a picture called *Invasion of the Body Snatchers*, for God's sake! They'll think that I'm demented!" [*Laughs*] How do you explain *that* away? Even now, people who don't know it and haven't seen it, they kind of snicker, you know? Don Siegel wanted to call it *Sleep No More*.

In 1955, before Body Snatchers *had been released, you were already telling interviewers that the title was dreadful. You also said about it, "I suppose it will appeal to the science fiction kids."*

[*Gasps*] Oh, dear...oh, Lord! It's terrible you can't *bury* your past, isn't it? It's always there to haunt you!

I just thought it was interesting that you were so frank about your own first movie.

You know, if you haven't learned the "studio speak," you say things like that. I don't like "studio speak," I don't like the hypocrisy. The publicity woman at Fox used to come on the set every single day, Sonia Wolfson. She was a terribly nice woman, but terribly...*driving*. She'd come on with the pencil poised on the paper and say, "Now, what did you do last night?" And it used to drive everybody crazy. I remember Robert Taylor really *telling* her—he made it up to such a degree, she fled scarlet-faced, and she never asked him *that* question again [*laughs*]! Publicity people would also *make up* things that weren't said, and that was really so terrible, because people *believe* what they read. If you're quoted as saying something that you didn't even say, you can never get away from it.

Once you married Greg Bautzer, obviously you didn't worry about where your next meal was coming from, and yet you stuck with your acting career.

Well, because I was under contract and Fox wouldn't let me go. I *begged* to be let out, because they wouldn't allow you to do *anything* [beyond the movie work], especially in television. When Martin Manulis and Houseman sent me the script for the Scott Fitzgerald "Winter Dreams" [episode of *Playhouse 90*], it was such a wonderful story, it was such a part of Americana, I went to Buddy Adler and I said, "Let me do this." He said, "No. None of our people can do television." I said, "But we can't *learn*, we can't *stretch* ourselves. Where do we learn if we just go from film to film to film? That's not a learning process." So I made him read it and they all discussed it, and then they said, "All right, she can do it." So at least I broke *that* open, I was able (*while* I was under contract) to do three *Playhouse 90*s, because after a while they were recognized as being prestigious.

But you couldn't get Fox to let you out entirely.

That's right. And they kept giving me pictures like *The Lion* [1962] with Bill Holden, which was going to be shot in Kenya. I was assigned to that, and I told them, "I can't *go*, I've got a child who's *two*. If I take him to Kenya, I don't want him to have his head stuck on a pole!" (The Mau Mau thing was still going on then.) So I was suspended for the length of that. *No Down Payment* [1957] they also assigned me to, and I said, "I can't imagine why anybody is *making* this picture!" I said, "This is the most boring thing—life in a housing development, for God's sake?! Absolutely not." So I was under suspension for a good deal of the time. These contracts were in their [the studios'] grace and favor; the actor couldn't say, "Look, thanks a lot. I'm off." And if you're suspended, the length of the [shooting of the] picture is added to the end of your contract. The head of the William Morris Agency, who was a friend of my husband's and a very nice man, said he wanted to represent me and he tried to get me [away from Fox].

Foreign film posters promised a bit more of Wynter than was actually seen in the movie.

But Buddy Adler had some kind of a problem, he wanted to teach me some kind of a lesson, and he wouldn't let me go. I was there for seven years, and I could do nothing about it.

You were in one of the scariest episodes of The Alfred Hitchcock Hour, *"An Unlocked Window" with female impersonator T.C. Jones.*
It was great fun—Louise Latham and I were falling down laughing all the time. She has a mad sense of humor, and we just laughed our way through it. Poor T.C. Jones was not allowed to go to the commissary for lunch, 'cause they didn't want to tip the ending [Jones played a female nurse who turns out to be a male killer]. And every time he wanted to go to the loo, he'd stand there outside the men's room in his nurse's outfit and his false eyelashes, counting the men going in, waiting for them to come out and then making a dash for it and hoping to God nobody would walk in on him [*laughs*]. He was so good in it, the crew didn't refer to him as a man, they would say, referring to him, "Tell her to move over to the left a little bit," "Put a little more light on her." One evening he says to me, "The car's broken down. You wouldn't give me a lift home, would you?" I say sure. So we're driving along, it's evening, Santa Monica Boulevard, and I notice people at a stoplight kind of...looking at us. I thought nothing of it. We went on, and it happened again. At that point, I turned around and I looked at him in the seat next door to mine, and there he was in a T-shirt, with his little furry chest, lipstick, the eyelashes still on... and a bald head [*laughs*]! And this was in 1964, when these things weren't quite as "taken for granted" as they are nowadays! I can't tell you how fast I drove that man home once I realized!

What brought you to Ireland?
They were making *Shake Hands With the Devil* [1959] here and the studio sent me. I had never been to Ireland before. I made a lot of friends here. And then I came back when John Huston asked for me for *The List of Adrian Messenger* [1963]—I played the mother of Huston's son Tony. I had never ridden side-saddle before, and I had to ride side-saddle; had to play in hunting sequences side-saddle; had to drive a Land Rover, and nobody ever bothered to ask whether I could do it or not [*laughs*]! So I did it! I bought the land here in 1966, built a house. But my son was at school, so I stayed in America until he went to university and was able to drive and stuff. That's when I started spending more and more time here. I love it, but the winters are pretty hard. They're long and gray, and I was snowed in twice this year.

So what's the best movie you were in?
You know, there really *wasn't* a best. The best workout was, of course, the *Playhouse 90* work. Also [the TV series] *Twelve O'Clock High*—I had a wonderful time there. I did three of those, and they were love stories that were kind of tragic. *Unresolved* love stories, like *D-Day, the Sixth of June*. But I finally gave up. In the end, I found myself doing *a Magnum, P.I.* And even though it was a *Magnum*, and Tom Selleck is the loveliest man in the world, and the whole thing was fun, I found myself at one stage with a gun in my hand, playing some wicked person. And I thought, "Hang on here. Here's a grown woman with a gun in her hand, and this is

supposed to be entertainment? What am I doing here?"

So, to get back to your question, the *Playhouse 90*s were my favorites. As for the films, I don't know. *The View from Pompey's Head* was fun, *D-Day* was lovely, and *Sink the Bismarck!* [1960] I enjoyed. But there really aren't any movies that I did anything astonishing *in*, or *with*. I never read my own publicity, just as I don't see pictures that I've done. Once lived, once done—that's it. Onward!

Dana Wynter Filmography

As Dagmar Wynter

Night Without Stars (Europa/General Film Distributors/RKO, 1951)
White Corridors (General Film Distributors/Rank, 1951)
Lady Godiva Rides Again (*Bikini Baby*) (British Lion/Carroll Pictures/Walter Reade, 1951)
Something Money Can't Buy (General Film Distributors/Universal, 1952)
The Woman's Angle (Associated British-Pathe/Stratford Pictures, 1952)
It Started in Paradise (General Film Distributors/Astor, 1952)
The Crimson Pirate (Warners, 1952)
Colonel March Investigates (Criterion/Eros, 1953)
Knights of the Round Table (MGM, 1953)

As Dana Wynter

The View from Pompey's Head (*Secret Interlude*) (20th Century–Fox, 1955)
Invasion of the Body Snatchers (Allied Artists, 1956)
D-Day the Sixth of June (20th Century–Fox, 1956)
Something of Value (MGM, 1957)
In Love and War (20th Century–Fox, 1958)
Fraulein (20th Century–Fox, 1958)
Shake Hands with the Devil (United Artists, 1959)
Sink the Bismarck! (20th Century–Fox, 1960)
On the Double (Paramount, 1961)
The List of Adrian Messenger (Universal, 1963)
If He Hollers, Let Him Go! (Cinerama, 1968)
Airport (Universal, 1970)
Santee (Crown International, 1973)
Le Sauvage (*The Savage*; *Lovers Like Us*) (1975)

Index

Page numbers in boldface refer to photographs.

Absolutely Glamorous (tv) 281
Accident (1967) 161
Ackerman, Forrest J 219
Adelman, Gary 224
Adler, Buddy 304, 306
Adventures of Ozzie... (tv) 142, 145
Agar, John 281
Ah, Wilderness! (stage) 141
Aherne, Brian 245, 247
Al Capone (1959) 71
Aldon, Mari 196
Aletter, Frank 142
Alexander, Max 227, 228, 230, 231, 236
Alfred Hitchcock Presents/Hour 80, 82, 151, 153, 161–73, **162**, **164**, **165**, 174–75, 176, 177, 178, 306
All Quiet on the Western Front (book) 244
All Summer Long (stage) 113
Allardice, James 172–73, 175
Allegret, Marc 235
Allen, Irwin 23
Allen, Lewis 159–60
Allen, Woody 192
L'Amante di Paride see *Loves of...*
Amazing Stories (tv) 86
The Amazing Transparent Man (1960) 244, 245
Ambler, Eric 177
Ames, Allyson 213, 214, 216, 217, 218, **218**, 221–22, 223, 225
Anders, Luana 115, 118
Anders, Merry 288, **288**, **290**
Anderson, Robert 115
The Andersonville Trial (stage) 27
Andromeda Strain (book) 72, 73, 75
Andromeda Strain (1971) 61, 72–5, 74
Anna Karenina (1935) 187
Antosiewicz, John vi
The Apple Cart (stage) 169
Argosy (magazine) 287, 291
Arkoff, Samuel Z. 120
Armendariz, Pedro 286
Arness, James 22, **259**, **261**, **263**, 264, **265**, 267
Arsenic and Old Lace (stage) 19–20
Ashworth, Jay 215
The Assassin (stage) 16–17
The Astounding B Monster (webzine) vi
At War with the Army (stage) 172
At War with the Army (1950) 172
L'Atlantide (1961) 245
Atlas (1960) 44, 52–55, **53**
Atmar, Ann 213, **216**, 217
The Atomic Man (1956) 39
Audrey Rose (1977) 177–78, **178**
Auntie Mame (1958) 18
Babes in Bagdad (1952) 244
Bad and the Beautiful (1952) 241
Badiyi, Reza 88, 89
Baker, Diane 78, 83

Balaban, Harry **129**
Balter, Allan 283
Bankhead, Tallulah 158–59
Banks, Joan 198–99
Barnett, Buddy vi
Barretts of Wimpole Street (1934) 187
Bartholomew, Dave vi
Bates, Ralph 137
Batman (tv) 227
Battlestar Galactica (tv) 14
Bau, George 197
Bau, Gordon 197
Baumann, Marty vi
Bautzer, Greg 271, 295, 304
The Beachcomber (tv) 85
Beast from Haunted Cave (1959) 44, 48–51, **49**
Beckley, Tony 135
Bee, Molly 148
The Beginning or the End (1947) 152
Bel Geddes, Barbara 175
Bela Lugosi Meets a Brooklyn Gorilla (1952) 101
Belinsky, Bo 104
Bender, Russ 107
Bennett, Joan 301
Bergerac, Jacques 283, **284**, 286, 287, 292
Bernardine (stage) 112, 113
Bernay, Lynn 45
Bernds, Edward 22
Bernstein, Leonard 130
Bernstein, Shirley 130
Betz, Carl 257, 258
Beyond the Time Barrier (1960) 244–45
Biano, Solly 22, 194, 203, 218
The Big Sky (1952) 17
Bishop, Julie 233
The Black Cat (1934) 232–34, 237
Black-Eyed Susan (stage) 295
Blair, George 286
Blanchard, Mari 37, 196
Bliss, Lela 31
Bloch, Charles B. 283–84, 285–86
Bloch, Robert 82, 83, 173
Blondell, Joan 82, 83, 84
Blood Legacy see *Legacy of Blood*
Bloom, Claire 61, 68
The Blue Dahlia (1946) 160
Bluebeard (1944) 227, 234, 236–40
Boeing Boeing (1965) 132, 133
Bogdanovich, Peter 233, 234, 238
Bohnen, Roman 4
Bohus, Ted vi
Bonanza (tv) 14, 39
Bonnie and Clyde (1967) 217
Borzage, Frank 183, 184, 245
Boulton, Davis 68
Bow, Clara 255
The Boy from Oklahoma (1954) 260
Boyne, Gil 288, 289

Bradbury, Ray 161, 166, 167
Brahm, John 174
Brando, Marlon 114, 166
Brandt, Carolyn 222
Brasselle, Keefe 195
Breakthrough (1950) 194, 195, 196, 197
Breen, Joe 194, 195–96, 203
Brent, Romney 254
Bridges, James 161, 164, 166
Bridges, Lloyd 149–50
Bringing Up Buddy (tv) 142
Broder, Jack 96, 98, 99, 100–01, 102, 103, 104, 106, 107, 108–09
Broder, Madelynn 101
Broeske, Pat vi
Bronson, Charles 124, 199, 200, 201, 202
Bronsten, Nat 11
Brooke, Hillary 33
Brown, Ginny vi
Brown, Phil 1–15, **3**, **5**, **7**, **9**
Brummer, Dick 221, 224
Brunas, John vi
Brunas, Michael vi
Bunny Lake Is Missing (1965) 69
Burns, Ronnie 141, 142
The Burns and Allen Show see *George Burns and Gracie Allen*
Burr, Raymond 209
Burroughs, Edgar Rice 184–85
Buttram, Pat **162**, 168
Bwana Devil (1952) 123
The Caine Mutiny Court Martial (stage) 27
Campbell, William 289
Camping with Henry and Tom (stage) 27
Campo, Wally 51
Cantor, Eddie 204
Cape Fear (1962) 92
Captain Sirocco see *The Pirates of...*
The Carlssons 37
Carmel, Roger C. 72
Carnegie Hall (1947) 231, 236
Carnival of Souls (1962) 88, 89, 90, 91, 92, **93**, 95
Carnival of Souls (1999) 88–95
Carol, Sheila 49, 51
Caron, Leslie 151, 164
Carradine, David 239
Carradine, John 41, 238, 239
Carreras, James 137
Carreras, Michael 135
Carruthers, Benito 135
Casey, Taggart 99, 107
Cassini, Oleg 270
Castle, William 78, 83, 175, 287
The Cavern (1966) 238, 240, 245–7
Cecil, Henry 171
Cell 2455, Death Row (book) 289
Chandler, Jeff 271
Chandler, Raymond 159–60

Chaney, Lon 19, 20–21, 68
Chaney, Lon, Jr. 5, 6
Chaplin, Charles 159
Chaplin, Sydney 40
Chapman, Marguerite 245
The Chapman Report (1962) 97
Chessman, Caryl 128, 289, 291
Chiller Theatre (magazine) vi
ChiPs (tv) 227
Christ in Concrete (book) 10
Christian, Paul *see* Hubschmid
A Christmas Carol (1938) 27
A Christmas Carol (stage) 16, **26**, 27
Churchill, Sarah 62
Churchill, Winston 62
Clarembard (stage) 80
Clark, Dane 228
Clark, Susan 71
Clarke, Robert vi, 243
Clement, Kevin vi
Clifford, John 89, 90
The Cobweb (1955) 113
Cocchi, John vi
Cochran, Steve 214
Cohen, Herman 108, 144
Cohen, Mickey 291
Cole, David 17
Collins, Richard 10, 13–14
Colman, Booth 16–28, **18**, **21**, **24**, **26**
Columbo (tv) 283
Combat (tv) 33
The Command (1954) 257, 266
Conlon, Tom 184
Considine, John W., Jr. 184
Conte, Richard 176
Conway, Gary 45
Cooke, Alistair 298
Cooper, Gary 14
Coppola, Francis Ford 212, 221, 223, 270
Coray, Jerome 251
Corey, Jeff 44, 45
Corman, Gene 44, 48, 50–51
Corman, Roger 44–48, 50, 52, 53, 54, 55, 103, 104, 112, 115, 116, 117
Cortez, Stanley 100, 104, 106
Cossa, Paolo 41, 42
Cotten, Joseph 172
The Couch (1962) 78, 82
Craven, Wes 91, 92, 95
Crawford, Joan 20–21, 78, 82, 83–84, 198–99
Cregar, Laird 174
Crichton, Michael 72, 75
Crime Wave (1954) 124
The Crucible (stage) 59
Cult Movies (magazine) vi
Cult of the Cobra (1955) 29, 37–39, **38**
Cummings, Robert **157**
Curtis, Donald 36
Curtis, Tony 75, 132, 287
Curtiz, Michael 63
Cushing, Peter 137
D-Day, the Sixth of June (1956) 303, 306, 307
DaCosta, Morton 18
Dahl, Roald 164, 176–77
Dalton, Abby 45
Daly, James 110
Dalzell, Archie 286, 287
Damato, Glenn vi
Damn Yankees (stage) 250
Damon, Mark 117
Danger (tv) 62

Dante, Joe vi
Danziger, Edward J. 243, 244
Danziger, Harry Lee 243, 244
Dark Side of Genius (book) 156–58
David, Saul 69, 71, 72
David Copperfield (1935) 187
Davis, Bette 84
Davis, Luther 12
Day, Doris 247, 248
Day of the Bad Man (1958) 266
The Day of the Triffids (1963) 106
Dead Man's Eyes (1944) 6
The Deadly Bees (1967) 133–36, **134**
Dean, James 113
Death of a Salesman (stage) 27
Death Valley Days (tv) 284
Deathwatch (1966) 57
de Bont, Jan 76
Decameron Nights (1952) 33
DeCarlo, Yvonne 200
Deep in My Heart (1954) 268
Deep Space (1987) 58
DeEyre, David 79
DeFelitta, Frank 177
Demara, Fred 287, 288, **288**, 291
Demy, Jacques 248
Dern, Bruce 168
Desire in the Dust (1960) 82
de Toth, Andre 124, 126, 127, 194, 197, 200–03, 207, 208
Detour (1945) 227, 240
Devon, Richard 45, 46, 48
de Wilde, Brandon 173
Dial M for Murder (1954) 169
Di Donato, Pietro 10
Dietrich, Marlene 244
Disney, Walt 22, 265
Dmytryk, Edward 8–10, **11**, 14
Dr. Goldfoot and the Bikini Machine (1965) **105**, 107
Domergue, Faith vi, 29–43, **30**, **32**, **35**, **38**
Donahue, Elinor 141
The Doris Day Show (tv) 247–48
Dors, Diana 173, 175
Douglas, Gordon 21, 72, 261, 264
Douglas, Kirk 17, 285
Dracula (stage) 250–54, 255
Dracula (1931) 232, 251–52, 255
Driscoll, Bobby 141
Duel at Silver Creek (1952) 29, 33, 40
Duke, Patty 177
Dukesbery, Jack vi
du Maurier, Daphne 296
Dunne, Irene 8, 12
Du Pont Show of the Month (tv) 79
Dwan, Allan 211
E.T. The Extra-Terrestrial (1982) 35
The Eddie Cantor Story (1953) 195
Edens, Roger 268
Edwards, George 99–100, 103
Eisley, Anthony 96, 101, 103, 104, 107
Elhardt, Kaye 102, 103
Elliot, Biff 107
Ely, Ron 19
End Over End (book) 61
Entertainment Tonight (tv) 89
Erdody, Leo 238
Escort West (1959) 39
Evans, Maurice 17, 18, 19, 20, 25
The Eve of St. Mark (1944) 126
Evelyn, Judith 79
Everett, Chad 177

The Face That Launched a Thousand Ships see Loves of Three Queens
The Fall of the House of Usher (1960) *see House of Usher*
Fame (tv) 109
Family Affair (tv) 141
Fangoria (magazine) vi
Fanny (stage) 280
Farrow, John 40, 180
Farrow, Mia **191**, 192
Father Knows Best (tv) 106, 141, 149
Faulkner, Ed 102, 106–07
Fedderson, Don 141, 142, 149
Feist, Felix 180
Ferrer, Jose 268
Ferrer, Mel 31, 151–52, 164, 171
Field, Margaret 243
Field, Sally 243
Fields, Verna 222
Finlay, Frank 133
Fisher, Eddie 204
Fitzgerald, F. Scott 304
Fitzgerald, Michael vi, 29
Florey, Robert 80, 174
Flynn, Errol 196, 204, 209
Follow That Dream (1962) 78
Fontaine, Joan 33
For Whom the Bell Tolls (book) 244
Ford, John 225
Forest, Michael 44–60, **46**, **47**, **49**, **53**, **57**
Fortier, Bob 214, **215**, 222
Fowler, Gene, Jr. 144, **144**
Fowley, Douglas 270, 273, 275, 279, 280
Foy, Bryan 126, 194
Fraker, William A. 213, 214, 216
Francis, Anne 117
Francis, Freddie 133–34, 137, 139
Franco, Francisco 244
Frankenheimer, John 286, 295, 297
Frankenstein (1931) 19, 113, 253
Franz, Arthur 195
Fraser, Shelagh 2–3
Fredericks, Ellsworth 297
Freeborn, Stuart 11
Freed, Bert 258
Fregonese, Hugo 31, 33, 36, 39, 42
Fresco, Clint A. P. vi
Fresco, Erin vi
Fresco, Rufus vi
Fresco, Tigger vi
Friendly Persuasion (book) 114
Friendly Persuasion (1956) 114
Frith, Christopher vi
Fromkess, Leon 236, 237, 238
Frye, Dwight 252
Fulton, John P. 156
Gabel, Martin 170
Gabor, Eva 295
Gaby (1956) 113, 114
Galactica 1980 (tv) 16
Galloway, Nancy 22
Gardner, Ava 221
Garfield, John 199
Gaynor, Mitzi 114
Gazzara, Ben 120, 296
Gendron, Pierre 236, 237
The George Burns and Gracie Allen Show (tv) 141–42
The George Gobel Show (tv) 172
Giant (1956) 113
Gibbons, Cedric 186
Gidding, Nelson 61–77, **63**

Index

Gielgud, John 7, 177
Gigi (1958) 296
Gilleran, Tom 56
Gingold, Michael vi
Girl of the Night (1960) 117
Gist, Robert 21
Give Us This Day (1949) 10
The Glass Menagerie (stage) 7, 8
Gless, Sharon 177
Goddard, Paulette 244
Goodbye, My Fancy (1951) 198–99
Gordon, Barry 166
Gordon, Bert I. 80–81
Graham, Barbara 61, 64
Grand Hotel (stage) 12
Gray, Billy 106
Gray, Sally 11
The Great Impostor (1961) 287
Green, Dr. Richard 73
The Green Berets (1968) 106
Greenlaw, Charlie 201, 203
Greer, Dabbs 199
Griffith, Andy 63
Griffith, Charles B. 52
Grodin, Charles 200
Grossman, Adam 91, 92
Guillermin, John 59
Guinness, Alec 1
Gwenn, Edmund 262, 264, 267
H. M. Pulham, Esq. (1941) 5
Haas, Dolly 174
Habe, Hans 225
Habe, Marina 225
Hackett, Joan 169
Haggard, H. Rider 184
Hagman, Larry 245–46, 247
Haliday, Bryant 113
Hall, Conrad 213, 214, 223, 225
Hall, James Norman 214
Hall, Jon 105–06
Hamill, Mark 3
Hamlet (stage) 17, 18, 20
Hammerstein, Oscar 112
Hammett, Dashiell 130
Happy (tv) 142, 147
Hardt, Eloise 216, 225
Hardwicke, Cedric 169–70
The Harlem Globetrotters (1951) 7
Harper (1966) 213
Harper's (magazine) 160
Harrigan, Nedda 251
Harrington, Curtis 40
Harris, Julie 61, 65, 66, 67, 68
Harris Against the World (tv) 142
Harrison, Joan 151, 155, 159, 161, 163, 167, 177
Harrison, Paul 41
Hart, Susan vi, **105**
Harvey (stage) 21
Harvey, Herk 88, 89, 90, 95
Hatch, Richard 14
Hatton, Rondo 6, 7
The Haunting (1963) 61, 64–69, 67, 75–77; (1999) 75–77
The Haunting of Hill House (book) 61, 64, 65, 66, 67, 68
Hawaiian Eye (tv) 103
Hawks, Howard 17, 96–97
Hayden, Harry 31
Hayes, Allison 283
Hayes, Helen 7, 17
Hayward, Louis **243**
Hayward, Susan 61, 65–66, 271
Haze, Jonathan 47, 48

Hecht, Ben 168
Hedren, Tippi 80
Hefner, Hugh 271, 277
Heisler, Stuart 31, 33
The Helen Morgan Story (1957) 63
Hellman, Monte 48, 49, 51, 54
Helm, Anne 78–87, **79**, **81**, **86**
Helm, Peter 81
Helmore, Tom 18
Hepburn, Audrey 171
Hepburn, Katharine 109, 110, 184
Hercules (1959) 44, 52
Herring, Moree 228, 232
Herrmann, Bernard 167
Heston, Charlton 134
The Hidden Room (1949) 8–11, **9**
High School Hellcats (1958) 145
Hill, Arthur **74**, 166, 177
Hiller, Arthur 161, 163
Hiller, Wendy 177
Hilligoss, Candace 88–95, **90**, **93**
The Hindenburg (1975) 68
Hirschfeld, Al 174
Hitchcock, Alfred 80, 154, 151, 155, 156–59, 161–66, **164**, **165**, 167–78
Hoey, Dennis 96, 109–10
Hoey, Michael A. 96–111, **105**, **109**
Holden, William 304
Holliman, Earl 150
Hollywood Television Theatre (tv) 151, 164
Homolka, Oscar 174
The Honeymooners (tv) 207
Hopkins, Anthony 177–78
Horvath, Charles 201
Hotel (tv) 36
A House Is Not a Home (1964) 56
The House of Seven Corpses (1973) 41
House of Usher (1960) 115, 117
House of Wax (1953) 122–28, **123**, **125**, **129**, 131, 194 208, **195**, **198**, **202**, **205**, **206**, 260
Houseman, John 151, 155, 159–60, 167, 295, 304
Howard, Leslie 113
Hubschmid, Paul 70
Hudson, Rock 257
Hughes, Howard 29, 31, 32, 80
Hughes, Kathleen 39
Hughes, Ken 39
The Hurricane (1937) 106
Huston, John 306
Huston, Tony 306
Hyman, Eliot 270–71
Hyman, Stanley Edgar 65
The Hypnotic Eye (1960) 283–93, **284**, **288**, **290**
I Can't Escape (1934) 228, 231
I Want to Live! (1958) 61, 64, 66, 67, 69
I Wanted Wings (1941) 1, 5
I Was a Teenage Werewolf (1957) 141, 142–45, **143**, **144**, **147**, 148, 150
Immoral Mr. Teas (1959) 271–72
The Incredibly Strange Creatures Who Stopped... (1963) 222
Incubus (1965) 211, 212–26, **215**, **216**, **218**
Indusi, Joe vi
Inherit the Wind (stage) 27
The Innocents (stage) 17
The Interns (1962) 82
Invasion of the Body Snatchers (1956) 294, 297–304, **299**, **302**, **305**
Ireland, John 41

It Came from Beneath the Sea (1955) 29, 36–37
It Takes a Thief (tv) 221, 222
Jackson, Brad 45–46
Jackson, Shirley 61, 64–65
Jacob's Ladder (1990) 92
Jane Eyre (stage) 109–10
Jayne, Jennifer 139
Jeans, Isabel 296
Joan of Lorraine (stage) 254
Joanou, Phil 86
Johansson, Paul 94
Johnson, Richard 61, 65, 67, 68
Johnson, Tom vi
Jones, Carolyn 124, 127, 298
Jones, Margo 250, 254
Jones, Spike 273
Jones, T. C. 164–66, 306
Jones-Moreland, Betsy 45
Jonson, Ben 4
Journey of Honor (1992) 170
Journey to the Unknown (tv) 151, 177
Journey's End (stage) 17
The Jungle Captive (1945) 1, 4, 6, 7
Just Suppose (stage) 113
Kane, Joe vi
Karatnytsky, Christine vi
Karloff, Boris 16, 18–20, 75, 232, 233, 234, 253
Karloff, Dorothy 18
Karloff, Evelyn 18–19, 20
Karloff, Sara 18, 19
Katzman, Sam 36, 37
Keith-Johnston, Colin 17
Kennedy, Douglas 245
Kerr, Deborah 112
Kerr, Frederick 112–131
Kerr, Geoffrey 112–13
Kerr, John 112–21, **116**, **119**, **120**
Khartoum (1966) 134
Kilburn, Terry 27
King and Country (1964) 161
King Kong Lives (1986) 58–59
King Richard and the Crusaders (1954) 260
Kinsolving, Lee 56
Kirk, Phyllis 122–31, **123**, **125**, **129**, **130**, 194, 196, 197, 200, 204
Klugman, Jack 142
Knight, Shirley 271
Kraft Playhouse (tv) 62
Kramer, Earl 110
Kramer, Stanley 110
Kruger, Otto 6, 7
Laemmle, Carl 227, 228, 230, 231, 232, 233, 235
Laemmle, Carl, Jr. 228, 230–31, 232, 235
Laird, Jack 176
Lamarr, Hedy 233, 235, 237
Lampert, Zohra 92
Lancaster, Burt 135–36
Landis, Jessie Royce 254
Landon, Michael 142, **143**, 144–45, **144**, 148, 150
Lane, Priscilla 156
Lang, Fritz 234
Lang, Jennings 301
LaPaglia, Anthony 154
LaPaglia, Jonathan 153–54
Latham, Louise 306
Laughton, Charles 20
Lawford, Peter 122, 129, **130**, 131, 258
Lebon, Yvette 245

LeBorg, Reginald 6, 40
Lee, Christopher 170
Lee, Lila 231
Legacy of Blood (1973) 34, 40–41
Le Gallienne, Eva 151, 155
Legend of Mandinga (1961) 99, 106
Leigh, Janet 174
Leigh, Suzanna 132–40, **134, 136, 138**
Leinster, Murray 96, 97, 99, 102
LeRoy, Mervyn 232
Leslie, Joan 31
Let's Scare Jessica to Death (1971) 92
Levine, Joseph E. 220
Lewis, Eddie 8, 12
Lewis, Jerry 172
Lewton, Val 66
Lieber, Perry 33
Liebowitz, Sam 168
Life (magazine) 4, 79, 122
Life and Legend of Wyatt... (tv) 279
Lifeboat (1944) 158–59
Lime, Yvonne 141–50, **143, 144, 147, 149**
The Linden Tree (stage) 20
The Lion (1962) 304
Lipton, Lawrence 287
List of Adrian Messenger (1963) 306
Lithgow, John 86
Live a Little, Love a Little (1968) 97
Livingston, David 151–52
Lloyd, Norman 151–79, **153, 155, 157, 178**
Locke, Sondra 176
Lockwood, Gary 81, **81**
The Lodger (1944) 174
Lomond, Britt 96, 99
The Lone Ranger (tv) 62, 227
Lorre, Peter 160, 161, 166
Losey, Joseph 160–61
The Lost Continent (1968) 132, 135, **136,** 137
Lovejoy, Frank 126, **129,** 197–99, 201, 202, 203, 204, 258
Loves of Three Queens (1953) 235
Loving You (1957) 142, 150
Loy, Myrna 130
Lucas, George 1, 2, 3–4, 222
Lucas, Tim vi, 211
Lugosi, Bela 232, 233, 250–55
Lugosi, Lillian 232, 250, 252, 253, 254
Lund, Lucille 234–35
Lust for a Vampire (1971) 132, 137
Lyon, Francis D. 39
M (1931) 160
M (1951) 160, 161
Mabry, Moss 261
Machlin, Milton 291
MacMurray, Fred 266
MacRae, Gordon 198, 207
MacRae, Sheila 207
Macumba Love (1959) 270, **272,** 273–77, **275, 278,** 279–81
Magers, Boyd vi, 29
Magic Sword (1962) 78, 80–82, **81**
Magnificent Ambersons (1942) 106
Magnum, P.I. (tv) 306–07
Malden, Karl 72
Maltin, Leonard 89
A Man for All Seasons (stage) 27
The Man from Planet X (1951) 227, 242–44
Man in the Shadow see Violent...
The Man Who Came to Dinner (stage) 142
The Man Who Never Was (tv) 295

Manchurian Candidate (1962) 286
Mander, Miles 110
Mankiewicz, Don 61
Mann, Anthony 285
Manners, David 233
Mansfield, Jayne 196
Manulis, Martin 295, 304
Mara Maru (1952) 204, 209
Marchand, Nancy 79
Maria Stuart (stage) 16
Marley, J. Peverell 201
Marnie (1964) 171
Marshall, Herbert 159, 160
Marshall, Peter 246, 247
Marshall, Tony **147**
Martin, Dean 172
Martin, Mary 114
Martin, Tony 268
Martucci, Mark vi
Mason, James 107
Mason, Pamela 102, 107
The Master of Ballantrae (1953) 196
Matheson, Richard 86
McCarthy, Kevin vi, 294, 298, **299,** 300, 301, 302–03
McCarthy, Mary 303
McCay, Peggy 199
McClintic, Guthrie 113
McClory, Sean 263–64, **263,** 265
McCord, Ted 214
McCormack, John 183
McDonnell, Dave vi
McDowall, Roddy 25–26, 177
McNally, Stephen 40
McPherson, John 153
McQueen, Steve 161, 166
McVey, Patrick 251
Medium Cool (1969) 84
Meet McGraw (tv) 197–98
Melcher, Martin 247–48
The Men (1950) 114
The Merchant of Venice (stage) 27
Merck, Wallace 59
Mescall, John J. 233
Meyer, Russ 224, 271
Michea, Elaine 217
Mihajlovic, Dragoljub 217
Miles, Vera 123, 170–71, 196, 297
Milestone, Lewis 159
Milland, Ray 159
Miller, Dick 53
Miller, Ken 46, 144, **147,** 148
Miller, Larry 91, 92
Miller, Marvin 108
The Millionaire (tv) 141, 142
Milos, Milos 213, 217
Minnelli, Vincente 112
Mirisch, Walter 301
Mission: Impossible (tv) 283
Mitchell, Cameron 85
Mitchum, Robert 32, 39–40
The Model Shop (1969) 248
Mohammad, Messenger of God (1977) 59–60
Mommie Dearest (book) 83–84
Monash, Paul 61–62
The Monster from Earth's End (book) 96–97, 98, 102, 103
Montalban, Ricardo 118
Montgomery, Robert 129
Moore, Joanna 170–71
Morgan, Bob 200
Morgan, Helen 63

Morgan, Miles 113
Morley, Robert 132, 161, 169
Morris, Barboura 54, 55
Morros, Boris 236
Morrow, Jeff 34
Morrow, Vic 33
Moss, Sterling 166
Mossman, Ted 215
Mother Goose a Go Go (1966) 85
The Mummy (1932) 19, 75
The Mummy Lives (1993) 75
Mundy, Meg 17
Murphy, Audie 40
Murphy, Barry vi
The Music Man (stage) 257, 268
The Music Man (1962) 18
Mutiny on the Bounty (book) 214
My Favorite Martian (tv) 250
My Three Sons (tv) 141, 142
Mystery of the Wax Museum (1933) 19, 122, 124, 197
The Naked Dawn (1955) 240
The Naked Jungle (1954) 266
Natalka Poltavka (1937) 234, **235**
Navy vs. the Night Monsters (1966) 96–109, **97, 98, 108,** 110, 111
Neal, Patricia 176
Neill, Roy William 110
Nelson, Gene 39
Newman, Paul 213
Newmar, Julie 281
Newton, Robert 10–11
Nielsen, Ray vi, 180
Night Gallery (tv) 176
Nightmare in Wax (1969) 78, 85
Nilsson, Harry 137
Nimoy, Leonard 57
Ninth Life (book) 291
No Bail for the Judge (book) 171
No Down Payment (1957) 304
No More Ladies (stage) 16
Nolan, Kathy 148
Nord, Eric "Big Daddy" 287
Norman, Leslie 135
Norton, Elliot 295
Notorious (1946) 168
Novak, Kim 39, 271
Oakland, Simon 66
Oberon, Merle 268
O'Brian, Hugh 279
O'Brien, Pat 211
Obsession see The Hidden Room
O'Connell, Brian vi
Odds Against Tomorrow (1959) 61
Oh, Men! Oh, Women! (stage) 13
O'Hanlon, George 195
Olson, James 74
O'Meara, Sara 141, 145–48, **149**
Omnibus (tv) 110, 151, 153
One-Eyed Jacks (1961) 166
Onionhead (1958) 63
Operation Pacific (1951) 196
Ophuls, Max 31
Ordung, Wyott 107
Orr, William T. 63, 203–04, 258, 260, 262
Oscar Wilde (1960) 132
O'Sullivan, Maureen 180–93, **181, 182, 183, 185, 187, 188, 189, 190, 191**
Oswald, Gerd 56
Otash, Fred 287
The Outer Limits (tv) 16, 44, 56, 212, 214, 225
Paar, Jack 287

Index

Pahlen, Victor 241
Pajama Tops (stage) 270, 281
Palm Springs Weekend (1963) 97
Palmer, Lilli 257–58
Paradise, Hawaiian Style (1966) 132, 133
Paradise, Suzanna Style (book) 139
Parker, Fess 22, 265, **265**
Parnum, John E. vi
Parrish, Leslie 58
Parsons, Louella 32
Parton, Regis **32**, 33, 34, **35**
Pastorini, Dan 275
Pat and Mike (1952) 211
Patri, Dan vi
Patterson, Lee 39
Paul, Louis vi
Payne, John 37
The Pearl of Death (1944) 110
Peckinpah, Sam 22, 300
Pellicer, Pina 166
Penn, Leo 120
Perkins, Anthony 75, 114
Peter Pan (stage) 20
Peyton Place (tv) 120
The Phantom of the Opera (1925) 68
The Phil Silvers Show 78–79
The Philadelphia Story (stage) 110
Phillips, Bobbie 91, 92, 94
Picerni, Paul 123, 124, **129**, 194–210, **195**, **198**, **202**, **205**, **206**
Pickens, Slim 168
Picket Fences (tv) 250
Pierce, Arthur C. 96, 101, 108, 109
Pierre of the Plains (1942) 4
The Pirates of Capri (1949) 240–42
Pit and the Pendulum (1961) 112, 115–18, **116**, 119, 120–21
Pitt, Ingrid 137
Planet of the Apes (1968) 25
Planet of the Apes (tv) 16, 23–26, **24**
Playboy (magazine) 270, 271, 277–79, 281
Playgirls and the Bellboy (1962) 270
Playhouse 90 (tv) 295, 296–97, 304, 306, 307
Polanski, Roman 219
Pollexfen, Jack 242
Powell, William 130
Power, Tyrone 211
Preminger, Ingo 7–8
Preminger, Otto 7, 69
Presley, Elvis 78, 97, 107, 132, 134, 135, 142–44, 150
Price, Dennis 139
Price, Mary 204
Price, Vincent 112, 115–16, 117, 118, **119**, 122, 123, **123**, **125**, 126, 127, **129**, 194, 197, 199, 200, 204–07, **205**, 208, 295
The Private Lives of Adam and Eve (1960) 270
Private Property (1960) 212
Provost, Jeanne vi
Provost, Oconee vi
Psycho (book) 173
Psycho (1960) 114, 172, 173, 175
Psycho (1998) 175
Psycho Sisters (1972) 40
La Rabia see *The Rage*
The Rage (1963) 281
The Rage Within see *The Rage*
Raiders from Beneath...(1964) 22
Rainmaker (1956) 142, 145, 149–50
Rains, Claude 32, 40, 167–68

Rathbone, Basil 16, 17–18, 40, 81
Rathbone, Ouida 40
Raven, Mike 137
Reagan, Nancy 148
Reagan, Ronald 8, 148
Rear Window (1954) 175
Reason, Rex **32**, 33, 34, 35
Reed, Walter 270, 275, 277, 279, 280
Reeves, Steve 44, 55
Reid, Kate 73
Remarque, Erich Maria 244
Renoir, Jean 159, 164, 166
The Respectful Prostitute (stage) 17
Reville, Alma 173–74, 176
Rey, Alejandro 166
Reynolds, Burt 70, 71, 148
Richard, Dawn **147**
Riding Shotgun (1954) 208, 257
Ripps, Mike 274, 277
Rippy, Leon 59
Robbins, Cindy 144, **147**, 148
Robert Montgomery Presents (tv) 129, 294
Robinson, Chris 51
Rodann, Ziva 270, 277
Rodgers, Richard 112, 295
Rogers, Will, Jr. 141, 260
Role of Script Supervision (book) 227
Romanoff and Juliet (1961) 22
Rooney, Barbara Ann 217
Rooney, Mickey 147, 213, 217
Rosenberg, Max J. 133
Rosenstein, Sophie 30
Roth, Philip 166
Rougas, Michael **147**
Rubin, Stanley 257–58
Rubinstein, Artur 269
Run for Your Life (tv) 120
Ruric, Peter 233
Russell, Gail 159, 160
Russell, Jane 31
Ruthless (1948) 240, **243**
Sabotage (1936) 174
Saboteur (1942) 151, 156, **157**, 168
Sabrina Fair (stage) 13
The Saga of the Viking Women... (1957) 44, 45–48, **46**, **47**
St. Benny the Dip (1951) 243
St. Elsewhere (tv) 151, 153, 178
Salerno Beachhead see *A Walk in...*
Salt to the Devil see *Give Us...*
Sande, Walter 107
Santa Fe Passage (1955) 37
Sargent, Mike **98**, 102
Saxon, John 238, 246, 247
Sayer, Jay 48
Schallert, William 264
Schary, Dore 211
Schenck, Aubrey 20
Schermer, Jules 64
Schiaffino, Rosanna 247
Schlitz Playhouse of Stars (tv) 8, 12
Schnee, Charles 64
Schreiber, Lew 158–59
Schüfftan, Eugene 238, 239
Schwalb, Ben 286
Scott, Elliot 68
Scott, Randolph 208, 260
Scott, Zachary 39
Scourby, Alexander 79
Scrivani, Rich vi
Sea Hunt (tv) 284
Séance on a Wet Afternoon (1964) 220

Selleck, Tom 306
Sergeant Bilko see *Phil Silvers Show*
Sergeant Preston of the Yukon (tv) 62
Serling, Rod 176
The Servant (1963) 160–61
Seven Days (tv) 151–54, **153**, 160, 179
Shake Hands with the Devil (1959) 306
Shakespeare, William 58
Shatner, William 58, 211, 213, 217–18, **218**, 222
Shaw, Artie 220–21
Shaw, George Bernard 169
Shaw, Irwin 16–17, 220–21
Sheffield, Johnny **182**, **183**, 192
Sherdeman, Ted 262
Sherwood, Robert E. 112
Shirley Temple Storybook (tv) 78, 79
Showgirls (1995) 91
Sidney, Sylvia 174
Siegel, Don 40, 299–300, 301, **302**, 303
Silvera, Frank 166
Silvestre, Armando 281
Sinatra, Frank 50, 284
Sinatra, Richard 50, 51
Sink the Bismarck! (1960) 307
Skager, Mona 212, 218, 221, 223
Ski Troop Attack (1960) 44, 48, 49, 51, 52
Skolsky, Sidney 195
Skullduggery (1970) 69–72, **70**
Slezak, Walter 280
Smith, C. Aubrey 20
Smith, John 34
So Evil, My Sister see *Psycho Sisters*
Soby, Peter 88–91, 94
Sofaer, Abraham 80
Sole Survivor (1982) 92
"Some Words with a Mummy" (short story) 75
Son of Dracula (1974) 132, 137–38
Sondergaard, Gale 240
Song o' My Heart (1930) 183–84
Sons and Lovers (1960) 134
Sorel, Sonia 238, 239
Sorrell, Helene 258
South Pacific (stage) 114
South Pacific (1958) 112, 113–14, 116, 117
Sparber, Hershel 59
Spartacus (1960) 284, 285
Speedway (1968) 97
Spellbound (1945) 151
SPFX (magazine) vi
Spiegel, Sam 170
Spielberg, Steven 35, 222
Spin a Dark Web (1956) 39
Spinout (1966) 97
Spoto, Donald 156–58
Squire, Katherine 166
Stack, Robert 194
Stalag 17 (1953) 211
Star Trek (tv) 44, 56–58, 218, 222
Star Trek: Voyager (tv) 16
Star Wars (1977) 1–4, **3**, 35
Stark, Ray 270–71
Starlog (magazine) vi
Starr, Ringo 132, 137, 139
Stay Away, Joe (1968) 97
Steckler, Ray Dennis 222
Steele, Barbara 115, 118
Stefano, Joseph 173, 225
Stensgaard, Yutte 137
Stevens, Connie 148
Stevens, Leslie 211, 212, 213, 214, 215, 216, 217, 218, 221, 222, 224, 225

Index

Stevens, Onslow 263, 264
Stevens, Robert 161, 169, 172, 174, 254
Stevens, Warren 135
Stewart, David J. 173
Stoney Burke (tv) 212
Strait-Jacket (1964) 78, 82–84
Strange Illusion (1945) 227
Strange Woman (1946) 233, 235, 237
Stranger Wore a Gun (1953) 260
Strasberg, Susan 40
Streets of San Francisco (tv) 120
Striker, Fran 62–63
Stritch, Elaine 251, 253, 254
Stromberg, Hunt 237
Stromberg, Hunt, Jr. 254
Studio One (tv) 79, 294
Sturges, Preston 31
The Subject Was Roses (stage) 191
Subotsky, Milton 133
Sullavan, Margaret 230
Suspense (tv) 62, 250, 254, 294
Suzuki, Pat 70
The Swarm (1978) 133
S.W.A.T. (tv) 227
Swift, Susan 177, **178**
The Swingin' Maiden (1964) 80
The System (1953) 257, 258
Szwarc, Jeannot 176
Tales of the Unexpected (tv) 151, 164, 176–77
Tamblyn, Russ 61
Tandy, Jessica 161
Tarzan (tv) 19, 23
Tarzan and His Mate (1934) 180, **185**, 186
Tarzan Escapes (1936) 180, **187**
Tarzan Finds a Son! (1939) 180, **181**, 191–92
Tarzan the Ape Man (1932) 180
Tarzan's New York Adventure (1942) 180, **182**, 189, 192
Tarzan's Secret Treasure (1941) 180, **183**, 192
Tate, Sharon 219
Taurog, Norman 97, **105**
Taylor, Anthony M. 211–26, **221**
Taylor, Don 161, 167
Taylor, Robert 268, 303, 304
Taylor, Rod 22
Tea and Sympathy (stage) 112, 113
Tea and Sympathy (1956) 112, 113–15
The Teahouse of the August Moon (stage) 13
Temple, Shirley 79, 219
Templemore, D. M. 70
The Tender Trap (stage) 13
Terror in the Haunted House (1959) 99
Terry, Phillip 107
Thalberg, Irving G. 228
That's My Boy (1951) 211
Them! (1954) 21–22, 257, **259**, 260–67, **261**, **263**, 265
They Shall Not Die (stage) 168
The Thin Man (tv) 122, 128, 129–30, **130**, 131
The Thing from Another World (1951) 36, 96–97, 101
This Is My Love (1954) 29
This Is Your Music (tv) 257
This Island Earth (1955) 29, **32**, 33, 34–36, **35**
Thomas, Harry 107, **108**
Thomas, Kevin 109
Thompson, Marshall 38

Three Indelicate Ladies (stage) 250, 254
Thriller (tv) 16
Thunder in the Sun (1959) 270, 271
Thunder Over Texas (1934) 235–36
Thunder Over the Plains (1953) 124
Tickle Me (1965) 97, 99, 107
Tillman, Edwin 106
Time Travelers (1976) 23
The Time Tunnel (tv) 23
Timeslip see The Atomic Man
Timpone, Tony vi
Tisch, Laurence 131
Tobey, Kenneth 36
The Today Show (tv) 270, 271
Todd, Richard 303
tom thumb (1958) 132
Tonge, Philip 17
Towers, Harry Alan 75
Trendle, George W. 62–63
Trilling, Steve 30, 122, 203, 262
Trintignant, Jean-Louis 245
Trois Étoile (tv) 132
Turner, Lana 221
TV Guide (magazine) 39, 122
Twelve O'Clock High (tv) 306
The Twilight Zone (tv) 56, 86
Twilight Zone–The Movie (1983) 33
Ulmer, Arianné vi, 227, 233, 238, 239, **240**, 241, **242**, 244, 245
Ulmer, Edgar G. 227, 228–30, 231–32, **231**, 233–36, 237, 238, 239–41, **240**, 242, **242**, 243–46, 247–49
Ulmer, Shirley 227–49, **229**, 235, 237, **242**, **243**, 246
Uncharted Seas (book) 135
Under Ten Flags (1960) 22
The Uninvited (1944) 159
Universal Pictures (book) 29
The Unseen (1945) 159–60
The Untouchables (tv) 194, 208
The U.S. Steel Hour (tv) 79
Vail, Justina 152
Van, Bobby 102, 103, 106
Van Doren, Mamie 96, 103–04, 107, **108**
Van Dyke, W.S. 181
The Veil (tv) 19
Vendetta (1950) 29, 31, 33–34, 36
Vercors 69
Vertigo (1958) 171
Video Watchdog (magazine) vi, 211
VideoScope (magazine) vi
Vidor, King 5
The View from Pompey's Head (1955) 303, 307
Violent Stranger (1957) 39
The Virginian (tv) 20–21
Volpone (stage) 4
von Stroheim, Erich 234
Voyage to the Bottom…(tv) 23
Voyage to the Prehistoric Planet (1965 tv movie) 40
Wachsberger, Nat 245
Wake of the Red Witch (1948) 110
A Walk in the Sun (1945) 109
Walker, June 112, 113, 120
Wallis, Hal B. 132, 133, 135, 139, 142
Walston, Ray 250–56, **252**
Wanamaker, Sam 10
Wanger, Walter 64, 297, 298–99, 300, 301–02, 303
Warner, Barbara 266
Warner, Jack L. 31, 63, 97, 126, 127, 196, 203, 204, 258, 262, 266, 269
Warner, Joan 231, 236

Warren, Gloria 31
Waterloo Bridge (1931) 112
Watts, Charles 145
Wayne, David 160
Wayne, John 106–07, 110
Weaver, Brian vi
Webster, Ben 16
Webster, Margaret 16
Weird Woman (1944) 1, 4, 5, 6
Weissmuller, Johnny 180, **181**, **182**, **183**, 184, **185**, 186–87, **188**, **189**,
Weld, Tuesday 81
Weldon, Joan 123, 196, 257–69, **259**, **261**, **263**, **265**, **268**
Welles, Orson 71, 106, 151, 179
Wellman, William, Jr. 273, 277
Wells, Jacqueline *see* Bishop, Julie
Wesson, Dick 198, 199
West, Jessamyn 114
West, Red 107
West, Sonny 107
West Side Story (1961) 65
Westerns Women (book) 29
Westmore, Frank 25
Westworld (1973) 75
Wexler, Haskell 84
Whale, James 112, 230
What Ever Happened to Baby Jane? (1962) 84
What Falls Away (book) 192
Wheatley, Dennis 135
Where Danger Lives (1950) 29, 32, 36, 39–40
White, George 107
Whitmore, James 264, 267
Whitty, Dame May 16
Wilcox, Collin **162**, 168, 171
Wilder, Billy 286
Wilkinson, June 270–82, **274**, **275**, **276**, **278**
Williams, Esther 186
Williams, Grant 82
Williams, John 169
Williams, Lucy Chase vi
Williams, Wade vi
Willson, Henry 30, 31–32
Wilson, Richard 71
The Winslow Boy (stage) 17
Winwood, Estelle 81
Wise, Robert vi, 61, 64, 66, 68–69, 72, 73, **74**, 75, 76, 77, 177
Witney, William 39
Wolf, John 176–77
Wolff, Frank 48, 49, 50, 51, 52, 55–56
Women of the Prehistoric Planet (1966) 99, 100, 101
Woodfield, William 283–93, **285**
The World of Suzie Wong (1960) 273
World Without End (1956) 16, **21**, 22
Worley, Jo Anne 271
Wray, Fay 122
Wright, Teresa 168
Wyler, William 114, 227, 228
Wynter, Dana 294–307, **296**, **299**, **302**, **305**
You Shall Know Them (book and play) 69
Young, Ned 199
The Young Marrieds (tv) 199
The Young Set (tv) 130
Young Widow (1946) 31
Zanuck, Darryl F. 158, 297
Zorro (tv) 99
Zubatkin, Marc vi

www.ingramcontent.com/pod-product-compliance
Ingram Content Group UK Ltd.
Pitfield, Milton Keynes, MK11 3LW, UK
UKHW050542150426
5217IPUK00026B/2040